Other Books by Walter Kaufmann

Nietzsche
Critique of Religion and Philosophy
From Shakespeare to Existentialism
The Faith of a Heretic

POETRY

Goethe's Faust: A New Translation
Cain and Other Poems
Twenty German Poets

TRANSLATOR AND EDITOR

The Portable Nietzsche
Existentialism from Dostoevsky to Sartre
Judaism and Christianity: Essays by Leo Baeck
Philosophic Classics: Thales to St. Thomas
Philosophic Classics: Bacon to Kant
Religion from Tolstoy to Camus

HEGEL

HEGEL

REINTERPRETATION, TEXTS, AND COMMENTARY

WALTER KAUFMANN

1965

DOUBLEDAY & COMPANY, INC., GARDEN CITY, NEW YORK

*All translations in this volume are the author's.
Most of the material, including Chapter IX and
most of Chapter VII, has never been translated before.*

LIBRARY OF CONGRESS CATALOG CARD NUMBER 65–13982
PRINTED IN THE UNITED STATES OF AMERICA

ONULP

FOR MY MOTHER

who read the *Phenomenology* in 1914,
in return for her copy of the book

Was du ererbt von deinen Vätern hast,
Erwirb es, um es zu besitzen!
FAUST, 682 f.

Preface

The aim of this book is as simple as its execution is difficult: to establish a comprehensive reinterpretation of Hegel—not just of one facet of his thought but of the whole phenomenon of Hegel.

That this is worth doing, few will question. It is generally agreed that Hegel was one of the greatest philosophers of all time, and no philosopher since 1800 has had more influence. A study of Hegel enriches our comprehension of subsequent philosophy and theology, political theory and literary criticism. Indeed, recent intellectual history cannot be understood apart from him.

Since 1905 a great deal of new material has come to light, including many important Hegel manuscripts as well as letters and documents. Most of it has never been translated into English, and British and American monographs on Hegel have persistently ignored it.

What needs to be done, however, has not yet been done in German or French either. Many German studies of Hegel are very erudite, and in the two-volume works by Franz Rosenzweig, Theodor Haering, and Hermann Glockner the manuscript discoveries made early in this century are taken into account. But since the last of these volumes appeared in 1940, new material has been published and the critical edition of Hegel's works has progressed. Moreover, Rosenzweig confined himself to Hegel's political philosophy; Haering required thirteen hundred pages to reach Hegel's first book and then, after giving that a few pages, stopped; and Glockner, after a thousand pages, finished with Hegel's first book, and devoted only a few pages to Hegel's later work.

It is a worthy ambition to publish volumes that can be consulted repeatedly in libraries, but only a book that can be read straight through before being referred to again and again can establish a really new interpretation.

In the body of this book the reader will find Hegel and not me. But in the Preface some autobiographical remarks may be forgiven if they help to explain my approach. They might even help some readers in their approach to Hegel.

In our living room in Berlin, where I grew up, a large picture of Kant hung over a green tile stove in one corner. On the flat surface of the stove, which was never used, reposed a huge seventeenth-century Bible, and Kant was flanked by smaller portraits of Fichte and Hegel. In a sense, I have lived with Hegel since I was four.

Next to Fichte, the wall was covered with German literature from Lessing to the present. At right angles with that, on the wall facing Hegel, the center bookcase was devoted to philosophy. But though we had Kant's "works" and an incomplete set of Nietzsche, there were only a few volumes by Hegel. It was not until I was a graduate student that I started seriously on those, having read only the *Philosophy of Right* in college.

It was in the summer of 1942, after I had passed my "Prelims" at Harvard and got married, that I first read the *Phenomenology* and the *Encyclopedia*. One might study Hegel with one's teeth clenched, but I read him in a honeymoon spirit.

It was a delight to find again and again that after considerable effort one could make sense of passages that at first had seemed quite incomprehensible. Georg Lasson, who had contributed prefaces in a spirit of loving discipleship, was my friend; Rudolf Haym, who was quoted as having disparaged the *Phenomenology,* was not. Josiah Royce, too, remarked that Haym had not done justice to the book, and it was not until much later that I read Haym and found his book one of the best on Hegel. But that summer the point was to comprehend the incomprehensible, not to read unsympathetic criticism; and the presumption was that his critics had not understood Hegel, which was true enough in most cases.

In one of my weekly reports on my reading, I criticized Royce's image of Hegel. My professor made a notation on the paper for me to see him, and then invited me for lunch at the Faculty Club. Since I thought that he looked like Bismarck, and I had never set foot inside a faculty club, I was apprehensive. The menu came, and I ordered something from the middle. Then my professor said: "Waiter, bring *me* an apple!" While I had to eat, I was told that I was confused, that all German philosophers were confused, that Kant and Hegel had been confused, and that Royce had tried to make some sense of Hegel. In one way at least I was in good company.

My honeymoon with Hegel is long passed. The discovery that what at first makes no sense is after all by no means meaningless too often leads to joyous assent. The Heidegger vogue is a striking example. But recognition of an author's meaning is one thing, comprehension another. When a philosopher is exceptionally difficult, most readers leave him alone or soon give up. The few who persevere and spend years figuring him out naturally do not like to be experts on something that is not worth while. So one is tempted to suspend criticism and concentrate on exegesis. Heidegger actually encourages and inculcates this approach: in immensely repetitive essays, particularly on Hölderlin and the pre-Socratics, he practically preaches exegetical thinking. It is one of the many important differences between Hegel and Heidegger that Hegel distinguished clearly between such thinking and comprehension. Comprehension without critical evaluation is impossible.

One of the glaring faults of most "existentialism" is this lack of seriousness. One remains at the surface and is edified. For all the usual protestations of ultimate seriousness, there is something exceedingly playful about Kierkegaard's manipulation of language and examples, about what Heidegger does with words, and—in their philosophical writings—about Sartre's brilliance and Camus's gambits. They ask us, in effect, to suspend our critical faculties and not to take things too exactly. In Kierkegaard's terms one might say that they ask to be read on the aesthetic plane. In "existentialist" writers this seems even more ironical than it would be in Hegel's case.

Hegel often failed in the same way, and in his case, too, this is ironical because he called his philosophy "science." But in principle he was clear on this point. Comprehension requires sympathetic immersion as well as criticism: we must enter not only into a train of thought, but also into its subject matter; and insofar as possible we must take the author's positions more seriously than he himself took them. Only in that way can we hope to make progress beyond him.

Indeed, we are not doing Hegel justice when we say that, in spite of his frequent lapses, he was clear about this in principle. This suggests that the standard itself is an old one. In fact, nobody has done so much to establish it as Hegel did.

It is often difficult to fuse sympathy and criticism. Most writers on Hegel fail in one respect or the other, if not in both. On the whole, the most scholarly German studies are too close to their subject, while most of those who have written on him in English do not really seem at home with him. His world is after all not theirs.

This is illustrated by the divergent attitudes toward Hegel's early period. Recent German scholarship has become so immersed in it that it often does not get around to even an attempt at any critical consideration of his mature thought. British and American scholarship, on the other hand, has refused altogether to immerse itself in Hegel's development, and as a result usually fails to comprehend his thought from the inside.

Perhaps my own experience of having lived with Hegel for so many years, while also living with Goethe and Nietzsche, existentialism and—in the flesh—American students and colleagues, has helped to establish a proper balance between closeness and distance. And it may be fortunate, as well as unusual, that the closeness came first and the distance afterwards. It would not be in Hegel's spirit to try to go back to him; but to take him seriously and go beyond him is not to betray him.

The question remains how any one book can significantly advance the comprehension of Hegel as a whole. Monographs on a single aspect of his thought seem less problematic; but Hegel himself never tired of insisting on the importance of a comprehensive approach, while stressing the shortcomings of essays that renounce any whole view and confine themselves exclusively to details.

Two approaches have been tested more than once and do not seem to help most students of Hegel where help is needed most. The *first* leads us to Hegel by way of his predecessors: Richard Kroner, for example, in his two-volume *Von Kant bis Hegel*. But most students would rather not plod through such detailed accounts of Fichte and Schelling; and Hegel himself, in his lectures on the history of philosophy, gave Kant, Fichte, and Schelling together as much space as he gave to Aristotle alone, or to Plato.

When G. R. G. Mure devotes the first half of his slim *Introduction to Hegel* to Aristotle, this is therefore not as perverse as it appears to be at first glance; but still this approach is far-fetched. Too little space remains for Hegel himself, and moreover one could begin instead with Plato or Spinoza. This method is needlessly indirect.

The classical representative of the *second* approach is Kuno Fischer. In his two-volume *Hegel* he gives a play-by-play account of the major works, one by one, paraphrasing or, where the text becomes really obscure, quoting. In Germany he has had few imitators: if that was what was wanted, he had done it; but many philosophers probably felt that he had altogether discredited this approach by leading it to the absurd.

The two most widely read English studies, however, represent variations of this method. W. T. Stace's one-volume work on *The Philosophy of Hegel* is misnamed: it gives a play-by-play account only of the third edition of Hegel's *Encyclopedia*. Moreover, it is based on William Wallace's inadequate translations and ignores all primary and secondary sources not available in English. J. N. Findlay's *Hegel* deals with the other major works, too, but also disregards all primary and secondary sources that have not been translated into English and, like Stace, totally ignores Hegel's development.[1]

Goethe said: "Works of nature and art one does not get to know as they are finished; one has to catch them in their genesis to comprehend them to some extent."[2] Hegel tried to show, beginning with his first book, that this same consideration applies to philosophy, as well. And it certainly should be applied to Hegel himself.

The reader of the *Phenomenology* or the *Logic* does not so much need to be told what happens, section by section, as he wants to know how these books are to be taken: what Hegel attempted to do—and what he did in fact. A detailed discussion of a very few sample sections is likely to be far more helpful than a thumbnail digest of almost all.

The reader who is interested in comparing Hegel with Kant's *Critique of Pure Reason* or Aristotle's *Metaphysics* will have no

[1] For a detailed appraisal see my critical notice of the book in *Mind*, April 1961, 264–69.
[2] Letter to Zelter, August 4, 1803.

trouble in finding good translations of both, as well as helpful books
about Kant and Aristotle. The crucial influence on Hegel of Kant's
philosophy of religion and of Lessing, Goethe, and Schiller is not
nearly so easy to determine for oneself; therefore, *these* influences
have been discussed in the first chapter, along with Hegel's development to the age of thirty. People seriously interested in Hegel are
more likely to have Kant's *Critique* and some Aristotle on their
shelves than Schiller's *On the Aesthetic Education of Man;* hence
this work, which made a tremendous impression on Hegel and influenced his terminology, is liberally quoted in section 7.

In sum, the method of this book was dictated by its subject
matter. I did not impose on Hegel a procedure that had worked
on some other subject, say Nietzsche. To put it into Hegelian language: the movement of this book, from beginning to end, comes
out of the subject matter itself.

To be very specific: The idea of the first chapter has already
been explained. The second deals with Hegel's early publications:
a pamphlet, a dissertation, and five philosophical articles. None of
these essays is reported on, paragraph by paragraph. In every instance, the account is selective and stresses what is relevant for
an understanding of Hegel's books.

The third chapter deals with the *Phenomenology* but is also
meant to facilitate the comprehension of Hegel's later writings. This
chapter includes sections on Hegel's terminology—here key terms
are taken up, one by one—and on Hegel's dialectic.

The fourth chapter deals with Hegel's next book, the *Logic,*
originally published in three volumes. Here, naturally, more has to
be said about the dialectic; further terms have to be discussed;
and, as in the case of the *Phenomenology,* the idea of the whole
work needs to be considered at some length. There is also an excursus,
apropos of Hegel's treatment of being and nothing, on Hegel vis-
à-vis Heidegger.

The fifth chapter deals with Hegel's system and the various
editions of the *Encyclopedia,* for this is the book that presents the
famous system, and there are several markedly different editions
of it. A little philological exactitude helps us greatly in understanding Hegel's own conception of his system.

The two lecture cycles on aesthetics and philosophy of religion
are available in complete English translations and should offer no

special difficulties to those who read the present book. But the two cycles on the philosophy of history and the history of philosophy do present problems and are therefore taken up in Chapter VI. The *Philosophy of History* is probably Hegel's best known book; but in the more demanding sense of that word, it is scarcely "known" at all, and it is not really one of Hegel's "books." The critical edition of 1955 has not been translated, and its findings have never yet been used in any major study of Hegel, in German or in English. And a great many misconceptions stand in the way of comprehension. The same applies to the little known three-volume *History of Philosophy,* and to the critical edition of the introduction to that work. So the sixth chapter is devoted to "Hegel on History."

This book bears no relation to any dissertation and is plainly not the place for an effort to demonstrate philosophical acuity. What is needed is not for somebody to score on Hegel by tripping him up on numerous details, which would not be especially difficult, but rather an attempt to fashion a comprehensive new interpretation. Because so few of the relevant texts are accessible to most students, and even the majority of scholars have ignored them, a great many quotations have been included. To give the usual footnote citations without quoting would have been strictly academic: it might give some scholars a comfortable feeling that the references are given, but few indeed would be in a position to look up the relevant passages.

Since there are limits to how much one can quote decently without breaking up the text too much, a great deal of the documentation has been saved for Chapter VII where it is presented in chronological order, in such a manner that, I hope, most readers will enjoy reading this chapter straight through when they come to it. Indeed, this may be a pleasant and effective way of letting Hegel's development pass in review once more, by way of letters and contemporary reports. Incidentally, almost none of this material has ever been translated before, nor has any biography or study of Hegel's intellectual development ever been published in English. Even in German one still has to supplement Rosenkranz's *Life* of 1844 with more recent publications, above all the four volumes of correspondence published after World War II.

What is still needed after that is a new and sound translation of a major Hegel text, with a commentary that follows it paragraph for paragraph. The text chosen for this purpose is the long preface to the *Phenomenology;* the reasons for this choice will be seen at a glance by looking at the mottoes of Chapter VIII.

The book ends on a light note: a translation of Hegel's little essay, "Who Thinks Abstractly?" It is philosophically interesting and should put to rest the myth that Hegel had no sense of humor.

The table of contents may suggest that the book is composed of independent sections. It is not. The book was written in one sweep and is meant to be read that way. The section titles follow Hegel's example in two ways: they appear only in the Contents and not in the text, and they represent afterthoughts. They are intended to show at a glance what topics are discussed at some length later on, to help those reading the book to locate earlier passages once more, and to be useful to readers who have finished the book but wish to consult it on various points.

In the Chronology the left column is devoted to Hegel's life and writings, the right column to contemporary events.

Contents

Chronology

*–born   †–dies

	1729	Lessing*; Moses Mendelssohn*
	1732	Haydn*
Georg Ludwig Hegel (father)*	1733	
Maria Magdalena Fromm (mother)*	1741	
	1743	F. H. Jacobi*
	1744	Herder*
	1746	Kant, *Thoughts about the True Estimation of Living Forces* (1st book)
	1749	Goethe* Aug. 28
	1756	Mozart*
	1759	Schiller*; Handel†; Robert Burns*
	1762	Fichte*
	1764	Winckelmann, *Geschichte der Kunst des Altertums*
	1765	Leibniz, *Nouveaux essais* (posthumously)
	1766	Lessing, *Laokoon*
	1767	A. W. Schlegel*
	1768	Schleiermacher*; Winckelmann†
parents marry, Sep. 29	1769	Napoleon*
Hegel,* Aug. 27	1770	Beethoven*; Hölderlin*; Wordsworth*
	1772	F. Schlegel*; Novalis*; Coleridge*
Christiane (sister)*	1773	Fries*
		Goethe, *Götz* (1st play)
	1774	Goethe, *Werther* (1st novel)
	1776	U. S. Declaration of Independence
		Hume†; Herbart*
Christiana Charlotte Johanna Fischer (mother of Hegel's illegitimate son)*	1778	Voltaire†; Rousseau†
	1779	Lessing, *Nathan;* Gluck, *Iphigenia in Tauris*
	1780	Lessing, *The Education of Mankind*

	1781	Lessing†
		Kant, *Critique of Pure Reason;*
		Schiller, *The Robbers* (1st play);
		Voss, *Odyssey* tr.
mother† Sep. 20	1783	Kant, *Prolegomena;*
		Mendelssohn, *Jerusalem*
	1785	Kant, *Grundlegung;*
		Jacobi, *On Spinoza's Doctrine*
	1786	Frederick the Great†
		Mozart, *Figaro*
		Jacobi, *Against Mendelssohn's Accusation*
	1787	Kant, *Critique of Pure Reason,* 2d rev. ed.;
		Goethe, *Iphigenia in Tauris;*
		Schiller, *Don Carlos;*
		Uhland*; Gluck†
		Mozart, *Don Giovanni & Eine kleine Nachtmusik*
graduates from Gymnasium;	1788	Schopenhauer*; Eichendorff*; Byron*
Tübingen University		Kant, *Critique of Practical Reason;*
		Mozart, *Jupiter Symphony*
	1789	French Revolution;
		Jacobi, *On Spinoza's Doctrine,* 2d rev. ed.;
		Schiller, ". . . Universal History"
M.A., philosophy, Tübingen	1790	Kant, *Critique of Judgement;*
		Goethe, *Faust: A Fragment*
Marie von Tucher (wife)*	1791	Mozart, *Magic Flute & Requiem* and†
	1792	French begin repeated invasions of Germany;
		Fichte, *Critique of All Revelation* (1st book);
		Shelley*; Rossini*
Fragments on folk religion	1793	Louis XVI guillotined;
(published 1907); final the-		Kant, *Religion within the Bounds of Mere Reason;*
ological exam, Tübingen;		Christianity abolished in France and replaced
goes to Bern, Switzerland,		by cult of reason;
as tutor		Napoleon rises from captain to general;
		Schelling's 1st article (68 pp. on myths)
	1794	Robespierre guillotined;
		Fichte, *Wissenschaftslehre* (Doctrine of Science)
"The Life of Jesus" & "The	1795	Prussia appeases France to be able to partic-
Positivity of the Christian		ipate in 3d partition of Poland;
Religion" (published in		Kant, *Eternal Peace;*
1907)		Schelling, *Of the Ego;*
		Schiller, *On the Aesthetic Education of Man;*
		Goethe, *Wilhelm Meister's Apprenticeship;*
		Keats*
Hike in Bernese Alps; quits	1796	French again invade southern Germany; Napo-
Bern		leon's brilliant Italian campaign;
		Goethe, *Wilhelm Meister's Apprenticeship,* Books
		VII and VIII;
		Burns†

Goes to Frankfurt am Main as tutor	1797	Kant, *Metaphysics of Ethics* (2 vols.); Schelling, *Ideas for a Philosophy of Nature;* Hölderlin, *Hyperion,* Part I; Schubert*
	1798	French take Rome & imprison pope in France; Napoleon's Egyptian campaign; Napoleon First Consul; Kant, *Anthropology;* Fichte, *System of Ethics* & charged with atheism;
"The Spirit of Christianity and its Fate" (published 1907); father,† Jan. 14		Schelling, *On the World Soul*
	1799	Fichte, *Appeal to the Public* & leaves Jena for Berlin; Schelling, *First Draft for a Philos. of Nature;* Schleiermacher, *On Religion;* Hölderlin. *Hyperion,* Part II; Heine*; Balzac*
	1800	French invade Bavaria; Kant, *Logic;* Fichte, *Vocation of Man* & *Closed Trade State;* Schelling, *System of Transcendental Idealism;* Schiller, *Wallenstein*
Moves to Jena, publishes "The Difference between Fichte's & Schelling's System"; Latin dissertation on planetary orbits; defense of theses Aug. 27 (on 31st birthday): Privatdozent, beginning of university career.	1801	Fichte, *Sun-clear Report;* Schleiermacher, *Monologues;* Schiller, *Mary Stuart;* A. W. Schlegel, *Hamlet* tr.; Novalis†
Co-editor (with Schelling) of *Critical Journal of Philosophy;* in vol. I: "On the Nature of Philosophical Criticism . . ."; "How Common Sense Construes Philosophy . . ."; "Relation of Skepticism to Philosophy . . ."	1802	Napoleon becomes Consul for Life; Schelling, *Bruno;* Schiller, *Maid of Orleans;* Novalis, *Writings* (2 vols.) & *Heinrich von Ofterdingen* (2 vols.)
In vol. II (last vol.): "Faith and Knowledge or the Philosophy of Reflection . . . Kantian, Jacobian, and Fichtean"; "On Scientific Modes of Treatment of Natural Law . . ."	1803	Schelling, *Lectures on the Method of Academic Studies* & *Ideas for a Philosophy of Nature,* rev. ed., & leaves Jena for Bavaria & founds *New Journal for Speculative Physics;* Fries, Reinhold, Fichte, and Schelling & *Philosophical Doctrine of Right;* Herder†
Elected assessor by Jena Mineralogical Society	1804	Napoleon crowned Emperor; Kant†; Krug succeeds to Kant's chair at Königsberg; Fries, *System of Philosophy;*

	Schelling, *Philosophy and Religion;* Schiller, *Tell;* Beethoven, *Fidelio*
Promoted to Ausserordent- licher Professor (with Fries); fall: begins to lecture on history of philosophy for the 1st time; winter: begins writing his *System;* Fries prof., Heidelberg	**1805** Napoleon becomes King of Italy and wins the Battle of the three Emperors at Austerlitz, de- feating the Tsar and Austrian Emperor; Fries, *Knowledge, Faith, and Intimation;* Goethe, *Rameau's Nephew,* tr.; Beethoven, *Eroica;* Schiller†; Rosenkranz (Hegel's first biographer)*
Sep.: first mention of "Phe- nomenology" as title of Part I; Oct.: book completed night before battle	**1806** Napoleon's victory in the Battle of Jena finishes Holy Roman Empire (founded 800 A.D. by Charlemagne); Napoleon enters Berlin; Fichte, *The Basic Features of the Present Age & The Way to the Blessed Life;* Schleiermacher, *On Religion,* 2d ed.; Beethoven, *Violin Concerto*
Jan. 1: honorary member, Heidelberg Physical Society; Preface of *Phenomenology* sent to publisher Jan. 10; Ludwig (illegitimate son),* Feb. 5; removal to Bamberg to edit newspaper; Apr.: *Phenome- nology* (1st book); sister be- comes governess	**1807** Napoleon dismembers Prussia; Fries, *New Critique of Reason* (3 vols.) & *Fichte's Newest Doctrine;* Schelling publishes a lecture; Beethoven, *Fifth Symphony*
Fall: leaves Bamberg; Rektor of Gymnasium, Nürnberg; duties include instruction in philosophy	**1808** Fichte, *Addresses to the German Nation;* F. Schlegel, *On the Language and Wisdom of India;* Goethe, *Faust,* Part I; Beethoven, *Sixth Symphony;* D. F. Strauss*
	1809 Schelling, *Philosophical Writings,* vol. I (all that appeared), otherwise no book from 1807 to 1812; Goethe, *Elective Affinities;* Beethoven, *Emperor Concerto;* Haydn†
Apr.: engaged; marries, Sep. 16	**1811** Fries, *Outline of Logic* & *System of Logic*
Logic, vol. I, Part I; Susanna (daughter)* and †	**1812** Napoleon's Russian campaign, Georg Ludwig (Hegel's only brother) falls; Grimm, *Märchen,* vol. I; Beethoven, *Seventh & Eighth Symphonies*
Logic, vol. I, Part II; Schulrat as well as Rektor; Karl (son)*	**1813** Napoleon beaten at Leipzig; Schopenhauer, *On the . . . Principle of Reason* (1st book);

		Kierkegaard*; Wagner*; Verdi*; Nietzsche's father*; Büchner*; Hebbel*; Grimm, *Märchen*, vol. II
Immanuel (youngest son)* sister retires ill	1814	Napoleon exiled to Elba; Fichte†
	1815	Napoleon returns; Waterloo; St. Helena; Schelling, *On the Deities of Samothrace*
Logic, vol. II; calls to Heidelberg, Berlin, & Erlangen; Professor, Heidelberg	1816	Schopenhauer, *On Vision and Colors*; Rossini, *Barber of Seville*; Fries leaves Heidelberg for Jena
Encyclopedia (one-vol. system); Ludwig (illegit. son) joins family	1817	Wartburg festival
Professor, Berlin; Ludwig attends Französisches Gymnasium	1818	Marx*
	1819	Schopenhauer, *World as Will and Representation*; Goethe, *West-Eastern Divan*; Jacobi†
Sister temporarily in asylum	1820	
Philosophy of Right (last book)	1821	Napoleon†; Keats†; Dostoevsky*; Baudelaire*; Flaubert*; Goethe, *Wilhelm Meister's Wanderjahre*
	1822	Shelley† Heine, *Poems* (1st book); Beethoven, *Piano Sonata*, op. 111
	1823	Beethoven, *Ninth Symphony*
	1824	Byron†
Ludwig quits bookstore job, enters Dutch colonial army	1825	Beethoven, *Quartet*, op. 132
Ludwig goes to Batavia	1826	Jefferson†; Voss (Homer tr.)†; Heine, *Travel Images* (4 vols. −1831)
Encyclopedia, rev. ed. (almost twice the size of the 1st ed.)	1827	Heine, *Buch der Lieder*; Beethoven† Blake†
	1828	Schubert† Goya† Tolstoy*
	1829	F. Schlegel†
Encyclopedia, 3d rev. ed.; Rektor, University of Berlin	1830	July Revolution in Paris
Aug. 28: Ludwig† Nov. 14: Hegel dies of cholera	1831	
Feb. 2: Sister's suicide; pupils begin ed. *Works*, 18 vols. (−1840; meanwhile 2d ed. begins)	1832	Goethe†

Abbreviations

The following abbreviations have been used for works cited often:

B   *Briefe von und an Hegel,* 4 vols. (1952–60)

C   Commentary on V–PG in Chapter VIII

D   Chapter VII of the present book

Dok.   *Dokumente zu Hegels Entwicklung,* ed. Hoffmeister (1936)

E   Hegel's *Encyclopedia,* 3rd ed. (1830)

EGP Hegel's *Einleitung in die Geschichte der Philosophie,* critical ed. by Hoffmeister (1940)

H   Cross references to *sections* of the present book

PG   Hegel's *Phänomenologie des Geistes,* ed. Lasson (1907)

Ros.   Rosenkranz, *Hegels Leben* (1844)

VG   Hegel's *Die Vernunft in der Geschichte,* critical ed. by Hoffmeister (1955). All references are to Hegel's own MS unless the page number is followed by an "L" to indicate that the citation is based on the students' lecture notes.

V–PG Hegel's *Vorrede* (Preface) to the *Phänomenologie*

WK   Kaufmann, *From Shakespeare to Existentialism* (Anchor ed.)

HEGEL

CHAPTER I:

Early Development and Influences, 1770–1800

Misconceptions about Hegel begin with his very name. On the cover of the English translation of some of his early writings, he is called "Friedrich Hegel." The professor who for a generation was the authority on Hegel at Harvard usually called him Georg Hegel, as if he and Georg were on a first-name basis.[1] But although Hegel addressed both Schelling and Hölderlin with the familiar *Du,* he signed his letters to them *Dein Hegel.* And they called him *Du* but also signed their last names. Germans did not use first names as much as Americans do, and although Hegel's full name was Georg Wilhelm Friedrich Hegel, one has to read a lot of letters before one finds a very few that are signed with a first name. Indeed, when his widow wrote his best friend a few days after Hegel's death, she referred to him as "Hegel." But Hegel's letters to his sister and wife are signed—"Wilhelm."

Another, much more important, misconception is that Hegel's life was utterly uneventful; nothing worth talking about ever happened, so one might as well proceed straight to his philosophy. In fact, one cannot understand Hegel's philosophy at all adequately if one ignores his life and times, and there have been few periods in history when so much happened. Hegel himself taught, most notably but by no means only in the preface to his *Philosophy of Right,* that "philosophy is its age comprehended in thought"; and far from being a web spun in an ivory tower, his own thought was intimately related to what happened during his life time. This

[1] In the *New York Times Book Review,* August 2, 1964, his picture was captioned "Georg Hegel."

is true not only of his philosophy of history or his political philosophy but also of his whole conception of philosophy and his own mission.

First of all, Hegel lived through the whole of the great age of German literature. Lessing was born in 1729, Goethe in 1749, and Schiller in 1759; Hegel, like Hölderlin and Beethoven, in 1770. Goethe's youthful storm and stress masterpieces, *Götz* and *Werther,* appeared when Hegel was a child, and so did Lessing's *Nathan,* which Hegel was to quote more often than any other work in his early writings on religion. All the works of Goethe's and Schiller's maturity were published when Hegel was old enough to take in their appearance. He was seventeen when Schiller's *Don Carlos* and Goethe's *Iphigenia* came out, and though the former might be expected to appeal more to a boy of that age, we shall see later how decisively *Iphigenia* influenced his intellectual development.

Hegel was twenty when Goethe's *Faust: A Fragment* appeared, soon to be hailed, even in its incomplete form, as the greatest German play yet written. And he witnessed Goethe's Protean development from style to style: after the consummation of storm and stress and German classicism, he went on in the nineties, when Hegel was in his twenties, to publish *Wilhelm Meister,* the great *Bildungsroman* that established a new genre in German letters. Soon the romantics, whose movement took shape in the nineties, tried to surpass Goethe's *Meister;* and Hegel experienced the high tide of romanticism not only as a contemporary but as the work of young men of his own age. Of the two brothers Schlegel who led the romantic revolt, one was three years his senior, the other, Friedrich, two years his junior; Schleiermacher, the theologian of the circle, was two years older than Hegel; Novalis, their greatest poet, two years younger. And Hölderlin, the lonely outsider who is now widely considered the greatest German poet next to Goethe, was Hegel's closest friend. In his thirties, Hölderlin struggled against schizophrenia and finally succumbed, to spend the rest of his long life completely deprived not only of his genius but of his reason, little more than a vegetable.

Music meant much less to Hegel than literature, and neither his collected works nor his published letters contain a single reference to Beethoven, which seems odd because one would suppose that Hegel would have greatly admired at least some of Beethoven's symphonies. Neither does he mention Haydn though it seems that on at least one occasion he heard a Haydn symphony;[2] but he several times registered his admiration for Mozart.[3] And he loved Rossini's *Barber of Seville*.[4]

Hegel was nineteen at the time of the French Revolution; and four years later—the same year that Kant published his long awaited book on *Religion within the Bounds of Mere Reason*— Christianity was abolished in France and replaced by the cult of reason. There was an apocalyptic note in the air which soon vibrated through German philosophy.

At the time of the Declaration of Independence Hegel was six, and America was very far away, but France was not far away at all, and in 1792 the French began their repeated invasions of Germany. What happened in France during the quarter of a century from the Revolution to Waterloo was not just French history but also German history, and not just history but again and again a matter of life and limb. Napoleon's meteoric rise and brilliant campaigns were never far from one's mind—or body— and Hegel finished his first book, the *Phenomenology*, in Jena, the night before Napoleon finished the Holy Roman Empire, which had lasted over a thousand years, in the Battle of Jena.

It is well to remember that there was little peace in Europe from the time Hegel was twenty until the time he was forty-five— his only brother fell in Napoleon's Russian campaign in 1812— and that during his last sixteen years, of which he spent thirteen as a professor in Berlin, he enjoyed peace for the first time since his childhood. Though he had thrilled to the Revolution and later to Napoleon, even after the Battle of Jena, it is hardly surprising that Hegel came to appreciate the so-called Restoration.

What happened in far-off America interested him less. In a sense

---

[2] B IV, 419.

[3] *Aesthetik*, Glockner's ed., XII, 376; XIV, 171 f., 194, 203, 524. The first and the last two passages praise *The Magic Flute*. Cf. D 1797 and Gustav Parthey, *Jugenderinnerungen*, II, 406, quoted in the Appendix to Fischer, 2d ed., 1236: "After a performance of Mozart's *Don Giovanni*, 'Hegel, in his awkward diction, expressed such a warm love for this music that *Musikdirektor* Klein said to us afterwards: only now have I become really fond of this stuttering philosopher.'"

[4] *Aesthetik*, XIV, 207, and B III, 59 ff., 64, 68. The first two passages also refer to Mozart's *Figaro*.

that *was* history rather than a genuine part of his life. In another sense, it seemed to Hegel that the United States had not yet entered world history—and would not do so until the frontier had been conquered.

"If the forests of *Germania* had still existed, there would have been no French Revolution. . . . America is thus the land of the future in which, in times to come, possibly in a fight between North and South America, some world-historical significance is to be revealed. . . . It is not the philosopher's business to prophesy. As far as history goes, we must rather deal with what has been and with what is—in philosophy, on the other hand, with what neither merely has been nor merely will be but with what *is* and is eternally: with reason, and with that we have enough to do" (VG 209 f. L).

2

This concern with reason is characteristic of Hegel's philosophy, but it does not imply any desiccation of the emotions or a lack of feeling for passion. Indeed, in the same cycle of lectures on the philosophy of history from which we have just quoted, Hegel also said—and these words we have in his own manuscript, not just in his students' lecture notes: "Thus we must say quite generally that *nothing great* in the world has been accomplished *without passion*" (VG 85; emphasis his).

Hegel's reputation has suffered from the scorn of Kierkegaard; Kant's has had no similar fate. Yet it was surely Kant much more than Hegel who resembled the popular image of the professor: Kant's life was extremely secluded and uneventful; his philosophy issued from his mind without much outside stimulation; and his manner was, more often than not, almost grotesquely pedantic. Kant's stature is secure and these observations are not offered in a vain attempt to detract from it. But it is extremely odd that what is true in his case and admitted not to affect the greatness of his merits is so widely assumed to diminish Hegel's stature and even to make him ridiculous, although in Hegel's case it is *not* true. Compare Kant on the passions with Hegel:

"Passions are cancers for pure practical reason and often incurable. . . . It is folly (making a *part* of one's aim the *whole*) that strictly contradicts reason even in its formal principle. Therefore the passions are not only, like the affects, *unfortunate* moods that are pregnant with many evils, but also, without exception, wicked, and the most benign desire, even if it aims at what belongs (considering the matter) to virtue, e.g., to charity [*Wohltätigkeit*], yet is (considering the form), as soon as it degenerates into a passion, not only *pragmatically* pernicious but also *morally* reprehensible. An affect brings about a momentary collapse of freedom and of the dominion over oneself. Passion renounces them and finds its pleasure and satisfaction in a slavish mind. . . . Nevertheless the passions have also found their panegyrists (for where do these fail to appear once malignancy has invaded principles?) and it is said 'that never has anything great in the world been achieved without violent passions, and Providence itself has wisely planted them in human nature as springs of action.'—Of the various *inclinations,* without which, as natural and animalic needs, living nature (even that of man) cannot get along, one may concede this. But that they should be allowed to become *passions,* or actually were meant to, that Providence did not want, and to represent them from that point of view may be forgiven to a poet (namely, to say with Pope: 'if reason be a magnet, then the passions are winds'[5]); but a philosopher must not allow this principle to come near him, not even to praise it as a provisional institution of Providence which intentionally placed it in human nature until mankind would reach the proper degree of culture."[6]

This long passage is doubly relevant: Hegel and Kant do not merely offer us a neat contrast, but Hegel's attitude and philosophy must be appreciated as an important departure from the outlook of his great predecessor. To be sure, Hegel did not go nearly so far in the opposite direction as the German romantics did: he sought to integrate Kant and romanticism in a single system.

If we imagined Kant as a student at Tübingen—or elsewhere,

---

[5] Kant probably meant *Essay on Man,* Epistle II, 107:

> On life's vast ocean diversely we sail,
> Reason the card, but passion is the gale.

[6] *Anthropologie* (1798), §71; unchanged in the 2d rev. ed. (1800, Warda ✠198), §78. (In the *Akademieausgabe* and in Ernst Cassirer's edition of Kant's *Werke,* both of which claim to follow the text of the 2d ed., it is §81.) This Kant passage, which I have never seen paired with the well-known Hegel quotation, shows that Bartlett's *Familiar Quotations* is wrong in assuming that Hegel's dictum was original with him. The "panegyrists" may refer to Helvetius, *De l'esprit,* Essay III, Chapters 6–8.

for that matter—we could scarcely picture him choosing Hölderlin for his closest friend, as Hegel did. Even Goethe did not warm up to Hölderlin, and Schiller, who patronized him for a while, always found him a little embarrassing, as Goethe's and Schiller's correspondence shows.

3

It is usually either ignored or simply taken for granted that Hegel and Hölderlin were friends; but surely it throws some light on Hegel's character that this man should have become the closest friend he ever had. They studied together at Tübingen, then parted in 1793 to become tutors in different cities but kept corresponding; and in 1797 Hölderlin found his friend a post as a tutor in Frankfurt am Main where he himself had the same sort of job. After a while Hölderlin moved to near-by Homburg, but until Hegel gave up this kind of work in 1799, when his father's death temporarily improved his financial position, Hegel and Hölderlin saw a great deal of each other.

A fellow student at Tübingen, Leutwein, being two years older than the two friends, left the university in 1792 to become a vicar and later a Latin teacher. In 1798 he published a textbook, and in 1839, eight years after Hegel's death, he wrote down some reminiscences of Hegel as a student. They were used in a newspaper story which Rosenkranz quoted in his Hegel biography (1844), with the comment: "These mythical traditions are on the whole not incorrect when we compare them with the contents of authentic sources . . ." (28 f.). The first-hand memoir itself was also published in 1844 in *Jahrbücher der Gegenwart* (675 ff.) and has since been reprinted by Hoffmeister who also judges that "the report is not worthless, if one makes allowance for Leutwein's vanity and narrow perspective" (*Dok.*, 428-30).

". . . A certain joviality and tavern ease [*Kneipenbehaglich-keit*] also made him pleasant company. But one thing should not be forgotten, namely that his behavior was somewhat bohemian [*etwas genialisch*], which was not always in accord with the cloister statutes; altogether, his morality may have been better than his legality, which led to his subsequent change. Otherwise he was considered a *lumen obscurum*. . . ."

Leutwein claims that Hegel's change was brought about when another student was ranked above him, and Hegel was dropped to fourth place in his class instead of being third. This was probably due in part to his behavior, and it supposedly deeply hurt Hegel although he would not admit it. How much truth this bit of amateur psychology may contain is at best uncertain. "At least, metaphysics was not Hegel's special interest during the four years when I knew him. His hero was Rousseau in whose *Emile, Social Contract,* and *Confessions* he was always reading. He thought that this reading liberated him from certain general prejudices and tacit assumptions or, as Hegel put it, fetters. He found special pleasure in the Book of Job on account of its unruly natural language. Altogether, he struck me as at times somewhat eccentric. His later views he acquired only abroad, for in Tübingen he was not even really familiar with father Kant."

The above mentioned newspaper added another story, apparently based on the recollections of another alumnus, which Rosenkranz also quoted: "Hegel is said to have been the most enthusiastic speaker on freedom and equality, and, like all young men at the time, fervently admired the ideas of the [French] Revolution. One morning, on a Sunday—it was a beautiful, clear spring morning—he and Schelling with a few other friends are said to have gone to a meadow not far from Tübingen to put up a freedom tree. A freedom tree! Wasn't that a prophetic word? In the east, where the founder of Critical Philosophy [Kant] had around that time broken Dogmatism, the word of freedom had been sounded; in the west it had emerged from the rivers of blood that had been spilt for it. . . ."

That Hegel did not immerse himself in Kant while at Tübingen is surely true. The year after they left Tübingen, Hölderlin wrote him, "Kant and the Greeks are almost my only reading," and the evidence of Hegel's early writings, too, indicates that he got up Kant on his own, after he had finished his formal studies. Even then it was at first only Kant's views of religion, published in 1793, and his moral philosophy, recapitulated and developed in the same book, that concerned him. The *Critique of Pure Reason* he did not study closely until much later, and his image of Kant was always determined decisively by Kant's *Moralität* and its striking contrast with the *Sittlichkeit*[7] of the Greeks, as interpreted in Goethe's *Iphigenia* and in Schiller's "Letters" *On the Aesthetic Education of Man.*

[7] Another type of morality, more fully explained in H 6 and 21.

4

That Hegel was very precocious and exceedingly intelligent, there can be no doubt. When he was sent to Latin school at five, his mother had already taught him the first declension and the nouns that go with it, and his diary, published first by Rosenkranz and later reprinted by Hoffmeister, shows that at fourteen—the age at which it begins—he covered many pages with entries in Latin. Müller has suggested in his big book on *Hegel* that "in the process his German style contracted a chronic cold" (16), but Hegel's writings of the nineties, which were not designed for publication, show us an extremely vigorous and picturesque German prose. The corruption of his style came later. What is true is that its ills are patently influenced by Latin: the excessive length of Hegel's sentences points in that direction no less than his heavy reliance on both personal and relative pronouns which makes it imperative for the English translator to break up the sentences; only the gender shows—and even that sometimes does not show conclusively—to what these pronouns are meant to refer.

On July 5, 1785—still at the age of fourteen—Hegel records how upon the death of his favorite teacher, Löffler, he bought from his library twelve books which he lists with their respective prices, all very neatly:

1. *Greek*
    1. Aristoteles de moribus
    2. Demosthenes oratio de corona
    3. Isocrates opera omnia
2. *Latin*
    a. PROSE
    4. Ciceronis opera philosophica
    5. A. Gellii noctes Atticas . . .
    b. POETRY
    8. Plautus
    9. Catullus, Tibullus, Propertius, Gallus, Claudianus, and Ausonius . . .

Ten days later, on the fifteenth, Hegel recounts how he took a walk with Professor Cless: "We read in Mendelssohn's *Phaidon* [1776], only . . . the introduction, namely the character of Socrates.[8] Anytus, Melitus, and Crito [*sic!* instead of Lycon who is mentioned with the other two by Mendelssohn] were the three monsters [*Scheusale*] who got death for him from the timid senate and the rabid mob." It seems that Hegel first learnt of Socrates' trial and death not from Plato's *Apology, Crito,* and *Phaedo,* but from Moses Mendelssohn.

Rosenkranz reports how at sixteen Hegel made a complete translation from the Greek, still extant in 1844, of Longinus' book *On the Sublime.* "He was naturally inclined toward Greek much more than toward Latin and for that reason exerted himself more on his Latin lest he get behind. His wide reading made his Latin style a little far-fetched; he enjoyed rare and unusual phrases."

Also at sixteen, he studied Tyrtaius, the *Iliad,* Cicero, and Euripides; in the spring of 1788 Aristotle's *Ethics,* and that summer Sophocles' *Oedipus at Colonus.* "The reading of Sophocles he continued unabated for several years. He also translated him into German and later, probably under the influence of his friendship with Hölderlin, tried to render not only the dialogues but even the choruses metrically, but was not particularly successful. As the still extant translations show, he occupied himself most with *Antigone,* which to him represented the beauty and profundity of the Greek spirit most perfectly. His enthusiasm for the sublimity and grace of the ethical pathos in this tragedy remained constant all through his life.—Beginning on April 5, 1786, he translated the *Encheiridion* of Epictetus. In this case he copied the Greek text a chapter at a time, so the extant manuscript looks somewhat variegated in its alternation of Greek and German script." He also translated Tacitus and large parts of Thucydides—the latter probably while he was a tutor in Bern. Rosenkranz also lists some of the German authors he read (10–15).

In the midst of his entries for January 1, 1787, after mentioning his work on Longinus, Cicero, spherical trigonometry, and Virgil, Hegel notes: "In the afternoon I wanted to read only a little in *Sophiens Reise,* but I could not tear myself away from it until eve-

[8] Hoffmeister, *Dok.,* 403 f., has called attention to the lasting influence of Mendelssohn's characterization on Hegel's conception of Socrates.

ning when I went to the concert." Rosenkranz not only included this item in Hegel's diary, in the Appendix of his *Life;* he also said in passing on page 9 that the young Hegel did not avoid girls "any more than he excluded novels from his reading, as indeed he simply could not tear himself away from *Sophiens Reise.*" This passing mention, though not the diary, may have come to Schopenhauer's attention, for the latter, who never tired of denouncing Hegel in the most abusive terms, is said to have boasted: "My companion is Homer, Hegel's companion is *Sophiens Reise von Memel nach Sachsen.*" Glockner comments that we cannot infer "that the boy Hegel actually finished the six-volume *Schmöker;* on the contrary: on the following days there is no further reference to it" (I, 409). While this is as true as can be, one might add: and if he had?[9]

All this should give us a fair picture of Hegel up to the time he left the Tübingen *Stift* in 1793. The famous *Stift* was a kind of Protestant theological seminary and resident college which in those years graduated many men who later achieved renown in German academic life, including F. I. Niethammer and H. E. G. Paulus who in later years became Hegel's friends.

To sum up, Hegel was an extremely bright and industrious boy and came to Tübingen with a thorough grounding in classics, fluent in Latin and Greek, and at home in German literature. His scientific training, too, was good for the times. At the University, where at twenty he took an M.A. in philosophy, he enjoyed the freedom of being away from home and worked much less hard than before. He was sociable and liked to drink with the other students, but his closest friend was Hölderlin with whom he was united by a common love of the Greeks, of poetry, and of philosophy. He also was close to Schelling who, five years younger than Hegel and Hölderlin, was something of a boy wonder at the *Stift.* In 1793 when Hegel was writing those fragments on folk religion which form the earliest

[9] The novel was written by Johann Thimoteus Hermes (1738–1821), published 1769–73; 2d ed., 1776. It presents a picture of the period and of a sensitive soul, in the form of letters. *Schmöker* is a derogatory term for a readable but worthless book.

Hegel's diary entry is discussed by Kuno Fischer, I, 9, who gives the impression that Hegel ignored books of lasting value for the sake of such trash. It is also Fischer who introduced the Schopenhauer quote into the literature, claiming that it came from a letter Schopenhauer wrote to his student, L. Bähr. The published letters to Bähr, however, contain nothing like it; nor does the whole three-volume edition of *Der Briefwechsel Arthur Schopenhauers*, ed. Arthur Hübscher, Munich, Piper, 1929, 1933, 1942.

part of his so-called *Theologische Jugendschriften,* full of sarcastic and then still unpublishable contrasts of the glorious Greeks and the wretched Christians,[10] Schelling published his first article, at the age of eighteen: sixty-eight pages "On Myth, Historical Legends, and Philosophical Dicta in the Most Ancient World"; and before he was twenty-five he had published five books and become the foremost disciple of Fichte, who was then, after Kant, Germany's most famous philosopher. By 1815, when Schelling's meteoric career seemed to have fizzled out long ago though he was only forty, he had returned to the concerns of his first article, and when he came once more into the limelight as an old man, ten years after Hegel's death, his lectures on the philosophy of mythology and revelation were heard by, and greatly influenced, Kierkegaard.

5

From Tübingen Hegel went to Bern, Switzerland, as a tutor (*Hauslehrer*). Kant and Fichte, too, had held such positions early in their careers, and so did, just a little later, Herbart before he came to teach philosophy at Göttingen and Königsberg.

In Bern, Hegel was entirely on his own for the first time, and he tried to clarify his thoughts about religion. He had taken his final examinations in theology three years after his M.A. in philosophy, but there is no trace of any religious crisis in his development. Emphatically, he was not a believer, and this did not bother him in the least. Kant's outright scorn of "religious delusion," "fetishism," *Afterdienst,* and *Pfaffentum* in the fourth and last part of *Religion within the Bounds of Mere Reason* (1793) clearly did not offend Hegel in the least, although Kant extended to institutionalized religion in general such abusive terms as Luther had directed only against the Catholic church. *Pfaffe* is a derogatory name for a parson or priest, *Pfaffentum* an even more scathing term for clericalism; *Afterdienst* though scrupulously followed in Kant's semi-scholastic fashion by a parenthesis with a Latin equivalent "(*cultus spurius*)" brings to mind the backside, which Luther often used in composite words to suggest a perversion. Yet the young theology student accepted Kant's views on these matters without the least hesitation.

[10] They are omitted in the English translation but discussed at length in the chapter on "The Young Hegel and Religion" in WK 131–40, which also contains many long representative quotations from these fragments.

The second section of the last part of Kant's book is entitled "On the *Afterdienst* of God in a Statutory Religion" and begins: "The true and only religion contains nothing but laws, i.e. practical principles of whose unconditional necessity we can become conscious and which we recognize as revealed by pure reason (not empirically). Only for the sake of a church . . . can there be statutes, i.e. decrees which are considered divine but which are arbitrary and accidental for our purely moral judgment. To consider such a statutary faith . . . essential for the service of God and to make it the supreme condition of divine pleasure in man, is a RELIGIOUS DELUSION, and its observance is an *AFTERDIENST*. . . ." The words printed in capital letters are set off by Kant in much larger type. §2 of the same section begins:

"First, I presuppose the following proposition as a principle that requires no proof: EVERYTHING BESIDES LEADING A GOOD LIFE THAT MAN SUPPOSES HE CAN DO TO PLEASE GOD IS MERE RELIGIOUS DELUSION AND *AFTERDIENST* OF GOD." And in §3, which links *Pfaffentum* and *Afterdienst* in its title, Kant says: "From a SHAMAN among the Tunguses to the European PRELATE who rules church and state at once, or . . . between the wholly sensuous MOGULITZ who in the morning lays the paw of a bear's hide on his head with the brief prayer 'Do not slay me!' to the sublimated PURITAN and Independent in CONNECTICUT, there is certainly an imposing distance in MANNER, but not in the PRINCIPLE of faith; for as far as that is concerned they all belong to one and the same class, namely that of those who place their divine service in that which in itself does not make a man better (in the faith in certain statutary propositions or the performance of certain arbitrary observances). Only those who find divine service solely in the outlook of leading a good life differ from these people by advancing to an entirely different principle that is far superior to the former. . . ." And, a few pages later: "*PFAFFENTUM* is the constitution of a church insofar as FETISHISM rules in it, and this is found wherever it is not ethical principles but statutory commandments, rules of faith, and observances that constitute what is basic and essential."

In the final pages of the book, Kant attacks belief in miracles and, among other things, comments on prayer: "*Prayer,* considered as an *internal, formal* divine service and thus as a means of grace is a superstitious delusion (making a fetish); for it is a *wish de-*

clared to a being that needs no declaration of the inner mind of those who wish—and thus nothing is done and none of the duties incumbent on us as commandments of God are fulfilled, and God is really not served. A wish of the heart to please God in all we do and omit, i.e. the state of mind accompanying all our actions that we do them as if they were done in the service of God—that is the *spirit of prayer* which can and should be present in us 'unceasingly.' But to clothe this wish (even if only internally) in words and formulas, that can at most have merely the value of a means to animate repeatedly this state of mind in ourselves, but cannot bear any immediate relation to divine pleasure and therefore also cannot be a duty for everybody; for a means can only be prescribed to those who *need* it for certain ends, but by no means everybody needs this means (of speaking in fact *with himself* while pretending, which seems more understandable, that he is speaking *with God*). . . ."

It was this book, published the year Hegel left Tübingen for Bern, that prompted his initial enthusiasm for Kant—not the *Critique of Pure Reason,* which had appeared when Hegel was eleven. Liberal Protestant theology, of course, did not find it necessary to break with Kant, but Hegel, at twenty-four, thinks it would be fun "to disturb the theologians as much as possible . . . as they amass Critical [i.e., Kantian] building materials to strengthen their Gothic temple; to make everything difficult for them, to whip them out of every nook and subterfuge," and he trusts that among the pieces they are taking "from the Kantian stake to prevent the conflagration of dogmatics they surely also carry home live coals." In the same letter to Schelling (see D 1795) he expresses some concern lest Fichte's *Critique of All Revelation* (1792) may not open a loophole for those who want to go back to old-style dogmatics.

What aroused Hegel's concern was not Kant's radicalism but rather his division of man into mutually conflicting parts. He objected not to Kant's impieties or blasphemies but to the nature of Kant's *Moralität,* which consists in the triumph of reason and duty over inclination. *Hegel's departure from Kant was prompted by a higher regard not for traditional Christianity but for the Greeks, and his image of the Greeks, like Hölderlin's, was profoundly influenced by Goethe and Schiller.*

6

From the start of his philosophical development, Hegel accepted Kant's repudiation of any supra-rational statutary religion as well as Goethe's and Schiller's conception of *Sittlichkeit* as embodied, for example, in Goethe's Iphigenia who is a completely harmonious ethical personality. The time has come to consider Goethe's play briefly. It is the greatest achievement of German classicism and as beautiful as it is noble. Like nobody before him, Goethe succeeded at one blow in bringing the Greeks to life in eighteenth—and nineteenth—century Germany. Winckelmann and Lessing had talked about the Greeks and taught their countrymen, including Goethe, to think about them in a different way, but Goethe made a new generation, including Hegel and Hölderlin, see and hear them. Suddenly, Sophocles' Antigone ceased to be merely the heroine of a tragedy written in the fifth century B.C.; her spirit was present even now and represented a live option and an alternative to Kant's *Moralität*.

Goethe's play is barely longer than *Antigone,* has only five characters (Iphigenia, Orestes, Pylades, the King of Tauris, and his messenger), and is written for the most part in iambic pentameters; but three times Iphigenia's soliloquies break this mold with all the sublimity of a Sophoclean chorus: in the last scene of Act I, in the first scene of Act IV, and above all in the final scene of the fourth act, in the so-called *Parzenlied* whose presence one still feels in Hölderlin's poetry, especially in his *Schicksalslied* (*"Ihr wandelt droben im Licht . . ."*).

It may seem far-fetched to link this play with Sophocles' *Antigone,* which Hegel loved so much and which Hölderlin, already fighting for his sanity, translated; after all, Euripides wrote an *Iphigenia in Tauris.* But in Euripides' play the king, Thoas, is tricked, and Iphigenia, Orestes, and Pylades carry off the divine image, a statue of Artemis, thus fulfilling the condition for Orestes' purification from the crime of his matricide. Goethe turned Iphigenia into an embodiment of *Sittlichkeit* comparable to *Antigone.* No brief quotation can give any adequate idea of this, but these six lines (from Act V.3) certainly echo Sophocles' tragedy:

THOAS: An ancient law commands you and not I.
IPHIGENIA: We covetously seize upon a law
             That serves our passion as a needed weapon.
             Another law, more ancient, speaks to me
             And bids me to resist you, the command
             That makes the stranger sacrosanct.

Goethe's Iphigenia, unlike Euripides' but like Sophocles' Antigone, stands for love and humanity against hate and cruelty. In a tremendous speech, later in the same scene, she decides to be honest with the king and confides in him, as in a comparable situation Sophocles' Neoptolemus breaks his previous resolve and is honest with Philoctetes. And even as her *Humanität* has restored her brother's mind earlier in the play, it now prevails over the king's resolve to sacrifice the strangers to the goddess, and over Orestes' eagerness to fight; the king allows them to leave in peace—after Orestes explains in his last speech that the plan to carry off the divine image was the result of a misunderstanding. Apollo had commanded him to bring to Greece the sister from the sanctuary in Tauris and promised that if he did this his curse would be lifted: Orestes had assumed that the image of Apollo's sister, Artemis, was meant but now realizes that it was rather his own sister, Iphigenia, who has already freed his mind from the Furies that haunted it ever since he slew his mother.

We should recall how in the speech that culminates in the *Parzenlied* Iphigenia speaks first of robbing "the holy, much revered image entrusted to me," and then, eight lines later, cries out to the Olympians, "And save your image in my soul!" Goethe's change of Euripides' plot does not revolve around a superficial ambiguity: what is truly divine and has the power to purify a man is not a statue or anything supernatural but a harmonious ethical personality whose pride does not preclude humility and whose outstanding courage and honesty are employed in the service of love.

Kant, too, felt free to speak of the divine while expressly ruling out all traditional Christian overtones—and Hegel followed Kant and Goethe in this respect; but unlike them, he has often been misunderstood on this point. To understand him, we have to consider him in the context of his times.

In several ways, Hegel is closer to Goethe than to Kant. He fully accepts and shares Goethe's enthusiasm for the Greeks, as well as the association of the Greeks with an ethic of harmony and humanity. Later, in the *Phenomenology,* Hegel celebrates the brother-sister relationship as the highest possible ethical relationship. He twice mentions and quotes *Antigone* in this context, and no attentive reader can fail to notice that the whole discussion revolves around Sophocles' play. While he does not refer to Goethe's play at that point, there can hardly be any doubt that he thought of it, too—and that, since he, like Goethe, had one sister, the play had also struck a deeply personal chord in him. In any case, Goethe's *Iphigenia* is cited by Hegel in 1795 (Nohl 98; WK 141) and again in "Faith and Knowledge" in 1802 (302); and above all we have his comments on *Iphigenia* in his lectures on aesthetics:

"With Goethe, on the other hand [as opposed to Euripides], Iphigenia becomes a goddess and trusts the truth in herself, in the human heart." "Goethe, with infinite beauty, interprets the ambiguous divine pronouncement . . . in a humane and conciliatory manner: the pure and holy Iphigenia is the sister, the divine image, and the protector of the house." "In this as in every other respect, the profound beauty of this poem cannot be admired enough."[11]

7

Besides Kant and Goethe, Schiller influenced the young Hegel deeply—indeed, not only the *young* Hegel. We still have Hegel's first reaction in a letter to Schelling, April 16, 1795, to Schiller's important essay "On the Aesthetic Education of Man, in a Series of Letters," which had just appeared that year in Schiller's journal, *Die Horen:* Hegel called it "a masterpiece" (see D).

Schiller pays generous tribute to Kant (1 and 15 n.)[12] and also mentions "my friend Fichte" twice (4 n. and 13 n.), very favorably, but in fact he is much too conciliatory and unpolemical when he says, right after the second reference to Fichte: "In a

[11] *Werke,* ed. Glockner, XII, 309–12. Later in these lectures, Hegel remarks that the play is "excellent but not in the strictest sense dramatically alive" and in this connection cites Schiller's critique of *Iphigenia.* Hegel also calls it "a truly poetic model" of a conciliatory ending in the tradition of the *Eumenides* and *Philoctetes* (*ibid.,* XIV, 506 and 539).

[12] The numerals in parentheses refer to the twenty-seven letters, the "n's" to Schiller's footnotes.

transcendental philosophy . . . one easily gets into the habit of thinking of the material merely as an obstacle and of representing the senses . . . as necessarily opposed to reason. While such a way of thinking is not in any way implicit in the *spirit* of the Kantian system, it might well be implicit in the *letter*."[13] Surely, the former *was* Fichte's position, and the conception of morality as the triumph of reason over opposing inclinations was the very heart of Kant's practical philosophy. As long as I am prompted by inclination, I am not moral, according to Kant, even if my inclinations coincide with my duties; and to like to do what is moral is not moral.

Kant insists on this point again and again; for example, in his first book on ethics, the *Grundlegung* (1785), in Section I, not only for several pages immediately after the concept of duty is introduced in the eighth paragraph, but also later in the same work. In his *Critique of Practical Reason* (1788) he writes:

"The concept of duty thus demands of an action, *objectively*, agreement with the law, but of the maxim of the action, subjectively, respect for the law as the sole way in which the will is determined by the law. And on this rests the difference between the consciousness of having acted *in accordance with duty* and *from duty*, i.e., from respect for the law; the former (legality) is also possible if only inclinations determined the will, but the latter (*morality*), moral worth, must be found solely in this: that the action was done from duty, i.e., solely for the sake of the law.

"It is of the utmost importance for all moral judgments to attend with the greatest possible precision to the subjective principle of all maxims in order that all morality of actions be found in their necessitation *from duty* and from respect for the law, not from love and sympathy for that which the actions should bring about."[14]

This *Moralität* is obviously quite different from the *Sittlichkeit* of Goethe's Iphigenia; and Schiller, though too full of admiration for Kant to attack him by name, is entirely on Goethe's side. Without mentioning Kant, he once gave the classical formulation of the rigoristic position which he could not accept—in a series of distichs called "The Philosophers":

[13] On the first page of his first published essay (*The Difference* . . . , 1801), Hegel says: "The Kantian philosophy required that its spirit be distinguished from its letter. . . ."
[14] Pp. 144 f.; *Akademieausgabe*, V, 81; i.e., a little less than one-third through I.I.3.

CONSCIENTIOUS SCRUPLE
Gladly I serve my friends, but alas out of inclination;
And though this pains me oft, virtuous I am not.

DECISION
There is no other counsel, but you have to try to despise it
And with abhorrence do that which your duty commands.[15]

Schiller tried on the level of popular philosophy what Goethe had done poetically in *Iphigenia:* to present an image of man as a harmonious whole. Of course, he, too, was a poet, and some of his epigrams in the "Letters" are memorable: "One is just as much a citizen of one's age as one is a citizen of one's state" (2); "The artist is, to be sure, the son of his age, but it is to his discredit if he is also its pupil or, worse, its favorite. May a beneficent deity tear the suckling away in good time from his mother's breast to nourish him with the milk of a better time and let him mature to his majority under distant Greek skies" (9). The contrast between the present age and ancient Greece is crucial for Schiller's essay—and for Hegel's development.

This contrast is developed particularly in the sixth letter where the totality and harmony of the classical Greek are juxtaposed with the fragmentation of modern man. Schiller comes very close to saying that Kant's dissection of man reflects the modern condition: "Among us, one is almost tempted to claim, the faculties of the mind [*Gemütskräfte*] express themselves as separately in experience as the psychologist differentiates them in theory, and we see not only single subjects but whole classes of people develop only a part of their dispositions while the rest, as in crippled plants, are scarcely suggested in faint traces."[16]

"The abstract thinker therefore often has a *cold* heart because he dissects the impressions which after all stir the soul only as a whole; the business man often has a *narrow* heart because his imagination, imprisoned in the uniform sphere of his occupation, cannot expand to take in other ways of thinking. . . . Gladly I concede to you that, however little pleasure the individuals can feel in this fragmentation of their nature, yet the species could not have made

---

[15] Hegel quotes the last line in his *Philosophy of Right*, §124. Schiller's *Letters* are discussed in Hegel's *Aesthetik, Werke,* Glockner's ed., XII, 96 ff.
[16] Cf. V–PG II.3.2.

progress in any other way. The appearance of Greek humanity was unquestionably a maximum that neither could tarry nor climb higher on this stage. It could not tarry there because the understanding one possessed even then could not possibly help separating itself from feeling and intuition to strive for distinctness of knowledge; and it could not climb higher because only a certain degree of distinctness can coexist with a certain fullness and warmth. The Greeks had reached this degree, and if they wished to progress to a higher form [*Ausbildung*] they, like we, had to give up the totality of their nature to pursue truth on separate ways. To develop man's manifold dispositions, there was no other means than to oppose them to each other. This antagonism of forces is the great instrument of culture, but also no more than an instrument; for as long as it persists one is only on the way to culture. . . .

"It is equally certain that the power of human thought would never have achieved an analysis of the infinite or a critique of pure reason if reason had not isolated itself in a few isolated individuals who were called on to do so. . . . But will such a spirit who is, as it were, dissolved into pure understanding and pure intuition be fit to exchange the strict fetters of logic for the free development of the poetic power and to grasp the individuality of things with a faithful and chaste mind?"

This important letter (6) ends with a call for the restoration of the harmonious totality of our nature. It is clearly implied that this does not involve a return to a past golden age but rather a harmony that is higher and more advanced than was the Greeks', because it will retain the advances made possible by the sacrifice of such harmony in the intervening centuries.

Hegel's agreement with Schiller—when he first read this essay at twenty-four, but also in his later work, especially but not only in the *Phenomenology*—is so far-reaching, and Schiller is so much easier to understand than Hegel, that some reflection on such passages as these is invaluable for the student of Hegel. Hegel, too, sees through Kant's analysis of the mind and the bifurcation of man into sense and reason to the human reality that is mirrored in this point of view. Indeed, what Schiller does here in relation to Kant becomes for Hegel a paradigm of philosophical comprehension. Also, Hegel accepts the idea that what is unfortunate for the individual and may look like a step down and something negative may in fact serve the progress of humanity. Specifically, he agrees that a totality may have to fall apart before it can be reconstituted on a higher level.

In a way, the Greeks are models of humanity, and their *Sittlichkeit* is superior to Kant's *Moralität;* but for the reason just given, *Antigone* is considered in the *Phenomenology* (with the highest admiration) *before* Kant's *Moralität,* which is considered in an extremely critical vein. When Hegel in his later works reversed the sequence of *Moralität* and *Sittlichkeit,* he did not change his mind but merely ceased to deal with specifically Greek *Sittlichkeit* and discussed instead the higher harmony that might come after Kant.

There are many smaller points in Schiller's essay that are relevant to the *Phenomenology*. Hegel's scornful remarks about "edification" (V–PG I.II.9) should be related to the conclusion of the twenty-second letter where Schiller derides some readers: "His interest is either moral or physical; only what it should be, aesthetic, it is not. Such readers enjoy a serious and grand poem like a sermon, and one that is naïve or witty like an intoxicating drink. And if they had sufficiently bad taste to demand *edification* from a tragedy or epic . . . , they will inevitably be offended by an Anacreontic or Catullian poem."[17]

But it is a remark at the beginning of the next letter (23) and, above all, the first paragraph of the twenty-fourth letter that most obliviously influenced the *Phenomenology*.[18] "There is no other way to make the man of the senses rational than to make him aesthetic first" (23). In other words, Schiller suggests that there is a particular sequence through which man has to advance to rationality. This idea is elaborated a little later on:

"Thus one can distinguish three different moments or stages of development which both the individual human being and the whole species must traverse necessarily and in a determinate sequence if they are to fulfill the whole sphere of their destiny. Owing to accidental causes which may lie either in external influences or in

[17] Cf. also Hegel's Jena "aphorism" ⅗66: "One demands of philosophy, since religion has been lost, that it should aim at *edification* and replace the pastor" (Ros. 552; *Dok.* 371).
[18] This was recognized by Glockner who called attention to the importance of these letters for Hegel (II, 68–78), but up to this point our accounts are quite different.

the arbitrary freedom of man, the various periods can of course become longer or shorter, but none can be skipped entirely, and their sequence, too, cannot be reversed either by nature or by the will. Man in his *physical* condition merely suffers the power of nature; he divests himself of this power in his *aesthetic* condition; and he dominates it in his *moral* condition."

Hegel's *Phenomenology* recognizes many more than three stages; he is not quite so emphatic and clear on the point of the "determinate sequence"; and he does not echo the final sentence just quoted. But he does not only take over the conception and the terminology of "moments or stages of development [*Momente oder Stufen der Entwicklung*]"; he also develops the idea that "The individual must also pass through the contents of the educational stages of the general spirit" (V–PG II.3.3): indeed, this is the central idea of the whole *Phenomenology*.

The influence of Schiller's terminology on Hegel's extends beyond the examples given so far. In a footnote (12), for example, Schiller finds very suggestive such German locutions as *ausser sich sein* (being beside oneself); "*in sich gehen* [to go into oneself], i.e., returning into one's ego. . . . Of a man who has fainted one does not say, he is beside himself but rather, *er ist von sich,* i.e., he has been forcibly removed from his ego, for he is not in it. Therefore, one who comes to again is merely said to be *bei sich,* which is entirely compatible with being beside oneself." Here was a precedent for Hegel's later attempt to use *an sich, für sich,* etc., as suggestive philosophical terms.[19]

Schiller distinguishes the sensuous drive and the form drive before he introduces in the fourteenth letter what has become the best known term of the essay: the play drive [*Spieltrieb*]. At the beginning of the next letter he couples the first drive with *life,* the second with *form* (*Gestalt;* but the drive he calls *Formtrieb*), and then adds: "The object of the play drive, represented in a general schema, we can then call *living form.*" It is not irrelevant that Schiller was a playwright: in German, too, a play can be called *ein Schauspiel,* and performing it is called *es spielen,* playing it. While Hegel's *Phenomenology* is not a play, it brings before us— if it does not play with—living forms.

A similarity that is more obvious may be found in Schiller's

19 See C II.1.8, 10, 30; II.2.10.

triad: two opposed drives are synthesized, and their apparently mutually exclusive objects—life and form—give way to living form. If one did not know that it was said by Schiller near the end of the fifteenth letter, one would surely assume that it was Hegel who had said: "It is neither grace nor is it dignity that speaks to us out of the glorious face of the Juno Ludovisi; it is neither of these because it is both at once." In fact, Hegel says much the same, only not nearly so concisely, in the penultimate paragraph of Section III.1 of his preface to the *Phenomenology:* ". . . such expressions must no longer be used where such otherhood is sublimated. . . ."

Even the characteristic Hegelian term *aufheben,* rendered "sublimate" throughout this book, is encountered in Schiller. The word, of course, is common and can mean "cancel"—and in Hegel's usage it almost always means at least that—but it can also mean "preserve" and, thirdly, "lift up." Often Hegel uses *aufheben* to suggest all three meanings at once, as in the example just given. When Schiller uses the word in the middle of the fourteenth letter, the meaning might merely be "cancel"; but in the middle of the eighteenth letter there is a passage that has a definitely Hegelian ring: "beauty *unites* these two opposed states and thus sublimates the opposition. But because both states remain eternally opposed to each other, they cannot be united in any other way than by being sublimated."

A similar passage occurs in the twentieth letter: "Man cannot immediately move from feeling to thought; he must *take a step back* because only when one determination is sublimated again [here the meaning seems to be "cancelled"] the opposite determination can appear. . . . The determination that he received through sensation therefore has to be retained because he must not lose reality; but at the same time it must be sublimated insofar as it is a limitation because an unlimited determinability is supposed to take place. Thus the task is to annihilate and at the same time to keep the determination of the condition, and this is possible only in one way: by *opposing another determination to it*. The scales balance when they are empty; but they also balance when they contain equal weights."

Elsewhere, reason is coupled with the absolute and unconditional, while "the understanding remains forever within the sphere of the conditional" (24).[20] For Hegel, too, the understanding remains satisfied with simple propositions, consisting of subjects and predicates that in the nature of the case are only conditionally true, while reason seeks to transcend simple dogmatic propositions to give an unconditionally true account whose form, as he argues in the preface to the *Phenomenology,* can only be a whole system.

In the same crucial letter, incidentally, from which we have quoted the conception of the three stages, Schiller quotes eight lines from Goethe's *Iphigenia.* Another idea that is widely associated with Hegel also comes out of Schiller's essay: the contrast of two types of infinity.

"Some do not realize that the freedom in which they quite rightly find the essence of beauty is not lawlessness but the harmony of laws, not arbitrariness but the highest inner necessity; others do not realize that the determinateness which they just as rightly demand of beauty consists not in the *exclusion of certain realities* but in the *absolute inclusion of all,* and that it is thus not limitation but infinity" (18).

"The condition of the human spirit *before* all the determination given to it through sense impressions is a determinability without bounds. The endlessness of space and time is given to the imagination for its free use, and because, *ex hypothesi,* nothing is posited in this wide realm of the possible, and hence nothing is excluded either, one may call this condition of the lack of all determination an *empty infinity,* which should not by any means be confused with an infinite emptiness" (19).

"When the latter, the lack of all determination that issues from want, has been represented as an *empty infinity,* then the aesthetic freedom of determination . . . must be considered a *replete infinity* . . ." (21).

Schiller's explanations of his terms are clearer, as his prose is generally, than Hegel's. Moreover, Hegel seems to presuppose that his readers have encountered some of his terms before—presumably in Schiller—and therefore does not bother to define them when he first introduces them. The first edition of the *Phenomenology* (1807) numbered 750 copies; there was no second edition until after Hegel's

---

[20] Cf. also Goethe: "Reason depends on what becomes, the understanding on what has become. The former does not ask: for what? The latter does not ask: from where? Reason delights in development; the understanding wants to arrest everything to use it" (*Wilhelm Meisters Wanderjahre,* 1821; *Maximen und Reflexionen* #555).

death; and he probably counted on readers who were familiar with Schiller and Kant, even if they had not studied Fichte and Schelling.

Even so, the three Schiller quotations on the two types of infinity may not be entirely clear. To begin with the first, the point seems to be that a work of art is structured through and through, and precisely for that reason inexhaustible. Or, to use the crucial term in this connection: it allows for an infinity of interpretations—not because there is nothing there and hence anything goes, but because so much is there, even if not, as Schiller's hyperbole suggests, "all."[21]

The second quotation seems perfectly clear, except for the final clause. What *is* the difference between the empty infinity of uninhabited time and space on the one hand and an infinite emptiness on the other? Here Schiller may be speaking as a poet who is sensitive to the connotation of phrases: "infinite emptiness" is a phrase that qualifies emptiness, which is felt to be something bad, and the adjective raises the badness to the highest possible degree; while "empty infinity" qualifies infinity, which is considered vast and sublime, and the adjective, without negating this sublimity, merely tells us something more about it.

Schiller's use of *Geist* is similarly suggestive and brings out one more reason—though there are enough in any case—why this term, so important in Hegel's work, must be translated "spirit" and not "mind." After juxtaposing the sensuous drive and the form drive, Schiller prepares to introduce their synthesis, the play drive, in the fourteenth letter. Toward the end of the preceding letter he says that both of these opposed drives require some limitation, but the sensuous drive must not be weakened into "physical incapacity and a bluntness of the emotions which is always merely contemptible. . . . Character must assign to temperament its bounds, for sense may lose *only to the spirit.*" *Geist,* in other words, is the heir of the sensuous drive *and* of the form drive; it is not—and this is important for understanding Hegel—primarily an epistemological faculty or organ of knowledge, like "mind," but above all, though neither Schiller nor Hegel places this most appropriate word in the center of the discussion where it belongs, *a creative force.*

Schiller prefers to speak of a play drive without attempting any definition of play—until he finally says in the last letter (27): "An

---

[21] In Freud's terminology, it is overdetermined.

animal *works* when a lack is the driving spring of its activity, and it *plays* when an abundance of force is this driving spring, when the excess of life spurs itself into activity. Even in inanimate nature one finds such a luxury of force and a laxity of determination which one might call . . . play." An excellent example of such "play" in inanimate nature is found in Hegel's diary of a trip through the Bernese Alps during the summer of 1796—the year after Schiller's essay had appeared—in Hegel's description of the Staubbach falls (see D).

Schiller's central contrast of abundance and lack prefigures Nietzsche's contrast of romantic and Dionysian art in *The Gay Science* (1887, §370): "Regarding all aesthetic values I now avail myself of this main distinction: I ask in every single case, 'Is it hunger or overflow which has here become creative?'" Schiller's wretched suffering in the military school he attended from 1773 till 1780, where play was frowned upon and his own first play, *The Robbers,* had to be written in direct defiance of regulations—it was published at his own expense, anonymously, in 1781, when he was still a regimental doctor under army discipline—supplies some relevant overtones to his celebration of "play." For him this word meant freedom and the overflow of creative energy—not what the same word might mean to a bored bourgeois.

Incidentally, from 1775 to 1780 Schiller's military academy was in Stuttgart (before that it had been in a small town in Württemberg), and as late as 1782—the year when Hegel, also in Stuttgart, turned twelve—Schiller was imprisoned by the Duke of Württemberg and expressly forbidden to write any more "comedies" (!) or to communicate with anybody outside Württemberg. Later that year, Schiller fled from his native state, and the following year he became theater poet in Mannheim in Baden, the same state where the universities of Heidelberg and Freiburg are located. In the fall of 1789 he became a professor of history at the University of Jena, on the recommendation of Goethe who was then in the state government at Weimar. It was not until 1794 that the two poets became close friends.

For Schiller, brought up in a brutally inhuman way, "play" was a word that carried special weight, and his biography helps us to understand one of the most famous dicta of the *Letters:* "man plays only where he is human in the full meaning of that word, and *he is wholly human only where he plays*" (15). Such a biographical-psychological approach, of course, leaves open the question whether Schiller is right. The glance at his upbringing lets us see part of what he had in mind—something at least about which he is right. In play man throws off constraints imposed upon him from outside and— Schiller is not speaking of "games that go on in real life" and which have established rules—he becomes autonomous. Indeed, when Schiller says directly before the dictum quoted that "man ought *only to play* with beauty, and he ought to play *only with beauty,*" he leaves little doubt that he associates play with artistic creativity. Here—this is his central claim—man is not fragmented, but the whole man is involved; such activity is not that of a specialist, or rote, but wholly human.

Karl Vorländer, one of the leading Kant scholars of his genera- tion, has called this essay *"die philosophische Hauptschrift Schillers"* and recorded how not only Goethe liked it but Kant, too, found it "excellent" and took notes on it with the intention of writing a re- view to which, being seventy-one, he unfortunately did not get around.[22] But what are we to say of Schiller's writing *about* beauty instead of merely writing poems or plays to create beauty? Is he defying his own counsel *"only to play* with beauty"? No, there is something playful about his way of writing.

It is understandable that Schiller, precisely because he loved and admired Kant, felt embarrassed by "the gruesome form which one would like to call a philosophical chancery style";[23] and we feel grateful to Schiller for writing so much better. But he departs de- liberately not only from Kant's scholastic-bureaucratic prose but from what one might call entirely rational procedures. As Schiller argues in the passages quoted above, it required some fragmenta- tion of man and the exclusive cultivation of reason in some to create works like the *Critique of Pure Reason;* but now the time has come

---

[22] *Die Philosophie unserer Klassiker* (1923), 111 f.
[23] Letter to Goethe from Jena, September 22, 1797. Cf. also the letter to Goethe from Jena, December 22, 1798: "I am very eager to read Kant's *Anthropology.* The pathological side of man that he always stresses, and that may perhaps have its place in an Anthropology, pursues us through almost everything he writes, and this is what gives his practical philosophy such a peevish appearance. It is surprising and lamentable that this cheerful and jovial spirit has not been able to clear his wings completely from the filth of life and actually has not quite overcome certain gloomy impressions of his youth, etc. There is still something in him that, as in Luther's case, reminds one of a monk who has opened up his monastery but been unable to destroy its traces altogether." Both Goethe and Schiller objected not to Kant's critique of Christianity but to his retention of a doctrine of radical evil in human nature.

for a new harmony, and we must "exchange the strict fetters of logic for the free development of the poetic power" which alone can "grasp the individuality of things with a faithful and chaste mind" (6). Schiller's prose style in this essay is thus of a piece with its contents. And when he plays with the various locutions that make use of the German reflective pronoun *sich;* or pairs one drive with life, the opposed drive with form, and then the play drive with living form; or when he plays with the meanings of the German *aufheben,* or plays off against each other two types of infinity, he engages in the activity he commends. And here Hegel follows in Schiller's footsteps.

Hegel's preface to the *Phenomenology* has been characterized as his break with romanticism, and it certainly contains a scathing critique of many facets of that movement. But while Goethe and Schiller are sometimes considered romantics in the English-speaking world, Hegel, like Goethe, Schiller, and most of the leading romantics themselves, saw Goethe and Schiller as *die Klassiker* and understood romanticism as in large part a revolt against them. And even if the essay here discussed should strike twentieth-century readers as typically romantic, Hegel certainly never turned against Schiller. The *Phenomenology* ends with a quotation from a Schiller poem (slightly adapted in keeping with Hegel's habit in such matters), and throughout the book, for all its insistence on raising philosophy to the level of a science, the influence of Schiller's *Letters* is writ large, not least in the matter of style. Hegel accepts Schiller's vision of a new totality here and now, of classical Greece reborn on a higher level in early nineteenth-century Germany, and of a style that projects this new fusion of the faculties. Hegel's *Geist* is closer to Schiller's *Spieltrieb* than it is to the understanding which, in Schiller's phrase, "remains forever within the sphere of the conditional." And the subject of the *Phenomenology* is clearly a pageant of living forms.

But we are twelve years ahead of ourselves: the *Letters* appeared in 1795, the *Phenomenology* in 1807. And to understand Hegel's initial reaction we can make use of one final quotation from the *Letters:* "Reason has achieved what it can when it finds and proclaims the law; courageous will and living feeling have to execute it. When truth is to triumph in the struggle with forces, it must itself first become a *force* and put up some *drive* as its advocate in the realm of phenomena; for drives are the only moving forces in the world of feeling" (8).

Kant had expressly denied this in his *Critique of Practical Reason,* saying: "How a law can be by itself and immediately a ground of determination of the will (which is, after all, the essential feature of all morality), that is for human reason an insoluble problem and the same as how a free will can be possible."[24]

8

Hegel's early writings on religion need not be discussed here at any length because my analysis of them, supported by many characteristic quotations, is easily accessible elsewhere.[25] It will suffice here to stress a few points. The earliest fragments, which contrast folk religion and Christianity, have already been mentioned (H 5): they were written before Schiller's *Letters* appeared. Here the main tendency is precisely the same as Schiller's, and our last quotation from the *Letters* might have served as a motto for Hegel's fragments. This is the point on which he, too, differs with Kant.

Stylistically, these fragments are quite different from both Kant's book on religion and Hegel's later style. There is nothing of "a philosophical chancery style." In place of Kant's pedantic abusiveness which operates with nasty nouns, employed with scholastic precision (H 6), Hegel operates with vivid images and sarcastic contrasts of wretched Christianity with glorious Greece. A few very brief illustrations may show this:

Christians have "piled up such a heap of reasons for comfort in misfortune . . . that we might be sorry in the end that we cannot lose a father or a mother once a week"; while for the Greeks, who were honest and courageous, "misfortune was misfortune, pain was pain."

The Greeks' religious festivals were joyous and celebrated "the friendly gifts of nature"; at the greatest Christian festivals people appear in church "in the color of mourning, with downcast eyes," and, celebrating "universal brotherhood, many are afraid that through the brotherly goblet they might be infected with a venereal

---

[24] Part I, Book I, Chapter 3, 2d paragraph; *Akademieausgabe,* V, 72.
[25] "The Young Hegel and Religion" in WK 129–61.

disease by someone who drank from it before. And lest one's mind remain . . . wrapped in a holy feeling, one must reach into one's pocket in the midst of things and put one's offering on a plate."

In the same vein, Hegel juxtaposes Jesus and Socrates. Here he goes beyond the polemics of the Enlightenment, beyond Lessing's courageous attacks on the orthodoxy of his time, beyond Kant's book on religion, beyond Herder's sharp critique of Christianity in the fourth volume of his *Ideas on the Philosophy of Human History* (1791), and beyond not only Schiller's publications but even Schiller's very frank letters to Goethe. Contrasts of *Jesus'* faith with faith *in* Jesus, and *Jesus'* teaching with Christian teachings *about* Jesus were no longer unusual; but Jesus himself, even when his divinity was questioned, was still immune from criticism. In Hegel's contrast it becomes clear that he considers Jesus by no means the most admirable teacher of virtue but inferior to Socrates and really rather unattractive.

Socrates aimed to enlighten men instead of delivering sermons, and he did not limit the number of his close friends to twelve: "the thirteenth, fourteenth, and the rest were as welcome as the preceding ones." He did not insist on uniformity and had no wish to create "a corps that would have one spirit and bear his name forever"; he associated with men of higher caliber. And Socrates, unlike Jesus, "did not offend anyone by swaggering self-importance or by using high-flown and mysterious phrases of the sort that impress only the ignorant and credulous."

These passages (Nohl 33 f.; WK 134 f.) are of considerable interest to students of the history of ideas because Hegel's image of Jesus is so unattractive—incomparably more so than Nietzsche's in *The Antichrist;* for Nietzsche, like almost all other critics of Christianity, finds Jesus admirable, albeit pathological. These fragments are also of crucial importance for anyone who wants to understand the puzzling phenomenon of Hegel. One ought to be perplexed at finding a philosopher with such a firmly established reputation for conservatism and obscurity, writing in such a radical vein, with clarity, vigor, and stylistic brilliance. Those who ignore these fragments cannot begin to understand the man and his development.

Hegel went on to ridicule the Sermon on the Mount: Christian teachers would not dream of reproaching a man whose coat was stolen for not giving up his pants as well; the clergy plays a solemn part in connection with oaths though Jesus expressly forbade them; and the fault in these matters cannot be said to lie merely with the clergy: Jesus' teachings make very limited sense. "When it was a matter of judging a case in accordance with the law of the courts, Christ attacked the administrators of these laws. But even if they had been the most irreproachable of men and quite of his own mind, they still would have had to judge irrespective of that, in accordance with the laws. The judge must often speak differently from the human being and condemn what as a human being he might pardon."

Nor does Hegel side with Luther; on the contrary: "He took from the clergy the power to rule by force, over men's purses, too, but he himself still wanted to rule over their opinions" and he was far "from any idea of the worship of God in spirit and truth" (Nohl 41 f.; WK 135 ff.).

Two points about these early fragments are of the utmost importance. First, one should note *how* radical Hegel was in his early twenties. Second, his prime concern, like Schiller's, was from the start—to quote a later passage from his early writings (Nohl 266; WK 154)—"to restore the human being again in his totality." He felt that this all-important task, left undone by Kant, could not possibly be accomplished by Christianity; like Schiller, he turned to the Greeks; but unlike Schiller, he turned not to art but to religion —what he then called folk religion.

In this connection, one may note that in the *Phenomenology* we do not yet encounter Hegel's later triad of art, religion, and philosophy: there, Greek art and religion are fused under the heading *"Die Kunstreligion"* or "art religion." In the early nineties, however, Hegel wondered whether a new folk religion might raise a whole people to a high moral level. Such a religion, Hegel says expressly, would aim at morality as the highest end of man; it would not do violence to any human conscience or coerce anyone; and it "must not contain anything that universal human reason does not recognize—no certain or dogmatic claims which transcend the limits of reason"—not even doctrines that "transcend reason without contradicting reason" (Nohl 48 ff.; WK 138). What Schiller wants from art, Hegel wants from religion—if only such a religion were possible. But would it be possible?

9

In 1795, the year he read Schiller's essay, Hegel wrote two essays, again not intended for publication but to clarify his own thinking. The first was a life of Jesus.

Pierre Van Paassen says in a postscript to his own *Why Jesus Died* that in 1940, when the Nazis confiscated his library, it included "no less than seven thousand 'lives' and critical studies of Jesus' deeds and utterances, all . . . published within the last three quarters of a century."[26] The pioneers in this genre were David Friedrich Strauss (1808–74), and Ernest Renan (1823–92). Strauss, one of Hegel's students, whose "Life" appeared in German in 1835, created a sensation, inaugurated "a new epoch in the treatment of the rise of Christianity,"[27] and was translated into English by George Eliot, with a Latin preface by Strauss, in 1846. Renan's "Life" appeared in French in June 1863—and "before November sixty thousand copies of it were in circulation."[28] Since then, "Lives" have mushroomed, but when Hegel put his hand to his attempt, the idea was by no means hackneyed.

Hegel's "Life" has never been properly understood. It is plainly a tour de force. That there should be no trace of anything supernatural in connection with either the birth or the period after Jesus' death and burial, and no miracles, is not surprising. But Hegel's "Life" begins, "Pure reason, incapable of any limitation, is the deity itself": a bridge between the abolition of Christianity in France and the institution of the cult of reason in 1793, on the one hand, and Hegel's later philosophy on the other. And Hegel's Jesus teaches not what the Jesus of the Gospels teaches but rather Kant's ethic.

He demands only "the service of reason and virtue" and rejects faith, and he says such things as: "What you can will to be a universal law among men, valid also against yourselves, according to that maxim act—this is the basic law of ethics . . ." and, "Oh, that men had stopped there and never added to the duties imposed by reason a lot of other burdens to bedevil poor humanity."[29]

26 Dial Press, New York 1949, p. 269.
27 *Encyclopaedia Britannica*, 11th ed., article on Strauss.
28 *Ibid.*, article on Renan.
29 Nohl 122, 87, 102; WK 140 f.

This is plainly Hegel's attempt to write a scripture for such a folk religion as he had envisaged. Kant is made to speak vivid and forceful German, worlds removed from his chancery style, and his ethic is made more palatable by being put into the mouth of a thoroughly humanized Jesus. Absurd? Obviously; and Hegel had no mind to publish it. On the contrary, it may have been at least partly the grotesqueness of this effort that persuaded him once and for all that man could *not* be restored in his totality and harmony by religion.

Later the same year, Hegel wrote his first major essay, "The Positivity of the Christian Religion," translated into English by T. M. Knox (1948). At the outset, Hegel assumes with Kant that "the end and essence of all true religion, and of our religion [Christianity], too, is the morality of man" (Nohl 153; WK 141). Two pages later he defines "positive" as meaning "founded on authority and placing the worth of man not at all, or at least not only, in morality." Positive religion is what Kant had called statutory religion, and the influence of Kant's book on religion is writ large throughout Hegel's essay.

Again, Hegel is more radical than Kant. Of course, he was in his twenties while Kant had been almost seventy when his book appeared, and Kant had to worry about the censor while Hegel was not writing for publication. The style of the "Positivity" is very close to that of the fragments on folk religion: vivid detail, powerful examples, trenchant sarcasm. Jesus is treated more respectfully, but the originality of the essay still lies in Hegel's argument that the "positivity of the Christian religion" must be charged in no small measure to Jesus himself.

Hegel's theme is similar to Erich Fromm's popular juxtaposition of humanistic and authoritarian religion in his widely read Terry Lectures on *Psychoanalysis and Religion* (1950), but Hegel, even at twenty-five, is incomparably more profound. Instead of accepting, as Fromm does, the conciliatory cliché that Jesus' manner and teachings were humanistic, Hegel brings out, as few free-thinkers of the Enlightenment or the nineteenth century did, the "positive," authoritarian, irrational, not purely moral aspects of Jesus' manner and teaching. Hegel finds extenuating circumstances in the alleged rawness of Jesus' Jewish audience—extenuating circumstances, not grounds for acquittal. This is important both for an understanding of the young Hegel's conception of Jesus, and because in the course of this essay Hegel seems to have gained the enduring conviction that a humanistic religion is an impossibility. Admittedly, he does not put the point this way; but even as he never expected salvation from Christianity, henceforth he no longer places his hopes on religion—any religion, even a new type of religion.

10

The following year, in 1796, Hegel took a long hike into the Bernese Alps and kept a diary.[30] Those who have mentioned this diary at all—it has never before been translated—have often given an utterly misleading impression of it, as if Hegel had been completely obtuse to nature and had written little but: as for the mountains, all one can say about them is that they are there.

In fact, his diary shows a wide open mind, eager to assimilate all kinds of observations about natural phenomena and the way of life of people living in the mountains. It is true that there is more concern with information than with aesthetic experiences, but it appears that the great peaks were in the clouds and Hegel never saw the stunning views of Jungfrau, Mönch, and Eiger that luckier tourists find unforgettable. His whole trip was done by foot, much of it in the rain, and the poor weather did not keep him from penning some of the most sensitive impressions ever recorded of waterfalls.

The difference between his response to waterfalls and walls of rock is not unconnected with his later philosophy. What attracts and entrances him is life and motion, while motionless rigidity repels him. One should hesitate to read philosophy into such matters, but anyone will find on reading Hegel's own descriptions of the falls (in D) that if his comments have any fault it is that they are so very philosophical. And that is why the diary deserves mention at this point. It is of a piece with Hegel's protest against the frozen dogmas and statutes of positive religion and his quest for a living harmony.

The diary was written in July and August. Also in August, Hegel wrote a poem, "Eleusis," which he inscribed "For Hölderlin" and mailed to his friend in Frankfurt. Part of this long poem and also parts of another poem—one of two that Hegel wrote for his bride

30 Parts are included in D.

during the month of their engagement, in 1811—are included in D, in English. None of Hegel's poems is in any way outstanding, nor did he ever publish any of them. "Eleusis" was published by his biographer, Rosenkranz, in 1844 and has been discussed now and then in the literature. The style is close to Hölderlin's, though far less successful.

In October, Hölderlin found Hegel a job similar to his as a tutor in Frankfurt and wrote to ask him to come and live near him. Hegel complied gladly. In Frankfurt Hegel wrote another long essay, "The Spirit of Christianity and Its Fate," which has also been rendered into English, complete. Here Jesus is made to teach the *Sittlichkeit* of the Greeks, of Goethe's Iphigenia, and of Schiller's *Letters* rather than Kant's *Moralität.* "A man who wished to restore the human being again in his totality," after Jewish *Moralität* and insistence on law had led to "the human being's division against himself," had to offer an ethic that did not involve "acting from respect for duty and in contradiction to one's inclinations" (Nohl 266; WK 154).

Although the discussion of fate prefigures some pages in the *Phenomenology,* the essay has little originality or importance. To be sure, *this* reading of the Sermon on the Mount is more appealing to many twentieth-century theologians and lay Christians than the Kantian tour de force of the "Life of Jesus." Many comparable attempts in this vein since Hegel's time come to mind. But this whole genre is rather insipid: it is as pointless as it is easy to read into Jesus one's own ethic, whatever that may be; and Hegel was quicker than most to realize this because he himself had put two very different moral outlooks into Jesus' mouth, one after the other. He could hardly persuade himself of the historical probability of his second attempt, or of the worthwhileness of a third and fourth effort. While Schelling, as Hegel was to put it later, carried on his education in public, issuing book after book, sometimes several in one year, Hegel filed this latest attempt in a desk drawer, where it belonged.

11

The only thing Hegel published in the eighteenth century was an anonymous translation: *Confidential Letters about the Former Legal* [staatsrechtliche; sur le droit de ce pays] *Relationship be-*

tween the Land of Vaud and the City of Bern: From the French of a Deceased Swiss (1798). The original had appeared in 1793, and the author Jean Jacques Cart, a lawyer, was *not* dead in 1798. Hegel added a preface, condensed the text considerably, and added notes. His preface ends:

"The events speak loud enough for themselves; the only point can be to get to know them in their abundance; they scream aloud over the earth:

Discite justiciam moniti

[Learn the justice of the admonition!]; but the deaf will be seized cruelly by their fate."

Franz Rosenzweig, best known as a Jewish existentialist and co-translator, with Martin Buber, of the Hebrew Bible into German, established himself as a scholar with an important two-volume work on *Hegel und der Staat.* He discussed this translation at length, comparing it with the original, and he juxtaposed the words quoted with Hegel's later attitude—"the resigned self-limitation to the 'understanding of that which is.'[31] . . . Here the accent still lies entirely on will and deed: to be sure, the events are to speak; but they are to do more than speak; they shall 'scream,' teach aloud, and admonish: *discite justiciam moniti!"* (I, 50).

In January 1799 Hegel's father died. Hegel does not seem to have been very close to him, and there is no evidence that the event produced any trauma in the young philosopher. It did, however, improve his financial circumstances slightly, and he gave up tutoring forever.

12

In 1800 Hegel decided to rewrite his essay on "The Positivity" but did not get beyond the introductory section. By the time he had finished that, it was plain that a revision would not do: a really new essay would be called for, and this remained unwritten.

"The following essay does not have the purpose of inquiring whether there are positive doctrines and commandments in the Christian religion. . . . The horrible blabbering in this vein with its endless extent and inward emptiness has become too boring and

31 The context of this phrase is cited at the end of H 21, text for note 19.

has altogether lost interest—so much so that it would rather be a need of our time to hear the proof of the opposite of this enlightening application of universal concepts. Of course, the proof of the opposite must not be conducted with the principles and methods with which the education of the times favored the old dogmatics. Rather, one would have to deduce this now repudiated dogmatics out of what we now consider the needs of human nature and thus show its naturalness and its necessity. Such an attempt would presuppose the faith that the convictions of many centuries—that which the millions, who during these centuries lived by them and died for them, considered their duty and holy truth—were not bare nonsense or immorality" (Nohl 143; WK 158).

Hegel is not so much changing his mind as his point of view: he finds what he had developed earlier not false but rather too obvious and onesided. His earlier insights require, we might say, to be *aufgehoben:* they must be abandoned in favor of a fresh start from the opposite direction; an essay has to be written to negate them; but in the end they would have to be preserved in a treatment that would not be as onesided as either of the two preceding efforts. The onesidedness in this case was historically conditioned: a point originally worth making has been picked up by so many writers and developed at such length that it "has become too boring and has altogether lost interest"; and now it might be "a need of our time" to restate the opposite view which it has become all too fashionable to denounce—but to restate it, of course, not in its earlier and discredited form but at a higher level, making full use of contemporary insights.

To be specific: Of course, Christianity as a positive religion embodied a great deal of nonsense and immorality; but that is so obvious that the point no longer needs laboring. Now it would be more interesting to show to what extent it contained also some truth and contributed some good.

The question could be said to be one of emphasis. In his twenties, Hegel emphasized the dark side of Christianity. In his later work, he stressed the bright side—the contributions of Christianity. The difference in emphasis is radical, but Hegel's conception of Christianity never did change radically. When he treated Christianity sympathetically, it was only to commend it as an important, if somewhat benighted, anticipation of modern philosophy. He no longer contrasted it unfavorably with the popular religion of Greece because, like Schiller in the *Letters* we have considered, he came to believe that the harmony of ancient Greece had to be disrupted to make way for a higher development which could now be consummated—not in religion which is incapable of restoring man in his totality, but in philosophy. At will, Hegel could now make a great point of the inadequacy of Christianity, which he considered too obvious to stress, or of the way in which it was a stage on the road to knowledge, which he considered more difficult and decided to do.

13

He was not, of course, the first to make this constructive attempt: among those who had traveled the same road before him was Lessing whose essay on "The Education of Mankind" (1780) bears a motto from Augustine: *Haec omnia inde esse in quibusdam vera, unde in quibusdam falsa sunt;* "all this is therefore in some respects true, as it is in some respects false."

Lessing's preface, less than a page long, ends: "Why shouldn't we rather see in all positive religions[32] nothing but the way in which the human understanding everywhere could not but develop and shall continue to develop, instead of either smiling at one of them or getting wroth? This our scorn, this our indignation nothing should deserve in the best world, and only religions should deserve it? God's hand should be involved everywhere, only not in our errors?"

The essay, which consists of one hundred short paragraphs and runs only a little over twenty pages, views history as the education of mankind and distinguishes three stages. The first is represented by the Old Testament which allegedly taught virtue by holding out punishments and rewards in this world (§16). The New Testament occupies the second stage and inculcates "an inner purity of the heart, with a view to another life" (§61). Even if Jesus' disciples "had no other merit besides securing for a truth that Christ seemed to have intended only for the Jews a more general circulation among the nations, they would on that account alone deserve to be reck-

[32] It may have been Lessing who suggested this use of "positive" to Hegel.

oned among the succorers and benefactors of mankind. But that they amalgamated this one great doctrine with other doctrines whose truth was less evident and whose usefulness was less considerable, how could that have been any different? Let us not scold them for that but rather inquire seriously whether even these amalgamated doctrines have not given human reason a *push* in a new *direction"* (§§62–63).

"Indeed, it was most necessary that every people should have considered this book for a time as the *non plus ultra* of its knowledge. For the boy, too, must consider his elementary textbook that way at first, lest his impatience to finish with it tear him along to matters for which he has not yet laid the foundation" (§67).

"And why should it not be possible that a religion whose historic truth is, if you will, in such a bad way, should nevertheless lead us toward more proximate and better concepts of the divine, of our nature, of our relations to God which human reason on its own should never have hit upon?" (§77).

"It is not true that speculation [this was to become one of Hegel's favorite words] about these matters has ever done mischief and been disadvantageous for civil society.—This reproach is to be lodged not against speculation but against the nonsense, the tyranny, of preventing such speculations, . . ." (§78).

Finally Lessing announces "the time of a *new and eternal evangel"* (§86) and relates his own conception of history to medieval heretics who speculated about three ages of the world and the antiquation of Christianity. Three paragraphs still deserve special notice. "Let me not despair of you [Providence] even if your steps should seem to me to go backwards!—It is not true that the shortest line is always the straight one" (§91). Not only is Lessing right as far as education is concerned, but this insight, which he here puts so concisely, remains one of Hegel's central convictions.

The same is true of this dictum: "Precisely the way on which the species reaches its perfection, every individual human being (one earlier, one later) must have traversed, too" (§93). But how, asks Lessing, is this possible in one life? Is it possible in one and the same life to be first a Jew, then a Christian, and then to surpass both stages? "Hardly!—But why couldn't every single human being have been present in this world more than once?" (§94). In the end Lessing suggests the possibility of transmigration.

This last suggestion Hegel did not take up. He had learned from Goethe's great example that a man can consummate in one and the same life, first, storm and stress, then classicism, and then transcend both stages. And about 1800 Hegel may also have felt that he himself had similarly developed through a variety of points of view regarding Christianity: he had quite recently passed through an anti-Christian stage and was now ready for Lessing's mature perspective, firmly stationed on Lessing's third and highest level.

In his *Phenomenology* Hegel accepted, along with much else that we have cited from Lessing, the idea of §93, but interpreted it as our task here and now (V–PG II.3.3). It is therefore a little odd when Royce suggests in his *Lectures on Modern Idealism* (150), and Jean Hyppolite duly echoes this suggestion in his *Genèse et structure de la Phénoménologie de l'esprit de Hegel* (1946, 23), that the stages of the *Phenomenology* "may be compared to different incarnations or transmigrations, as it were, of the world spirit." This idea shows some *esprit* but misses the crucial demand on the reader to "pass through the contents of the educational stages of the general spirit, but as forms that have long been outgrown by the spirit, as stages of a way that has been prepared and evened for him" (V–PG II.3.3). While Lessing's essay ends: "What have I got to lose? Is not all of eternity mine?"—actually this was Lessing's last book and he died the following year—Hegel wants us to traverse the whole road right now as we read the *Phenomenology,* which he offered originally as the introduction to his system. What is to follow after the *Phenomenology* will presuppose that the readers have reached the level that the world spirit has reached in our time.

Much later, Hegel was to say: "Of all the glories [*Von allem Herrlichen*] of the ancient and modern world—I know pretty well all of it, and one should and can know it—the *Antigone* [of Sophocles] appears to me in this respect as the most excellent and satisfying work of art."[33] The frightening boast and demand are important for an understanding of Hegel. In his time it was still possible to read, and to have read, all the masterpieces of the Greeks and Romans, and of European literature and philosophy, and to try at the same time to keep up with the sciences. Hegel's philoso-

[33] *Aesthetik,* ed. Glockner, XIV, 556. Similar encomia of *Antigone* are found XIII, 51, and XVIII, 114.

phy confronts us as the work of a man who has not shunned this tremendous effort. Those who have done less are likely to re-capitulate in their philosophies doctrines held, and criticized and transcended long ago. But one who has done what Hegel has done can say of his philosophy what Hegel says toward the end of his lectures on the history of philosophy:

"To this point the world spirit has got now. The last philosophy is the result of all earlier ones; nothing is lost, all principles are conserved. This concrete idea is the result of the *exertions of the spirit* through almost twenty-five hundred years (Thales was born 640 B.C.)."

It is widely supposed that it is at least arguable that Hegel may have thought that history, and particularly the history of philosophy, ended with him. The evidence to the contrary is conclusive. Even this far-from-modest section begins *"The present standpoint* of philosophy is . . ."; and soon after the passage just quoted Hegel says (on the same page): "No philosophy transcends its age [*Keine Philosophie geht über ihre Zeit hinaus*]."

Five pages later, two pages before the end of the whole three-volume lecture course, Hegel says: "Now this is the standpoint of the present time, and the series of spiritual formations is for the present concluded with this.—Herewith, this history of philosophy is *concluded.*"

There is no ambiguity whatsoever in Hegel's phrasing: what is here rendered as "the present time" is in the original *der jetzigen Zeit;* "for the present" is *für jetzt;* and "this history" is *diese Geschichte.* That Hegel believed that there would be further history after him was made clear in section 1 when we discussed the passage in his course on the philosophy of history in which he calls America "the land of the future." But if one drops "for the present" and changes "this history" to "the history" in the above quotation, then, of course, it must seem as if he had held the fantastic view so often attributed to him.

CHAPTER II:

The First Seven Essays, 1801–1803

14

When Hegel arrived at the University of Jena in January 1801 to attempt a university career, he had an excellent grounding in the Greek and Roman classics, he had done graduate work in theology, and he had received decisive impulses from the work of Kant and Schiller, Goethe and Lessing. But he had published nothing, except an anonymous translation (H 11).

There was no question in his mind about his chosen field: philosophy. As a student he had been close to Schelling who, though five years younger, had meanwhile made a name for himself as a philosopher. But after an extremely good and friendly letter from Schelling, dated June 20, 1796, shortly before Hegel left Bern, their correspondence had ceased. Hegel did not revive it until November 2, 1800, shortly before he went to Jena where Schelling had been teaching philosophy as an Associate Professor (*ausserordentlicher Professor*) since 1798.

On his arrival in Jena, Hegel and Schelling resumed their friendship and soon decided to edit jointly a new journal, *Kritisches Journal der Philosophie*. Now, if not before, Hegel worked hard to acquire a thorough knowledge of ancient and modern philosophy. By the time the *Journal* was discontinued in 1803, when Schelling left Jena for Bavaria—Würzburg at first, Munich in 1806—Hegel had assisted H. E. G. Paulus in preparing a new edition of Spinoza, and his own publications showed the range of his scholarship.

His first real publication was a pamphlet of a little over one hundred pages whose title page, translated, reads like this:

Difference

of the

Fichtean and Schellingian

System of Philosophy

in

Relation to Reinhold's Contributions toward a Readier
Examination of the Condition of Philosophy at the
Beginning of the Nineteenth Century, 1st Installment

by

Georg Wilhelm Friedrich Hegel
Doctor of Worldly Wisdom

Jena

in the academic bookstore

at Seidler's

1801

On the first level this was an extended review of a work by Reinhold, who was then considered much more important than he is now. Born in 1758, he was a monk for some time before he converted to Protestantism and made a name for himself by developing Kant's philosophy along new lines. Fichte succeeded to his chair at Jena when he went to Kiel in 1794. (Reinhold died in 1823.)

On the second and more important level, Hegel considered it his first task in philosophy to absorb and fully understand Fichte and Schelling.

Schelling had not yet broken with Fichte whose foremost disciple he was held to be. Hegel articulated the differences between their respective philosophies.

On the third, and for us by far the most important level, it is symptomatic that the phrase that leaps at us from the title page is "System of Philosophy." Not only Reinhold is mere foreground; even Fichte and Schelling are, though to a lesser extent. The writer is

most fundamentally concerned with a system of philosophy—not
Fichte's or Schelling's, or his own particular system, but *the* system
toward which recent philosophy, indeed all philosophy, has been
developing.

After a short preface we encounter an introductory section of
which Lasson thinks that it may have been added after the essay
was finished, "just as he later placed his famous preface before the
Phenomenology. . . . This chapter on 'Several forms that are encountered in contemporary philosophy' resembles that preface to an
extraordinary extent in its tendency."[1]

Indeed, the short preface to the *Difference* ends with an apology
for the immediately following pages that might come straight from
the first pages of the *Phenomenology:* "Regarding the general reflections with which this essay begins—about need, presupposition,
basic propositions, etc., of philosophy—they have the shortcoming
that they are general reflections, and they are prompted by the fact
that with such forms as presupposition, basic proposition, etc., the
approach to philosophy is still obstructed and covered up, and it is
therefore needful to a certain extent to enter into these questions
until the day when only philosophy itself is discussed."

The first chapter has several sections with their own subtitles,
the first few of which might come from the preface to the *Phenomenology:* "Historical view of philosophical systems"; "The need for
philosophy"; "Reflection as an instrument of philosophy"; "Relation of speculation to healthy common sense"; "Principle of a
philosophy in the form of an absolute basic proposition [*Grund-
satz*]". . . .

A few quotations from the early sections may give an impression
of Hegel in 1801 at his best: "The living spirit that dwells in a
philosophy demands, in order to reveal itself, to be born [again]
by a kindred spirit. Before an historical attitude that, prompted by
some interest, is after information about opinions, it passes by as a
strange phenomenon without revealing its inside" (9).

"The true peculiarity of a philosophy is the interesting individuality
in which reason has organized a form for itself out of the building
materials of a particular age; in this the individual, speculative reason finds spirit of its own spirit, flesh of its own flesh; it beholds
itself in this as [both] one and the same and as another living

[1] *Erste Druckschriften* (1928), xx. All subsequent page references to Hegel's
early writings refer to this volume, edited by Lasson.

being. Every philosophy is complete in itself and, like a genuine work of art, contains the totality. Just as the works of Apelles and Sophocles, if Raphael and Shakespeare had known them, should not have appeared to them as mere preliminary exercises for their own work, but rather as a kindred force of the spirit, so, too, reason cannot find in its own earlier forms mere useful preliminary exercises for itself. And if Virgil did consider Homer such a preliminary exercise [*Vorübung*] for himself and his refined age, his work has therefore remained a post-liminary exercise [*Nachübung*]" (12).

This is the end of the first section; the second begins: "When we consider more closely the particular form that a philosophy bears, we see how it springs on the one hand from the living originality of the spirit who in it has restored through himself the rent harmony and given form to it through his own deed; on the other hand, from the particular form of the bifurcation [*Entzweiung*] from which the system issues. *Bifurcation* [or discord] is the source of *the need for philosophy* . . ." (12).

What Hegel once sought in a perhaps possible new religion, and what Schiller sought in play, play writing, and art, Hegel now seeks in philosophy. Nor does he consider the restoration of harmony a fringe benefit of philosophy; the need for philosophy *is* the need for the restoration of harmony.

In the sentences that follow, Hegel contrasts reason and understanding (as Schiller did in his twenty-fourth Letter, H 7) and finally says: "To sublimate such oppositions that have become fixed is the sole interest of reason. This interest does not mean that reason is against opposition and limitation in general; for necessary bifurcation is a factor of life which forms itself through eternal opposing, and totality is possible in the highest liveliness only through restoration out of the highest separation. Reason is only against the absolute fixation of bifurcation by the understanding. . . . When the power of unification disappears from the life of men and opposites have lost their living relation and reciprocity [*Wechselwirkung*] and gain independence, then the need for philosophy originates" (13 f.).

"The need for philosophy can be called its *presupposition*. . . . That which people call the presupposition of philosophy is nothing else than the expressed need. Because the need is thus posited for reflection [which always bifurcates], there have to be two presuppositions.

"The first is the absolute itself; this is the goal that is sought. It is already there; how else could it be sought? Reason merely produces it by liberating consciousness from limitations; this sublimation of limitations is conditioned by the presupposed unconditionality.

"The other presupposition would be the emergence of consciousness out of totality, the bifurcation into being and not-being, into concept[2] and being, into finitude and infinity . . ." (16).

Hegel's approach to philosophy, at least at the time when he himself approached philosophy, was clearly at least in part existential. But he did not look on philosophy as a solitary individual in isolated anguish but rather as a man willing to generalize as Plato and Aristotle had generalized when they suggested that philosophy begins in wonder or perplexity. Hegel adds the historical observation that philosophy is born of the alienation of man—an alienation that is as painful as it is necessary for human excellence. But we have already discussed this question in connection with Schiller's sixth Letter (H 7).

Why, it may be countered, do we need philosophy? Why won't common sense do? In his discussion of that, Hegel says: "As soon as such truths of common sense are taken by themselves and isolated . . . they appear slanted and as half-truths" (21). And: "Speculation therefore understands common sense, but common sense does not understand what speculation does" (22).

In his very next essay, Hegel made common sense his central theme. But the two points here mentioned state very important points forcefully and concisely. The trouble with common sense is that, like Scripture and popular proverbs, it can usually be cited on both sides of any issue—which shows, to revert to Hegel's formulation, that the so-called truths of common sense are half-truths. And even as our dreams do not furnish us with a coherent view of the world in which both our dreams and our waking experiences can find their place, so, too, common sense is not only self-contradictory (as our dreams, too, are mutually incoherent) but unable to integrate the insights of philosophy, while philosophy can understand and integrate common sense.

To that end philosophy must issue in a system. And Hegel, even in his first published essay, insists on this necessity (34 *et passim*)

[2] Not yet used here in the same sense as in Hegel's later writings. When rendering *Begriff* in its later technical sense, I capitalize Concept.

and attacks the view that philosophic truth can be comprehended in single basic propositions (25 ff.). Both of these points are later developed further in the preface to the *Phenomenology*.

From the long discussion of Fichte only two points require a place here. Hegel claims that Fichte does not properly understand freedom and says of his work on natural law (1796): "And in this ideal of a state there is no activity or movement that is not necessarily subjected to some law, taken under immediate supervision, and to be observed by the police and the other rulers, so that p. 155, Part II, in a state based on a constitution in accordance with this principle, the police know pretty well where every citizen is at every hour of the day and what he does" (67). And a footnote ridicules Fichte's suggestion that everybody have a passport which should be produced when cashing a check—a point echoed much later in Hegel's preface to *The Philosophy of Right*.

About three pages after this very long footnote, Hegel says in his critique of Fichte's *Sittenlehre* (1797): "But when in ethics the commanding power is placed in man himself, and something commanding and something obeying are absolutely opposed in him, then the inner harmony is destroyed; discord and absolute bifurcation constitute the nature of man" (70).

For our purposes it does not matter how fair Hegel was to Fichte or how well he understood his two immediate predecessors: that could not be decided without a detailed examination of all of Fichte's and Schelling's works referred to—as well as those not cited—by Hegel and would therefore lead us much too far afield. What we wish to understand here is not Fichte or Schelling but Hegel, and our central consideration in the discussion of this essay has been to throw light on his development, his approach to philosophy, and his later work.

15

To obtain the right to lecture at the university as a *Privatdozent,* Hegel had to write a Latin dissertation and defend a few Latin theses. He chose twelve theses of one short sentence each, altogether a single page in print, and defended them on his thirty-first birthday.

Hegel's *Dissertatio philosophica de Orbitis Planetarum* (On the

Orbits of the Planets) comprises only about twenty-five pages. The most striking fact about it is surely that Hegel had the competence to write a dissertation on such a subject. He had always maintained a keen interest in the sciences. After he had become principal of the Gymnasium at Nürnberg in 1808 he often took the place of sick teachers, "and the students were especially surprised when, without ado, he continued the instruction not only in Greek and other such subjects but also in differential and integral calculus" (Ros. 250).

A few lines in the first paragraph of the dissertation are worth quoting in this connection: "Thus there is no more sublime and purer expression of reason, none worthier of philosophical contemplation than that living being [*animali illo*] which we call the solar system. And when Cicero praised Socrates for bringing philosophy down from the heavens and introducing it into the lives and homes of men, such praise must either be considered low or be interpreted by saying: philosophy cannot acquire any merit concerning the lives and homes of men unless it comes down from heaven, and therefore it must use every effort to rise to the heavens."

The dissertation is now remembered mostly for its last two pages where Hegel, as a kind of postscript, adds a few remarks on the distances between the planets. "They exhibit the relation of an arithmetical series; but because in the natural order no planet corresponds to the fifth member of the series, people believe that nevertheless one exists as a matter of fact between Mars and Jupiter, traversing the heavens without our knowing it—and they search for it assiduously." Hegel then points out that in Plato's *Timaeus* we find another series of numbers: "Timaeus, to be sure, is not referring to the planets but teaches that the demiurge constructed the universe according to this rule. The series of these numbers is: 1, 2, 3, 4, 9, 16, 27, if it is permitted to read 16 instead of the 8 in the text. If this series should indicate a truer natural order than that arithmetical progression, it would be clear that between the fourth and fifth member there is a large interval in which one need not miss a planet."

The discovery of asteroids between Mars and Jupiter around that very time has prompted some attacks on Hegel, as if he had determined by speculative deduction that something could not be the case even while science discovered that, on the contrary, it was a fact. Rosenkranz commented long ago, by way of defending

Hegel: "Hegel wrote his dissertation in the spring and summer of 1801, but evidently did not yet know of Piazzi's discovery of Ceres on January 1, 1801. Nor could he know of the discovery of Pallas by Olbers, March 28, 1802, any more than of Juno's in 1804 or Vesta's in 1807. The clamor that has been raised about the philosopher's demonstrating the planet away on his podium, while the astronomers discover it to tweak his nose, is therefore an entirely empty and puerile *Schadenfreude*"[3] (154 f.). While Rosenkranz rightly stressed the hypothetical mode of Hegel's remark, his defense did not join the issue as ably as Glockner's did, almost a hundred years later:

"He did not proceed speculatively but stuck to the empirical data—while, conversely, the astronomers did not want to credit these data and, for purely theoretical reasons, searched for a further planet whose distance from the sun would correspond to the presumed arithmetical series. The true facts of the case are thus that the scientists 'speculated' while the philosopher stuck to experience and merely tried to look for a law that would correspond to the facts" (II, 238).

The last words suggest what *is* questionable in Hegel's procedure: Is it the philosopher's task to show how what is for a time considered right is also rational? Is it his job, to use a modern term, to "rationalize" the views, scientific and moral, which are current in his day? Should he not, on the contrary, remind his contemporaries of the uncertainty of their beliefs and "facts"? Should he not, in Nietzsche's words, stand "in opposition to his today" and be "the bad conscience" of his age? (*Beyond Good and Evil* 212.)

Certainly, the mature Hegel, whom we know through his books and lectures, represents a very different conception of philosophy from Nietzsche's. And Glockner's final words are plainly suggested in part by his knowledge of the later Hegel. In connection with the dissertation and Hegel's other early writings it would be wrong to raise this issue. The remark about *Timaeus* and the planets, which even involves an admitted emendation of the text—and at that a text that admittedly does not concern the planets—has a somewhat playful, if not ironic, tone. It is Hegel who is trying to tweak the scientists' noses. But when the new discoveries be-

---

[3] Delight at somebody else's embarrassment or misfortune.

came known in Jena, he included them in his lectures on the philosophy of nature.

Later, Hegel did try more and more to show how the world is rational; but he certainly did not try to justify common sense. Indeed, as we shall soon see, one of his very first publications was devoted to an attack on common sense.

16

Hegel's next efforts were concentrated in the new *Critical Journal of Philosophy*. It lasted only through 1802 and 1803, and each year there were three issues. As Schelling had another journal of his own, Hegel wrote the "Introduction" for the first issue, subtitled "On the nature of philosophical criticism in general and its relation to the present condition of philosophy in particular."

Hegel here gives credit to Kant and Fichte for having "set up the idea of a science, and especially of philosophy as science"; but he derides the pretensions of so many philosophers who now claim that they offer a science and a system and says, "that thus such a multitude of systems and principles comes into being" that one may feel reminded of "the condition of philosophy in Greece when every more eminent philosopher elaborated the idea of philosophy in accordance with his individuality. At the same time philosophical freedom and superiority over authority and the independence of thought among us appear to have grown to such an extent that it would be considered shameful for a philosopher to name himself after an already existing philosophy; and thinking for oneself supposes that it has to proclaim itself only by means of that originality which invents an altogether new system of one's own." Hegel goes on to distinguish "what is original in a genius from the *peculiarity* which considers and proclaims itself as originality."

It is highly unlikely that either Hegel or Schelling considered this introduction, which was unsigned like all the contributions of the two friends that made up the six issues, as an oblique attack on Schelling: surely, the introduction to such a joint venture would have been the last place for that. And yet Hegel had only just published his first essay, juxtaposing Fichte's and Schelling's systems, and Schelling himself had meanwhile written, for publication in his own journal, "Presentation of My System of Philosophy."

Hegel himself had also begun to work out a system and had mentioned this to Schelling in his letter of November 1800, when he resumed contact with him before joining him in Jena. But Hegel neither now nor later ever thought of his system as *his* system, nor did he claim the kind of originality he mocks in the "Introduction." On the contrary, the ideas just cited remain characteristic of Hegel's mature work. This is especially clear in the preface to the *Phenomenology:* Hegel insists that philosophy must take the form of a system but does not offer us one system among others, as if *his* system were more original than others; neither does he offer us *his* philosophy. On the contrary, there is only one philosophy; and this is part of what he means when he speaks of elevating philosophy to the level of a science.

On another point in the "Introduction" he did change his mind, or at least his way of putting his point. He attacks the fashion of popularizing philosophy and probably means to include some of Fichte's recent books, then goes on:

"Philosophy is by its nature something esoteric, neither made for the mob nor capable of being prepared for the mob. It is philosophy only by being altogether opposed to the understanding, and thus even more to healthy common sense, which means the geographical and temporary limitations of a group of men. Compared with this, the world of philosophy is an inverted [*verkehrt* might also be translated as topsy-turvy] world. When Alexander had heard that his teacher had published some writings about his philosophy, he wrote him from the heart of Asia that he should not have made common what they had philosophized together, and Aristotle defended himself by saying that his philosophy had been made public and also not made public. Thus philosophy must indeed recognize the possibility that the people rise to it, but it must not lower itself to the people. But in these times of freedom and equality in which such a large public has formed that does not want to be excluded from anything but considers itself good for everything, and everything good enough for itself, the most beautiful and the best have not been able to escape the fate" of leveling.

In the *Phenomenology* Hegel takes quite a different line, insisting in the preface that the time has come to make philosophy scientific and, like science, common property, available to all; and he alludes in this connection to the ideals of the French Revolution. In 1802 he says that philosophy must be esoteric; in 1807 he insists that it must not be esoteric. Yet the contradiction is largely, if not entirely, verbal, as Aristotle's reply suggests. In 1807 Hegel emphasizes that philosophy must be available to reason and not restricted to some cosy clique; in 1802, that philosophy makes great demands on reason and that those who would join in its possession must rise to its level and not shirk the necessary effort. These claims are not renounced in 1807; on the contrary, they are restated emphatically. It is even possible that the word "esoteric" was suggested by Schelling in mutual discussions of this manifesto— Schelling used it in his own work around that time—and that Hegel merely did not object to the term as long as he could give it his own interpretation.

Near the end of the introduction, Hegel alludes to Schiller's *Letters*. He condemns those who pull down philosophical systems to the level of "the ever changing and mere news; yet one should not confuse this craving for change and novelty with the indifference of play which is in its greatest levity at the same time the most sublime and indeed the only true seriousness." While the appreciative use of "indifference" comes from Schelling's work, this encomium of play is plainly influenced by Schiller.

17

Hegel contributed two interesting essays to the first two issues of the *Critical Journal,* both in the form of review articles—one on common sense, the other on skepticism. The first bears the title "How common sense takes philosophy, shown through an analysis of the works of Herr Krug," and then, in the style still current in reviews, lists three of Krug's books, one published in 1800, two in 1801.

Wilhelm Traugott Krug (1770–1842) is no longer remembered in the twentieth century, except for a footnote early in Hegel's Philosophy of Nature (E §250; the note was inserted in the second edition of 1827): "Herr Krug once asked . . . that the philosophy of nature should perform the trick of deducing *merely* his writing pen.—One might perhaps have held out hope to him for this achievement and the respective glorification of *his* writing pen when science would have progressed far enough one day and would be in the clear with everything more important in heaven and on earth, in the present and the past, and nothing more important would be left to be comprehended."[4]

In the early years of the nineteenth century, Krug was far better known than Hegel. Born the same year, Krug had obtained a chair of philosophy at Frankfurt on the Oder in 1801; and, notwithstanding Hegel's attack of 1802, Krug succeeded to Kant's chair in Königsberg the year Kant died. In 1809 he accepted a call to Leipzig.

We shall consider Hegel's essay only to throw light on Hegel. In the original edition it runs twenty-five pages, in Lasson's critical edition sixteen. The first point worth citing here concerns realism and idealism:

". . . Hr. Kr. [i.e., Herr Krug] divides dogmatism . . . into idealism, which is said to deny the reality of the outside world, and realism when it *admits* and *claims* this reality. But in this division, precisely transcendental idealism has been left out, for this does not merely admit—in a philosophical sense one cannot speak of admitting—but *claims* the reality of the external world as well as its ideality, and the theoretical part of the *Wissenschaftslehre* does not aim at anything else than a deduction of the reality of the external world" (145). Although the point may be elementary, it is still overlooked in some discussions of Hegel.

On the next point many readers, including seasoned philosophers, will surely side with Krug; but on this matter, too, Hegel was not to change his mind. "Common sense places the absolute on exactly the same level as the finite, and extends to the absolute the demands that are made regarding the finite. Thus it is demanded in philosophy that nothing should be set up unproved. Common sense immediately notes the inconsistency that has been committed, for it notes that the absolute has not been proved. With the *idea* of the absolute its *being* is said to be posited immediately; but, the common understanding objects, it can quite easily think of something and form an idea of something without its being necessary for that reason that this something that has been

---

[4] Professor W. E. Hocking of Harvard used to say in class that Hegel had ridiculed Krug's challenge to him to deduce his writing pen, but that a really good philosophy of nature ought to be able to accomplish such a deduction.

thought of must also have existence, etc. Thus Hr. Krug will reproach geometry that it is not a science complete in itself, as it
claims to be, for it fails to prove the existence of the infinite
space in which it draws its lines.—Or does Hr. Krug consider
God or the absolute a kind of hypothesis which philosophy incurs,
just as *one* physics permits itself the hypothesis of empty space,
a magnetic, electric matter, etc., in whose place *another* physics
might posit quite different hypotheses?" (147 f.)

The central point at issue here is the one Kant raised in his
celebrated refutation of the ontological argument for God's existence when he tried to prove a point about the concept of God
by likening it to the concept of a hundred dollars (1781, 599).
Hegel here sides against not only Krug's common sense but Kant;
and he never accepted Kant's treatment of the ontological argument, but always insisted that God, or the absolute, is *sui generis*.

The discussion of Krug's pen is worth quoting almost in full.
It is much longer here than in the *Encyclopedia* footnote, and it is
rarely realized to what extent the later Hegel drew on his earlier,
much less well-known work. The passage also provides a nice
sample of Hegel's ponderous sarcasm.

"It is funny how Hr. Kr. is nevertheless so gracious that he does
not want to take the philosopher who poses as a master in philosophy quite literally by his word; so he demands only *something
little,* only the deduction of one definite notion, e.g., of *the moon*
with all its characteristics, or of a rose, a horse, a dog, wood, iron,
clay, an oak, or merely of his writing pen. It looks as if Hr. Kr.
had wished to make things easy for the idealists with such demands
by picking out of the solar system only a subordinate point, the
moon, or, as something still much easier, his writing pen. But
doesn't Hr. Kr. comprehend that the determinatenesses which are
incomprehensible in transcendental idealism belong to the philosophy of nature, of whose difference from transcendental idealism
he does not seem to know anything—insofar as they, unlike Hr.
Kr.'s pen, belong in philosophy at all? In the philosophy of nature
he can find a *Dedukzion* (a word whose meaning is as bad here
as its spelling) of one of the things he proposes, of iron. Does Hr.
Kr. have so little of an idea of philosophical construction that he
supposes that the moon could be comprehended without the entire
solar system, and does he have such a feeble notion of this solar
system that he does not see that the knowledge of this system is the

most sublime and supreme task of reason? If Hr. Kr. had even a remote intimation of the magnitude of this definite task or of that which is in general at the present moment the first concern of philosophy, namely to place God once again absolutely right in front at the head of philosophy as the sole ground of everything, as the only *principium essendi* and *cognoscendi* [principle of being and of knowledge], after he has been placed long enough *alongside* other finite things or entirely at the end, as a postulate [by Kant in his *Critique of Practical Reason*] that issues from an absolute finitude—how, then, could it occur to him to demand the deduction of his pen from philosophy? A dog, an oak, a horse, a reed are, to be sure, like Moses, Alexander, Cyrus, Jesus, etc., something more excellent, and both lines of organization [nature and history] are closer to philosophy than Hr. Krug's pen and the philosophical works he has authored. The philosophy of nature points out to him how he should have to comprehend the organization of an oak, rose, dog, and cat; and if he has the inclination and zeal to contract his human individuality to the stage of life of a rose or a dog in order to comprehend and grasp their living being completely, let him make the attempt. But he cannot expect this from others. And it would be better if he tried to expand his nature to the greatest individualities, such as Cyrus, Moses, Alexander, Jesus, etc., or even only of the great orator[5] Cicero; then he could hardly fail to comprehend their necessity and to consider the construction of these individuals, as well as the series of the appearances of the world spirit which one calls history, more capable of a construction. But from the demand for a deduction of his pen he will have to desist entirely toward this end . . ." (148 f.).

Again, Hegel states at the outset of his career what he never again states so fully, though he never changed his mind about it. And he makes clear his distaste for talk of deduction, his preference for "comprehension," and his conviction that it is the task of the philosophy of nature to comprehend the rationality of the solar system, and of the philosophy of history to comprehend the "necessity" of a "Cyrus, Moses, Alexander, Jesus, etc."

Since the times of Kant, who developed a major hypothesis in astronomy, science and philosophy have parted ways to such an extent that hardly any philosophers are left with any inclination

5 Krug's identification.

to do philosophy of nature: one does philosophy of science instead. Similarly, philosophy of history is turning more and more to reflection on historiography and historical method and dealing less and less with the *content* of history—with the major events or such individuals as Hegel enumerates. But the boundaries of philosophy are not permanent; division of labor continues; and the fact that over a century or two ago some philosopher still did something that is now done by members of other departments at the better universities should not preclude attempts at sympathetic comprehension of Hegel's position. He maintained that reason must not resign itself to the view that nature and history are completely arbitrary: on the contrary, it must seek to determine to what extent that which it studies is rational.

The fact remains that Hegel uses "necessary" as an inclusive antonym of "arbitrary," as if everything for which good reasons can be given and which was not, therefore, arbitrary could be reasonably called "necessary." Another example of this unfortunate terminology was encountered earlier, in the penultimate sentence of the quotation at the beginning of Section 12, where Hegel speaks of "naturalness and necessity." Indeed, for him "natural" and "necessary" and "rational" may almost be said to form a trinity. Whatever can be shown to have been "natural" under the circumstances and therefore in keeping with rational expectations and not arbitrary, he is apt to call "necessary"; but this does not mean that he claims to be able to "deduce" it in any reasonable sense of that word. It does mean that he claims to "comprehend" it.

The extreme sarcasm of the words that immediately follow the last brackets in our long quotation about the pen does not stand alone. Two further examples may illustrate Hegel's biting humor. Krug had mentioned that he hoped to write a work covering the whole of philosophy, as Hegel puts it, "in eight volumes, namely seven volumes of contents and one volume of *subject* index." A page later, Hegel writes:

"Otherwise, *even the word* 'reason' is not used by Hr. Kr. in the three works before us, insofar as they relate to philosophy. Excepting the *Letters on the Wissenschaftslehre,* one encounters it a couple of times in the genitive . . . (to which we also call Hr. Kr.'s attention lest it happen to him that in the seven volumes of philosophical sciences reason should not be mentioned at all, or only in the genitive, and this subject should then be missing from the subject index, volume 8)" (153).

Our last example involves the name of the unfortunate Krug, which means pitcher: "In the light of the above, the synthetism of Hr. Kr. must be thought of like this: Imagine a pitcher in which Reinholdian water, stale Kantian beer, enlightening syrup called Berlinism, and other comparable ingredients are contained by some accident . . ." (155).

Lasson may be right when he says in his introduction to Hegel's *Erste Druckschriften:* "Presumably, he would not have had to wait fifteen years before being offered an academic chair, if the first impression the scientific world received from him had not been that of a polemical spirit of uninhibited sharpness who employed with mastery the whole scale of literary weapons from rough Swabian rudeness to cutting scorn and cold contempt.[6] After a short time, Hegel himself stopped writing this sort of thing . . ." (xii f.).

It may be noted that when Hegel chose to write this way he mastered these accents every bit as well as Kierkegaard did roughly fifty years later in his uninformed attacks on Hegel. It is not the least value of a study of the young Hegel that it shows what an utter caricature Kierkegaard's image of the totally unhumorous Professor Hegel was, and how little the Dane understood his man (Cf. H 68).

18

Having attacked common sense in the first issue of the *Journal,* Hegel criticized skepticism in the second. This time he reviewed Gottlob Ernst Schulze's *Critique of Theoretical Philosophy,* a work that had appeared in two volumes (1801/02), both well over seven hundred pages long. Schulze (1761–1833) was Professor of Philosophy at Helmstedt since 1788. In 1810 he accepted a call to Göttingen. Eight years before his new work, Schulze had attracted a great deal of attention with his critique of Kant. And now an extremely favorable review of the first volume had appeared in a popular literary supplement—and was reprinted by Hegel and

---

[6] Cf. Ros. 165: "Hegel had a rough wit that appeared now as naïve [?] irony, now as cutting satire, now as absolute [?] humor, in manifold ways, in an inexhaustibility of new and fitting images."

Schelling in the same issue with Hegel's review, in an appendix consisting of a collection of similar material. This item they entitled: "Outbreak of popular joy over the destruction at long last of philosophy [*Ausbruch der Volksfreude über den endlichen Untergang der Philosophie*]." It began: "It is time at long last that the blanket be taken away from the philosophers that has covered their eyes with darkness for over two thousand years. *Patience is not infinite. . . .*"

Hegel's review article bears the title "Relation of skepticism to philosophy, account of its various modifications, and comparison of the most modern with ancient skepticism." By now Hegel shows considerable mastery of the history of philosophy, by no means only of the development of skepticism. Indeed, no great modern philosopher before Hegel had ever shown any comparable knowledge of his predecessors. The article is seventy-four pages in length (fifty-one in the critical edition) and cannot be summarized here. We shall begin by considering four passages.

The first deals with the persistent disagreement among philosophers. Does this not discredit philosophy? Says Hegel: "But when Hr. Sch. has seen that the striving of so many men who are venerable for their talents and zeal has been unsuccessful when they tried to seek out the ultimate grounds of our knowledge, this can at most be considered a very subjective way of seeing. Leibniz, e.g., expresses quite a different way of seeing in the passage which Jacobi made one of his mottoes: *j'ai trouvé que la plupart des sectes ont raison dans une bonne partie de ce qu'elles avancent, mais non pas tant en ce qu'elles nient.*[7] The superficial view of philosophical quarrels reveals only the differences of the systems, but even the old rule, *contra negantes principia non est disputandum,*[8] shows us that when philosophical systems fight with each other—it is another matter, admittedly, when philosophy fights with un-philosophy —there is agreement on principles which are superior to all success and fate and which do not show themselves in what the fight is about and therefore escape that gaping which always sees the opposite of what is happening before its eyes" (163).

The problem of philosophical disagreement thus concerned Hegel from the start, and instead of simply ignoring it and giving reasons for his own views, he made it the very basis of his own philosophy.

---

[7] I have found that most sects are right in a good part of what they affirm, but not so much in what they deny.
[8] One cannot argue against those who deny principles.

As we have seen (H 12), Hegel came to believe in 1800 "that the convictions of many centuries" were not "bare nonsense or immorality." Extending this faith to the great philosophers, he was confronted by the task of finding what truth each had seen: if one could only recapitulate all the insights of all one's predecessors one should be able to develop a philosophy far superior to any that had ever gone before.

To be sure, Hegel has not shown that Leibniz and Jacobi were right; and in fact they were surely wrong. A catalogue of all the affirmations of all sects through the ages and over the globe would approximate an encyclopedia of nonsense and immorality. But the opposite of Leibniz's dictum comes much closer to the truth of the matter: most sects are wrong in what they affirm but right in a good part of their negations. Sectarians are good at seeing the errors committed by other sects, but blind to the errors of their own affirmations. And in philosophy, too, the great contributions of the great philosophers may be found in their superb criticisms of errors, whether those of religions, common sense, or other philosophers; but men who had shown brilliance and genius in this respect usually went on to offer untenable affirmations of their own, which had to be criticized in turn by their successors. In this way there has been cumulative insight and progress of a sort: more and more illusions have been stripped away, and men gradually come to realize that more and more of their supposed knowledge was spurious. As Socrates insisted, as long as men begin by thinking that they know what in fact they do not know, he may be wisest who realizes how little he knows (*Apology* 21). Socrates overstated the point with his characteristic love of paradox and spoke of knowing "nothing," which makes for needless confusion. But it makes good sense and is by no means merely an ironic point to say that wisdom consists in realizing how many beliefs are false, and that the history of philosophy, as the love of wisdom, has been a progressive disillusionment.

This view is not nihilistic: it does not suggest that all philosophers are equally wrong and nothing is ever gained; on the contrary, the suggestion is that there is progress and that philosophic insight is cumulative. "Instead of seeing the history of philosophy as an accumulation of fantastic systems, one may view it as the gradual analysis of, and liberation from, one illusion after another, a stripping away of fantasies, a slow destruction of once hallowed truths that are found to be errors. . . . Philosophers have rarely given *good* reasons for what was believed previously. Much more often, their denials, their heresies, their exposures of long unquestioned doctrines continue to be taught."[9]

This view, of course, is not Hegel's view. He came to think that *positive* knowledge was cumulative, and that construction could be expanded progressively. A critic may find fault with his affirmation, while applauding his rejection of the view that philosophy has been a waste of time because the great philosophers did not agree with each other.

In any case, the view suggested here is not meant to imply that philosophers *never* have any positive insights that prove to be true and important, or that *only* their criticisms of other views are worth remembering. There are exceptions; for example, some philosophers have made brilliant psychological observations, and philosophers have contributed more than their share of penetrating epigrams. Moreover, their way of looking at things and problems—and of seeing problems where none had been seen before—is often enlightening and of great educational value. But when it comes to their *arguments,* the best of these are generally criticisms, not ingenious defenses, of accepted views.

These, to repeat once more, are not Hegel's ideas, and it is high time to return to his essay on skepticism. His next point requires no critical comment: it is important because it is so characteristic of Hegel's thought down to his last period. "Taking everything into account, it seems that Hr. Schulze considers only theoretical philosophy as speculative philosophy, while he considers the other parts of the latter as one knows not what; or rather, one nowhere sees a trace of an idea of a speculative philosophy which is neither particularly theoretical, nor practical, nor aesthetic philosophy" (165). For Hegel the last two are not only important branches which must not be forgotten over the first; there are, strictly speaking, no branches; philosophy is a totality nourished as much by man's thinking about ethics and his study of art and literature as it is by reading epistemology and metaphysics.

In keeping with this, Hegel also attends to the human reality behind skepticism, to Pyrrho, the ancient founder, and to *ataraxia* —the imperturbability the Greeks sought through skepticism. And

[9] Kaufmann, *The Faith of a Heretic,* section 5, where examples are given.

of this Hegel says: "From this positive side it is also clear that this skepticism is not alien to any philosophy. The apathy of the Stoic and the indifference of the philosopher in general, must recognize themselves in this *ataraxia.*"

The last passage from Hegel's essay to be considered here deals with the problem announced in its title: "Without the determination of the true relation of skepticism to philosophy, and without the insight that skepticism is intimately at one with every true philosophy, and that thus there is a philosophy that is neither skepticism nor dogmatism and thus both at once, all the histories and tales and new editions of skepticism cannot lead to anything. . . . Even Diogenes Laertius mentions in his manner that some call Homer the originator of skepticism because he speaks differently of the same things in different situations; that many of the dicta of the seven sages, too, are skeptical. . . . But even more Diogenes adduces as skeptics Archilochus, Euripides, Zeno, Xenophanes, Democritus, *Plato,* etc. In brief, those whom Diogenes echoes had the insight that a true philosophy necessarily also has a negative side which is turned against everything that is limited, and thus against the pile of the facts of consciousness and their undeniable certainty as well as against the bigoted concepts in those magnificent doctrines which Hr. Schulze considers inaccessible to reasonable skepticism, against this whole soil of finitude on which this modern skepticism has its nature and truth—and thus true philosophy is infinitely more skeptical than this skepticism. What more perfect and separate document and system of genuine skepticism could be found than the *Parmenides* in Plato's philosophy. This embraces and destroys the whole territory of this knowledge by means of the concepts of the understanding. This Platonic skepticism does not issue in any *doubting* of these truths of the understanding which knows things as manifold, as wholes consisting of parts, a coming to be and passing away, a multiplicity and similarity, etc., and which makes objective affirmations of this sort; it issues in a total negation of all truth of such a kind of knowledge. This skepticism . . . is itself the negative side of the knowledge of the absolute and immediately presupposes reason as the positive side" (173 f.).

It might seem that the view of philosophical progress advanced a couple of pages back as *not* Hegel's is, after all, part of his view. Unquestionably, Hegel emphasizes the importance of negation; his early essays and articles were essentially critiques; and his students did not fail to be struck by this aspect of his thought. Rosenkranz relates an episode that seems to have occurred almost four years after the publication of the essay on skepticism, when Hegel first offered his course on the history of philosophy while he was working on his *Phenomenology:*

"The course on history of philosophy Hegel gave at night by artificial light. . . . As one form of speculation emerged after the other in the lectures, only to be submerged again, and finally—the listeners had never expected this—the *Schellingian* system, too, took its turn, a rather old man from Mecklenburg jumped up in horror after the conclusion of one lecture, when Hegel had already gone, and shouted, 'But this is *death* himself, and thus all must perish.' This prompted a vivacious discussion among the students in which Suthmeier finally gained the upper hand and explained with pathos: to be sure, this was death and had to be death, but in this death was life which, purified by it, would unfold ever more gloriously" (217).

The student who spoke last seems to have had the right idea about Hegel. Common sense and the inadequacies of the rigid concepts of the understanding are criticized by Hegel along with the limitations of his predecessors; but the main thrust of his effort became more and more constructive. Even in 1802 Hegel was trying to give final form to his system.

19

As the essay on skepticism proceeds, Hegel attempts a detailed analysis of ancient skepticism and its various stages, and of the ten so-called tropes or modes of early skepticism[10] he says:

"The content of these modes proves even better how far removed they are from any tendency against philosophy, and how they are directed solely against the dogmatism of common sense: not one is aimed at reason and its knowledge, but all of them are aimed quite clearly only against the finite and the knowledge of the finite— against the understanding. . . . This skepticism is thus not at all

[10] See Sextus Empiricus, *Outlines of Pyrrhonism;* complete in a bilingual edition in the Loeb Classical Library; selections, including the various modes, in Kaufmann, *Philosophical Classics: Thales to St. Thomas* (Englewood Cliffs, New Jersey, Prentice-Hall, 1961), 570–76.

directed against philosophy but, in a not particularly philosophical but rather popular manner, against common sense or the common consciousness which clings to the given, the fact, the finite (whether this be called appearance or concept [i.e., concept of the understanding; Hegel later used Concept in a different sense]) and sticks to this as something certain, secure, and eternal. These skeptical modes show the common consciousness the unreliability of such certainties in a manner that lies close to it. For they also invoke appearances and finitudes, and from their difference and the equal rights of all of them to prevail—from the antinomy that is thus recognizable even in the finite—such skepticism recognizes the untruth of the finite. It may therefore be considered the first stage on the way to philosophy, for the beginning of philosophy has got to be the advance above the truth which is offered by the common consciousness, and the intimation of a higher truth. The most modern skepticism, with its certainty about the facts of consciousness, should therefore be referred above everything else to this ancient skepticism . . ." (184).

This crucial contrast between ancient and modern skepticism is further developed by Hegel (especially on page 192)—and taken up again twenty-five years later in the second, revised edition of Hegel's *Encyclopedia* (1827, twice the size of the first edition of 1817). There, §39 concludes:

"*Humean* skepticism, by the way, should be well distinguished from *Greek skepticism*. Hume's assumes as basic the *truth* of the empirical, of feeling, of intuition, and from that base contests general determinations and laws—because they lack justification from sense perception. Ancient skepticism was so far from making feeling and intuition the principle of truth that, on the contrary, it turned first of all against the senses. (On modern skepticism in relation to ancient skepticism, see Schelling's and Hegel's *Crit. Journal of Philosophy,* 1802, vol. I, issue 1.)"

Actually, Hegel's article had appeared in issue 2, but he did not catch this error when he made "3600 significant changes" in the third, revised edition (1830),[11] though he did go over this paragraph and, after "*Humean* skepticism," inserted the words "to which

[11] This figure is found in the critical edition of the *Encyclopedia*, p. xxx. In this edition, Hegel's slip is corrected without any indication that his text has been changed. Lasson, who gave the same figure earlier in his editions of 1905 and 1911, p. 503, did not correct this error.

the above reflections refer pre-eminently." Schulze is no longer mentioned in the *Encyclopedia* although in 1814 he had published an *Encyclopedia of the Philosophical Sciences*—the very title Hegel used three years later, even down to the subtitle "to be used in connection with his lectures." Of course, books designed toward that end were legion, and other philosophers, too, had published such "Encyclopedias" for some time.

In any case, the fact that Hume has taken Schulze's place is hardly connected with the matter of the book title. For the *Critical Journal* Hegel had written review articles, using books that had just appeared as points of departure for dealing with what he considered especially important topics. He began with the dogmatism of common sense, using Krug as a foil; then took up skepticism, using Schulze. Both men had reputations that at that time far exceeded Hegel's own.

Next, Hegel wrote a long article for the *Critical Journal,* entitled "Faith and knowledge, or the philosophy of reflection of subjectivity in the completeness of its forms, as Kantian, Jacobian, and Fichtean Philosophy."[12] In an important way this article belongs with the two preceding ones, as becomes obvious as soon as we turn to the second or third edition of the *Encyclopedia.*

In both of these editions (but not in the first), Part I, which is called "The Science of Logic," begins with what Hegel calls a *Vorbegriff* or preliminary analysis (§§19–83); and this is subdivided as follows:

A. First attitude of thought toward objectivity; metaphysics.

B. Second attitude of thought toward objectivity.

    I. Empiricism.

    II. Critical Philosophy.

C. Third attitude of thought toward objectivity; immediate knowledge.

The first point that meets the eye as one considers this plan is that Hegel, confronted with four outlooks that he considered sin-

---

[12] *Glauben und Wissen (Erste Druckschriften,* 221–346). Müller's reference (196) to *"Wissen und Glauben* (252 Seiten)" is doubly in error but by no means typical of his book.

gularly important, made a triad of them by lumping together two of them as B.I. and B.II. He would not always have done that; indeed, when he published his *Logic*[13] in three volumes in 1812, 1813, and 1816, he did almost the opposite. Though the tables of contents of all three volumes abound in triads, the title page of the second volume actually calls it: *"Science of Logic:* First Volume: Objective Logic; Second Book: The Doctrine of Essence." The third volume contained "Subjective Logic." As late as 1813, then, Hegel was capable of presenting something that had three parts as I.1, I.2, and II.

In the cases at hand, the three or four "attitudes of thought toward objectivity" are not in any case exhaustive: all three are severely criticized, and the point of this preliminary analysis is to establish the need for Hegel's own approach. Hegel's criticism of all four is at bottom the same: all of them fail to subject crucial philosophical terms to analysis.

Dogmatism—or, as the table of contents says, metaphysics—ascribes such predicates as "has existence" to God; "finitude or infinity" to the world; and "simple, composite" to the soul; but "One has failed to inquire whether such predicates are in and for themselves something true, and whether the form of the proposition could be the form of truth" (§28). The task remains of analyzing such concepts as well as the concept of a proposition.

"The basic illusion in scientific empiricism is always this: that it uses the metaphysical categories of matter, force, and, of course, one, many, generality, also infinite, etc., and furthermore makes *inferences* following the thread of such categories, while presupposing the forms of inference and using them—and all the while it does not know that it thus contains and does metaphysics and uses these categories and their connections in an entirely uncritical and unconscious manner" (§38).

After metaphysics and empiricism—or dogmatism and positivism—Kant is similarly taken to task for finding only four antinomies and dealing with these as he does, instead of realizing that a comprehensive analysis of Concepts is needed. (See especially E §48 and H 42.) "Immediate knowledge" (Jacobi) is obviously open to the same charge.

---

[13] *Logic,* in the present book, refers to Hegel's work with that name; Logic, to that branch of his system which he called "Logic"; and logic, to what that term means ordinarily.

In Hegel's discussion it is not as evident as it must seem from what has been suggested here that the central complaint is always the same. Indeed, this has generally gone unnoticed. But once it is noticed, the inclusion of this preliminary analysis in the so-called Lesser Logic becomes clear, and one need no longer wonder why this introductory part was not placed before the *Encyclopedia* as a whole (in a position comparable to the preface of the *Phenomenology*), with the Logic beginning only after this is completed. The main point of this introductory survey is to establish the need for the Logic, not for the whole *Encyclopedia*. For the Logic is nothing else than Hegel's comprehensive analysis of philosophical Concepts and their relations to each other.

We are now twenty-five years beyond 1802 when Hegel's articles appeared in the *Critical Journal*. In retrospect we can see that these articles are not mere juvenilia which the student of Hegel's mature work might as well ignore. It is striking how Hegel, at the beginning of his literary career, singled out in his *Journal* articles, first, the dogmatism of common sense; then, the modern skepticism which he later called empiricism and associated with Hume, and which others (e.g., Lasson, *Erste Druckschriften*, xxxi) may prefer to call positivism; and then, in "Faith and Knowledge," Kant and Jacobi. When we take into account that these articles were written at a time when Hegel was trying hard to finish and publish his system, it becomes clear that the "preliminary analysis" of twenty-five years later was not added merely as a pedagogical device but reflects to some extent Hegel's own approach to philosophy. Finally, the reader who finds that in the *Phenomenology* Hegel disposes of skepticism in a famous section of less than half a dozen pages ought to know that five years earlier Hegel had published a long article on the subject in which he had shown himself to be thoroughly familiar with its development from Pyrrho to Gottlob Ernst Schulze.

20

Of Hegel's long article on "Faith and Knowledge" Lasson says in his critical edition: "It seems as if the author had written it in a certain condition of rage, without allowing himself time enough to work over the style in any way. It was unfortunate for the manner in which his first printed essays have been judged that in the old edition of his works precisely this treatise was placed at the beginning of his collected writings; thus the readers got the impression that Hegel at this time, whether intentionally or not, expressed himself in language that is involuted and hard to understand, although this is not at all true of his other critical essays. Moreover, in the first printing the monster of a sentence which concludes the treatise is broken in the middle, resulting in an impossible anacoluthon" (xxxiv).

It is symptomatic of the way Hegel was edited in the collected works that three words were changed slightly in that last sentence: The first change was unnecessary and unhelpful; the second quite as ungrammatical as the original reading to which Lasson refers (Lasson altered the verb form in a different way, resulting in a grammatical reading); and the third change falsified Hegel's meaning for no good reason at all.

Lasson is also sharply critical of the *contents* of the essay, in which he finds "the typical ingratitude of those who complete a great development against their predecessors, without whom this completion would not have been possible" (xli). We shall again skip the polemic against Hegel's immediate predecessors. But the introduction reverts to the problems with which the young Hegel had dealt before he came to Jena, particularly in "The Positivity" and in the attempt to rewrite that essay in 1800 (H 12), and shall therefore be quoted here in part. For the essay on "Faith and Knowledge" marks an important stage on Hegel's way from a critique of the "positive" and irrational faith of Christianity to the attempt to find knowledge by means of philosophy.

We begin at the beginning of the essay: "Culture has raised the most recent times so high above the ancient opposition of reason and faith, of philosophy and positive religion, that this juxtaposition of faith and knowledge has acquired an altogether different meaning and has been removed into philosophy itself. That reason should be the handmaid of faith, as one used to say in bygone times—a position against which philosophy relentlessly claimed its absolute autonomy—such notions or expressions have vanished; and reason, if that which gives itself this name deserves it, has asserted itself to such an extent within positive religion that even a fight of philosophy against what is positive, miracles, *et al.*, is considered something dated, and obscure, and Kant's attempt to reanimate the positive form of religion by giving it a meaning from his own philosophy failed—not because the peculiar sense of these forms was changed, but rather because they no longer seemed worthy of even this honor. Yet the question remains whether triumphant reason has not suffered the very fate that the triumphant strength of barbarous nations usually suffers from the defeated weakness of cultured nations: retaining the upper hand as far as external dominion is concerned, while being defeated in spirit by the vanquished. The glorious triumph of enlightening reason over what, with its small measure of religious comprehension, it took for the faith that opposed it, looks different when examined in this light: neither is the positive element that it fought religion, nor has that which triumphed remained reason, and the offspring which descends triumphantly upon this corpse, [posing] as the common child of peace that unites both, contains as little reason as genuine faith.

"Reason, which had in any case degraded itself by understanding religion only as something positive and not idealistically, could not do better than have a look at itself after this fight, to gain self-knowledge, and to recognize the fact that it was nothing by placing that which was better than it, as long as it is merely understanding, in a *faith* as something that is *beyond, outside and above* it—as has happened in *the philosophies of Kant, Jacobi, and Fichte*—and thus reason again makes itself the handmaid of a faith. According to Kant, the supra-sensible cannot be known by reason; the supreme idea does not also have reality. According to Jacobi, reason is ashamed of begging, and to dig it has neither hands nor feet; man is granted only the feeling and consciousness of his ignorance of the true, only intimations of the true in reason, which is here merely something generally subjective and instinctive. According to Fichte, God is something incomprehensible and unthinkable; knowledge knows nothing except that it knows nothing, and has to flee to faith. According to all three, the absolute, according to the old distinction, cannot be against any more than for reason; it is above reason.

"The negative procedure of the Enlightenment, whose positive side was, for all its vain pretensions, without any kernel, obtained a kernel by grasping its own negativity and by liberating itself from shallowness by means of the purity and infinity of the negative. On the other hand, the objects of its positive knowledge could therefore be merely finite and empirical things, while the eternal had to remain beyond. For knowledge, the eternal thus remains empty, and this infinite empty space of knowledge can be filled only with the subjectivity of longing and intimation. Formerly, it was considered the death of philosophy if reason were to renounce its being in the absolute, simply excluding itself altogether from it and adopting a merely negative attitude toward it; but now just this became the highest point of philosophy. . . .[14]

"The great form of the world spirit, however, which has recognized itself in these philosophies, is the principle of the North and, religiously considered, of Protestantism: it is the subjectivity for which beauty and truth present themselves in feelings and dispositions, in love and understanding. Religion builds its temples and altars in the heart of the individual, and sighs and prayers seek the God whose contemplation one denies oneself in view of the danger for the understanding, which would look upon that which is contemplated as a mere thing, and upon the sacred woods as so much wood. To be sure, the internal, too, must become external, the intention must attain actuality in the deed, the immediate religious feeling must find expression in external agitation, and the faith which flees the objectivity of knowledge must become objective for itself in thoughts, concepts, and words. But the understanding separates quite sharply the objective from the subjective, and the objective is considered devoid of value and altogether nothing; and subjective beauty must fight against precisely the necessity according to which the subjective becomes objective . . . and beautiful feeling giving way to painless contemplation would become superstition.

". . . It is precisely its flight from the finite and the firmness of this subjectivity that reduce the beautiful to mere things for it, the sacred woods to pieces of wood, the images to things that have eyes and do not see, ears and do not hear. . . ."

Hegel's sentences are often awkwardly long, but he has by no means lost the power of vivid imagery that distinguished his early writings on religion, and what he says is of considerable interest. The "positive" religion, which the Enlightenment—and Hegel himself only seven years earlier—attacked and discredited, was religion

---

[14] This whole paragraph forms a single sentence in the original. The last two lines and the following paragraph have been omitted here.

without any religious spirit; and the enlightened reason that was so completely victorious that there was really no point any more in continuing the fight, was not reason at its best either, but, one might almost say, a reason devoid of the spirit of reason. It stuck to the finite and was thus mere understanding, to return to Schiller's distinction. Nor did reason fail to develop some sense of its own inadequacy: its nemesis was that it excluded itself from the infinite, which had been the true goal of the religious spirit—and thus reason ended up, as it had done in the Middle Ages, as the handmaid of faith.

Kant might seem to be a rationalist of sorts and somewhat scholastic in his manner, while Jacobi might strike us as an irrationalist and, quite unlike Kant, an apostle of feeling. But Kant already remarked that he had done away with knowledge to make room for faith, and in this respect he and Jacobi are at one, while Hegel, like Plato and Aristotle, Spinoza and Leibniz, insists that precisely the divine and eternal is the proper subject of philosophical inquiry and knowledge.

What Kant and Jacobi have done, however, should not be understood as the failure of a couple of individuals; rather, they represent the consummation of Protestantism. They have done on the philosophical level what the iconoclasts of the Reformation did on the material level. The understanding, which is glued to the finite, sees divine images only as idols that have eyes and do not see, and the sacred grove only as so much wood. But no reasonable person should look upon a Greek statue of Apollo in that spirit: reason must seek to comprehend the infinite in the finite, the eternal in what is here and now. Hegel opposes the philosophers who deny themselves the contemplation of the infinite and eternal, supposing that it dwells forever beyond reason; on the contrary, it is the task of reason and philosophy to contemplate the spirit in *this* world.

The long last sentence of this essay constitutes a paragraph of over twenty lines. To make sense of it, we have to change one verb form. But the sentence is interesting and points ahead to the end of the *Phenomenology of the Spirit*. Early in this sentence we encounter the phrase: "the feeling on which the religion of modern times [Christianity] rests: God himself is dead." The words "God is dead," now widely associated with Nietzsche, occur more than once in Hegel's writings; but Hegel, unlike Nietzsche whose dictum had for that very reason a far greater impact, proceeds beyond the death to the resurrection.

Later in the same sentence Hegel speaks of "the speculative Good Friday, which used to be [considered] historical," and of restoring "this in the whole truth and hardness of its godlessness, from which hardness alone—for the cheerfulness, less thorough manner, and greater singularity of dogmatic philosophies and natural religions must disappear—the highest totality in all its seriousness . . . can and must be resurrected, at the same time all-embracing and into the most cheerful freedom of its form."

Thus Hegel's essay ends, in German, with the words: *auferstehen kann und muss,* can and must be resurrected, or can and must rise again. As we shall see, the *Phenomenology* ends with a comparable image: there the famous "speculative Good Friday" is replaced by a vision of Golgotha.

21

In the last two issues of the *Critical Journal* Hegel published a long article "On the scientific modes of treatment of natural right, its place in practical philosophy, and its relation to the positive sciences of law" (1802/3).[15] Parts of it are so much worse stylistically than anything Hegel had written before that one is led to wonder whether it marks a great turning point in his development. Some of the early pages are exceedingly obscure, and their darkness is not relieved by the brilliant imagery that distinguished "Faith and Knowledge." One feels that something has gone wrong and recalls a remark Rosenkranz makes early in his biography of Hegel:

"His handwriting became firm in 1786 [when he was sixteen] and exhibits an unfaltering flow and great distinctness of the letters. . . . Only in the Jena period he begins to rewrite and abbreviate frequently. Beside the more vigorous larger writing there appears a smaller one whose lines fluctuate up and down, press the letters together, and go over from the round flow to a pointed form" (17).

There can be no doubt that the prose becomes more and more

15 Lasson's critical ed. is found in *Schriften zur Politik und Rechtsphilosophie,* 2d rev. ed., 1923.

inhibited and less and less clear. Glockner says: "The last chapter is the weightiest thing [*das Bedeutendste*] Hegel wrote before the *Phenomenology*" (II, 323). But this is doubtful. What is certain is that in that chapter, too, one encounters an amazing lack of clarity and forthrightness. On two facing pages in the discussion of comedy, for example—even now Hegel feels that tragedy and comedy belong to a discussion of ethics—there are two sentences that extend, respectively, over twenty-five and twenty-seven rather long lines; and this excessive length is in no way functional.

In the nineties, when he wrote to clarify his own thinking without any intention of publishing his essays, he wrote with clarity and vigor, but then came to feel that his criticisms, however powerful, were facile and tedious; what was needed was writing in a constructive vein. He set out to develop a system of philosophy, arrived at Jena with a plan on which he continued to work, but he could not finish it to his own satisfaction. So he began to publish review articles in a journal that he himself edited: again, his criticisms were vigorous, to say the least—really too vigorous, considering the victims, Krug and Schulze. While Kant, Fichte, and even Schelling, still in his mid-twenties, had made names for themselves with their own contributions to philosophy and were assured of enduring fame and inclusion in any history of philosophy, Hegel, now in his thirties, was either expounding the giants—one of them his junior by five years—or doing battle against Krug and Schulze. One gathers that he felt deeply dissatisfied with himself, and this vexation added to his aggressiveness. It seemed high time to write more than a review article—and the long piece on Natural Right represents an effort in that direction—but on the other hand Hegel felt that what was really needed was no mere article but a system. And the system, though in some ways clear in his mind, was nowhere near completion.

Rosenkranz praises this long article, but is as far as Glockner from taking into account these considerations. He is right when he says, "It was here that he first allowed his own system to emerge more definitely" (172), but he fails to note the strain this involved. And when he adds a page later, "This treatise in its ethical loftiness would be worthy of a legislator!" he forgets to tell his readers that no legislator could afford such obscurity. He continues: "Though Hegel later presented all these concepts more distinctly, in greater detail, in a more artfully systematic manner, in his *Philosophy of Right,* one must yet insist that the originality of their conception is more beautiful in this more youthful form, fresher, and indeed in parts truer."

This is surely meant to be high praise and will so strike admirers of the *Philosophy of Right.* The point is, very briefly, that in this essay Hegel criticizes Kant's *Moralität*—his objections to the categorical imperative include points still made in many classrooms— and then goes on to expound his own conception of *Sittlichkeit.* In a moment we shall illustrate both points. First, however, let us pursue a little further our analysis of the way in which Hegel's style reflects a profound predicament.

The crucial point can be put succinctly: Hegel is doing what on his own convictions he should not be doing; and he is unable to do what he feels he ought to do. The system that is wanted is not ready, and the form in which he does present his thoughts strikes him as unsuitable. We shall see in the next chapter how this vexation persists through the *Phenomenology*—both the body of that book and the long preface. In a different way it marks *all* of Hegel's work. Throughout, there is a deep cleft between his peculiar gifts and his intentions, his genius and his convictions. A more harmonious person would hardly have looked upon harmony as such a high and significant goal.

In the nineties Hegel's writings were, for the most part, far from obscure. On the rare occasions when he permitted himself to write in a vein that he himself considered really unworthy of a philosopher—for example, in the brilliant little essay "Who Thinks Abstractly?" (Chapter IX)—his prose and his thoughts were clear and forthright. But he felt strongly that he ought to be doing something that in fact he was not able to do, and his curiously inhibited and frustrated style mirrors the fatal strain between his gifts and his intentions.

In criticizing Kant's moral philosophy Hegel makes much of its lack of content: "Now it is precisely one's interest to know what is right, what duty; one asks for the content of the moral law, and it is solely this content that matters. But it is of the essence of the pure will and pure practical reason that they abstract from all content; and therefore it is inherently self-contradictory to seek any moral legislation, which would have to have content, from this practical reason, since its essence consists in not having any content."

Kant's imperative or moral law "that a maxim of your will must at the same time be valid as the principle of a universal legislation" won't work: "there is nothing that couldn't be made a moral law in this way" (350 f.). Hegel then considers some of Kant's examples which, according to Kant, cannot be universalized because that would involve a contradiction; and Hegel suggests that these cases are analogous to the maxim that we should help the poor: "When one thinks that the poor would be helped universally, then there would be either no poor at all any more or *only* poor people; so none would remain who could help, and in both cases help would become impossible. The maxim, then, universalized, does away with itself" (355).

To find a content, Hegel proceeds beyond Kant's *Moralität* to *Sittlichkeit;* and later he says: "We remark here also a hint of language that, otherwise rejected, is fully justified by the preceding: it is of the nature of absolute *Sittlichkeit* to be something general or *Sitten* [customs]; so the Greek word which designates *Sittlichkeit* [i.e., *ethos*] and the German one both express its nature superbly well. And the recent systems of *Sittlichkeit,* since they made being-for-oneself and the single person their principle, . . . could not misuse these words to designate *their* subject, but accepted the word *Moralität* which, to be sure, according to its origin, points in the same direction [toward *mores*], but because it is rather more an artificially constructed word it does not so directly resist its worse [individualistic, Kantian] meaning" (388 f.). In the original, this quotation forms a single sentence of sixteen lines; but unlike many another passage it is clear and unambiguous.

Hegel's point obviously depends on German usage and cannot be rendered into English. *Sittlichkeit* is a plain German word, not a specifically philosophical term, and one need not be interested in etymologies or know foreign languages to perceive its close connection with *Sitte* (custom). Kant, to be sure, had called his first major work on ethics *Grundlegung zur Metaphysik der Sitten* (1785) and had later followed it up with a two-volume *Metaphysik der Sitten* (1797), and the following year Fichte had published his *System der Sittenlehre;* but Hegel felt, not without justice, that all these references to *Sitten* (customs) were quite misleading: after all, Kant's ethic was patently not founded on custom but rather on the solitary

individual's ratiocination about his maxims. Kant had also introduced the word *Moralität,* which, unlike *Moral,* is a rather artificial
term; and Hegel, wanting to distinguish the Kantian ethic from his
own, employs this label for Kant's while appropriating *Sittlichkeit*
for his own.

When he says "that the absolute ethical [*sittliche*] totality is nothing else than a people [*ein Volk*]" (368), we should recall his
early fragments about folk religion (*Volksreligion*) with their glorification of the Greeks (H 8), as well as the fact that in 1802 and
1803 one could scarcely speak of a German people, a *deutsches
Volk.* Hegel's discussion of *Sittlichkeit* in his long journal article is,
moreover, supported by frequent citations of Plato and Aristotle
(eight, mostly long, quotations), and one passage from Gibbon on
the demoralization in the Roman empire.

The only other quotation in the last half of this long article comes
from Diogenes Laertius: ". . . and concerning *Sittlichkeit* the word
of the wisest men of antiquity is the only truth: being ethical
[*sittlich*] means living in accordance with the customs [*Sitten*] of
one's country; and concerning education, what a Pythagorean once
said in answer to the question what might be the best education for
one's son: 'Making him the citizen of a people with good institutions' [Diogenes Laertius VIII.16]" (392).

Before he published this article, Hegel had written a *System
der Sittlichkeit* which was published in full only over a century later
by Lasson; but Rudolf Haym read the manuscript, and what he said
about Hegel's notion of *Sittlichkeit* applies also to the journal article:
"Hegel's ethics rested on the same basis, which was the most fundamental and ultimate basis of his whole way of thinking. . . . It
rests on the contemplation of the ethical life [*auf der Anschauung
des sittlichen Lebens*] of the classical peoples: its character is colored through and through by Greek antiquity. It is, to state the
whole truth, according to its contents a description, and according
to its philosophical form an absolutizing of the private and public,
of the social, the artistic, and the religious life of the Greeks."[16]

Not only does Hegel speak of "the absolute ethical totality" in
the passage just quoted; a few lines before that he introduces, italicized, "*absolute Sittlichkeit.*" As Haym remarks, "There is complete proof that he did not yet envisage art, religion, and philosophy

16 *Hegel und seine Zeit* (1857), 160.

above and after the ethical spirit as a still higher manifestation and realization of the absolute spirit. . . . For the present, the real realization of the absolute spirit in ethical communal life was for him the altogether true and highest realization of this spirit; the ethical spirit *was* for him the absolutely absolute. Thus it had to be in accordance with the innermost motive of Hegel's way of thinking, and thus it had to be in accordance with the substantial idea of his philosophy. That motive was the restoration of the content of life in classical antiquity. This idea was the realization of that which was merely thought. . . . Necessarily, the restoration of classical life was shipwrecked by the conditions of modern life. Necessarily, therefore, this restoration had to flee into the form of idealism, into the form of philosophy. And necessarily this form, in turn, had to save its own right by proclaiming itself, i.e., thinking, as in the final instance a still truer realization of thought than that which thought receives in the ethical actuality of the state. . . . We shall see *later* that to the end Hegel decided *alternately* now in favor of the absoluteness of the objective and real appearance of the absolute spirit in the state, now in favor of the absoluteness of its 'absolute,' i.e., ideal, appearance in art, religion, and philosophy. We learn *for the present* that of these two decisions the latter was altogether the later one, and that in 1802, in the first bloom of his philosophical conception, he wanted to reach the true and actual end . . . with the ethical spirit" (161 f.).

Haym is completely right in stressing the overwhelming importance of classical Greece for Hegel's philosophy. In a brilliant book on *The Tyranny of Greece over Germany*,[17] Professor E. M. Butler of Cambridge University dealt with Winckelmann and Lessing, Goethe and Schiller, Hölderlin and Heine, Nietzsche and Stefan George. She might well have included Hegel under that suggestive title. What Haym does not recognize clearly enough is that Hegel's admiration for the Greeks was centered in Athens and based in large measure on the fusion there accomplished of art and religion with the ethical life of the citizens. Art, religion, and public life can hardly be disentangled even in retrospect: to which of them would one assign the Parthenon, the great statues of Zeus and Athena and Apollo, or the gatherings at which Aeschylus and Sophocles, and a little later Sophocles and Euripides, vied for the first prize?

[17] Cambridge University Press, 1935; Beacon Paperback, 1958.

When Hegel in effect declared himself for the primacy of the ethical realm, this *included* art, religion, and philosophy; he *never* set the state above these. Nor is it true that "to the end Hegel decided alternately now in favor" of the one, now in favor of the other. In his first book, the *Phenomenology,* which Hegel himself compares to a ladder (II.2.5), art and religion, which are treated together, and philosophy, which is treated next and last, occupy the top rungs, above both *Sittlichkeit* and *Moralität.* And in Hegel's system—not only in the first edition of 1817 but also in the thorough-going revision of 1827 and in the last edition, published a year before Hegel's death—the ethical life and the state mark the pinnacle of what he calls objective spirit, while absolute spirit, which comprises art, religion, and philosophy, rises above that.

Hegel's reason for assigning such a high place to the ethical life and the state is that, largely under the influence of the example of Athens, he views them as the matrix in which art, religion, and philosophy develop. Hegel no more chooses between ethical life and philosophy than he chooses between philosophy and art; and he is aware of the fact that the Greeks, too, did not think of making any such choice.

Not all of this was as clear to him in 1802 as it was when he finally published his system. In 1802, as a matter of fact, Hegel had tried to complete a long essay on "The German Constitution."[18] He had finished over 130 pages before abandoning the project. The first sentence had been: "Germany is no longer a state." The question had been what might be done about it. As Pelczynski says, "One of Hegel's purposes in writing *The German Constitution* was to expose that hypocrisy and to make his countrymen face reality" (14), but beyond that his suggestions were "hopeless and impractical" (16); and this was plainly the main reason he gave up the project.

For the very same reason, his long journal article could not cure his profound malaise. It was all very well to contrast Athens with Kant, but as Hegel himself insisted in his critique of Kant: "It is precisely one's interest to know what is right, what duty; one asks for the content . . . and it is solely this content that matters." In the end, Hegel had not got far beyond suggesting that the ancient

---

[18] Translated by T. M. Knox and discussed by Z. A. Pelczynski in *Hegel's Political Writings* (1964). Original in Lasson's ed. of *Schriften zur Politik und Rechtsphilosophie.*

Athenian knew his duties and knew what was right, which, even if entirely true, was not really much help here and now. After all, as Hegel put it on the last page but two of his journal article, the Germans were "a dissolved people."

What Haym sensed, rightly enough, was that Hegel was a man deeply at odds with himself; but in the passage we have quoted Haym did not analyze this tension aright. We should rather say that there was in Hegel, especially but not only at that time, a conflict between activism and quietism. Thus Hegel wrote in his introduction to *The German Constitution:* "The thoughts contained in this essay cannot have any other aim or effect upon publication than the understanding of that which is,[19] and thus to promote calmer contemplation as well as the ability to endure it. . . ." (5)[20]

Hegel was not satisfied to find harmony in art, as Schiller and some of the romantics had suggested. He lacked the artistic genius that enabled Schiller to find peace and happiness in writing plays and poems. Like Plato and the Pythagoreans, he felt that the individual in isolation could not attain what he most wanted, apart from an ethical community. But that was out of reach, and meanwhile philosophical "understanding of that which is" might give one the strength to endure what is, without putting on blinders.

The conception of philosophy as therapy has come to be widely associated with Wittgenstein, who said in his *Philosophical Investigations* that "The philosopher treats a question—like a disease" (255) and who compared philosophical methods to "different therapies" (133). For Hegel, too, philosophy was a kind of therapy —but in the tradition of Spinoza and the Stoics. The young Hegel was not a professor who, sitting at his desk, felt confident that he was omniscient, though this is, more or less, the popular image of the man. In fact, he was at odds with himself and the world, desperately needed the therapy of philosophy, but for many years did not succeed in mastering it sufficiently to cure himself.

[19] These are the words quoted by Rosenzweig in the passage cited in H 11.
[20] The sentence, though short, is extremely awkward. Knox renders it into elegant English, but his "tolerant attitude" misses the sadness and force of Hegel's *Ertragen* (endure).

CHAPTER III:

The Phenomenology

22

In 1803 Schelling left the University of Jena, and the *Critical Journal*, which Hegel and Schelling had edited together, was discontinued. Now Hegel stopped publishing—until his first book appeared in 1807.

The articles in the *Journal* had been unsigned, and about one of them, not mentioned so far, there was a dispute after Hegel's death: some of the disciples of each editor claimed authorship for him. It speaks greatly for Haym's understanding of Hegel—one might also say, his feeling for Hegel—that he believed "with certainty" that the error lay "on the side of the disciples of Hegel who were over-zealous for the fame of their master" (155 f.). A subsequently discovered list of his own publications in Hegel's hand proved Haym right: the disputed article was by Schelling. Yet Haym was anything but a partisan of Schelling, and although he is often remembered as a severe critic of Hegel, his critique was always blended with admiration. Looking back on the *Journal*, he wrote: "Three quarters of the whole *Journal* were notoriously written by the second editor. Three quarters of this *Journal* are truly important [*bedeutend*] and a treasure of the most profound and thoughtful discussions; a fourth quarter contains partly repetitions of what Schelling had said long before, partly a series of more or less clever notions [*geistreichen Einfällen*], of polemical little skirmishes, of romantic-ingenious rudenesses and elegant frivolities: this fourth quarter is notoriously the property of the first editor. Schelling put his real literary activity around this time into his *Neue Zeitschrift*" (157). The last point is important: it would not have occurred to anyone to judge Schelling mainly by his contributions to the *Critical Journal.* But Haym goes much further: "Hegel's achievements surpassed those of his friend already in 1802," although Hegel himself never betrayed any sense of superiority (158).

No doubt, hindsight is required for this judgment. If Hegel had died before writing his *Phenomenology,* Schelling might still be included in histories of philosophy, but Hegel certainly would not be mentioned. Nor did he at the time attract attention comparable to Schelling's renown. And Hegel himself knew it.

His energy now went into two closely related projects: his lectures and the attempt to prepare his system for publication. During his first term, beginning late in 1801, Hegel announced "Logic and Metaphysics" and had eleven students. He also announced a course jointly with Schelling, but apparently this did not materialize. In the summer of 1802 he devoted himself entirely to his literary labors—and announced a book with the title "Logic and Metaphysics or *Systema reflexionis et rationis";* and when he announced a course on the same subject that winter, he mentioned that this text would appear in the spring. In the summer of 1803 he proposed to cover the whole of philosophy and referred to a text that he would soon publish with Cotta in Tübingen. During the next two years, until the summer of 1805, his announcements did not refer to any book but only promised lectures *ex dictatis.*[1] He also lectured repeatedly on philosophy of right.

In the winter of 1803/4 he promised to read *ex dictatis* on "System of Speculative Philosophy" and specified three parts: first, Logic and Metaphysics, or Transcendental Idealism; then the Philosophy of Nature; finally, that of Spirit.[2] The following summer he did not lecture, while in the winter of 1804/5 he repeated this course for thirty students, and after that he always had between twenty and thirty. In the summer of 1805 he offered the same

[1] For all of this, see Ros. 160 ff., and Haering, "Die Entstehungsgeschichte der Phänomenologie des Geistes." Cf. also Haering, II, 479 ff., and Hoffmeister's introduction to his edition of the *Phänomenologie* (1952), xxviii ff. Otto Pöggeler, "Zur Deutung der Phänomenologie des Geistes" (*Hegel Studien,* I, 1961), p. 279, disagrees with Haering but later, on pp. 284 f. and 288 f. corroborates the essential points.
[2] In the Latin announcements the word used is *mentis.* This is almost the only reason—and an utterly insufficient one (see H 34 and 65) for translating Hegel's *Geist* as "mind" instead of "spirit."

course again—and again promised a book that was evidently meant to cover his whole system in one volume.

In the winter of 1805/6 he lectured for the first time on the history of philosophy; he also repeated philosophy of nature and spirit under the title *Realphilosophie*[3]; and for the first and only time he offered a course on mathematics in which Gabler, who after Hegel's death succeeded to his chair at Berlin, was one of his students. In his course announcements for that winter he did not promise a book. The announcements, of course, were composed a few months before, presumably late in the summer; but that winter he actually signed a contract for a book with a publisher in Bamberg, Goebhardt. The title in the no longer extant contract seems to have been "System of Sciences"—according to Haering, *"probably* already . . . with the specification 'First Part,' but *certainly still without any mention of a 'Phenomenology.'* According to the announcement for the summer of 1806, this first part was still supposed to contain . . . the *Logic,"* probably together with a brief introduction (122).

During the summer of 1806 he again offered Philosophy of Nature and Spirit, as well as a second course on Speculative Philosophy "in which he lectured for the first time on Phenomenology and Logic, and which he also announced again for the winter of 1806" (Ros. 162). That summer, the introduction kept growing, and around August—certainly not before—when Hegel wrote his announcement for the winter semester 1806/7, the title "Phenomenology" occurs for the first time. Hegel announced: *Logicam et Metaphysicam sive philosophiam speculativam, praemissa Phaenomenologia mentis ex libri sui:* System der Wissenschaft *proxime proditura parte prima* and *Philosophiam naturae et mentis ex dictatis.*[4] Indeed, as late as September 20, 1806, Hegel's announcement in the *Intelligenzblatt* of the *Jenaer Allgemeine Literatur Zeitung* promised, in German, that he would offer "Speculative Philosophy or Logic and Metaphysics, preceded by Phenomenology of the Spirit . . . according to his textbook" and "Philosophy of Nature and Spirit . . . according to dictated sentences."

This is the first occurrence of the words "Phenomenology of the Spirit," and in context the implication is clearly that the volume

---

[3] For Hegel's *Jenenser Realphilosophie,* the lectures of 1803/4 and 1805/6, see Bibliography II. D. 5 and 6.
[4] The Latin is translated in the next sentence.

about to appear will contain mainly Hegel's "Logic and Meta-physics" which he always treats as one subject. The Phenomenology will be only the introduction of volume one, not the whole of volume one, much less a separate major work. According to the contract with the publisher, the first half of the volume was supposed to be printed by Easter 1806; in fact, this was not done: Hegel had the greatest difficulties in actually getting this book written. He finally mailed the first half of the manuscript to Jena on October 8 and finished the remainder the night of October 12–13. But the title "Phenomenology of the Spirit" was apparently chosen only in August—for the introductory part of volume one—and as late as September Hegel still seems to have hoped that the same volume would also accommodate, even as its main part, Logic, on which he had copious notes.

In January he read proofs and mailed the *preface* to Bamberg —another ninety-one pages as printed in the original edition. Early in April he saw the first copies of the book. It had not been conceived and written the way most people imagine Professor Hegel to have written his books. It was the work of a tormented spirit.[5]

Hegel writing the *Phenomenology* is worlds removed from the serenity of Holbein's Erasmus, standing at his desk, a timeless image of the sober scholar. He is far closer to the world of Dostoevsky's novels. So far from its being true that his life was a blank and his thoughts remote from the concerns of flesh and blood, dictated solely by cold, if perverse, logic, the full measure of his torment has not yet been suggested.

Goebhardt had not been eager to publish Hegel's book, and Niethammer, Hegel's best and most loyal friend, had signed a commitment that he personally would pay for the entire printed edition if Hegel did not furnish the whole manuscript by October 18. Only on that condition, the publisher had paid Hegel a badly needed advance. Hegel got off half of the manuscript ten days before the deadline, but then Napoleon moved in, finished off the Holy Roman Empire, founded by Charlemagne in 800, in the Battle of Jena, and on October 13 occupied the city. The night from the twelfth to the thirteenth Hegel finished the book—appalled by the thought that the first half might well have got lost on the way, and wondering whether

---

[5] Cf. Müller, 163: "Simply to copy this book without thinking probably would require not much less time than the months in which it originated."

he dare to mail the second half. On the eighteenth he writes
Niethammer that he has been advised "that such circumstances set
aside all obligations," but when the first mail leaves again he will
send the balance. Meanwhile there had been a big fire in Jena as well
as some looting. That was how the book was finished—except for the
preface, which was done in January.

23

By then, one might suppose, all was peace. But on February 5,
Christiana Charlotte Johanna Burkhardt, neé Fischer, gave birth
to an illegitimate child, Ludwig, Hegel's son. Those who have
written about Hegel have hardly ever mentioned this fact—in almost all cases because they did not know it, in a very few because
they considered it indelicate. Glockner not only fails to mention
both the mother and the son in his two-volume work, although he
devotes a chapter of 195 pages to "Hegel's Personality"; he concludes a footnote about women to whom Hegel wrote letters with
the words: "Nothing suggests that any of these relationships gave
rise to a moral problem about which Hegel ever thought seriously"
(I, 283).

There are at least two reasons for *not* omitting some discussion
of Ludwig. If one ignores him, one cannot really understand the
state of mind in which Hegel wrote his first book; and, secondly,
the boy's birth did introduce a very serious moral problem into
Hegel's life. The first of these points should be fairly clear by now.
The *Phenomenology* was written in a few months' time, under an
immense strain. It was not written with a clear outline in mind, as
if Hegel had known exactly what he proposed to do and then had
done it. For years he had announced a book and not been able to
write it, though he kept accumulating pages and pages of drafts
and lecture notes. Meanwhile, not only Schelling had published
book upon book; J. F. Fries, three years Hegel's junior, who together with Hegel, had begun his academic career at Jena in 1801,
and been made Associate Professor there in 1805, also together
with Hegel, had later that year accepted a chair at Heidelberg; and
Krug, born the same year as Hegel, had published enough to obtain
the chair at Königsberg when Kant died in 1804. The point was not
just one of honor, prestige, or money, though Hegel was in desperate

straits financially; the question was whether he, now over thirty-five, could or could not write a book. And that was tied up with the problem of whether he could resolve his philosophical difficulties, clarify his thoughts, and resolve his intellectual torments along with his other vexations.

Jena, a great intellectual center before Hegel arrived, associated with Goethe and Schiller, Fichte and the early romantic movement, as well as Schelling, had by then lost its lure. Everybody who was anybody was leaving—and after the Battle of Jena there was no winter semester for Hegel; there was the urgent necessity of finding a job somewhere else; and early in 1807 he went to Bamberg to edit a newspaper.

In the spring of 1806, when he finally had begun to write, seeking clarification in the process, without any clear idea what exactly would happen on paper, he made a woman in Jena pregnant, and knew it as he kept writing away and found that the book was radically changing under his hands. By October, the introductory part had grown into such a fat book that there could be no thought of including even the first third of the system, the Logic. But the deadline had to be met, the French army was on the spot, and his days at the University of Jena were numbered. So he cut the umbilical cord.

Then in January, when the boy's birth was expected any day, Hegel suddenly added his immensely long preface to the introduction to his system, although that introduction already began with an "introduction" of nineteen pages. Some of those who know Hegel's writings best consider this preface Hegel's most important essay. (See the quotations that precede my complete translation of the preface.) On February 5, Ludwig was born.

Who was the mother? Rosenkranz, in his biography, and Karl Hegel, in his edition of his father's letters, observed complete discretion, as if neither mother nor son had existed; meanwhile rumors grew and were not refuted. Even in 1954, the long note on this matter at the end of the third volume of the critical edition of the letters (433 ff.) gave a misleading picture of the mother. The crucial document appeared only in the fourth volume, in 1960, without any comment on its significance.

The document in question is an excerpt from the Jena records of baptism: "Christiana Charlotte Burkhardt, born Fischer, the abandoned wife of a servant of a count, for the third time an illegitimate son, Georg Ludwig Friedrich. . . . Day of birth: 5 February, 1807, at 12 noon. Day of baptism: 7 February, 1807. Godfathers: Herr Friedrich Frommann, book dealer here; Herr Georg Ludwig Hegel [the father's brother], Lieutenant in the Royal Württemberg Regiment Crown Prince. (Former births: 18 October, 1801: in dishonor, a daughter: Auguste Theresia.[6] 9 March, 1804: for the second time in dishonor, a son, who died 30 November, 1806.)" The entry further indicates that the mother was an only child, that her father was a court messenger—her mother is not mentioned—and that she was born May 8, 1778.

In sum: she was almost eight years younger than Hegel, but she was not plunged into dishonor by Hegel; and in view of her past and the prejudices of the time, it would hardly have been very surprising if Professor Hegel had done his best to forget the whole affair. But as he wrote Frommann from Bamberg, July 9, 1808: "I always have to regret grievously that so far I have been unable to tear her, who is the mother of my child and who therefore may demand every kind of duty from me, entirely out of her situation. To you I am greatly indebted for making it easier for me to make things a little easier for her." When the boy was four, he was given to Frau Frommann's sister, Sophie Bohn, who had been widowed in 1803 and in 1807 had moved to Jena with her own two sons to open a home for boys.

In 1811 Hegel married, while he was principal of the Gymnasium at Nürnberg. In the summer of 1816 he was finally offered a chair of philosophy, at Heidelberg. Thereupon he wrote Frommann, August 28, 1816, almost two months before he actually left Nürnberg: "My wife and I are resolved to have Ludwig live with us now." In the spring Ludwig joined the family, which by then consisted of two sons. The first child of Hegel's marriage, a girl born in 1812, had died soon after her birth. By then, Ludwig was ten, and his little brothers were three and four.

On April 19, 1817, Hegel wrote Frommann: "Voss has meanwhile brought us Ludwig. Just now I have told him of his mother's death, of which Voss informed me. It affected him more than me. My feelings have long got over her; I could only worry about unpleasant contacts between her and Ludwig—and thus indirectly

6 Ludwig's inscription in his sister's *Stammbuch,* March 26, 1823, and a farewell letter he wrote her August 27, 1825, show the depth of his feeling for her (B IV, 126, 130).

with my wife. . . . He shows a good head; he now attends the Gymnasium here which, to be sure, could be better. But I am amazed how much Latin he has learned this winter."

From Berlin, Hegel wrote Frommann, April 8, 1822, that Ludwig had been confirmed "eight days ago" and that he would like to find an apprenticeship for him in some business. From a letter of June 6, 1822, to the minister of education, Altenstein, we gather that Hegel was in financial straits. On July 9, he again discusses Ludwig's future with Frommann. Later, Ludwig entered Dutch military service and went to Batavia where he died of a fever August 28, 1831.

Before he embarked for the East Indies, the boy, then eighteen, wrote two desperate letters (B IV, 128 ff.). The first, dated July 11, 1825, was addressed to his sister's foster father. He complains that his "stepmother, who had two children of her own," had not treated him like her sons; "and so I always lived in fear, without loving my parents—a relationship that had to produce a constant tension." He would long have liked to run away, but lacked the means. He would have liked to study medicine, "but I was told there could be no thought of that; I should work for a businessman! I told them before that I would hardly stay there as I did not feel born for business; the answer was that in that case one would cease to support me.—And this has really happened now." He has enlisted for six years and will get out again, he writes, June 24, 1831. He has found a few congenial young men. "If you could give me some information about the circumstances of my dear mother, about the final circumstances of her death, and her relation to Herr Hegel, I should be obliged to you. I am in such uncertainty about all this; yet these are things that are very close to me."

The other letter, to his sister, dated August 27, 1825 (his father's birthday), is written aboard ship. It is much shorter and ends: "Farewell! Your brother, who loves you unto death."

24

Some professors find a measure of fulfillment, or at least some relief and release of tension, in lecturing. Not Hegel. Even as a student he had been criticized for his poor oral delivery and his weak voice. On November 27, 1803, Goethe wrote Schiller: "In connection with Hegel I have been wondering whether one could not secure a great advantage for him if one could teach him something about the technique of speaking. He is a truly excellent human being; but his utterances are open to too many objections." Schiller had replied: "I am delighted that you are getting better acquainted with Hegel. What he lacks one will scarcely be able to give him." On March 14, 1807, just before the *Phenomenology* appeared, Goethe wrote his friend Knebel how glad he was that Hegel was about to publish a book: "I am eager to see at long last a presentation of his way of thinking. He has such an excellent head, and he finds it so difficult to communicate his ideas."

Rosenkranz describes Hegel as a lecturer at Jena as follows: "Without the least consideration for rhetorical elegance, devoted through and through to the subject, deeply stirred by the tendency of the present age, always striving on and yet often quite dogmatic in his expression, Hegel captivated the students with the intensity of his speculation. . . . An odd smile revealed the purest benevolence; yet at the same time there was something sharp, even cutting, painful, or rather ironic about it. It reflected the tragic trait of the philosopher, the hero who wrestles with the riddle of the world.

"On the students en masse Hegel had no influence whatever. They knew of him only as an obscure oddity; and whoever wanted to hear not only the older professors but also for once one of the younger lecturers preferred to hear Fries, who was trying to work his way up at the same time as Hegel. But a small circle of adherents and admirers clung to him that much more firmly, and their enthusiasm increased immensely, especially during the last years of Hegel's stay in Jena" (215 f.).

Rosenkranz has also recorded for us how Hegel's last lecture at the University of Jena ended:

"The Phenomenology was Hegel's last lecture in Jena. He concluded his course on Speculative Philosophy September 18, 1806, with these words:

'This, gentlemen, is speculative philosophy as far as I have got in developing it. Consider it a beginning of philosophizing which you will carry further. Ours is a significant epoch, a time of ferment, when the spirit has made a jerk, transcended its previous form, and is gaining a new one. The whole mass of previous notions, Concepts, the bonds of the world, have dissolved and collapse like a dream image. A new emergence of the spirit is at hand.

Philosophy above all must welcome its appearance and recognize it, while others, impotently resisting it, stick to what is past, and the majority constitutes unconsciously the mass of its appearance. Philosophy, however, recognizing it as what is eternal, must do it honor. Commending myself to your gracious recollection, I wish you merry holidays'" (214 f.).

On occasion, Hegel could be clear enough. Nor is the curious alternation of a powerful and straightforward style with all sorts of obscurities, including tapeworm sentences that demand to be construed, bit by bit, unique with him. When Hegel went to Jena to begin a university career, the greatest living philosopher—and the first world-historical philosopher to have written great works in German—was Kant; the most prominent German philosopher after Kant was Fichte. Both of them had set a curious precedent: they had written popular essays that proved them masters of clear and vigorous prose; but both had written their major philosophical works in highly academic language that bristled with obscurities. Kant's relatively simple and understandable *Grundlegung zur Metaphysik der Sitten* (1785), one of the great classics of ethics, contained a sentence that was a page and a half long.[7]

Leibniz had written philosophy in French and Latin, not in German. Alongside Kant another tradition had begun to form, spearheaded by Lessing and Schiller. But they were not professional philosophers, and philosophy was a mere sideline with both of them: they were poets, playwrights, and critics who had incidentally written essays that were of great interest philosophically. If anything, Kant's and especially Fichte's popular writings compromised this style in Hegel's eyes; for he did not like Fichte's popular essays, and in Kant's case there could be no question whatsoever but that his greatness and stature as a philosopher depended on those of his works that were written in a thoroughly forbidding style. If one wanted to enter the ranks as a worthy successor of Kant and Fichte, it seemed clear to Hegel—unfortunately—how one had to write. Looking into the past and reading philosophy in other languages did not change the verdict: in the more recent past, there was no philosophical work that Hegel admired more than Spinoza's *Ethics;* and going further back in time there was Aristotle, whom Hegel esteemed supremely. In time, it became Hegel's ambition to equal

[7] In Section II, 34 f.,: the whole paragraph following the long footnote about Sulzer.

Aristotle's achievement by fashioning a crowning synthesis of what philosophy had achieved up to his time.

Neither Aristotle nor Spinoza, nor Kant in his major works, had given a quarter to the general reader or shown the slightest concern for popularity. Nor had Plato in such late dialogues as the *Parmenides* and the *Sophist*. To enter the lists with them, Hegel decided to write like them, not like Lessing and Schiller—and not the way he himself had written before he came to Jena.

That something strange happened to Hegel has been noted by both Glockner and Müller. The former says, in spite of his own admitted admiration for Fichte (II, 227): *"Fichte threw him off course.* Without Fichte's precedent, Hegel would not have developed any dialectical method. Probably, he would have broadened Kantianism in a manner comparable to Schiller's" (II, 215). Müller writes: "Friend Schelling in Jena was Hegel's evil spirit and seducer. Like a spider he spins his system webs out of himself and catches and wraps up his prey. Irresistibly attracted by the Latinizing word floods, his animal prey plunges exultant into the nets of 'absolute indifference.' Hegel succumbed to the revel and attempted what he could not do—to 'speculate' and 'construe' with equal frivolity. After Schelling's fame as a pied piper had netted him a call to Würzburg . . . Hegel returned to his more genuine self. . . . In the preface to the *Phenomenology* he offered a public confession" (170 f.).

Both Glockner and Müller point to important facts, which, however, should be placed in the larger picture already suggested here. Hegel's debt to Fichte and Schelling is great indeed—and it is largely a negative debt, an encumbrance, even a curse. But G. R. G. Mure also had a point when he devoted the first half of his *Introduction to Hegel* to Aristotle, and Glockner does not exaggerate when he says in a footnote: "Future monographs will show how Hegel, in the years from 1802 to 1815, worked innumerable passages from Plato and Aristotle, partly in literal translations, into his philosophy. A surprising number of incidents has already been adduced by Wilhelm Purpus. . . ."[8] The first three sections of the *Phenomenology* ("Consciousness") are full of examples.

If I am right, Goethe and Schiller, not to speak of later Hegel scholars, did not quite understand Hegel's case. Unlikely as it may sound, he was *not* unable to write clearly, but he felt that he must

---

[8] II, 336; cf. 395 and Purpus, *Die Dialektik des Bewusstseins nach Hegel: Ein Beitrag zur Würdigung der Phänomenologie des Geistes*, Berlin, 1908.

and should not write in the way in which he was gifted. The only one who saw this clearly and stated it beautifully was Nietzsche. He was not a Hegel scholar, and his early admiration for Schopenhauer makes it surprising that he should have understood Hegel so well. But then it was also Nietzsche who said in *Ecce Homo:* "Who among philosophers before me was a psychologist?" (IV, §6.) Here is Nietzsche's analysis of Hegel, from the *Dawn* (§193):

"*Esprit and Morality.*—The Germans, who have mastered the secret of being boring with spirit, knowledge, and feeling, and who have accustomed themselves to experience boredom as something moral, are afraid of French *esprit* because it might prick out the eyes of morality—and yet this dread is fused with temptation, as in the bird faced by the rattlesnake. Perhaps none of the famous Germans had more *esprit* than *Hegel;* but he also felt such a great German dread of it that this created his peculiar bad style. For the essence of this style is that a core is enveloped, and enveloped once more and again, until it scarcely peeks out, bashful and curious—as 'young women peek out of their veils,' to speak with the old woman-hater, Aeschylus. But this core is a witty, often saucy idea about the most intellectual matters, a subtle and daring connection of words, such as belongs in the *company of thinkers,* as a side dish of science—but in these wrappings it presents itself as abstruse science itself and by all means as supremely moral boredom. Thus the Germans had a form of *esprit permitted* to them, and they enjoyed it with such extravagant delight that Schopenhauer's good, very good intelligence came to a halt confronted with it: his life long, he blustered against the spectacle the Germans offered him, but he never was able to explain it to himself."

This aphorism throws more light on "The Secret of Hegel" than Sterling's huge work with that title, either in its two-volume (1865) or its one-volume (1898) edition. This example shows that it was not an idle boast when Nietzsche said in *Twilight of the Idols* (section 51): "It is my ambition to say in ten sentences what everyone else says in a book—what everyone else does *not* say in a book."

25

The preface to the *Phenomenology* is full of excellent aphorisms—a few of them quite naked and unconcealed, so no reader can miss them. To be sure, they are buried in mammoth paragraphs to forestall any popular appeal. The book is called *System of Science, First Part,* and the appearance of the pages is forbidding enough to frighten away browsers. But the reader who perseveres is brought up short every now and then by a striking epigram. The pity is that Hegel, too, is brought up short, shocked at his own unscientific manner, and intent on making amends immediately. But after a while it happens again. It is as if he wore a garment that did not fit: the buttons keep popping, revealing his chest and, as it were, baring his heart; but every time he stops to sew them on again before he feels free to make another move, though it keeps happening again. It never seems to occur to him to give up the garment as a bad fit that might conceivably suit somebody else but obviously not him.

Many a witty observation or fine formulation is successfully concealed in a long sentence where even the few readers who find it are likely to mutter something like "couldn't be" and go on. Yet the preface is not constructed around a skeleton outline, as if the author's often pert observations were merely dispensable ornaments: it would be truer to call it a stream of thought that moves from core to core—to use Nietzsche's image.

One might wonder briefly whether Hegel might not have offered us aphorisms without wrappings, if he had not associated that form with the very feeble aphorisms Schelling had published just then[9] and with the effusion of other early romantics, like Friedrich Schlegel and Novalis, not to mention lesser names. But it was not merely the insubstantiality of these aphorists and the incomparably greater weight of the thought of Aristotle, Spinoza, and Kant that determined his choice of form. He was convinced that philosophy must become scientific rather than aphoristic or essayistic, and the point of the preface was in large measure to give his reasons. These reasons richly deserve consideration; perhaps no better case has ever been made out for a systematic approach to philosophy. What is so odd is merely that the preface itself—as Hegel admits with some embarrassment—is an example of the kind of writing that Hegel tries in this preface to banish from philosophy; and the book that follows, too, is at the opposite extreme from the scientific type of philosophy for which Hegel makes his plea. Yet many, if not most,

[9] "Aphorismen zur Einleitung in die Naturphilosophie" in *Jahrbücher der Medizin als Wissenschaft* (1806); *Werke,* VII (1860), 140 ff., 198 ff.

of those familiar with the whole corpus of Hegel's writings consider the *Phenomenology* Hegel's most original, brilliant, important, and interesting book.

Before we turn to consider the *Phenomenology* itself and some of the problems it raises, something further needs to be said about the book's immediate historical context; specifically, about the reaction of Kant to Fichte, and Fichte to Schelling.

26

Fichte was a tutor when he first read Kant. He was immensely impressed and, being without means, *walked* from Warsaw to Königsberg to call on the master in person. Kant was favorably impressed by Fichte and recommended the manuscript of Fichte's first book to his own publisher, who brought out Fichte's *Critique of All Revelation* in 1792. In the first copies, the author's name and preface were missing—not by Fichte's design—and since Kant's book on religion was then expected (it actually appeared the following year), the title and publisher gave rise to the rumor that this was Kant's work. Kant explained that it was not his but Fichte's, and praised the book. Overnight, Fichte was famous.

In 1793 he received a call to the University of Jena, and in May 1794 he began his lectures there. He was an unusually impressive lecturer, but his attempt to abolish the student fraternities led to his temporary exile from Jena in 1795. (See Hegel's letter to Schelling, August 30, 1795, in D.)

In 1798 Fichte, who was editing a philosophical journal with Niethammer, who later became Hegel's close friend, published an article on religion by F. K. Forberg (1770–1848), with a short preface of his own in which God is equated with the moral world order. Accused of atheism, he published a couple of vigorous defenses in 1799 and threatened to resign if reprimanded, which was construed as a resignation—and he was let go.

To understand Fichte—and Hegel as well—one should recall the last words of Kant's *Critique of Pure Reason*. After rejecting both dogmatism and skepticism, while insisting on a systematic approach, Kant had ended both the first and the greatly revised second edition: "The critical way alone is still open. If the reader has

had the kindness and patience to walk along this way in my company, he may now judge whether, if he will contribute his share to
make this footpath a highway, that which many centuries could not
achieve might not be attained before the present century runs out:
namely, to give human reason complete satisfaction about that
which has always engaged its curiosity, but so far in vain."

This conclusion of a book that was plainly one of the greatest
works of philosophy ever written struck Fichte as a challenge. Kant
had begun something that could and should be finished by 1800.
Fichte tried to do just that in his books on what he called *Wissenschaftslehre* and *System der Sittenlehre*. But now, in 1799, as
Fichte lost his professorship and had to leave Jena, Kant dissociated
himself from Fichte in a declaration published in the *Allgemeine
Literaturzeitung*.[10] He was then seventy-five, had had enough trouble with censorship himself, had kept on publishing his own books
—a dozen of them in the 1790s—and had not kept up with Fichte's
publications. He had no wish to be held responsible for Fichte's
opinions, whatever they might be.

Kant's statement read:

> "In response to the solemn challenge issued to me in the
> name of the public by the reviewer of Buhle's *Draft of Tran-
> scendental Philosophy,* in Number 8 of the *Erlangische Litera-
> turzeitung,* 1799, I herewith declare that I consider Fichte's
> *Wissenschaftslehre* a wholly untenable system. . . . Further,
> I must remark that the presumption of ascribing to me the
> intention that I had merely wished to furnish a *propaedeutic*
> for transcendental philosophy, not the system itself of this
> philosophy, is incomprehensible to me. Such an intention could
> never have entered my mind since I myself have praised the
> completed whole of pure philosophy in the *Critique of Pure
> Reason* as the best mark of the truth of it. Since the reviewer
> finally claims that the *Critique* is not to be taken *in accor-
> dance with its letter* in regard to what it literally teaches about
> sensibility, and that everyone who would like to understand
> the *Critique* must first master the proper (Beckian or Fichtean)
> point of view, because the Kantian letter, no less than the

---

[10] ⚹109, reprinted in *Fichte's Leben und literarischer Briefwechsel,* ed. I. H.
Fichte, vol. 2, 2d rev. ed. (1862), 161 f.

Aristotelian, kills the spirit: I herewith declare once more that the *Critique* is indeed to be understood in accordance with the letter, and is to be understood solely from the point of view of the common understanding which only requires to be sufficiently cultivated for such abstract investigations.

"An Italian proverb says: 'May God preserve us merely from our friends; regarding our enemies we will take care ourselves!' For there are benevolent so-called friends, who are well-disposed toward us but who in the choice of means to favor our intentions behave the wrong way (clumsy), but at times also fraudulent, crafty ones who plot our destruction while yet employing the language of benevolence (*aliud lingua promptum, aliud pectore inclusum genere*), of whom and whose traps one cannot sufficiently beware. But heedless of this, the critical philosophy, by virtue of its inexorable tendency toward the satisfaction of reason, both theoretically and morally-practically, must feel the calling that no change of opinions, no improvements, nor any doctrinal edifice of another form are in store for it; but the system of the critique rests on a complete, assured foundation, firm forever, and is indispensable for the highest aims of humanity also for all ages to come.

August 7, 1799.   IMMANUEL KANT."

Some of the intemperate language was probably intended for the reviewer and not for Fichte. The declaration manifests a profound irritation with all the current talk about the supposed difference between the letter and spirit of Kant's philosophy—Schiller's suggestion in his thirteenth letter (H 7) had fallen on fertile ground—and with all the efforts to complete what Kant had begun. Certainly, the declaration is not an appealing document.[11]

Fichte owed far too much to Kant to feel that he himself could publish a reply. So he wrote Schelling a letter, which Schelling was to publish in the same journal, where it duly appeared in ※122

---

[11] Karl Popper, *The Open Society and Its Enemies,* rev. ed., 1950, misrepresents this episode thoroughly and omits all mention of the charge of atheism and Fichte's dismissal. Popper says, in italics: "I have seen so far no history of philosophy which clearly states that, in Kant's opinion, Fichte was a dishonest impostor" (Chapter 12, 249, and note 58, 653 f.). This is wholly representative of Chapter 12, which deals with Hegel. (See WK Chapter 7.)

(*ibid.*, 163 f.). He was very respectful, furnished the context of words Kant had quoted from a letter he had written Fichte long ago—and thus showed how Kant himself had referred to his *Altersschwäche* (the weakness of old age). He also mentioned that Kant had long ceased to keep up with recent publications. And Fichte's published letter ends:

"It is only to be expected, dear Schelling, that, just as the defenders of the pre-Kantian metaphysics have not yet ceased telling Kant that he is occupying himself with fruitless subtleties, Kant should say the same to us. It is only to be expected that, just as they assert against Kant that their metaphysics still stands undamaged, unimprovable, and unalterable in all eternity, Kant should assert the same about his against us. Who knows where even now the young fiery head may be at work who will go beyond the principles of the *Wissenschaftslehre* and try to prove its errors and incompleteness. May heaven then grant us the grace that we may not take our stand on the assertion that these are fruitless subtleties and that we certainly will have nothing to do with them, but that one of us, or if this should be more than could by then be asked of us, instead of us some man educated in our school, may stand up and either *prove* the nullity of these new discoveries or, if he cannot do this, accept them gratefully in our name."

When Schelling himself turned out to be this young firebrand only two years later, Fichte lacked the grace for which he had wished. Until 1801 Schelling saw himself as Fichte's follower and felt that they both represented the same line. But Hegel's pamphlet on the *Difference of the Fichtean and Schellingian System of Philosophy* (1801) led Schelling to consider his own philosophy an advance over Fichte's comparable to Fichte's advance over Kant.

September 20, 1799, Fichte had written Schelling: "Our letters, my dear friend, have crossed each other. Meanwhile you will have received mine about Kant's advertisement [meaning the letter just quoted]. You take this matter as it well may be taken, but as I may not take it. To be sure, I am completely convinced that the Kantian philosophy, if it is not to be taken as we take it, is total nonsense.[12] But I think, excusing Kant, that he is doing himself an injustice, that his own philosophy was never especially fa-

[12] This judgment will be illuminated later in our discussion of Hegel vis-à-vis Kant, at the end of H 42.

miliar to him, and that by now he neither knows nor understands it any more; and of mine he certainly knows nothing except for what he has picked up on the wing from one-sided reviews. I now want to do nothing further than what I recently sent you. But if *you* wanted to do something, if you wanted to present your view to the public, this, I think, could be very good. You seem less partisan; you have a public that honors you; it is the external main proof of the correctness of the *Wissenschaftslehre* that a head like yours has absorbed it and that it is becoming so fruitful in your hands—a proof that people sometimes forget . . ." (*ibid.,* 304 f.).

Barely more than a year later, Fichte wrote Schelling a letter of which only a draft survives, which begins: "I had written you, my beloved friend, about some differences in our views, not as if I considered them obstacles for a common undertaking, which you surely do not believe either, but to give you some proof of my attentive reading of your writings. Only I should say to anyone else except you, whose truly divine power of divination I know [*wahrhaft göttliche Divinationsgabe*], that he was obviously wrong" (*ibid.,* 320).

On November 15, 1800, Fichte wrote Schelling about the latter's *System of Transcendental Idealism,* which had just appeared: "High praise is not fitting between us; in this regard only this much: everything is as it was to be expected from your genius [*von Ihrer genialischen Darstellung*]. About your *opposition* of transcendental philosophy and philosophy of nature I still cannot agree with you. Everything seems to depend on a confusion between *ideal* and *real* activity, of which both of us have been guilty here and there but which I hope to remove completely in my new essay . . ." (*ibid.,* 324).

On May 31, 1801, Fichte still wrote in the same spirit: "Mutual respect among men who work in the same science and who know, as I know of myself for eight years now, that they have seized on what is right, can only mean that they have supreme confidence in each other, always interpret each other by way of giving each other every benefit of the doubt, and where even that is no longer sufficient, hope that the erring friend, owing to his talent, will yet find the right way. That is how I have always behaved toward you, and you, when you had to consider me in error, have shown me the same attitude. Now only about me in relation to you. . . ."

After many pages of explanations, Fichte finally added a postscript on August 7: "So long, my dearest friend, this letter has been lying around, unsealed . . ." (*ibid.,* 340–48).

Schelling's reply of October 3, 1801, written after the publication of Hegel's essay on the *Difference,* has quite a different tone: ". . . The consciousness or feeling which you yourself had to have of this point forced you in your *Vocation of Man* to transfer the speculative dimension, because you actually could not find it in your *knowledge,* into the sphere of *faith,* of which, in my view, one cannot speak in philosophy any more than one could in geometry. You explained in the same essay, almost in these words: the truly primordial reality, i.e., presumably the speculative dimension, could nowhere be shown in knowledge. Is not this sufficient proof that your knowledge is not absolute knowledge but knowledge that is still somehow conditional . . . ? . . . You must forgive me when I say that your whole letter is permeated by a complete misunderstanding of my ideas, which is natural enough considering that you have not exactly exerted yourself to get to really know them. On the other hand, of all the ideas that you were kind enough to communicate to me in your letter, there was not one that was new [*fremd,* literally: strange] to me. I also know, as you will perhaps concede to me, partly from my own use, all the arts with which idealism is proved to be the only necessary system. These arts, which were fatal against all of your previous opponents, are without effect against me, since I am not your opponent, although you are, very probably, mine. I have already said above that I do not find your system false, for it is a necessary and integrated part of my own. . . . 'that I have not penetrated the *Wissenschaftslehre.'* . . . Of course, I have not penetrated it yet in this sense, nor do I intend ever to penetrate it in this sense—namely, in such a way that in this penetration I myself am penetrated. This opinion I have never had of the *Wissenschaftslehre,* and much less do I have it now, that I should consider it a book on which everybody must depend henceforth in philosophy and to which everybody has to be sent, although judgment in philosophical matters would certainly be made a great deal easier if all one needed for it were a written testimonial from you that one either understands or does not understand it" (*ibid.,* 348–57).

Fichte's reply of October 15 begins with a purely objective discussion of philosophical issues. Then it proceeds: "Your letter still has a second part which it is painful for me to touch on. Why is it that you cannot communicate yourself without insulting . . . ? Do be good enough to put yourself in my place and to think how I should have behaved regarding you when I had to declare that nobody, absolutely nobody had understood me."

An editorial footnote, written by Fichte's son, explains that the final allusion is to the mention of Schelling in Fichte's announcement of his new presentation of the *Wissenschaftslehre*. This is undoubtedly also the source of one of the most popular legends about Hegel, who is alleged to have died with the words: "Only one man has understood me, and he did not understand me either."[13] This story is not only untrue but quite out of keeping with Hegel's character and historical situation. In his last years in Berlin Hegel had many disciples who were applying his ideas in a variety of fields; some of them were themselves respected scholars; others made great reputations after he died. Hegel did not feel lonely and misunderstood. Fichte, on the other hand, did. He kept complaining in print; the most famous and obvious example was the book he had published in 1801, which Schelling mentions at the end of the letter just quoted: *Sun-clear Report to the Larger Public about the Real Nature of the Newest Philosophy: An Attempt to Compel the Reader to Understand.* Fichte's position could be paraphrased with just a dash of malice by saying that only one man had understood him—namely, Schelling—and that he had not understood him either. But when Fichte's fame was eclipsed by Hegel's, and a great many readers found Hegel's books more difficult than anything they had ever read, the dictum was ascribed to Hegel.

There had been no lack of provocation when Fichte, in his *Report on the Concept of the Wissenschaftslehre and Its Fate So Far* (1806), attacked "one of the most confused heads that the confusion of our day has produced, Friedrich Wilhelm Joseph Schelling," and said of him: "That the man thus showed his absolute ignorance of what speculation is and wants and his natural incapacity for speculation . . . is self-evident. . . ."[14] He never was given to pussy-footing; he was a passionate and whole-hearted man; and in his dealings with Schelling he had shown considerable

---

[13] Heinrich Heine, *Zur Geschichte der Religion und Philosophie in Deutschland* (1835), *Sämtliche Werke, Rechtmässige Original–Ausgabe,* V (1861), 211.
[14] *Werke,* vol. 8 (1846), 385.

nobility and had been not easily angered "but, being wrought, perplex'd in the extreme."

Now "the wheel is come full circle": Fichte saw his work in the same light in which Kant in 1799 had seen his, and disowned his erstwhile disciple, while the younger man saw the work of his predecessor as a mere stepping stone. Schelling had insulted Fichte, as Fichte had never insulted Kant, and Schelling was not in such straits as Fichte had been in when Kant dissociated himself from him: in these two respects, Fichte stands blameless. But the change in his estimate of the younger man's ability and work was more extreme and appalling than the transformation of Kant's judgment of Fichte had been. Still, the difference between Kant's age and Fichte's had been thirty-eight years, and they had never been close friends, while the difference between Fichte and Schelling was only thirteen years, and they had been very close for several years.

What matters in the present context is the lively sense of a progression with apocalyptic overtones. Since Hegel's death there has probably never been a time when there was any widespread agreement that some one individual was unquestionably the greatest living philosopher, and that the whole history of philosophy somehow led up to him. In the case of Kant there was such agreement, and not many philosophers in the twentieth century would dream of denying that no other philosopher in the last quarter of the eighteenth century was in his class. He was clearly one of the greatest philosophers of all time. And he himself said in the closing words of his greatest work: "before the present century runs out . . . human reason [might attain] complete satisfaction about that which has always engaged its curiosity, but so far in vain."

When the book appeared, nineteen years were left; when the second, comprehensively revised edition came out, only thirteen. Two years later the French Revolution broke out and convinced thousands of intellectuals that a new era was indeed at hand. Among those who took up Kant's challenge, Fichte was certainly the outstanding personality, and in 1798 Friedrich Schlegel, the leading spirit of the budding German romantic movement, said in his *Athenäums-Fragmente:* "The French Revolution, Fichte's *Wissenschaftslehre,* and Goethe's [*Wilhelm*] *Meister* are the greatest tendencies of the age."

Nobody today would rank Fichte with Kant; and Schelling, too, is of interest to few but historians. But in the years when Hegel was trying to write his first book, there was a widespread feeling that Kant's immense contribution required completion. This did not necessarily involve the presumption that the man who came after him would be greater than Kant, or even his equal. Moses led his people only to the borders of the promised land; Joshua conquered it.

Fichte had something of Joshua about him and, if nothing else, he broke the ice that might have frozen German philosophy after Kant. He convinced the younger generation that important work remained to be done. This is supremely relevant to an understanding of Hegel's philosophy.

A graduate student who writes his doctoral dissertation very quickly need not feel that it has to be a fair sample of the best he can do. But the longer he postpones his thesis—especially if meanwhile he offers sharp and at times condescending judgments about the work others turn out—the more the internal pressure mounts that his dissertation has to be a minor masterpiece. Schelling, who kept publishing book upon book, could afford to write one that was relatively unimportant. Hegel, in his mid-thirties, could not afford to publish a first book that might be on a par with Krug's and Schulze's works: if humanly possible, his volume had to be better than all the books that Schelling had turned out in such rapid order. Nor was that all—and this is the point at which the development from Kant to Fichte to Schelling becomes all-important.

Much more was at stake than Hegel's self-respect. He could either write something that would be, at best, another good book— one more respectable performance by a no longer quite young philosophy professor—or he could enter the lists against Fichte and Schelling and become the true Joshua. Or, if Joshua and the Judges had already done their work, he might try to capture the holy city.

The *Phenomenology of the Spirit* changed under Hegel's hands as he wrote it. But at no point was it meant to be just another publication. At no point was it intended as a solid contribution that would establish its author as the equal of, say, Fries. Dearly as Hegel would have liked to obtain a chair of philosophy, the stakes for which he was playing were incomparably higher. Human reason was to obtain, at long last, "complete satisfaction about that which has always engaged its curiosity, but so far in vain."

27

Hegel believed that this satisfaction had to be found in a comprehensive system. Most of his reasons for believing this he gave in the preface to the *Phenomenology*. Since a complete translation of this preface with a commentary on facing pages is offered later in this volume, it would be pointless to attempt any summary here. But a couple of important points may be added to the reasons Hegel himself gives.

The first was well stated by Haym in 1857: ". . . this is the character of the Hegelian system. I call it a *work of art of knowledge*. It wants not to dissolve the world of being and knowledge critically but to achieve the comprehensive unity of a beautiful whole. It wants not to uncover the perplexities of knowledge or gain clarity about the limits, the contradictions, and antinomies in the world of the spirit, but on the contrary to beat down these embarrassments and to reconcile these contradictions. It is, I say, the *presentation of the universe as a beautiful, living cosmos*. After the manner of ancient Greek philosophy it wants to show how in the world as a whole all parts serve and unite into a harmonic order" (96 f.).

Only the negative first half of the fourth sentence is misleading: Hegel assuredly made it one of his principal aims to uncover all the perplexities, limits, contradictions, and antinomies of the spirit, but—and this must have been in Haym's mind—not as finalities but rather as difficulties and discords that were finally resolved in his system. Here at last human reason gained "complete satisfaction." And instead of Haym's rather too general reference to "ancient Greek philosophy" we might say more precisely that Hegel meant to achieve the sort of synthesis that Aristotle had accomplished. Even as Aristotle had resolved the contradictions between some seemingly incompatible principles of the pre-Socratics by developing more comprehensive doctrines, like that of the four causes, which allowed him to integrate their insights and suggestions in his vision of the world, Hegel, too, had no wish to pit *this* principle against *that* philosopher, or this point against another, or doctrine against doctrine. He sought harmony and integration in a system the like of which no modern philosopher before him had been able to fashion.

The Sophists were the philosophers of the Greek Enlightenment, and Kant might in some ways be compared with Socrates. He was the greatest thinker of the Enlightenment, and by virtue of his genius he towered above it to such an extent that we think of him as a figure apart. The achievement of both was largely critical: they taught that men do not really know what they think they know—Socrates when he said, "he knows nothing, and thinks that he knows; I neither know nor think that I know" (*Apology* 21), Kant when he did away with so-called rational psychology, rational cosmology, and natural theology. And yet both stimulated those philosophers who came immediately after them to the boldest flights of speculative metaphysics.

Though some people consider Kant typically German, and Socrates strikes others as the most representative Greek, both were profoundly anomalous among their people. The genius of the Greeks and of the Germans was exceptionally imaginative and artistic, while Kant's and Socrates' gifts were somewhat deficient in this respect. No claim whatever about the endowments of the ordinary Greek or German is at stake here; nor do we know very much about the "average" ancient Greek. What we do know is that the Greek genius achieved its greatest triumphs in art and poetry; that even Thucydides, for all his sobriety and respect for fact, has an exceptionally developed aesthetic sense which we encounter also in Heraclitus and Parmenides, in Xenophanes and Empedocles; and that the beauty of Homer's and Sophocles' artistic imagination has never been surpassed. One might hesitate to generalize even so, because the usual clichés about national characteristics are so patently untenable; but the difference in this respect between the Greeks and, say, the Romans is surely unmistakable. Even the philosophy of the Greek Enlightenment, even the Sophists, did not altogether oppose this aesthetic bent: they taught their pupils how to fashion beautiful speeches. Socrates' rationalism and uncompromising critical intelligence were immediately put to surprising uses by Plato: in the *Apology* he fashioned a speech infinitely more beautiful than any written by a Sophist, and after that he had Socrates appear in dialogues, and before long he put into Socrates' mouth speculations more imaginative than any entertained by previous philosophers.

Kant's fate in Germany is somewhat similar. There was no great philosophical tradition yet, as there had been in Greece before Socrates. Nor were there epics and tragedies of the same order. But the genius that was unfolding even then was musical and poetic. There are not many non-German composers in a class with Bach, Handel, Haydn, Mozart, and Beethoven; and during their era German poetry was coming into its own, too. The great achievements of the period were triumphs of the artistic imagination. Kant, like Socrates, was an anomaly. In both cases we can discern precedents and, if pressed, reconstruct a tradition. But there is no denying that in an important sense they were outsiders—and quickly assimilated to tendencies for which they had had little sympathy.

In the second review of the *Phenomenology,* in 1810, it was suggested that "if one might call Schelling, as it were, the modern Plato, one could call him [Hegel] with greater justice the *German Aristotle.*"[15] The former comparison must seem far-fetched today because of the extreme disparity in stature. What the reviewer meant was that *"with Schelling the imagination is predominant,"* and that he had the power to carry his listeners and readers along with his splendid delivery. Hegel, on the other hand, seems to lack the poetic touch, is prosy by comparison, but the more imposing in his comprehensive solidity. There is no point now in pressing the parallel between Schelling and Plato; it is plainly not close at all. What matters is rather that by the time Hegel began to publish, Kant had already been amalgamated into a great new movement whose watchword was certainly not uncompromising critical intelligence.

Hegel did not build directly on the foundations laid by Kant, any more than Aristotle tried above all to see what could be made of Socrates' teaching. Nor was Hegel mainly a follower and reviser of Fichte and Schelling, any more than Aristotle was mainly an adapter of Plato. Both looked back on the whole of philosophy up to their own time and tried to do justice to all the insights of their predecessors. And they were not eclectics, but men who succeeded in developing a great total vision of the cosmos.

About this vision there is plainly something poetic in both cases. For all of Aristotle's and Hegel's scientific interests, their systems

15 K. F. Bachmann (1785–1855), who had studied under Hegel in Jena, in *Heidelberger Jahrbücher,* 1. Abteilung, pp. 145–63 and 193–209, cited in Hoffmeister's critical edition of the *Phänomenologie* (1952), xxxix ff.

represent imaginative achievements of the first order. While Alexander and Napoleon went out to conquer the world with their armies, Aristotle and Hegel sought to master it with their minds.

The three main parts of Hegel's system were fixed by the time he lectured in Jena: Logic and metaphysics, philosophy of nature, and philosophy of spirit. They will be considered in the next chapters. When he actually started to write up his system for publication, he began by constructing a ladder that might lead the reader all the way from simple sense certainty to the point of view from which the system was written. At most, this introduction was meant to occupy half of the first volume, probably less. Had Hegel's gifts and temperament been the way they are usually supposed to have been, he would have dispensed with this introduction, as almost all his British expositors have done, or at the very least he would have got it over as quickly as possible. But precisely this unprecedented enterprise gave him scope for his genius, and he wrote a book that invites comparison with Dante's *Divine Comedy*[16] and Goethe's *Faust*.

28

The basic idea of the *Phenomenology of the Spirit* is that a philosopher should not confine himself to views that have been held but penetrate behind these to the human reality they reflect. It is not enough to consider propositions, or even the content of consciousness; it is worth while to ask in every instance what kind of spirit would entertain such propositions, hold such views, and have such a consciousness. Every outlook, in other words, is to be studied not merely as an academic possibility but as an existential reality.

Even this might afford considerable scope for the imagination: one might draw one sharp vignette after another, probing characteristic weaknesses. But Hegel is fascinated by the sequence. How would a man come to see the world this way or that? And to what extent does the road on which a point of view is reached color the view? Moreover, it should be possible to show how every single view in turn is one-sided and therefore untenable as soon as it is embraced consistently. Each must therefore give way to another,

16 Ros. 206 f.; Haym, 239.

until finally the last and most comprehensive vision is attained in which all previous views are integrated. That way the reader would be compelled—not by rhetoric or by talk of compelling him, but by the successive examination of forms of consciousness—to rise from the lowest and least sophisticated level to the highest and most philosophical; and on the way he would recognize stoicism and skepticism, Christianity and Enlightenment, Sophocles and Kant.

This is surely one of the most imaginative and poetic conceptions ever to have occurred to any philosopher. The parallel to Dante's journey through hell and purgatory to the blessed vision meets the eye. The comparison with Goethe's *Faust* may be elaborated briefly.

Two quotations from "The First Part of the Tragedy" could have served Hegel as mottoes. The first of these passages (lines 1770–75) he knew from *Faust: A Fragment* (1790):

> And what is portioned out to all mankind,
> I shall enjoy deep in myself, contain
> Within my spirit summit and abyss,
> Pile on my breast their agony and bliss,
> And thus let my own self grow into theirs, unfettered,

though Hegel would scarcely have added, like Faust:

> Till as they are, at last I, too, am shattered.

These lines express much of the spirit of the book: the author is not treating us to a spectacle, letting various forms of consciousness pass in review before our eyes to entertain us; he considers it necessary to re-experience what the human spirit has gone through in history, and he challenges the reader to join him in this Faustian undertaking. As long as one does less than this, one lives with blinders on and is, to use an existentialist term, unauthentic. Most men prefer, to use a term from Jaspers' *Psychologie der Weltanschauungen* (1919), to live in a shell (*Gehäuse*), hiding from the many other possibilities. Hegel asks them not merely to read about such possibilities but to identify with each in turn until their own self has grown to the point where it is contemporary with the world spirit.

Hegel's *Phenomenology of the Spirit* is a "psychology of world views" but actually more existentialist than this title of the first great classic of twentieth-century existentialism would suggest. The title suggests what Kierkegaard would have called an "aesthetic" approach, an attitude of detachment and contemplation, perhaps of interest and occasional enjoyment or admiration, rather than impassioned involvement. That is why the passage quoted from *Faust* is so appropriate: the reader, like the author, is meant to suffer through each position and to be changed as he proceeds from one to the other. *Mea res agitur:* my own self is at stake. Or, as Rilke put it definitively in the last line of his great sonnet on an "Archaic Torso of Apollo": *du musst dein Leben ändern*—"you must change your life."

Another quotation from *Faust* that would be an appropriate motto was not included in the Fragment of 1790 and appeared in print the year after the *Phenomenology,* when the whole of Part One was published in 1808:

> What from your fathers you received as heir
> Acquire, if you would possess it! (682 f.)

We do not truly possess our humanity and culture as long as we live only in the present, in our own accidental environment. We have inherited priceless works of philosophy and literature but have to exert ourselves to master them and make them truly our own. In the process, to say it once more, we are bound to be changed.

The comparison with Goethe's play can be fruitfully extended by calling attention to the function of negation. In the Prologue of *Faust* (1808) the Lord says to Mephistopheles:

> I never hated those who were like you.
> Of all the spirits that negate
> The knavish jester gives me least to do.
> For man's activity can easily abate,
> He soon prefers uninterrupted rest;
> To give him this companion hence seems best,
> Who roils and must as devil help create. (337–43)

Goethe's "uninterrupted rest" invites comparison with Hegel's "inert simplicity" or "immediacy" in the preface to the *Phenomenology,* and as one reads the preface one cannot fail to note how similar the role of negation is in that book and in *Faust.* Even more obviously, men like to settle down in one position or another, and the negative power of criticism—and occasionally caricature worthy of a jester—keeps them moving up the ladder.

Later, in Faust's study, Mephistopheles himself explains the function of his negativity. To Faust's question, "Enough, who are you then?" he replies:

> Part of that force which would
> Do evil evermore, and yet creates the good.
> FAUST: What is it that this puzzle indicates?
> MEPHISTO: I am the spirit that negates.
> And rightly so, for all that comes to be
> Deserves to perish wretchedly;
> 'Twere better nothing would begin.
> Thus everything that your terms, sin,
> Destruction, evil represent—
> That is my proper element. (1335–44)

This is both a central motif of the *Phenomenology* and an essential feature of Hegel's later philosophy, especially of his vision of history. Every finite position is destroyed, but tragic as this perpetual destruction unquestionably is, in the long run it serves a positive end by leading to a greater good. History is the realm of sin, destruction, and evil, but out of these terrors and human agonies freedom emerges and grows. The sacrifices are not all in vain; the process is one that leads to salvation and a great vision. Without destruction and suffering the vision could never be had; without the negative, man would seek uninterrupted rest.

Kant already had tried to show in his *Idea for a Universal History with Cosmopolitan Intent* (1784) how what he called *antagonism* led to progress and would eventually compel nations to form a League of Nations (*Völkerbund*). His noble essay, as brief as it is suggestive, partakes of the vision of Isaiah. But Hegel is far closer to Goethe's *Faust* in his determination to digest all of human experience—and to the poet who fashioned "The Second Part of the Tragedy" (published only after Goethe's, and Hegel's, death), in his attempt to find a place in his work for an incredible number of figures, ideas, and details that almost any other great writer of the age would have excluded without the least hesitation.

What leads to this catholicity, also in *Faust II*, is by no means a didactic impulse—pedagogically, the result is in both cases impossible—but the artistic need of a vast spirit alienated from his environment. The Second Part of *Faust* and Hegel's *Phenomenology* are the creations of men as lonely as the exiled poet of the *Divine*

Comedy. Unable to settle down with any real contentment in this world as it is, and despairing both of changing it and of finding solace in human society, Hegel, like Goethe and Dante, created a world of his own, and instead of peopling it largely with figments of his imagination as many another writer has done, found places in it for the men and women and events he knew from history and literature, as well as a very few of his contemporaries—and did not really care greatly how much of all this would be recognized and understood. Of course, the reader is meant to grasp the structure of the whole, and the serious reader, who alone is of any interest to the author, is certain to recognize familiar faces at every turn, usually in unfamiliar surroundings; but not every detail is put in mainly for the reader's sake, for his instruction and the promotion of knowledge. A great deal is there because it happened just then to be of interest to the writer, and he was wondering where it belonged, how best to place it—how to fashion a cosmos of the totality of his cultural experience without suppressing anything that seemed to matter.

Indeed, never before had any major philosopher so patently enjoyed allusions, and so lavishly indulged in this pleasure. Let the cultured reader be rewarded for his pains; let the less educated be shamed into reading what they ought to have read along ago. Cliquishness is contemptible, but the mutual affinity and enjoyment of those members of the invisible church whose highly developed humanity gives them a great deal in common is one of the legitimate consolations for the misery of life.

This kind of writing was too new for Hegel to realize its peculiar dangers, and the immense pressure under which he wrote such a big book in so short a time did not permit him to reflect very much about the possible influence of his unusual style, many decades later. In the preface he pleaded belatedly that philosophy must become scientific—an unlikely epithet for the *Phenomenology.*

The highly allusive style turns the reader into a detective rather than a critical philosopher: one looks for clues and feels happy every time one has solved some small mystery; one feels that along with whoever else has figured things out one belongs on the author's side as opposed to the many who have not got the point. The question whether the author is right drops from consciousness.

Thus allusions replace arguments. Instead of remaining a preliminary that is almost taken for granted, understanding, because it has become so exceedingly difficult, takes the place of critical evaluation for which no energy seems to be left. It is so hard to get the point, and so few do, that the big problem is no longer whether the point stands up but rather whether one has got it. And the main division is not between those who agree and those who do not, but between those who understand and belong and those who do not.

The outstanding example of such a style in the twentieth century is Heidegger. He is anything but a follower of Hegel, and Hegel exposed some of Heidegger's principal confusions one hundred twenty years before Heidegger became famous. Heidegger does not invoke Hegel's example, but when his disciples are severely pressed in argument they not infrequently fall back on Hegel's precedent as their last line of defense.

We are considering the dangers of a style, not the originality, truth, or profundity of the content. Perhaps this is made clearer by touching on two other examples.

Under the Nazi dictatorship, speakers who opposed the government cultivated the art of allusion and innuendo. As one listened to, or read, say, Niemöller, what seemed to matter was the hidden content and, of course, his courage, and there was a feeling of fellowship among those who understood him and shared his enemies. Whether one agreed with him was wholly secondary. The same is bound to happen under any oppressive censorship that has not succeeded in extinguishing dissent, for example in Poland in the 1960s. What has become important and is discussed is how much somebody has got away with, how bold he has been, and whether he might have meant this or that; the question of truth is easily lost sight of. Obviously, nobody could infer that a Polish philosopher who depends on indirection and Niemöller in the thirties should be classed with Hegel as regards either their eminence or their beliefs.

What, then, accounts for this peculiarity of style of the *Phenomenology?* Certainly not political considerations, or any deliberate obscurantism. At bottom, it is the same impulse that lulls the critical intelligence to sleep in some of Plato's dialogues and in some of Nietzsche's writings, although both meant above all else to get us to think critically: the poetic impulse.[17]

17 Regarding Plato and Nietzsche, see WK Chapter 14: "Philosophy Versus Poetry."

29

Two examples may help to show what problems Hegel's allusiveness poses. Here is how Josiah Royce linked the *Phenomenology* with *Faust*—and Royce has been Hegel's foremost interpreter in the United States. Indeed, William James on "Hegel and his Method" in *A Pluralistic Universe* is really James on Royce; and it could be argued that Royce was Hegel's unauthorized deputy in America for a generation.

In his posthumously published *Lectures on Modern Idealism* (1919, now also in paperback) Royce devotes four chapters (out of ten) to Hegel, three of them to the *Phenomenology*. He devotes a page to Hegel's section on *Die Lust und die Notwendigkeit* (Pleasure and Necessity) and says:

"He begins this sort of life by taking form as Faust. The Faust-ideal in question is due to so much of that poem as was at that time known to Hegel, and is not the Faust-ideal that Goethe later taught us to recognize as his own. Hegel conceives the Faust of the poem, as it was then before him, simply as the pleasure seeker longing for the time when he can say, 'O moment stay, thou art so fair.' The outcome of Faust's quest, as far as it goes, is for Hegel the discovery that the passing moment will neither stay nor be fair. . . . Pleasure seeking means, then, the death of whatever is desirable about life; and Hegel foresees, for Faust himself . . . no escape from the fatal circle. At all events, the self is not to be found in this life of lawless pursuit of that momentary control over life which is conceived as pleasure. Such is Hegel's reading of the first part of Faust. He entitles the sketch, 'Pleasure and Destiny' " (190 f.).

Royce has no time for philological correctness. *Notwendigkeit* means necessity, not destiny. The *Phenomenology* (1807) did not offer any reading of *Faust I* (1808). "So much of that poem as was at this time known to Hegel"—i.e., *Faust: A Fragment* (1790)— jumped straight from the scene between Faust and Wagner to the lines "And what is portioned out to all mankind" (cited in the previous section), and this speech (in the Fragment these are the opening words of the first scene between Faust and Mephistopheles) hardly suggests "the pleasure seeker longing for the time when he can say, 'O moment stay, thou art so fair.' " This apostrophe to the moment, moreover, was not published until 1808 and, in context, has the very opposite meaning of that which Royce attributes to it. Faust says (lines 1692 ff.):

> If ever I recline, calmed, on a bed of sloth,
> You may destroy me then and there.
> If ever flattering you should wile me
> That in myself I find delight,
> If with enjoyment you beguile me,
> Then break on me, eternal night!
> This bet I offer.

MEPHISTO: I accept it.
FAUST: Right.

> If to the moment I should say:
> Abide, you are so fair—
> Put me in fetters on that day,
> I *wish* to perish then, I swear.

And as if all this were not emphatic enough, Faust says later in the same scene (lines 1765 ff.):

> Do you not hear, I have no thought of joy!
> The reeling whirl I seek, the most painful excess,
> Enamored hate and quickening distress.
> Cured from the craving to know all, my mind
> Shall not henceforth be closed to any pain,
> And what is portioned out to all mankind. . . .

At that point the scene in the Fragment begins.

Now the question remains whether Hegel's "sketch," as Royce calls it, is intended as a portrait of Goethe's Faust at all, and the answer is surely: No. What seems to have misled Royce is that on the first page of this section there are three allusions to *Faust;* but they do not establish that the next four pages are intended as a portrait of Faust.

If the point were merely that Royce had erred, it would scarcely merit mention, though this is by no means an isolated instance in his treatment of Hegel.[18] The matter gains importance when we take into account that Royce's "Lectures" were edited and very extensively revised before publication by J. Loewenberg, who in-

[18] Cf. C III.3.4.

herited the reputation of being the leading American Hegel scholar and who also edited what was for a long time the only Hegel anthology in English. When the "Lectures" were reissued in paperback, "with a new Foreword by John E. Smith," another authority on "Modern Idealism," nothing was done by way of mentioning or correcting any errors. And lest it be thought that all this is indicative of the state of American Hegel scholarship only, Kuno Fischer (p. 355) entitled his discussion of this section "Pleasure and Necessity (Faust)"—and Jean Hyppolite, in his French commentary on the *Phenomenology,* which exceeds the *Phenomenology* in length, still says *"Comme le premier* Faust *de Goethe, le seul alors connu, elle meprise l'entendement et la science . . ."* (271).

In fact, Hegel adapts four lines from Mephisto's soliloquy about Faust (1851 ff.): he uses, in considerably changed form, the first two and the last two lines of a seventeen-line monologue and thus characterizes a type. To begin with what Mephisto actually says, both in the Fragment and in the later version, two points are relevant: first, he plainly does not understand Faust and what he says is in important respects wrong about Faust; secondly, even so, what he describes is not a "pleasure seeker" but a man with an unbridled spirit whose "hasty striving is so great, it leaps over the earth's delights." Hegel's adaptation of the four lines has no longer any reference to Faust but expresses a thought so dear to him that in quite a different context, in the preface to his *Philosophy of Right,* he repeats this quotation almost literally, introducing it: "Mephistopheles, in Goethe—a good authority—says about this, roughly, what I have also quoted previously:

> Despise understanding and science,
> man's very highest gifts—
> then you have yielded to the devil
> and must perish."

These lines express Hegel's view of those who despise the understanding and science; they do not serve notice that what follows is "Hegel's reading of the first part of Faust."

This is obvious in the *Philosophy of Right.* But the whole style of the *Phenomenology* is such that the student and scholar are almost bound to ask themselves: What is the man talking about? *Whom* does he have in mind? Indeed—and this is crucial—the obscurity and whole manner of the text are such that these questions are almost bound to replace the question of whether what Hegel says is right. Until one knows about whom he is writing, one is often at a loss to say whether he is right; and at other times what he says is so plainly *not* right and his generalizations are so fantastic that the only way to understand how anybody could even think of saying such things is to refer his statements back to the individual of whom he was thinking.

30

Later in the *Phenomenology,* almost the whole chapter on *Sittlichkeit* revolves around Sophocles' *Antigone:* specifically, the first two of its three sections: "a. The ethical world, human and divine law, man and woman" and "b. The ethical deed, human and divine knowledge, guilt and fate." The last section of this chapter is much shorter than the first two.

It may sound odd to say that Antigone is "even" mentioned by name, but in the whole big book only thirteen men and women are named. Six are philosophers: Anaxagoras, Aristotle, Descartes, Diogenes, Kant, and Plato. Five more are historic, mostly writers or poets: Homer, Lichtenberg, Origen, Solon, and Sophocles. And two come out of tragedies: Hamlet and Antigone.

Fifteen others are plainly alluded to or quoted, ten of them historic: Aristophanes, Democritus, Diderot, Fichte, Goethe, Lessing, Leucippus, Schiller, Shakespeare, and Socrates; also Macbeth and Orestes, and Antigone's father and brothers—Oedipus, Eteocles, and Polyneices.

Sophocles' Antigone is mentioned and quoted at the end of Part V; the chapter on *Sittlichkeit* is the first one of Part VI. The heroine is quoted again, and again mentioned by name, in the middle of the section on "The ethical deed. . . ." But the interpretation of these sections does not depend on these quotations. These pages abound in statements that are simply outrageous in the form in which they are offered and that plainly cry out to be referred to Sophocles' tragedy.

For about three pages Hegel argues that "The feminine therefore has the highest intimation of what is ethical insofar as she is a sister," and that "The loss of the brother is therefore irreplaceable for the sister, and her duty to him is the highest one." In the second section we find out how "According to its content, however, the ethical deed has the aspect of a crime," and a little later that it "is based on the certain confidence in the whole into which nothing foreign, no fear, nor enmity is mixed." Soon after this, Antigone is mentioned and quoted the second time.

After that we hear about "two brothers" who, to begin with, have an equal right to the government: "These two therefore become opposed to each other, and their equal right to the power over the state destroys both as they are equally in the wrong. From the human point of view, the crime has been committed by the one who, not in possession, attacked the commonwealth at whose head the other stood. . . . But the one that was on its side, it will honor; the other one, however, . . . the government . . . will punish by depriving him of the last honors. . . ."

It would be almost perverse to argue against Hegel's two propositions about the sister: they are plainly *ad hoc*. To be sure, one can ask whether he was thinking *solely* of Antigone or perhaps also of Goethe's Iphigenia and her relation to Orestes, and of his own sister, Christiane. There are several sentences that plainly allude to Orestes, and a very good case could be made that he was thinking of all three brother-sister relationships. When he speaks of the Erinys, he is surely thinking of Orestes; but he may be thinking of Christiane's relation to himself when he says, "The brother, however, is for the sister the calm, even being par excellence." When he concludes that paragraph, "The loss of the brother is therefore irreplaceable for the sister," we are bound to think not only of Antigone's express words (lines 909 ff.) but also of Christiane's suicide, a few weeks after Hegel's death.

Assuredly, the *Phenomenology* is not a dull book. But in view of the claims with which the book is offered to us, the excitement it begets on the aesthetic plain is certainly not enough. As an ultra-highbrow puzzle and a treat for intellectuals, the book is wonderful, but what are we to make of its scientific pretensions?

Hegel claims, as we have seen, that a woman's relationship to her brother is ethically higher than her relationship to her husband, parents, or children. He argues that in the other relationships natural emotions are prominent, and the two persons are not so independent of each other; "But the unmixed relationship takes place between brother and sister. They are the same blood which, however, has attained in them its rest and balance. They do not desire each other, nor have they given this being-for-itself to each other or received it from each other; they are free individuality in relation to each other. The feminine therefore has the highest intimation of what is ethical insofar as she is a sister."[19] If we take these generalizations at face value, they are silly. One cannot rank human relationship this way, and it makes no sense to lay down once for all as a principle that a person is bound to have the highest intimation of what is ethical in this relationship rather than in that. Incidentally, the generalization that brother and sister do not desire each other is rather magisterial. But if we take the whole passage as special pleading for Antigone and an attempt to bolster her argument (lines 909 ff.), we find that this is not very good literary criticism either. Sophocles' Antigone suggests powerfully that there is nobody she loved as much as her dead brother; that she does not desire marriage with Haimon, her betrothed; that since Polyneices is dead she, too, wants to die (e.g., lines 72 ff.).

Rudolf Haym said long ago: "To say everything: the *Phenomenology* is *psychology reduced to confusion and disorder by history, and history deranged by psychology*" (243). Even this dictum, which the author himself italicized, is too kind: instead of mixing only history and psychology, Hegel offers us what Richard Wagner was later to call a *Gesamtkunstwerk,* leaving out little but music. Haym spoke of "a romantic masquerade." I should prefer to speak of charades: now a tableau, now a skit, now a brief oration—and what we are to guess may be the theme of a Greek tragedy or a character from Diderot's *Rameau's Nephew,* recently translated by Goethe; it may be the French Revolution or a philosophical stance, like stoicism or skepticism; medieval Christianity or the pseudo-science of physiognomy, or Kant's moral philosophy—and it is hardly surprising that somebody should guess Faust where Faust was not meant, especially since a few charades, which are not marked to distinguish them from the rest, do not represent anything in particular.

In only one respect is this image unfair: most of the tableaux are unmistakably identified, many in the table of contents and an appropriate section heading, others in the text. Moreover, Lasson of-

[19] Lasson's ed., 296. Baillie's tr., 475 f., renders the last sentence quite incorrectly. Ros. 208: although Hegel was undoubtedly thinking of *Antigone* in this section, "the characterization of the essence of manliness and femininity in general is a glorious success."

fered some helpful footnotes in his critical edition of the text, and
these were taken over by Hoffmeister and by Baillie in his translation. Still, part of the appeal of the book lies in the questions it
poses at every turn: Is Hegel thinking of Schelling? Does he mean
Jacobi? Is he referring to Iphigenia as well as Antigone? And: To
whom since Hegel's own time is what he says applicable?

With this last question we approach the greatness of the book.
All too often, Hegel is overly specific and has to drag in, for example, allusions to Antigone's brothers who destroyed each other
in the fight for Thebes, lest we miss his string of allusions to Sophocles' *Antigone.* Or he pontificates: "Actuality therefore contains,
concealed, the other side, foreign to knowledge, and does not show
itself to consciousness—does not show the son the father in the man
who insults him and whom he slays, nor the mother in the queen
whom he wifes."[20] One wishes Hegel had come out into the open,
saying something like: in some ways, Sophocles' tragedy—whether
Antigone or *Oedipus Tyrannus*—gives classical formulation to a
conflict or predicament that is representative of the human condition, or of a certain stage in the development of culture.

Haym is right that Hegel's "selection is absolutely arbitrary. As a
historical figure was especially familiar to the author or especially
present to his mind from recent reading, it is seized and made the
symbol of an allegedly necessary and indispensable stage of consciousness. . . . As absolute knowledge itself is nothing else than
thoughtful contemplation of things, but whitewashed and saturated
with an aesthetic conception of them, a romantic-fantastic confusion of what is the poet's business and what is the philosopher's
business, so, too, the phenomenological road to this knowledge consists in the perpetual poetic translation of abstract forces into con-
cretely historic ones, but even more in the constant interlarding
and mixing of both" (242–44). But although Haym is right, Hegel
could be defended on this score.

Why should he not seize on *Antigone* because he knows the play
so well, or on *Rameau's Nephew* because he has read it recently?
Why should he not choose his examples now from history and now
from literature? This is not what has gone wrong. The real fault
is that the overly heavy dependence on allusions makes Hegel's dis-

[20] Lasson's ed., 305. Baillie's tr., 490, mentions Oedipus by name, though
Hegel does not.

cussions too specific. What ought to be merely a vivid illustration becomes the subject matter itself. It is in this way that the poetic impulse takes over.

31

All this may seem so utterly damning that the reader may wonder how Hegelians from David Friedrich Strauss to Hermann Glockner could praise the *Phenomenology* as the greatest work of one of humanity's greatest thinkers, and how Ueberweg's superb multi-volume *Geschichte der Philosophie* could possibly say of it: "It is at the same time the most difficult and the most contentful of Hegel's works. The difficult, dark, condensed style compresses great masses of thought to the utmost."[21]

Probably the main reason the book has won such ardent admiration is that it is highly original and indeed unique, and insofar as it can be compared at all to any previous classic of philosophy one would have to adduce Plato's *Republic* or, conceivably, Spinoza's *Ethics*. Like Plato—and to a lesser extent, Spinoza—Hegel wrote a single volume in which he recreated the whole world from the point of view of a singularly cultivated and philosophically schooled sensibility. To organize such a wealth of material—indeed, in a sense "everything"—in the framework of one story is an astonishing feat, and it is exciting at every turn to see what he makes of this and how he understands and fits in that.

Beyond that, the conception of the book, which should be distinguished from its execution, deserves the greatest admiration. Instead of simply sitting down to write a book containing *his* philosophy, Hegel considers it essential to give an account of what man has thought so far. It is not enough to write one's own book, showing in footnotes here and there that one has read some Kant and Fichte, Krug and Schulze, Sextus and Hume, Plato and Aristotle, and to reveal something of one's general education by making an occasional bow to Homer or Goethe. Philosophers seem to disagree, and even if one supports one's own views with a few arguments, it is a foregone conclusion that others will find a few arguments to support

---

[21] . . . *vom Beginn des neunzehnten Jahrhunderts bis auf die Gegenwart*, 11th ed., ed. K. Oesterreich (1916), 77.

their different views: philosophy in that style is inconclusive and arbitrary. Instead of picking up a proposition from one book to controvert it and a quotation from another by way of agreement, one should try, if one bothers at all with the views of others, really to master each in turn—as an existential whole, keeping in mind that each belief is part of a larger view, and that each view requires a point of view which involves a human reality.

When Hegel asserts the ethical primacy for woman of the relationship to her brother, or when he speaks of the burial of another as the highest duty one can have toward him, he is not making these claims on his own behalf, as if he considered them timeless truths; he is trying to perform a marvel of empathy, not just reading *Antigone* and being effusive about its beauty or profundity but trying to see the world through Antigone's eyes. And he supposes that Antigone is not merely one figure in one old tragedy which he himself happens to like especially; he takes her to represent an ancient ethic—laws of which she says, in words that Hegel quotes before he commences his discussion of *Sittlichkeit,*

> Not now, nor yesterday's, they always live,
> and no one knows their origin in time.   (456 f.)

Her conception of the family and of *Sittlichkeit* is not merely hers but—Hegel thinks—*the* classical conception of it, which, however, comes into conflict with another conception, represented in Sophocles' tragedy by Creon. One does not have to engage in any special pleading for Hegel to suggest that the moral conflict between Antigone and Creon, as pictured by Sophocles, is not about a problem contrived by the poet: the issue is bound to arise where *Sittlichkeit* is conceived in a certain way—and that is what interests Hegel.

For all that, this particular portion of the *Phenomenology* is not one of the best. The point is only that even these pages, which are open to many objections, fit into the over-all conception of the book that has been presented here.

Philosophers may find the discussion of *Moralität,* a little later on, more to their liking; at the very least, Hegel's critique of Kant's morality retains considerable interest. I have no right, Hegel says implicitly, to present my own world view without coming to terms with Kant's. Nor is Hegel's world view altogether separate from his view of what he calls "the moral world view [*die moralische Welt-*

anschauung]," as if Hegel kept it back until the end to present it only after everybody else is criticized. As he views Antigone and Kant and all the other points of view he considers, he presents his own view of the world, section upon section.

In his critique of Kant a phrase recurs several times that is an important clue to Hegel's total conception: *aber es ist ihm damit nicht Ernst* (but he is not really serious about it).[22] That is Hegel's criticism of almost *all* the positions that pass in review: they are one-sided, and if they are not pushed to a tragic conclusion, like Antigone's in its collision with another, equally one-sided position, they are maintained—and this is the rule—in a half-hearted way, not seriously.

The views that are taken up in turn are not so much "shells," to use Jaspers's term once more, as they are halfway houses, and those who inhabit them dim the lights and move around carefully lest they discover the limitations of their intellectual homes. To remain faithful to his conception, Hegel must never condemn any view from his own point of view, externally: his criticism must always be internal and consist in taking each view more seriously than its professed opponents take it.

The crucial question of organization remains where so much material is to be considered. In the middle of the twentieth century, the most fashionable arrangement would probably be by types, as Jaspers's was in his *Psychologie der Weltanschauungen*. A merely arbitrary assortment would have the great disadvantage that important points of view might be overlooked. But Hegel's arrangement, over half a century before Darwin published his *Origin of Species* and impressed the idea of evolution on almost everybody's mind, was developmental.

Probably, he was influenced by Goethe's development from style to style, which suggested that there was a "logical" sequence—not "logical" in the ordinary sense, but rather in the way in which, to use a Hegelian image from the beginning of the preface, bud, blossom, and fruit succeed each other. Hegel assumes an organic necessity.

It does not seem to him that some of the views he considers are true and others false; but some are more mature than others, and

---

[22] In the section on *Die Verstellung:* in Lasson's edition, four times on p. 401 alone, and over half a dozen times after that; in Baillie's translation, 632 ff.

one might try to arrange them in an ascending series according to their relative maturity. This does not mean that what comes later is always better and more attractive. Early childhood has its unsurpassable charm, youth is in some respects never eclipsed; but for all that there is a developmental sequence that Hegel seeks to reproduce in the *Phenomenology*.

The idea is supremely suggestive and fascinating but, in the end, untenable. One could try to offer a history of philosophy, or of literary styles, or even of a whole culture in this vein, and in Hegel's three volumes of lectures of the history of philosophy something of this sort is in fact accomplished. Even a history of Christianity or of Hinduism could be written in this spirit, and since Hegel's time such evolutionary studies have become a commonplace. But a history of the world's religions in which all but the writer's own religion are treated as so many less mature stages on the way to truth can never be more than a piece of apologetics, though this genre flourished in the later nineteenth century and is not altogether extinct yet. The idea of arranging *all* significant points of view in such a single sequence, on a ladder that reaches from the crudest to the most mature, is as dazzling to contemplate as it is mad to try seriously to implement it.

Sometimes, to be sure, one can fruitfully relate two views by showing how the first, pushed to extremes (taken seriously), leads to the second. But any attempt to relate *all* points of view in a single chain of this sort is bound to be at best a virtuoso performance of which one might concede that the writer "plays" brilliantly, at worst a waste of time. The transitions of the *Phenomenology* fluctuate from one extreme to the other.

The idea of not sticking to the historical sequence is certainly defensible. What is earlier may at times represent a more mature stage. Hegel was also right in seeing that the way a view is reached is not necessarily external to the view itself: on the contrary, a knowledge of the development, including the prior positions, through which a man passed before adopting a position may make all the difference when it comes to comprehending his position.

To sum up: the greatness of the *Phenomenology* lies both in its conception, which is in part brilliant and fruitful, and in a lot of its detail; but some aspects of the conception are absurd, and some of the details bizarre.

32

The very table of contents of the *Phenomenology* may be said to mirror confusion. After the preface and the introduction, there are eight parts, each indicated by a Roman numeral:

    I.   Sense certainty, the this, and opinion.

    II.   Perception, the thing, and deception.

    III.   Force and understanding, appearance, and suprasensible world.

    IV.   The truth of self-certainty.

    V.   Certainty and truth of reason.

    VI.   Spirit.

    VII.   Religion.

    VIII.   Absolute knowledge.

These numbers and titles appear in the text as well as in the table of contents. Then, evidently as an afterthought, in the table of contents only and not in the text, the first three parts are lumped together under the heading—quoting from the original edition, which also specifies the page numbers and thus shows some interesting disparities at a glance:

    (A) Consciousness, pp. 22–100.

Part IV is preceded by a similar heading:

    (B) Self-Consciousness, pp. 101–161.

And the last four parts of the book are again lumped together, but without a title. Above Part V we read:

    (C) (AA) Reason, pp. 162[23]–375.

Above "VI. Spirit" we read:

    (BB) Spirit, pp. 376–624.

Above "VII. Religion":

    (CC) Religion, pp. 625–741.

And finally, above "VIII. Absolute knowledge":

    (DD) Absolute knowledge, pp. 741–765.[24]

The first three parts are not further subdivided, neither is Part VIII. All the other parts, which are longer, are.

---

[23] The original table of contents has "172," which is a misprint.
[24] The original reads: "741 to the end."

Part IV has only two subparts: "A. Independence and dependence of self-consciousness; mastership and servitude," and "B. Freedom of self-consciousness; stoicism; skepticism; and the unhappy consciousness." We shall return to this part in the next section.

Parts V, VI, and VII are all divided into A, B, and C; and each of these, in turn, with the exception of VI.B and VII.C, is in turn divided into a, b, and c. There the breakdown ends, except for V.A.a where the author could scarcely curb himself. Here matters become confused, and finally "Observance of the Organic" is broken down into alpha, beta, and gamma, and gamma, finally, into double alpha, double beta, and double gamma, and even under two of these subdivisions we find more than one descriptive title.

VI.B. is handled inconsistently: its three subdivisions are assigned Roman numerals: "I. The world of the spirit alienated from itself" (with a and b), "II. The Enlightenment" (with a and b), and "III. Absolute freedom and the Terror" (with no further subdivisions).

VII.C., "Revealed religion" has no subdivisions any more than "VIII. Absolute knowledge," which follows it.

The table of contents bears out that the work was not planned painstakingly before it was written, that Parts V and VI (Reason and Spirit) grew far beyond the bounds originally contemplated,[25] and that Hegel himself was a little confused about what he had actually got when he was finished. Of course, the above account also gives some idea of the actual contents of the book.

The first three parts deal with theory of knowledge and perception and are very heavily influenced by Plato and Aristotle. The fourth part we shall consider in a moment. Part V begins with over a hundred pages on theoretical reason, as it operates in the sciences, and this section ends, rather oddly, with a discussion of phrenology. The second half of Part V deals with practical reason and self-realization, and begins with the aforementioned discussion of "Pleasure and Necessity."

VI.A deals with *Sittlichkeit* and has been commented on above. VI.B is entitled "Spirit alienated from itself. *Bildung.*"[26] The further breakdown of this section has already been given. VI.C is

---

[25] Cf. also Hegel's letter to Schelling, May 1, 1807, in D, and Hegel's remarks in E §25.
[26] For a discussion of this word, see C I.3.4.

called "Spirit certain of itself. *Moralität*" and contains Hegel's critique of Kant's ethics.

Part VII begins with a few general pages in which the harassed author looks back on what he has done and tries rather desperately to rationalize it. He seeks to explain why it was all right to take up some forms of religion in the earlier parts, notably in the discussion of the unhappy consciousness (in IV) and of Antigone (in VI). But the worst is to come; speaking of all the preceding forms of the spirit, Hegel says: "Religion presupposes the whole procession of them [*den ganzen Ablauf derselben*] and is their *simple* totality or absolute self."[27] Then we get about ten rather poor pages about "A. Natural religion," mostly on Persia and Egypt, and wonder what he could possibly have meant: did religion of this sort, either as it really was or as Hegel here portrays it, presuppose the Enlightenment, the "absolute freedom" of 1789, and "the Terror" that ensued? Or did it presuppose comparable events? And what could one say in answer to these questions when it comes to "B. Art-religion" (meaning Greek religion) and "C. Revealed religion"? Only that Hegel finished the book under an immense strain; that faults are so easy to find in it that it is not worth while to adduce heaps of them; and that there is a great deal in the book that is infinitely more interesting.

33

By far the best part of the *Phenomenology* is its preface, included later in this volume. Next to that, Part IV, on self-consciousness, is most interesting. It begins with a few introductory pages which contain the dictum: "Self-consciousness attains its satisfaction only in another self-consciousness."[28]

Then we are offered one skit and three tableaux, all clearly labeled. In the skit, one self-consciousness encounters another. Here it is relevant that the connotations of the term are different in English and German. While being self-conscious often means being unsure of oneself and embarrassed, *selbstbewusst sein* means just the opposite: being self-assured and proud. Of course, the primary

27 Lasson's ed., 438; Baillie, 689.
28 Lasson's ed., 121; Baillie, 226.

meaning in both languages is the same: self-awareness. But while this sense is most important, the other connotations are relevant.

As self-consciousness encounters self-consciousness, pride meets pride, and each resolves to destroy the other in order to grow in self-assurance. Each aims at the other's death and risks his life. For Sartre, in *L'être et le néant,* this account is still paradigmatic. "The other" is the enemy.

What matters to Hegel is the comprehension of one particular relationship between one self-consciousness and another, namely that between master and servant. He construes it, in the first instance, as the result of the fight. The loser prefers servitude to death.

What follows made the profoundest impression on Karl Marx, who greatly admired the book and called it "the true birthplace and secret of the Hegelian philosophy."[29] The servant comes to live by his own work and thus becomes self-reliant and independent, while the master comes to rely on the servant's labor and thus becomes dependent. In *Das Kapital,* Marx writes: "As man . . . works on nature outside himself and changes it, he changes at the same time his own nature."[30]

With this neat and ironical reversal IV.A ends. IV.B is devoted to stoicism, skepticism, and the unhappy consciousness. The transition to the first of these three outlooks is easy to follow: the attitude of the servant who, despite his status, feels essentially self-reliant and independent may be characterized as stoicism. "This consciousness is thus negative against the relationship of mastership and servitude . . . to be equally free in fetters and on the throne, in spite of all the dependence of its individual existence."

Here the historical allusion is kept properly subdued: Those who do not know that one of the most famous Stoics was Marcus Aurelius, the Roman emperor, and another Epictetus, a slave, can still accept the point Hegel is making. The same is true of Hegel's sociological comment that stoicism "could appear as a general form of the world spirit only in an age of general fear and servitude,

[29] Quoted in Robert Tucker, *Philosophy and Myth in Karl Marx,* Cambridge University Press, 1961, 126, from Marx and Engels, *Historisch-Kritische Gesamtausgabe,* III, 153. Tucker himself argues that "when Marx speaks of Hegelianism he has in mind primarily the philosophy of history set forth by Hegel in his *Phenomenology*" (125). But Marx also wrote critical essays on *The Philosophy of Right* (see Bibliography).
[30] Vol. I, *Volksausgabe,* 133.

but also of general education which had taught men to think."

The implicit distinction is as sound as can be, and has often been overlooked by Marxists: the widespread acceptance of a point of view is determined sociologically, but the original development of it by some exceptional individual need not be. Some are, in Nietzsche's words, "untimely" and "born posthumously."

The transition to skepticism is plausible, too. "Skepticism is the realization of that of which stoicism is only the Concept—and the actual experience of what the freedom of thought involves; it is implicitly the negative and must present itself as such. . . . In skepticism the total insignificance and dependence of the other comes to be for consciousness. . . . The skeptical self-consciousness is this ataraxia of thinking oneself, the unchangeable and true certainty of oneself."

Stoicism is a halfway house: it denies the reality and significance of the external world, of such apparently real and significant matters as being a slave, being in fetters, being in pain, but does not seriously press the point that all this is unreal. Skepticism is serious about what stoicism merely says: the skeptic doubts that there really are fetters and thrones. In this way, perfect imperturbability and peace of mind are achieved.

Now Hegel must and does show how skepticism, too, is a halfway house; how it, too, is not truly serious about what it says. Briefly, "its acts and words always contradict each other. . . ." Though the skeptic claims to doubt the reality of his body and the external world, he acts in ways that show that he is not in earnest with his doubts. Actually, this more obvious point is made much less clearly by Hegel than another point: the skeptical consciousness has two conflicting conceptions of itself.

On the one hand, "it professes to be an entirely accidental, individual consciousness—a consciousness that is empirical and conforms to what has no reality for it, obeys what has no significance for it, and does and makes real what has no truth for it. But even as it thus considers itself as individual, accidental, and indeed animal life and a lost self-consciousness, it also makes itself, on the contrary, general and self-identical. From this self-identity, or rather in it, it falls back into that accidental and confused status, for precisely this self-moving negativity deals only with what is individual and busies itself with the accidental. This consciousness is thus the unconscious drivel that moves back and forth between the two extremes of the self-identical self-consciousness and the accidental, confused, and confusing consciousness. . . .

"In skepticism consciousness experiences itself truly as a consciousness that contradicts itself. From this experience a new form emerges which brings together the two thoughts which skepticism keeps apart. The thoughtlessness of skepticism about itself must disappear because in fact it is one consciousness that has these two aspects. This new form is one which involves the double consciousness of itself as self-liberating, unchangeable, and self-identical and of itself as absolutely self-confusing and perverse, as well as the consciousness of this its contradiction. . . . Thus the doubling which was formerly distributed among two individuals, the master and the servant, is turned into one; the doubling of self-consciousness in itself, which is essential for the Concept of the spirit, is thus present, but not yet its unity—and the unhappy consciousness is the consciousness of itself as a double being that only contradicts itself."

After Freud, the two poles of the skeptical self-consciousness of which Hegel speaks may perhaps be illustrated more vividly by considering the psychoanalyst's self-consciousness: On the one hand, he views his consciousness as empirical, accidental, and individual; he considers it unreliable and confused. On the other hand, he relies on it, considers it transempirical and objective, not merely personal but an instance of a general scientific consciousness. This, in any case, is the point Hegel makes about skepticism. It is another halfway house: now one puts on blinders and looks this way, ignoring what one sees at other times when one looks the other way. Sartre would call this *mauvaise foi* and say that the skeptical consciousness is in bad faith; it deceives itself. When skepticism is deprived of this subterfuge and forced to be in earnest, a new form of self-consciousness emerges: the unhappy consciousness that experiences itself as essentially divided against itself.

Even the preceding discussion of master and servant, stoicism, and skepticism is by no means compressed "to the utmost," as Ueberweg's *History* suggests, and the obscurity of Hegel's exposition is not due to terseness and the exclusion of all but the most essential points, but to the fact that an excess of Gothic detail often hides the basic structure of the argument. Now, with the unhappy consciousness, the author's poetic impulse takes over. In size, this account equals the analyses of mastership and servitude, stoicism, and skepticism taken together. And the reason for this is perfectly clear: Hegel becomes absorbed in allusions to the specific features of the medieval Christian mentality that, as he sees it, exemplified the unhappy consciousness.

Hegel never names Christianity; but Lasson is surely right when in his footnotes he asks us to recognize allusions to: God as judge, Jesus, the worship of Jesus, the Crusades, the consciousness of sin, asceticism, the priest as father confessor, prayers in Latin, and indulgences. Baillie in his English translation of the *Phenomenology* includes these footnotes; Royce, in *his* version of "The Contrite Consciousness" (included in Loewenberg's *Hegel Selections*) uses religious terms throughout—for example, "contrite" instead of "unhappy"—to render Hegel's more neutral words. Thus "pure consciousness" becomes "Devout Consciousness"; "bell" becomes "altar bell"; and "activity and enjoyment" once "service and communion," then "good works and communion." Royce's version is superscribed "freely translated."

The attempt to catch Hegel's allusions and the enjoyment of his cleverness or of some of his digs is bound to distract attention from the alleged "logic" of the development. The reader forgets the image of the ladder and wonders which of the many features of this tableau are in any sense necessary and essential to this stage; and the author, too, has plainly lost sight of the idea and plan of his book, and far from compressing his exposition severely, dwells at unnecessary length on irrelevancies.

Hegel evidently wanted to get some ideas about medieval Christianity off his chest, and the allusiveness of his style—no doubt, originally inspired by the recognition that all this concrete detail really did not belong here—greatly lengthened the discussion. His poetic impulse made the most of this opportunity to visualize and describe a state of mind and a period.

We can descry yet another motive. Hegel obviously was unable to continue the development that he had traced so brilliantly through several stages, beyond this point, to another stage.

Here was a divided consciousness that "places itself on the side of the changeable consciousness and considers itself insignificant; but as a consciousness of unchangeableness or simple being it must at the same time aim to liberate itself from the insignificant, i.e., from itself. . . . The consciousness of life, of its existence and activity, is only the suffering over this existence and activity, for in all this it has only the consciousness of its opposite as the essential—

and of its own nullity." This is still continuous with the preceding development from servitude to stoicism, and hence to skepticism. These transitions are among the most plausible in the whole book, and few indeed of the many other transitions can brook comparison with them. But what needed to be shown now was how the unhappy consciousness, too, is a halfway house, and how, taken in earnest and pushed to extremes, it gives way to another, more mature stage in the development of the spirit.

Not only was Hegel evidently unable to do this, he also wished to deliver himself of a lot of material about the attitudes reason adopts in the study of nature (approximately one hundred pages of it, as it turned out). So he followed up the discussion of the unhappy consciousness, and the seminal chapter on "Self-Consciousness" that ends with it, with an immensely long chapter on "Reason." He devoted the first of its three parts to "A. Observing Reason," which in turn begins with the "Observation of Nature" and ends with "Physiognomy and Phrenology." Hegel certainly did not manage to trace a necessary development from the unhappy consciousness to phrenology, any more than the development from Faust's abandonment of Gretchen in the dungeon, at the end of "The First Part of the Tragedy" to some of the more abstruse discussions in Part Two could be said to be organically necessary. Rather, the framework of the book is loose enough to permit the introduction of all sorts of ideas for which the writer would like to find a place.

The *Phenomenology of the Spirit* is a profoundly incongruous book and brings to mind some passages in Eckermann's *Conversations with Goethe* in which the poet insists that *Faust* "is after all wholly incommensurable, and all attempts to bring it closer to the understanding are in vain. One should also keep in mind that the First Part issued from a somewhat dark state of the individual. But precisely this darkness attracts people, and they exert themselves over it as they do over all insoluble problems" (January 3, 1830). Again: "This act, too, is to receive a character of its own so that, like a small world that exists for itself, it does not touch the rest and is united with the whole only through a faint relation to what precedes and succeeds it." Eckermann then suggested that the poet "uses the story of a famous hero merely as a kind of continuous thread on which he can string what pleases him. It is no different with the Odyssey and Gil Blas." Goethe agreed and added: "Moreover, what matters in a composition of this sort is merely that the several masses are significant and clear, while as a whole it always remains incommensurable, but precisely for that reason, like an unsolved problem, ever again lures people to repeated contemplation" (February 13, 1831).

34

Hegel himself, in his later years, called the *Phenomenology* his voyage of discovery. But in the preface he suggests that it is the Odyssey of the world spirit. He himself does not refer to Odysseus or use this image, and in connection with something he does say I have suggested in the commentary (I.3.4) that the *Phenomenology* is the *Bildungsroman* of the *Weltgeist,* the story of its development and education. But a comparison with the Odyssey is no less suggestive than this comparison with Goethe's *Wilhelm Meisters Lehrjahre.* In its search for a homeland where it can dwell in peace, the human spirit is shipwrecked again and again, has all kinds of adventures, many of them fantastic, and does not by any means seem to be making progress at every turn.

All of these comparisons with great works of literature are at odds with the prevalent conception of both Hegel and philosophy. They are bound to strike some readers as far-fetched. But Hegel's peculiar language bears out the present account and is not really comprehensible at all without some such reflections. Abstruse syntax that even a native reader of German must sometimes construe like Latin appears together, in the same sentence, with strikingly concrete imagery; and metaphysical speculation is fused with considerable poetic power. Almost like Shakespeare, Hegel often thinks in pictures; and although this comparison must seem perverse at first glance, it is important to realize that Hegel does not, like most philosophers, search for an image to illustrate his ideas: his difficulty often lies in getting across insight and image at once—or, in other words, in communicating his own vision. If the idea and its illustration were altogether separate in his own mind, he could offer the thought first and then, in the next sentence, an example, or first the concrete picture and then the lesson he wishes to draw from it. But he not only denies, like Aristotle, any Platonic *chorismos* or cleft between separately existing forms and concrete instances that imitate or participate in them; he resembles Plato in having a vision of the forms—not in another world, like Plato, but *in rebus,* in the images, skits, and tableaux that exemplify them. The same characteristics that make the book so difficult as a whole also make many sentences so exasperating: concrete images turn up out of season and resist being quickly dropped again. Hegel looks for terms that are not abstract—words that retain a sensuous core even when they are used in metaphysical prose. Consider a few examples:

Anschauung, firmly established by now in philosophical English as "intuition," in translations of Kant as well as other German philosophers, comes from *anschauen* which means to look at. Hence *Weltanschauung* is usually rendered "world view." (Cf. C I.2.2.)

An sich, always rendered "in itself," does not mean in German that a feature is hidden from view and literally inside, but rather that the feature is "on" the thing, visible "for us" (*für uns*) though not "for it" (*für sich*); nor does it exist separately, "for" or "by" itself" (another meaning of *für sich*). *An und für sich* (in and for itself) means that something is both "in itself" and "for itself" in the senses just specified. (Cf. C II.1.8, 10, 30.)

Aufheben (sublimate) means literally "pick up." Like every single one of the other terms explained so far, it is quite common in ordinary speech: it is what you do when something has fallen to the floor. But this original sensuous meaning has given rise to two derivative meanings which are no less common: "cancel," and "preserve" or "keep." Something may be picked up in order that it will no longer be there; on the other hand, I may also pick it up to keep it. When Hegel uses the term in its double (or triple) meaning—and he expressly informs us that he does (H 42)—he may be said to visualize how something is picked up in order that it may no longer be *there* just the way it was, although, of course, it is not cancelled altogether but lifted up to be kept on a different level. (Cf. H 42 and C II.1.16.)

Begriff (Concept) comes from *begreifen* which means "comprehend" but also has a sensuous meaning. *Greifen* means "grab" or "grasp"; the prefix intensifies the relation to the object. Thus *tasten* means to "feel (one's way)"; *betasten* means to touch something all over. Similarly, *dienen* means to serve; *bedienen,* to wait on somebody. *Denken* is think; *bedenken,* to think something over.

Begriff thus has the basic meaning of a thorough grasp, and this reverberates through Hegel's usage. (Cf. C I.1.3.)

Vorstellung (notion) comes from *vorstellen* (represent). The German verb occurs in the sense of: what is this supposed to represent? (*Was soll das vorstellen?*) *Eine Vorstellung* can mean, and in ordinary speech very often refers to, a theatrical performance. In the philosophical sense, the noun is most often connected with the verb form, *sich etwas vorstellen,* which means literally, to represent something to oneself, but is much less unusual and cumbersome. In everyday language it means as much as, to imagine something. Traditionally, translators of Kant and Schopenhauer have rendered *Vorstellung* as either "representation" or "idea." The former smacks of philosophical jargon, which the German term does not. That is why some translators prefer "idea"; but since Kant, Schopenhauer, and Hegel also often use the term *Idee,* which surely has to be rendered "idea," this solution is poor, too.

When Hegel uses *Vorstellung,* he generally has in mind a contrast with *Begriff.* He relies on two associations *Vorstellung* usually has in ordinary language: vagueness and a sensuous quality. Hegel's *Begriff,* on the other hand, is by definition precise, and it dispenses with visual aids. There is no English word that could serve as a perfect equivalent of *Vorstellung,* but "notion" is pretty good for at least two reasons. First, it is an ordinary word that does not stop one in one's tracks every time one comes across it in a sentence. Secondly, it suggests something vague and subscientific. Unfortunately, it has been widely used to render Hegel's *Begriff,* a task for which it is particularly ill fitted. A good test is the consistent use of "notion" for *Vorstellung* not only in the main part of this book but also throughout the translation of the preface to the *Phenomenology:* in every case it works far better than terms previously used. (Cf. C I.2.1.)

Geist is for Hegel "spirit" and not "mind." There are many reasons of which only three need be singled out here. The first is sweeping: in a very large number of passages, "mind" simply does not make sense, and only "spirit" will do; so even Baillie, though he entitled his translation *The Phenomenology of Mind,* had to use "spirit" again and again.

The second reason could be construed as merely an instance of the first: *Der heilige Geist* is the Holy Spirit, not "the holy mind," and "spirit," unlike "mind," has scores of biblical and religious associations. As a result, "spirit" has overtones and connotations that distinguish it from "mind" and bring it exceedingly close to the German *Geist*. This also explains why Hegel does not render the *nous* of Anaxagoras as *Geist* (VG 37 and 39), and why he claims that the Concept of *Geist* was introduced by Christianity (VG 47 L, 58 L). Indeed, we shall have to return to Hegel's conception of *Geist* when we consider his philosophy of history and its relation to Christianity (H 65; cf. C II.1.27 and III.1.3).

The third reason is in line with the central argument of this section. Who has ever seen "minds"? Minds are almost by definition invisible. They are postulated by philosophers as "ghosts in the machine," to use Gilbert Ryle's famous phrase from *The Concept of Mind;* their home is in epistemology and metaphysics. But many people, both in the Bible and since that time, claim to have seen spirits, and a *Geisterreich* (the "realm of spirits" Schiller envisages in the first stanza of his poem on *Die Freundschaft*) is nowhere near as abstract and metaphysical as "a realm of minds" would be.[31] Hegel concludes his *Phenomenology of the Spirit* with his own adaptation of the final two lines of Schiller's poem, in effect referring back to the book as a "realm of spirits." Throughout, we suddenly realize, Hegel has been conjuring spirits, letting them pass before us in a gigantic procession.

To appreciate the full significance of the end of the book, one must compare Hegel's adaptation of Schiller's lines with the original poem. Schiller celebrates friendship. Twice he speaks of the *grosse Geistersonne* (the great sun of the spirits) that the spirits seek "as streams flee to the ocean" and that he, too, wants to approach, arm in arm with a friend. Were he all alone in the universe, he says, he would dream up souls in the rocks and embrace them; we are dead as long as we hate, "gods, when we embrace each other lovingly"; "upwards, over the thousands of stages of innumerable spirits who have not created, this urge rules divinely. Arm in arm, ever higher and higher, from the Mongol up to the Greek seer," the dancing procession ascends. "Friendless was the great world master, felt a *lack* and therefore created spirits, blessed mirrors of *his* blessedness! Though the highest being found no equal, from the cup of the whole realm of souls foams for *him*—infinity." This prose translation, of course, can give no idea of Schiller's vigorous rhythms

---

[31] Whether some being has a mind, is a metaphysical question; whether, say, a horse has spirit or not, one can see.

and rhymes. But what concerns us is how Hegel ends his *Phenomenology:*

"The goal, absolute knowledge, or spirit knowing itself as spirit, has for its way the recollection of the spirits. . . . Their preservation, as free existence appearing in the form of the accidental, is history; but as comprehended organization it is the science of the appearance of knowledge. Both together, history comprehended, form the recollection and the Golgotha of the absolute spirit, the actuality, truth, and certainty of his throne, without which he would be something lifeless and lonely; only

> from the cup of this realm of spirits
> foams his infinity for him."

The *Phenomenology of the Spirit* ends with the death of God, with Golgotha; and this time the "speculative Good Friday" (to recall the image at the end of "Faith and Knowledge," published five years before) is not followed by any resurrection. To be sure, the tone of the ending seems affirmative; but we should not overlook a crucial word that Hegel has placed before the concluding quotation —a word that, being foreign to Schiller's text, carries an immense weight: *nur* (only). In Schiller's last stanza the presumption is that the infinity of the supreme being is mirrored by the whole realm of souls: though no single one equals the master's infinity, all the souls together do mirror it. For Hegel, the infinite God is dead: "only

> from the cup of this realm of spirits
> foams his infinity for him."

To put it into our own words: there is no supreme being beyond; the spirit is not to be found in another world; the infinite spirit has to be found in the comprehension of this world, in the study of the spirits summoned in the *Phenomenology.* "History comprehended" must replace theology.

Gestalten des Bewusstseins are also far more concrete than "forms of consciousness," though this is probably the nearest English equivalent. The first two lines of Goethe's *Faust* are relevant: *Ihr naht euch wieder, schwankende Gestalten . . .*

> You come back, wavering shapes, out of the past
> In which you first appeared to clouded eyes.

As we climb the ladder of Hegel's *Phenomenology,* we must first visualize each *Gestalt* and then get a firm grip on it and grasp it thoroughly to be able to climb over and beyond it.

But what is the meaning of "phenomenology"?

35

The word *Phänomenologie* was not Hegel's coinage. "The first who used the term 'phenomenology' at all and at the same time also used it to designate a part of his philosophical system was Johann Heinrich *Lambert* [1728–77]. The work in which he did this was called *New Organon or Thoughts about the Investigation and Designation of the True and Its Differentiation from Error and Mere Appearance* (2 vols., Leipzig 1764)."[32] The fourth and last part of this *Organon* was "Phenomenology or the Doctrine of Mere Appearance."

Herder picked up the term, particularly in two pertinent passages. In 1769 (in *Kritische Wälder* IV) he spoke of *"an aesthetic phenomenology,* which waits for a second Lambert." And in 1778: "If only we had . . . a real *phenomenology of the beautiful and the true . . .* !"[33]

Kant even thought of dedicating his first *Critique* to Lambert.[34] And on September 2, 1770—the week Hegel was born—Kant wrote Lambert: "It seems that an altogether separate, albeit merely negative, science (*Phaenomenologia generalis*) must precede metaphysics to determine the validity and limits of the *principles* of the sensibility lest they confuse our judgments about the objects of pure reason, as has almost always happened hitherto." And on February 21, 1772, Kant wrote Markus Herz that he had thought of writing "a work which might have a title like *The Limits of Sensibility and Reason.* I thought of two parts, one theoretical and one practical. The first contained in section 1, *phenomenology* in general, and in section 2, metaphysics, albeit only according to its nature and method. The second part also in two sections: 1. General principles of feeling and sense desire, 2. The first principles of *Sittlichkeit.* . . ."

Hegel probably knew Kant's letter to Lambert, as the correspon-

[32] Hoffmeister's introduction to his critical ed. of the *Phänomenologie* (1952), vii. The account and quotations that follow are based on pp. vii–xvii. Cf. Ros. 204.
[33] From *Wahrnehmungen über Form und Gestalt aus Pygmalions bildendem Traum.* Cf. Kant's *Werke,* Akademieausgabe, XV, 297.
[34] *Werke, ed. cit.,* XVIII, 64.

dence of the two men was published in 1786 and a few years later reprinted in Kant's *Kleine Schriften.* Novalis had also used the word a couple of times, once to say that "phenomenology is perhaps the most useful and comprehensive science," and Fichte had spoken of it in Lambert's sense, in 1804.[35] So the term was not new; but what Hegel offered under this title was.

Hoffmeister has argued that "the position of the *Phenomenology of the Spirit* in the whole of Hegel's system . . . corresponds precisely to that which Kant assigned to his *Critique of Pure Reason"* —on the one hand a preliminary treatise, on the other a work that contains what was to come after (xv). His points are interesting and may appeal to those who feel that neither philosopher ever succeeded in equaling the stature of his first great masterpiece. One can even add to Hoffmeister's consideration that both Kant and Hegel had taken a long time to publish their *magnum opus,* had collected thoughts and notes for many years, and then wrote their books in a single spurt in a few months. This genesis helps to explain some of the roughness of the prose as well as the fact that so much was stuffed into a single volume. But after all that has been said about the *Phenomenology* in this chapter, it should be plain that its differences from Kant's *Critique* far outweigh the similarities.

One difference among many is that what has just been shown about Hegel's terminology does not apply to Kant's, even though some of the very same words were used by Kant, too. What is true of the word *Phänomenologie* is true of most of Hegel's terms; they had been used before Hegel, but he gave them a new *nuance,* usually by carrying over into their technical use something of their sensuous core. For Hegel, *Schein* is not "mere appearance" in the sense of error and illusion. Nor does Hegel, like Kant, begin with a fixed contrast of noumena and phenomena from which he then derives "phenomenology." He knows that the Greek, like the German, root also means to shine, to become visible, and for him "phenomenology of the spirit" means the study of the *Gestalten des Bewusstseins,* the study of the spirits in which spirit manifests itself. The alleged archrationalist Hegel was much less of a rationalist than Kant.

The term "phenomenology" acquired new meanings after Hegel's death. Moritz Lazarus (1824–1903), for example, used it in his

[35] *Werke,* X, 195.

major work, *Das Leben der Seele* (1855–57, 3d ed., 1883), to distinguish the description of the phenomena of mental life from psychology which seeks causal explanations. This emphasis on description was equally marked in the usage of Edmund Husserl (1859–1938), with whom the term has come to be associated preeminently. When Husserl employed it to designate his own philosophy, Hegel's *Phenomenology* was an almost forgotten book, and Husserl did not choose the word to suggest a link with Hegel. He stood in an altogether different tradition: his master was Franz Brentano (1838–1917), a declared opponent of Kant and philosophical idealism. Brentano had resigned his Catholic priesthood after the proclamation of the dogma of papal infallibility in 1870 and had published a *Psychologie vom empirischen Standpunkt* in 1874.

It is not feasible to attempt a brief account of the meaning of "phenomenology" in Husserl's school. Husserl's views changed considerably in the course of his long life, and his leading disciples changed their ideas, too—indeed, they revised their own conceptions of philosophy—and they are far from agreeing with each other. Some of them, including Max Scheler and Martin Heidegger, did not remain disciples. The only major figure who admittedly owes a great deal both to Husserl's "phenomenology" and to Hegel's *Phenomenology* is Sartre.

36

The features of Hegel's style and sensibility that have been stressed here have often been overlooked. Unquestionably, Hegel also had rather stuffy ideas about what was academically proper and "scientific," and frequently his terminology, which makes good sense when one examines one or two terms at a time, degenerates into a jargon that obscures his meaning instead of making it more precise. This vice, of course, is not peculiar to him; if anything, it is more widespread one hundred fifty years after his time than it was in his day. Symbolism, technical terms, and footnotes can all be extremely useful, but it is common for professors to employ such devices beyond all reason, with an eye more to their preconceptions about what looks scholarly than to the clarity of their work. Just as some modern philosophers and literary critics, and a great many sociologists, give themselves scientific airs and say at length obscurely what might easily have been said briefly and clearly, Hegel, too, succumbed to this vice. In time, after he became a professor at Berlin and gained disciples, many of them caught this disease from him without catching his vision or genius, and his influence was certainly bad in part.

One illustration belongs in this chapter. On March 28, 1827, Goethe and Eckermann discussed *The Essence of Ancient Tragedy* by H. F. W. Hinrichs (1794–1861), and Goethe complained that such an originally vigorous man had been "so affected by Hegel's philosophy that an open-minded, natural view and thinking had been driven out of him, and an artificial and ponderous manner of both thought and expression had gradually been built into him, so we encounter passages in his book where our understanding simply stops and one no longer knows what one reads." As an example, Goethe read Eckermann a passage about the chorus that put him in mind of the witch's arithmetic in *Faust,* which was intended as humorous nonsense.[36] "What are the English and the French to think of the language of our philosophers when we Germans do not understand it ourselves?"

Goethe goes on to speak of Hinrichs's "idea of family and state" and of "potential tragic conflicts" connected with it. He adduces Sophocles' Ajax who "perished through the demon of an offended sense of honor, and Heracles through the demon of loving jealousy. In both cases there is not the slightest conflict between family piety and civic virtue, which according to Hinrichs are supposed to be the elements of Greek tragedy." Eckermann points out "that when he developed this theory he was thinking only of Antigone. He also seems to have considered only the character and actions of this heroine when he asserted that family piety appears at its purest in woman, and most purely of all in the sister, and that the sister can love only her brother in a wholly pure and sexless manner." " 'I should think,' Goethe replied, 'that the love of a sister for her sister would be still purer and more sexless! And we should not forget that there have been innumerable cases in which, known and unknown, the most sensual affection occurred between sister and brother.' "

Neither Goethe nor Eckermann seems to have realized the full extent of Hegel's influence on Hinrichs: they did not recall the treatment of Antigone in the *Phenomenology* (H 30).

[36] See WK 73.

37

One aspect of Hegel's thought and influence that so far has been neglected here can be summed up in one word: dialectic. But while almost everybody who has heard of Hegel associates him with this term, its meaning is far from clear. According to an ancient tradition (Diogenes Laertius IX.5), Zeno of Elea, renowned for his paradoxes, was the inventor of the dialectic; and Plato called the supreme science dialectic. Some Neoplatonists developed the idea that the course of the world is governed by a process with three stages: unity (*moné*), going out of oneself (*próhodos*), and return into oneself (*epistrophé*). In the Middle Ages, dialectic was one of the seven liberal arts.

In Kant's *Critique of Pure Reason,* dialectic becomes *die Logik des Scheins* (A 61, B 86): the logic of mere appearance, of error and illusion. Considering Plato's usage, it is rather odd that Kant explains his definition by saying: "Different as the meanings are which the ancients attached to a science or art, one can yet see for certain from their actual use of this term that among them it was nothing else than *die Logik des Scheins.* A sophistical art of giving one's ignorance, and even the illusions that one produced deliberately, the whitewash of truth by imitating the method of thoroughness, prescribed by logic. . . ." But half of the *Critique* (412 of the 856 pages of the first edition) is taken up by Kant's own "transcendental dialectic" which he defines as "a critique of this dialectical *Schein.*" This "is called transcendental dialectic, not as an art to stimulate such illusion dialectically (an unfortunately very viable art . . .) but as a critique of the understanding and of reason in respect to their hyper-physical use, to uncover the false illusion of their unfounded presumptions . . ." (A 63, B 88).

Kant's greatest achievement, then, his critical discussion of the "paralogisms" about the soul, the antinomies about the world, and the traditional proofs of God's existence—his attempt to destroy dogmatic psychology, cosmology, and theology—went under the name of "transcendental dialectic." His treatment of the antinomies was particularly impressive: thirty-six pages in the center of the book presented, on facing pages, four "theses" and four "antitheses," each followed by a "proof" and a "note." The first thesis was: "The world has a beginning in time and is also enclosed in boundaries spatially." The first antithesis: "The world has no beginning and no boundaries in space but is, in respect to both time and space, infinite." The four antinomies, said Kant, were due to the illicit use of reason, and he considered it one of the greatest accomplishments of his own work that he had succeeded in resolving these antinomies.

In an interesting note in the second edition, Kant called attention to the fact that his twelve categories of the understanding are arranged in four groups of three, and that the third category in each group is a synthesis of the two preceding it. (He did not use the word "synthesis" at this point; the passage is translated below, C III.3.11.)

Fichte introduced into German philosophy the three-step of thesis, antithesis, and synthesis, using these three terms. Schelling took up this terminology; Hegel did not. He never once used these three terms together to designate three stages in an argument or account in any of his books. And they do not help us understand his *Phenomenology,* his *Logic,* or his philosophy of history; they impede any open-minded comprehension of what he does by forcing it into a schema which was available to him and which he deliberately spurned.[37] The mechanical formalism, in particular, with which critics since Kierkegaard have charged him, he derides expressly and at some length in the preface to the *Phenomenology.*

Whoever looks for the stereotype of the allegedly Hegelian dialectic in Hegel's *Phenomenology* will not find it. What one does find on looking at the table of contents is a very decided preference for triadic arrangements. As already noted (H 32), Parts V, VI, and VII are all divided into A, B, and C, and all but one of these nine sections are further subdivided into three parts. But these many triads are not presented or deduced by Hegel as so many theses, antitheses, and syntheses. It is not by means of any dialectic of that sort that his thought moves up the ladder to absolute knowledge.

Skepticism, for example, is not the antithesis of stoicism, nor does Hegel make any effort to present it that way; rather he introduces

---

[37] Cf. G. E. Mueller, "The Hegel Legend of 'Thesis-Antithesis-Synthesis,'" and WK 166 ff. The only place where Hegel uses the three terms together occurs in his lectures on the history of philosophy, on the last page but one of the section on Kant—where Hegel roundly reproaches Kant for having "everywhere posited thesis, antithesis, synthesis" (*Werke,* ed. Glockner, XIX, 610).

it as a state of mind that is reached when stoicism is taken more seriously than its proponents are wont to take it and pushed to its "logical" conclusion. And the transition to the third member of that particular triad, the unhappy consciousness, is made in the same way: it is not offered to us as the synthesis of the two preceding stages but rather as the result of not allowing the skeptic to hide in bad faith in his halfway house (H 33).

When we turn to Hegel's discussion of the ethical world (H 30), we also do not find that the triads are reducible to theses, antitheses, and syntheses, much less that they are presented to us in that fashion. The three major divisions of Part VI, "Spirit," are "A. True spirit, *Sittlichkeit*" (with the discussion of Antigone in the first two of three subsections), "B. Spirit, alienated from itself, *Bildung*," and "C. Spirit certain of itself, *Moralität*." This triad is certainly closer to the popular conception of the dialectic. We move from a tradition-directed ethic to the alienated intellectualism of the Enlightenment and the French Revolution (which are discussed in the last two subsections of B), and hence to the inner-directed morality of Kant. Another author might have presented the spirit of the Enlightenment as the antithesis of Antigone's superstitious ethic, and then *Moralität* as the synthesis of *Sittlichkeit* and *Bildung*. But this is not what Hegel did. Hegel's account of Antigone's *Sittlichkeit* is overwhelmingly positive and full of admiration; and far from suggesting that all that was good in this stage is preserved in the higher synthesis of *Moralität*, he neither presents Kant's ethic as a synthesis nor does he extol it as the highest and most inclusive ethical point of view. One might expect him to do just that because after *Moralität* we proceed to "VII. Religion" and "VIII. Absolute Knowledge." But Hegel's discussion of Kant's *Moralität* is the *locus classicus* of his critique of Kant, and in his later books he still refers back to it as such. In his *Encyclopedia* and in the *Philosophy of Right,* incidentally, *Sittlichkeit* appears above *Moralität,* not, as here, below it on the ladder.

Readers with some understanding of Hegel have found his dialectic not in the triads of the table of contents but rather in the ironical reversal of the roles of master and servant, at the point where the servant becomes self-reliant because he depends on his own work, while the master comes to depend on the servant. Or they have found it in the instability of views and attitudes that, when adopted in earnest and pushed, change into other views and attitudes. Discerning students of Hegel, therefore, are likely to find the chapter on "Self-Consciousness" the most dialectical one in the book (H 33).

Whitehead was close in spirit to Hegel's dialectic when he said in his *Modes of Thought* (1938): "Both in science and in logic you have only to develop your argument sufficiently, and sooner or later you are bound to arrive at a contradiction, either internally within the argument, or externally in its reference to fact. . . . None of these logical or scientific myths is wrong, in an unqualified sense of that term. It is unguarded. Its truth is limited by unexpressed presuppositions; and as time goes on, we discover some of these limitations. The simple-minded use of the notions 'right or wrong' is one of the chief obstacles to the progress of understanding" (14 f.). "Panic of error is the death of progress" (22). "Philosophy is the criticism of abstractions which govern special modes of thought" (67). And: "The purpose of philosophy is to rationalize mysticism" (237).

Goethe was not only close in spirit to the dialectic of the *Phenomenology* but probably influenced it profoundly when he wrote in his great *Bildungsroman, Wilhelm Meister:* "Not to keep from error is the duty of the educator of men, but to guide the erring one, even to let him swill his error out of full cups—that is the wisdom of teachers. Whoever merely tastes of his error, will keep house with it for a long time and be glad of it as of a rare good fortune; but whoever drains it completely will have to get to know it, unless he be insane" (VII.9). This invites comparison with Hegel's aphorism: "What is most harmful is *trying to preserve oneself from errors.*"[38]

Royce put the matter well—oddly, not in one of the four chapters on Hegel, and without any particular reference to Hegel: "Without erring, and transcending our error, we, as sometimes suggested by the Socratic irony, simply cannot become wise. . . . Error is not a mere accident of an untrained intellect, but a necessary stage or feature or moment . . ." (79). Three pages later, right after a passage in which he discusses the French Revolution and refers to Nietzsche's will to power—again in a context devoid of any reference to Hegel—Royce hit on a very suggestive phrase, only to drop it immediately in favor of another which is not nearly so good: "All the greater emotions are dialectical. The tragedies of the storm and stress period, and of the classical and romantic literature, are por-

[38] Ros. 545; *Dok.* 363 (※44).

trayals of this contradictory *logic of passion* [my italics]. Faust asks the highest, and therefore contracts with the devil and destroys Margaret" (82). This example is not especially illuminating, and two sentences later Royce speaks of "similar literary expressions of the dialectics of the emotions. The fascination and the power of Byron are due to his contradictions. . . . Instances of the dialectics of the emotions abound in the European literature of the period. . . ."

Neither "logic of passion" (a fine phrase) nor "dialectics of the emotions" is very precise or rigorous; nor do we encounter any very rigorous procedure in the *Phenomenology;* nor does Hegel in that book make any great point of "dialectic." Some passages in the preface are undoubtedly relevant to his conception of dialectic, but they point more in the direction of the *Logic* than in that of the *Phenomenology:* the preface was intended as a preface to the whole system.

In the preface Hegel pleads for rigor and announces that "the time has come for the elevation of philosophy to a science," but the *Phenomenology,* whatever its virtues, is certainly neither rigorous nor in any reasonable sense of that word an example of "scientific" philosophy. It is well to keep in mind that even in the twentieth century *Wissenschaft* does not mean quite the same as "science." Max Weber, for example, in his widely discussed *Wissenschaft als Beruf* (1919) presents as a test case of the meaning of *Wissenschaft* a philologist's "making precisely this conjecture at this place in this manuscript" (10). In fact, Weber's conception of *Wissenschaft* is quite close to Hegel's (for a brief comparison, see C III.3.23). And the *Phenomenology* is certainly *unwissenschaftlich:* undisciplined, arbitrary, full of digressions, not a monument to the austerity of the intellectual conscience and to carefulness and precision but a wild, bold, unprecedented book that invites comparison with some great literary masterpieces. Hegel's later works are different in many ways from his first book, but we shall see in the next chapter that his dialectic never became the ritualistic three-step it is so widely supposed to be.

For the present we may conclude that the Hegel of the *Phenomenology* was still a man divided against himself and did not achieve the harmonious totality he sought. Like Schiller, he spurned the split in Kant's moral agent between duty and inclination; but he himself was quite similarly divided between what his reason told him ought to be done and what his genius was bent on doing. The classical formulations are Paul's: "what I would, that do I not; but what I hate, that do I" (Romans 7:15), and "ye cannot do the things that ye would" (Galatians 5:17). This phenomenon is generally associated with religion and morals, but it is at least as interesting—and deserves more study—in the case of writers and artists.[39] Hegel is a case in point.

It would be a serious mistake to assume without argument that Hegel's difficulty must be explained psychologically, as if—as Paul's dicta suggest—the intention were above reproach and the practice shamefully inferior. Hegel's difficulties were due in large measure to the inadequacy of his notion of what ought to be done.

His critique of romanticism in philosophy is brilliant and constitutes one of the chief excellences of his preface to the *Phenomenology*. His call for clarity and precision, and for expositions that appeal not merely to a clique of like-minded people but to all readers who are willing to take the necessary trouble to follow the argument—all this is not only plausible but beautifully presented. Even the plea for a systematic approach makes very good sense— at least up to a point. Our quotations from Goethe and Whitehead show this at a glance: not only the aphorist but also the essayist and writers of articles, monographs, and books in the area of their specialty are apt to taste now of this error and now of that—or always of the same error—settling down in some untenable halfway house without ever realizing what is wrong with it; they never develop their position sufficiently to discover the contradictions that would lead them on to more inclusive insights. They are afraid of error; but "panic of error is the death of progress."

What is wrong with Hegel's notion of what ought to be done can be stated here quite briefly. He assumes that philosophy requires a distinctive method of its own and sometimes writes as if he had such a method; but in fact, as we follow his procedure closely, we find that he did not. Instead of admitting this, he occasionally (though not nearly as often as is generally assumed) affected what are usually called dialectical deductions. These differ greatly from case to case and are certainly not reducible to any mechanical three-step; but what many of these cases have in common is the

---

[39] Cf., e.g., ". . . Dryden seldom could make his theory harmonize with his practice . . ." (M. T. Herrick, *The Poetics of Aristotle in England*, 1930, 69).

attempt to be rigorous in some way or other that does not really lend itself to rigor.

Right as Hegel is that it would be a mistake for philosophy to model itself on mathematical method, he is wrong in also departing from Descartes' quest for the greatest possible clarity and distinctness. Above all, he fails to recognize what is really the heart of scientific and rational procedure: *confronted with propositions or views, we should ask what precisely they mean; what considerations, evidence, and arguments support them; what speaks against them; what alternatives are available; and which of these is most probable.*

No quest for a system and no finished system can ever compensate us for the neglect of this canon—at least not scientifically; and aesthetically only if our intellectual conscience is underdeveloped and we are after all such romantics as Hegel expressly scorns. With this, we are already deep into, and beyond, Hegel's later thought. For this is the reason his prefaces and introductions are so often, and so notoriously, far superior to the works that follow. In this respect, the *Phenomenology* is no exception at all.

In his prefaces and introductions, Hegel—usually with apologies and a bad conscience—dispenses with what he considers the proper method and talks as, according to him, a philosopher ought not to talk. Here he is often at his best, feeling free, albeit regretfully, to communicate his vision and his many superb insights without, in one word, dialectic.

There is a legend abroad that the student of Hegel must choose in the end between the system and the dialectic, and it is widely supposed that the right wing Hegelians chose the system while the left wing, or the "young" Hegelians, including Marx, chose the dialectic. But I am by no means rejecting the dialectic in order to elect the system; I disbelieve both. And I am not so much rejecting the dialectic as I say: there is none. Look for it, by all means; see what Hegel says about it and observe what in fact he does. You will find some suggestive remarks, not all of them in the same vein, as well as all kinds of affectations; but you will not find any plain method that you could adopt even if you wanted to.

What, then, are we to make of McTaggart's emphatic dictum, at the beginning of his *Commentary on Hegel's Logic?* "The dialectical process of the Logic is the one absolutely essential element in Hegel's system. If we accepted this and rejected everything else that Hegel has written, we should have a system of philosophy. . . .

On the other hand, if we reject the dialectical process which leads to the absolute idea, all the rest of the system is destroyed . . ." (§2).

Although McTaggart was a brilliant man—for a short time both Bertrand Russell and G. E. Moore were greatly impressed and influenced by him—and much of what he had to say is interesting, he is wrong on this point, as becomes plain when he says in §4: "The whole course of the dialectic forms one example of the dialectic rhythm, with Being as Thesis, Essence as Antithesis, and Notion as Synthesis. Each of these has again the same moments of Thesis, Antithesis, and Synthesis within it, and so on. . . ." Like others, McTaggart imposed an alien pattern on Hegel. Findlay has said what needs to be said on this score:

"If one is to judge the value of the dialectical method, one must judge it for what it is, and not for what, on a one-sided interpretation of certain of Hegel's claims in regard to it, one thinks it ought to be. Otherwise we shall find ourselves in the position of McTaggart who, after being led to interpret the *Logic* in a manner flatly at variance with Hegel's statements, is then forced to jettison the whole of the remaining system as being the sort of semi-empirical venture which is not dialectically admissible" (75).

Findlay's *Hegel* comes close to the truth about the dialectic, but even he does not go far enough. The following understatement is revelatory: "The terms 'thesis', 'antithesis', and 'synthesis', so often used in expositions of Hegel's doctrine, are in fact not frequently used by Hegel: they are much more characteristic of Fichte" (69 f.). Moreover, Findlay's chapter on "The Dialectical Method" is balanced by an odd "Appendix: Dialectical Structure of Hegel's Main Works," in which "Dialectical Structure" is repeated eight times before the various tables of contents with their triads—a blatant misuse of the word "dialectical" on Findlay's own showing.

But to return to Hegel himself: What do we find if not a usable dialectical method? We find a vision of the world, of man, and of history which emphasizes development through conflict, the moving power of human passions, which produce wholly unintended results, and the irony of sudden reversals. If that be called a dialectical world view, then Hegel's philosophy *was* dialectical—and there is a great deal to be said in its favor. This is certainly an immensely fruitful and interesting perspective, and from the point of view of pedagogy, vivid exposition, and sheer drama it may be unsurpassed.

But the fateful myth that this perspective is reducible to a rigorous method that even permits predictions deserves no quarter, though by now half the world believes it.

The fact that Hegel himself never used the dialectic to predict anything, and actually spurned the very idea that it could be used that way, suggests plainly that Hegel's dialectic never was conceived as what we should call a scientific method, and that his deductions were admittedly ex post facto. In other words, Hegel's dialectic is at most a method of exposition; it is not a method of discovery.

CHAPTER IV:

The Logic

38

One of the better known early Hegelians, David Friedrich Strauss, best known for his *Life of Jesus* (1835) and for Nietzsche's youthful attack on him, published just before he died (1874), said:
"One may fittingly call the *Phenomenology* the alpha and omega of Hegel's works. Here Hegel left port in his own ships for the first time and sailed, albeit in an Odyssean voyage, around the world; while his subsequent expeditions, though better conducted, were confined, as it were, to inland seas. All the later writings and lectures of Hegel, such as his *Logic, Philosophy of Right,* Philosophy of Religion, Aesthetics, History of Philosophy, and Philosophy of History, are merely sections from the *Phenomenology* whose riches are preserved only incompletely even in the *Encyclopedia,* and in any case in a dried state. In the *Phenomenology* Hegel's genius stands at its greatest height."[1]

Should we, then, study the *Phenomenology* a little more instead of proceeding to consider the *Logic* and Hegel's system? This has been done. Royce, in his *Lectures on Modern Idealism,* devoted over seventy-five pages to the *Phenomenology* and less than twenty to "Hegel's Mature System."

Glockner reaches the end of the *Phenomenology* on page 537 of his second volume, and disposes of Hegel's later works in a few pages—less for the lot of them than he devoted to the early essay "On the Scientific Modes of Treatment of Natural Right" (H 21).

---

[1] *Christian Märklin* (1851), 53 f.; reprinted in *Gesammelte Schriften,* X, 224; quoted by Glockner, II, 539.

Haering goes even further: he requires thirteen hundred pages to reach the *Phenomenology,* gives that only twice as much space as he accorded the article on "Natural Right"—and then stops altogether. What at first glance seems madness makes at least a limited amount of sense. One does not read such large two-volume works on Hegel *instead* of reading Hegel himself; one reads them to get help in understanding Hegel. Toward that end, it can be argued, nothing helps more than an analysis of his early works. Even so Glockner and Haering put one in mind of the *Historisch-Kritische Gesamtausgabe* of Nietzsche's "works" (*Werke*), which began to appear in Germany while they were both working on their second volumes: five fat volumes of "works" appeared in chronological order; then the edition was discontinued during World War II— before it had reached Nietzsche's first book, published in his twenties.

The present volume is intended to help those who want to read Hegel. An analysis of the *Logic* or the *Philosophy of Right* does not enable the reader to understand the other mature works, or the early works. But if we now stopped here, the *Logic* and the system would still pose great puzzles.

39

Let us first consider Hegel's further biography briefly, insofar as it is relevant. How did Schelling react to the *Phenomenology?* The last letters the two men exchanged are translated in D, which also contains the other letters and documents cited in this section.

In January 1807 Schelling eagerly anticipated the book. In April Hegel wrote Niethammer about how he wanted to distribute the few first copies—and did not include Schelling. On May first, Hegel promised Schelling a copy "soon"; he made many interesting statements about the book and apologized for its defects; he suggested that the polemic in the preface, which many students still feel sure was directed against Schelling, was in fact aimed at his followers' "mischief"; and he not only stressed his eager anticipation of Schelling's reaction to the work but even expressed the hope that Schelling might review it.

November 2, Schelling wrote that he still had not got beyond the preface; he accepted Hegel's explanation of "the polemical part," but, unlike Hegel, referred to the possibility that the polemic could be construed as being aimed at him, and noted expressly that in the preface itself "this distinction is not made." The letter may be read as indicating that Schelling felt offended; but it was not peevish or nasty, and there is not the slightest reason for doubting that he meant it when he said in the end: "Write me soon again and remain well disposed toward Your sincere friend Sch."

It was not until July 30, 1808, that Schelling wrote Windischmann, registering his dislike for the book; he had evidently heard that Windischmann was reviewing it. In between, both Hegel and Schelling had undoubtedly expected to get another letter: Schelling, a reassuring and cordial answer to his own letter; Hegel, a letter reporting that Schelling had now finished the whole book and expressing his reactions to it.[2] Each waited, and neither wrote; and that was the end of their correspondence.

It is well known that the two men met once more in Karlsbad in 1829, by chance. It is almost always overlooked that in October 1812 Schelling paid Hegel a visit in Nürnberg, and in the fall of 1815 Hegel visited Munich and saw Schelling.[3] Thus the two men did not repeat the Kant-Fichte-Schelling pattern (H 26). And the situation was, of course, different from the start inasmuch as Hegel, who came into his own later, was five years older.

When writing letters to others about these late encounters, both men mentioned that they did not discuss philosophy, and the rapport of their early years was obviously a matter of the past. But they remained on civil terms.

In his lectures on the history of philosophy, Hegel took up Schelling as the last philosopher before he came to "the present standpoint of philosophy," his own. The discussion of "the present standpoint"—the editor of the lectures entitled this section "E. Result"—occupies just over eight pages; the immediately preceding lectures on "D. Schelling," almost forty pages. They begin:

"The most important—or, philosophically, the only important—

---

[2] Perhaps the only one to have seen this is Horst Fuhrmans, in his long account of "Schelling und Hegel: Ihre Entfremdung," in F. W. J. Schelling, *Briefe und Dokumente,* vol. I: 1775–1809, Bonn, 1962, pp. 451–553; see pp. 529–32.

[3] This is overlooked even by Otto Pöggeler, one of the editors of the critical edition of Hegel, in his dissertation on *Hegels Kritik der Romantik,* Bonn, 1956, p. 144; pp. 138–85 deal with "Schelling and the romantic philosophers of nature."

step beyond the Fichtean philosophy was finally taken by Schelling. The higher, genuine form that followed on Fichte is the Schellingian philosophy.

"Friedrich Wilhelm Joseph *Schelling,* born at Schorndorf in Württemberg, January 27, 1775, studied in Leipzig and Jena where he came to be close to Fichte. For several years now he has been secretary of the Academy of Fine Arts in Munich. His *life* cannot be covered completely or in decency since he is still living."

Kuno Fischer pointed out long ago that the biographical paragraph contains surprising mistakes.[4] Of the exposition that follows only a few sentences belong in the present context; the over-all structure of Hegel's lectures and the relative weight given to the philosophers he included belong in our discussion of his history of philosophy, later on, when we come to that part of his system (H 66).

"Schelling got his philosophical education before the public. The series of his philosophical writings is at the same time the history of his philosophical education and represents his gradual rise above the Fichtean principle and the Kantian content with which he began; it does not contain a sequence of elaborated parts of philosophy, one after the other, but a sequence of the stages of his education. When people ask for a final work in which his philosophy is presented most definitely, one cannot name one like that. Schelling's first writings are entirely Fichtean, and only by and by he emancipated himself from Fichte's form" (647 f.).

Not only is this true, nor does it merely show how Hegel related his own intentions and his own failure to publish a major work until he was thirty-six to his younger friend's publication of over half a dozen books before he was thirty; it also shows why it was so easy and almost natural for Hegel to see his own philosophy as the completion of Schelling's efforts, and indeed of the whole development from Kant beyond Fichte and Schelling.

Much later, when Schelling was called to the University of

---

[4] "A legion of inaccuracies! Schelling was born, not in Schorndorf but in Leonberg; in Leipzig he was not a student but a tutor; in Jena, not a student but a professor, even while Hegel was there, too; and he was a student at Tübingen, even for several years together with Hegel! Incomprehensible how Hegel could get into such a state of forgetfulness, and most reprehensible that the editor of his lectures has done nothing to correct such statements. Schelling was the companion of Hegel's youth and his friend, his model and guide on the way to philosophy" (II, 1148 n.). The last half sentence goes too far.

Berlin in 1841, ten years after Hegel's death, he reciprocated by relegating Hegel's philosophy, along with his own earlier philosophy, to the stage of merely "negative" philosophy, while demanding a new "positive philosophy," which he described in terms exceedingly close to Kierkegaard's later efforts. In fact, Kierkegaard was in the audience and tremendously impressed by Schelling's program, though he was to be disappointed by Schelling's later lectures.[5] Not only *Kierkegaard's* religious existentialism has roots in Schelling's later thought; Paul Tillich began his scholarly career with a dissertation on Schelling. And it was Schelling who coined the term "existential philosophy [*Existenzialphilosophie*]" to designate his later philosophy.[6]

While Schelling himself felt that his "positive philosophy" represented an altogether new stage in the development of philosophy, and a step beyond Hegel, readers of Hegel's preface to the *Phenomenology* should ask themselves whether Hegel's critique of romantic philosophy is not also applicable to the religious existentialism of the *old* Schelling, of Kierkegaard, and of Tillich.

The question of whether this critique was originally aimed at Schelling himself or only at his followers is more complex than meets the eye. Hegel associated Schelling with a stage in the development of modern philosophy—a stage that constituted definite progress beyond Kant and Fichte, though it, in turn, was not final and had to be transcended. It was certainly not his intention to vilify or ridicule Schelling, but, just as certainly, he wanted to show why one could not settle down in this halfway house. In his lectures on Schelling we find the sentences:

"Schelling surely had this notion in a general way, but did not push it to a conclusion in a definite logical manner; for Schelling it is immediate truth. This is a main difficulty in Schellingian philosophy. Then it was misunderstood, made shallow."[7]

The following distinction may be a little too fine, but it is unquestionably very close to the truth: Hegel was conscious of criticizing and going beyond Schelling; but he probably thought he

---

[5] For relevant quotations from Schelling's lectures and Kierkegaard's reactions, see my *Nietzsche* (1950), 102; Meridian ed., 105 f. and 377.
[6] In 1844, Rosenkranz already criticizes Schelling's *Existenzialphilosophie* (xviii).
We shall return to the late Schelling in H 68.
[7] Glockner's ed., XIX, 663.

was *ridiculing* only his followers and shallow imitators. The last sentences of the lectures on Schelling point also in this direction: "The form becomes rather an external schema; the method is the affixing of this schema to external objects. In this way formalism crept into the philosophy of nature; for example, in Oken—it borders on madness. Philosophizing thus became mere analogical reflection; that is the worst manner. Even Schelling had already made things easy for himself in part; the others have misused it totally" (683).

Some of the passages Rosenkranz quotes from Hegel's Jena lectures show that during the time he was working on the *Phenomenology* Hegel occasionally made this contrast crystal clear. Quotation is doubly worth while because Hegel's polemic is also interesting philosophically and supplements what he says against formalism in the preface to the *Phenomenology:*

"When studying philosophy, you must not take such a terminology for what counts, and you must not respect it. Ten or twenty years ago it also seemed very difficult to work one's way into the Kantian terminology and to use the terminology of synthetic judgments *a priori*, synthetic unity of apperception, transcendent and transcendental, etc.; but such a flood roars by as quickly as it comes. More people master this language, and the secret comes to light *that very common thoughts conceal themselves behind such bugbear expressions.*[8]—I remark on this mainly because of the current appearance of philosophy, especially the philosophy of nature; what mischief is being done with the *Schellingian* terminology! Schelling, to be sure, expressed a good meaning and philosophical thoughts in these forms—but this by way of *actually showing himself to be free* of this terminology, for in almost every subsequent presentation of his philosophy he used a *new* one. But the way this philosophy is now discussed publicly, it is really only the *superficiality* of thought that hides beneath it. Into the depths of this philosophy, as we see it in so many publications, I cannot introduce you, for it has no depth; and I say this lest you allow yourself to be *impressed*, as if behind these bizarre, hundred-weight words there must necessarily be some meaning.—What alone can be of

---

[8] The applicability of these remarks to Heidegger should be noted. But many a reader says instead, triumphantly and joyously: "See, it is *not* meaningless! How wonderful!" Or: "Look, he is saying what X or Y has said, too!"

interest is the amazement all this produces in the ignorant mass. In fact, however, this present formalism can be taught in half an hour. Just say, not that something is *long,* but that it reaches into *length,* and this length is *magnetism;* instead of *broad,* say it reaches into *breadth* and is *electricity;* instead of *thick,* corporeal, and it reaches into the *third dimension.* . . .

"I tell you in advance that in the philosophical *system that I present* you will not find anything of this flood of formalism. When I speak of this terminology and its use, as it rages at present, as I have done, I certainly distinguish *Schelling's ideas* from the use *his students make of them,* and I honor Schelling's truly meritorious contribution to philosophy as much as I despise this formalism; and because I know *Schelling's* philosophy, I know that its true idea, which it has reawakened in our time, is independent of this formalism" (184 f.).

The fact remains that in the *Phenomenology* "this distinction is not made," and quite a few phrases in the preface seem applicable to Schelling himself. For details, see the commentary, which also includes some pertinent quotations from Schelling's writings (C I.3.19; cf. C III.3.11).

Incidentally, Rosenkranz himself tells us elsewhere that Hegel's students at Jena had their doubts about Hegel's attitude toward Schelling: "A student, about to go from Jena to Würzburg, took leave of him. Hegel said to him: 'I have a friend there, too, *Schelling.*' Here, the enthusiasts remarked, the word *friend* had an altogether different meaning than in ordinary life" (217).

In any case, after the publication of the *Phenomenology* Hegel could no longer be considered Schelling's disciple. He had never seen himself that way to begin with; and when others did, it had made him angry. While the articles in the *Critical Journal,* which the two men had edited together, had been unsigned, there is one signed footnote near the end of the first issue:

"About the report . . . 'that Schelling has *brought* a valiant fighter from his fatherland to Jena, and *through* him *proclaims* to the amazed public that even Fichte stands far beneath his views,' I could not, with all circumlocutions and attenuations, say anything else than that the author of this report is a *liar,* which I therefore declare him to be with these clear words;

and this the sooner because I believe that in this way I shall earn the gratitude of a great many others to whom he is a burden with his drolleries, half-lies, digs in passing, etc.

DR. HEGEL."

The sort of comment he had got on the *Difference,* which he here protests, he was not likely to get on the *Phenomenology.* It was plain henceforth that he stood alone, "for himself," to use a Hegelian locution. But the book created no stir whatever. The first copies had been distributed in April 1807; the first review appeared in February 1809. A few months before publication of his book, the Battle of Jena had put an end to Hegel's university career at Jena, and he was not offered a teaching position at another university until 1816, the year his fourth volume appeared—the third volume of the *Logic.* That year he received three calls: to Heidelberg, where he actually went; to Erlangen; and to Berlin. The call to Berlin came just a little too late; when he got it, Hegel already felt committed to Heidelberg. But in 1818 Berlin asked him again, and then he accepted.

40

For a year and a half, beginning just before the *Phenomenology* appeared, Hegel was the editor of a newspaper in Bamberg. Interpreters generally dismiss this intermezzo as not particularly important for Hegel's development.

Rosenzweig suggests that Niethammer, Hegel's best adviser and friend by this time, thought it prudent for his younger compatriot to move at least into the horizon of the Bavarian government, which might eventually call him to a university post. "As a rather well-paid waiting post, which would support Hegel, who was without means since he had used up his patrimony, he took over the editorship of the *Bamberger Zeitung. . . .* While Hegel was editor, it appeared every weekday, was printed in the morning and distributed in the afternoon. It was not the truly local paper in Bamberg; those tasks [town affairs] were taken care of by the *Bamberger Korrespondent.* The *Bamberger Zeitung* furnished Bamberg" and a considerable area beyond it with news about Bavaria "and above all about European events" (II, 6 f.).

Haym, who made a point of reading all of the issues Hegel edited, tells us that "the readers were not burdened with any philosophical discourses. I have been able to find one, and only one, excursus that might remind an attentive reader of the author of the *Phenomenology*. . . . He tried here and there to obtain news in some special way and through private communications. In the main he had to rely on other papers, mostly French. But he was very correct and skilful in the composition of his material from these sources. A sure critical tact is notable whenever he seeks to review or reconcile contradictory reports. Everywhere he shows care and thoroughness. . . . To say everything: this newspaper was as well edited by Hegel as a poor newspaper could be edited by anyone" (270 f.).

In retrospect, the most interesting point about this episode is that in 1807 and 1808 Hegel was in such very close touch with day-to-day events—a far cry from the otherworldly ivory tower in which posthumous reputation has placed him. Moreover, and this is no less important, he was forced to publish six times a week what ordinary people would understand, and each issue had only four pages. So he learned to be brief, to cover a lot of material very concisely, and to finish things. In this respect, the year and a half at Bamberg were, after all, of crucial importance.

In the fall of 1808 Hegel became principal of the Gymnasium at Nürnberg; his duties specifically included instruction in philosophy; and he retained this position for eight years, until he went to Heidelberg. The only other towns where he lived that long were Stuttgart, where he was born, and Berlin, where he died.

When he went to Nürnberg he was not famous, although he had published a number of articles, as well as a book that has since been hailed as one of the great books of all time. He was thirty-eight, was immensely well read, personally knew some of the best known intellects of the time, and struck his students as an unusually impressive headmaster.

For him it was clear from the start that this occupation, too, could only be an intermezzo. For all that, it was the first real position in which he settled down, and he tried to meet its peculiar challenges. Perhaps the greatest of these was that he had to make clear philosophy for students in their teens who were not specializing in the subject. The way in which he tried to solve this problem became the pattern for his *Encyclopedia* and *Philosophy of Right*.

He aimed at clear outlines that could be readily remembered, at great brevity, and at definitive formulations. The organization henceforth becomes neat to a fault—triads everywhere (but not theses, antitheses, and syntheses). Brevity coupled with the desire to say a great deal in few words leads to reliance on jargon and a style that borders on the oracular. And the attempt to give his students definitive formulations, coupled with the fact that the boys were nowhere near his own level, introduced a decidedly dogmatic note into Hegel's prose.

This is a prime clue to "the secret of Hegel," which has been neglected. When he went to Nürnberg he had tried for years to complete his system, but had been able to complete for publication only an introduction which, with its 850 pages, was more than three times as long as the first edition of the system, the so-called *Encyclopedia,* when it finally appeared exactly ten years later.

Rosenkranz noted that the philosophy courses Hegel gave in Nürnberg constitute an intermediary stage between the *Phenomenology* and the *Encyclopedia* when he published Hegel's manuscripts covering the course, under the title *Propädeutik,* in volume XVIII of the original edition of Hegel's *Werke*. But what is of the utmost significance is that the otherwise enigmatic transformation of Hegel becomes perfectly clear and understandable when we consider his situation, first in Bamberg and then, above all, in Nürnberg.

Without that, one ought to be perplexed, though scarcely anybody seems to have been puzzled, by the incredible contrast between the young and the mature Hegel. In his youth he was a firebrand whose vitriolic criticisms of Christianity invite comparison with Nietzsche and do not even stop before the person of Jesus. He wrote with passion and vigor, and his sarcasm was radical. Then he went to Jena in quest of a university career, wrote articles for a scholarly journal, affected what seemed the right tone for that, and often became rather obscure—though not more so than many a young Assistant Professor of Sociology a century and a half later. Still, he could not curb his biting wit, and his great flair for the picturesque constantly broke through, sometimes even in the middle of long, hyper-academic sentences. Finally, his first big book appeared and turned out to be anything but stuffy or conventional. On the contrary, it was a Faustian book, wild, bold, and more than a little mad. And after that Hegel disappeared from view for a while, first in Bamberg, then in Nürnberg.

In the latter city he composed the first third of his system, the *Logik,* in three volumes (1812, 1813, 1816). This work still breathes at least some of the spirit of the *Phenomenology:* at the end of the preface to the first edition we are told how, when the *Phenomenology* appeared as the "first part" of Hegel's *System of Science,* the second volume was still to contain the Logic as well as the philosophy of nature and the philosophy of spirit; but now the first third of that projected volume has again grown beyond all bounds. And in the "introduction" that follows the "preface," we are told that one might say that the content of the Logic "is the account of God as he is in his eternal essence before the creation of nature and any finite spirit."⁹ Hegel himself emphasized these words in print. This work, which we shall consider shortly, is not as mad as these words may seem; in any case, it is still the labor of an utterly lonely genius.

When Hegel emerged from his obscurity to become a famous professor, it was hard to recognize the man with whom we have largely dealt so far. Anyone who seriously compares Hegel before the age of forty with the Professor Hegel of the last fifteen years of his life is bound to ask: Whatever happened to him? We can now answer that question in a single sentence: for eight long years the poor man was headmaster of a German secondary school.

<h1 style="text-align:center">41</h1>

Hegel's personal development during this period is adequately reflected in the documents furnished in D. In a letter of May 27, 1810, he describes life in the "dark regions" as one who has been there, speaks of "a few years of this hypochondria," and suggests that only devotion to "science" can cure it. On December 14, 1810, he describes human life with a consummate bitterness that is infinitely closer to Shakespeare or to *Candide* than to Leibniz or the popular image of Hegel.

Then, in April he became engaged to Marie von Tucher and wrote two poems for her. They are of no literary interest, but one of them has been translated in part, both to suggest the change in

⁹ This remark will be interpreted in H 42.

mood from the preceding year and to balance the rather odd tone of the two letters to his bride that followed. He had offended her by expressing a reservation in his postscript to his bride's letter to his sister: "insofar as happiness is part of the destiny of my life." Now he tried to explain and set things right. In September they married.

In 1812, their first child, a girl, was born and soon died. His brother, Ludwig, an officer who had been the godfather of Hegel's illegitimate son, Ludwig, fell in Napoleon's Russian campaign.

From letters of July and October we learn that Hegel was still on good terms with Schelling, and that he had also developed a friendly relationship to Jacobi, another butt of strong criticisms in the preface to the *Phenomenology*. In the October letter to his friend Niethammer, who was *Oberschulrat* in Munich, Hegel submitted his views about the teaching of philosophy at the secondary school level and related his own conception of Logic to Kant's: after all, Kant already had discussed traditional metaphysics under the heading of what he called "Transcendental Logic," especially in the second part, which he entitled "Transcendental Dialectic." And Hegel explained why he had no time for the fashionable talk about teaching students to philosophize instead of teaching them philosophy. He had doubts whether philosophy should be taught at all in secondary schools; probably, a good grounding in the classics would serve the students far better. But if philosophy were taught at all, then there should be some content, too, as in any other science.

In September 1813, we hear the beginning of Hegel's commencement address to his students in which he gave expression to his conservatism. That year he also became *Schulrat,* in addition to being headmaster of his school, and his wife gave birth to her first son, Karl. He was later to edit the second edition of Hegel's lectures on the philosophy of history, as well as the first collection of letters to and from Hegel.

In the fall of 1814 Marie Hegel gave birth to her second son; but in the spring, when she was still expecting, Hegel's sister suffered her first breakdown. While Hegel certainly lacked charm and was, all in all, not as attractive a figure as, say, Lessing, one can scarcely admire his letter to his sister (April 9, 1814) sufficiently: here his character appears at its best, and his wisdom, too, is impressive.

Now Christiane, the sister, moved in with the Hegels: their home became her home. In two letters of 1814 we witness Hegel's reactions to Napoleon's downfall and to the triumph of Prussia and her allies. Late in 1815, Christiane was well enough to leave.

On July 30, 1816, at long last, Hegel was offered a chair of philosophy. Fries had left Heidelberg for a professorship at Jena, where both he and Hegel had begun their academic careers at the beginning of the century, and now Daub, Professor of Theology at Heidelberg, wrote Hegel a long letter to invite him. On August 2, Hegel wrote Professor von Raumer a long letter about the teaching of philosophy at the university level; and on August 10, von Raumer forwarded it to Berlin, to the Minister of Education, who, it turned out, had asked him to interview Hegel. On August 15, the Minister wrote Hegel, telling him that the chair for philosophy was still vacant, but asking Hegel to judge for himself whether he had "the ability to give vivid and incisive lectures." Hegel did not receive the letter until the twenty-fourth, and wrote on the twenty-eighth, the day after his forty-sixth birthday, to answer the question put to him and inform the minister that meanwhile he had committed himself to Heidelberg. (All these letters have been translated in D; the correspondence with Erlangen, which also issued him a call around the same time, has been omitted.) Finally, in December 1817, the new minister, Altenstein, offered Hegel the chair in Berlin, vacant since Fichte's death in 1814, and Hegel accepted and went to Berlin in 1818.

42

The years just considered in such summary fashion were immensely productive ones for Hegel. It was in Nürnberg that he wrote and published the three volumes of his *Logic,* and in Heidelberg, during his brief stay there, he completed and published his system, in a slim volume.

In Berlin, he published his *Philosophy of Right* and the second and third editions of his *Encyclopedia.* It was also at Berlin that he attracted the devoted disciples who collected his writings after his death and included in his collected "works" four imposing cycles of lectures, mostly on the basis of student notes.

Although the *Logic* appeared in three volumes, in 1812, 1813, and 1816, Hegel conceived of it as having *two* volumes. The whole work he called *Wissenschaft der Logik* (*Science of Logic;* the word

Wissenschaft appears in the titles of all four of the works he himself published). Volume I contained "Objective Logic," volume II "Subjective Logic, or The Doctrine of the Concept." The first "volume," as is not unusual in Germany, appeared in two parts, with the "First Book" containing "The Doctrine of Being" and the "Second Book: The Doctrine of Essence."

In 1831 Hegel prepared a second edition of the *Logic* and completed an extensive revision of the first volume shortly before he died. The original edition, which is a great rarity, has never been reprinted. Few scholars have consulted it, and the date of the second volume is almost invariably given as 1812, instead of 1813. The textual variants, confined to the first volume, are not indicated in any extant edition. They are indicated in the following pages for two reasons. First, we have been following Hegel's development and would falsify it at this point if we attributed to his Nürnberg period what in fact was written nineteen years later, in Berlin. Secondly, Hegel did not write a book during his last ten years, but during his last year he revised the first volume of his *Logic* and the beginning of the preface to the *Phenomenology*.[10] Although many of his revisions are trivial, it is still of some interest to observe how the author of such bold works as the *Phenomenology* and the *Logic* revised his earlier works instead of writing new ones.

Hegel still found it immensely difficult to make a beginning. There is, first, a preface. (For the second edition, Hegel even added a second preface, dated November 7, 1831, exactly one week before his death.) But the preface comprises only eight pages, not more than ninety, as did that to his first book. Next comes an introduction that runs on for twenty-eight pages. Then comes a five-page section on "General Subdivision of the Logic"[11]; and then the "First Book" which begins with a section of thirteen pages, entitled "With what must the beginning of science be made?" Including the preface to the second edition, there are seventy-one pages of introductory text.

This would not be particularly odd if Hegel did not once again

---

[10] For the changes Hegel made in the preface, see my commentary in Chapter VIII. In the following pages "1812" stands for the first edition of the *Logik,* "1841" for the revised edition, cited according to its *zweite unveränderte Auflage* in Hegel's *Werke,* an unchanged reprint of the first posthumous edition of 1833.

[11] This section was rewritten in 1831; the introduction was revised and subtitled "General Concept of Logic."

cast aspersions on what he is actually doing. The "introduction" begins: "There is no science where the need is felt more urgently to begin with the subject matter itself, without preliminary reflections, than in the science of Logic." And more in the same vein. Hegel apologizes for his argumentative and historical style in these early pages, feeling that he ought to be properly "scientific" from the start; but he obviously feels at home in what he is doing and writes, on the whole, with surprising clarity and vigor. In this respect, his *Encyclopedia* and *Philosophy of Right,* with their crabbed, consecutively numbered paragraphs cannot compare with these for the most part extremely lucid pages.

Since Kant, we are told in the preface, the Germans have become *"a civilized people without metaphysics,"* which Hegel considers a "strange spectacle." In the introduction Hegel suggests that "ancient metaphysics had in this respect a higher concept of thinking than has become prevalent in recent times. For it assumed that what in things is recognized by thinking is what alone in them is truly true; thus not they in their immediacy, but only they as lifted into the form of thinking, as thought. This [Platonic and Aristotelian] metaphysics thus held that thinking and the determinations of thought were not alien to objects but rather their essence, or that *things* and the *thinking* of them (even as our language expresses some relation between them) agree in and for themselves. . . ."[12]

While Hegel is right about Plato and Aristotle, the etymologies of "thing" and *Ding* on the one hand, and "think" and *Denken* on the other seem to be actually different. Like Plato, Hegel takes pleasure in calling attention to linguistic points; and in the preface added to the second edition he commends the German language for containing words that "have not only different meanings but even opposed meanings," which he considers evidence of "a speculative spirit of the language; it can afford thinking a delight to hit upon such words and to find the reconciliation of opposites, which is a result of speculation but an absurdity for the understanding, present lexicographically in this naïve manner in a single word of opposite meanings. Philosophy therefore requires no particular terminology at all; of course, a few words have to be accepted from foreign languages, but words that by much use have already acquired citizenship; any affected purism would be most out of place where the subject matter is all-important."

[12] 1812, p. v; 1841, p. 27.

What matters to Hegel is not etymology as such. The point is that he does not see himself as one who comes to say: Ye have been told—but I say unto you. Rather he wants to bring into clear daylight and systematic order what is available before he begins. The motto is always Goethe's:

> What from your fathers you received as heir,
> Acquire if you would possess it.

One may also recall Mephisto's lines, in *Faust II,* published only after Hegel's (and Goethe's) death:

> Depart, "original" enthusiast!
> How would this insight peeve you: whatsoever
> A human being thinks, if dumb or clever,
> Was thought before him in the past.

Goethe also said on occasion that everything true has already been thought in the past; one merely needs to think it once more. And in a late poem, written in 1829 and entitled "Legacy [*Vermächtnis*]," he said:

> *Das Wahre war schon längst gefunden, . . .*
> *Das alte Wahre, fass es an!*

These lines are wholly in Hegel's spirit: "The true has long been found, . . . The ancient true, take hold of it!" Grasp it—or as Hegel might say, what matters is to comprehend it, *es begreifen.*

The prime example of an ordinary word that shows the "speculative spirit of the language" by having seemingly opposed meanings is, of course, *aufheben* (sublimate), which was explained briefly above in section 34. The first chapter of the *Logic* ends with a "Note" on this term:

"*Aufheben* and *das Aufgehobene* (*das Ideelle*) is one of the most important concepts of philosophy, a basic determination which recurs practically everywhere. . . . What sublimates itself does not thereby become nothing. Nothing is *immediate;* what is sublimated, on the other hand, is *mediated;* it is that which is not, but as a *result,* having issued from what had being; it is therefore *still characterized by the determinateness from which it comes.*

"*Aufheben* has in the [German] language a double meaning in that it signifies conserving, *preserving,* and at the same time also making cease, *making an end.* Even conserving includes the negative aspect that something is taken out of its immediacy, and thus out of an existence that is open to external influences, to be preserved. —Thus what is *aufgehoben* is at the same time conserved and has merely lost its immediacy but is not for that reason annihilated.[13] —Lexicographically, the two definitions of *aufheben* can be listed as two *meanings* of the word. But it should strike us that a language should have come to use one and the same word for two opposed definitions. For speculative thinking it is a joy to find in the language words which are characterized by a speculative significance; German has several such words. The double meaning of the Latin *tollere* (which has become famous through Cicero's joke: *tollendum esse Octavium*) does not go so far; here the affirmative definition reaches only as far as raising up. Something is *aufgehoben* only insofar as it has entered into a union with its opposite; in this more exact definition, as something reflected, it can suitably be called a *moment*. . . . More often, the observation will press itself upon us that philosophical terminology uses Latin expressions for reflected definitions, either because the mother tongue lacks pertinent expressions or, if it has them, as here, because its expressions remind us more of the immediate, and the foreign language more of the reflected. . . ."

As this passage on Hegel's most "dialectical" term suggests, his dialectic, even in the *Logic*, is not meant to flout the law of contradiction; it is not even intended to be counterintuitive. In fact, Hegel's delight at finding such a word as *aufheben* is plainly due to the opportunity it provides for him to appeal to the intuition that is embedded in the language. And his detailed explanation, as quoted, tries to overcome the rigid prejudices of the understanding by showing how both reason and intuition can make perfectly good sense of something that the understanding might be inclined to rule out without a hearing because opposite meanings *must* be mutually incompatible and therefore, if nevertheless combined, yield nonsense.

In his introduction to the *Logic*, Hegel is no less plain on this all-

---

[13] *vernichtet*. 1812: *verschwinden* (vanished). The remainder of this paragraph is not found in the first edition, which proceeds instead: "That which is *aufgehoben* may be defined more precisely by saying that something is here *aufgehoben* only insofar as it has entered into a union with its opposite; in this narrower definition it is something reflected and can suitably be called a *moment*.—Indeed, we shall have to observe frequently that philosophical terminology uses Latin expressions for reflected definitions."

important point, on which he has so often been misrepresented. Again it will be best to quote Hegel's own words:

"The [Kantian] *critique of the forms of the understanding* has led to the previously mentioned result that these forms have no *application to the things-in-themselves* [this is indeed Kant's own conclusion].—But this can have no other meaning [says Hegel, but not Kant] than that these forms themselves are something untrue. But by still being conceded validity for subjective reason and for experience, the critique has not effected any change in these forms but leaves them standing for the subject as they formerly were considered valid for the object. But if they are inadequate for the thing-in-itself, then the understanding, whose forms they are supposed to be, ought to tolerate them and be satisfied with them even less. If they cannot be determinations of the *thing-in-itself,* they can even less be determinations of the understanding which ought to be conceded at least the dignity of a thing-in-itself. The determinations of the finite and infinite are in the same conflict whether they are applied to time and space, to the world [where Kant elaborated their antinomies], or as determinations within the spirit; just as black and white yield a gray, whether they are united together on a wall or still on the palette: if our notion of the *world* dissolves as soon as the determinations of the infinite and finite are transferred to it, then the *spirit* itself, which contains both, is even more something that contradicts itself and dissolves itself.—It is not the qualities of the stuff or object to which they are applied or in which they are situated that can make a difference; for the object is characterized by contradictions only through and according to these determinations."[14]

Kant thought that antinomies arise only when the categories of the understanding are applied to the world as a whole, to what lies beyond all possible experience; it did not occur to him that anything might be wrong with the categories themselves. He simply took them, as Hegel puts it in the next paragraph, "out of Subjective Logic," or as Kant himself put it, from the traditional table of judgments. He failed to examine or analyze them as he should have done, and he never realized that there is something inherently odd or queer about the categories of the understanding.

Hegel discusses the same point in the introductory portion of the second and third editions of the *Encyclopedia* (cf. H 19): "This is

[14] 1812, vii f.; 1841, 29 f., unchanged.

the place to mention that it is . . . the categories for themselves which bring about the contradiction. This thought, that the contradiction which arises in reason through the determinations of the understanding is *essential* and *necessary,* must be considered one of the most important and profound advances of modern philosophy. But the solution is no less trivial than this point of view is profound . . ." (§48).

What is needed is a comprehensive review and analysis of our categories, and this is what Hegel attempts in his *Logic.* The point is to comprehend the concepts of being and nothing, of finite and infinite; then we shall see that they are all one-sided abstractions from a concreteness of which they are merely partial aspects. That is the heart of Hegel's *Logic;* that is the meaning of its much misunderstood dialectic.

The dialectic of the *Logic* is thus somewhat different from the dialectic of the *Phenomenology:* one could not possibly call it a logic of passion. As Hegel says in the penultimate paragraph of the introduction: "The system of Logic is the realm of shadows, the world of the simple essences [*Wesenheiten*], freed from all sensuous concretion. The study of this science, the sojourn and the work in this realm of shadows, is the absolute education and discipline of consciousness. Here it pursues tasks remote from sensuous intuitions and aims, from feelings, from the merely intended world of notions.[15] Considered from its negative aspect, these tasks consist in the exclusion of the accidental nature of argumentative thinking and the arbitrary business of allowing these or rather the opposite reasons to occur to one and prevail."[16]

Hegel still confronts us as another Odysseus: in the *Phenomenology* we followed his Odyssey, the spirit's great voyage in search of a home where it might settle down; in the *Logic* we are asked to follow him into the realm of shadows. There we moved in a world where the passions had their place; here the passions are left behind. We are to contemplate Concepts and categories—and see them as one-sided abstractions and mere shadows that are not what they seem.

[15] This term has been used so often to render *Begriff* that it may be well to remind the reader that in this book it is employed consistently to translate *Vorstellung.* (Cf. H 34).
[16] 1812, xxvii f.; 1841, 44. The only change: Hegel added "intuitions and."

We are now ready to understand in context a metaphor mentioned once before (end of H 40)—on the face of it, perhaps the maddest image in all of Hegel's writings: "The Logic is thus to be understood as the system of pure reason, as the realm of pure thought. *This realm is truth as it is without any shroud in and for itself.* One might therefore say that this content is the *account of God, as he is in his eternal essence before the creation of nature and any finite spirit*" (Introduction).[17]

The image of the realm of shadows seems superior, but what both metaphors have in common is the abstraction from the world and from concreteness. The suggestion that the Logic takes us back in some sense *"before the creation of nature and any finite spirit"* undoubtedly came from the structure of Hegel's system: he had decided to begin with the Logic, to follow that with the philosophy of nature, and to place the philosophy of spirit in the end; and the philosophy of spirit, as we shall see when we take it up in detail, deals with the human (or "finite") spirit.

One might suppose that the Logic should belong to the philosophy of (finite) spirit—and one might favor the abandonment of any attempt to offer a philosophy of nature. In the twentieth century, the philosophy of (natural) science seems to have replaced the philosophy of nature, which is now apt to strike us as an excrescence of romanticism; and once the philosophy of nature is thus transposed into the study of a human pursuit (natural science), one is bound to wonder whether Logic, too, cannot be absorbed into the philosophy of man, or philosophical anthropology.

Most of this problem can be postponed until we consider the system, but something can and must be said at this point about the status and priority of the Logic. Hegel plainly does not consider it a branch of psychology, and beyond that he claims some priority for it, even over investigations of nature, and, for that matter, over science. On both points he is far from being out of date. Indeed, he could be said to have effected a revolution in metaphysics which is as timely one hundred fifty years later as it ever was.

With Hegel, metaphysics ceases to be speculation about the nature of ultimate reality. He is still fond of speaking of "speculation" and "speculative," but as a matter of fact *he does not speculate about things of which we could say that the time for speculation is*

---

[17] 1812, xiii; 1841, 33. 1812: "truth itself as it is"; "and" was missing in the phrase "in and for itself"; and none of the words was emphasized.

long past because we now look to the sciences for verifiable hypotheses. With Hegel, analysis of categories replaces speculative metaphysics. He gives metaphysics the new meaning and content that it still retains with some of the best philosophers in the second half of the twentieth century.

The priority of a Logic that is conceived in this manner is illuminated in two passages in the preface to the second edition:

"The forms of thinking are first of all articulated and laid down in the *language* of man. . . . In everything that becomes for him something inward, any kind of notion, anything he makes his own, language has intruded; and what man makes into language and expresses in language, contains, shrouded, mixed in, or elaborated, a category. . . ."

". . . I have seen opponents who did not care to make the simple reflection that their ideas and objections contain categories which are presuppositions and themselves require criticism before they are used. Unconsciousness of this point goes amazingly far; it makes for the basic misunderstanding, the uncouth and uneducated behavior of thinking *something else* when a category is considered, and not this category itself. . . ."

All discourse, whether it is about nature, science, psychology, ethics, art, or religion, involves categories that are not unproblematic, although those who engage in such discourse very rarely realize that they are begging any number of questions by packing problematic assumptions into their categories. Therefore Hegel considers it right to begin with an analysis of categories—or with what he calls "Logic."

His position vis-à-vis Kant may be summed up briefly. As Hegel himself points out in his "General Subdivision of the Logic," Kant extended the meaning of "logic" by introducing his "Transcendental Logic"; and Hegel's "Objective Logic"—the first two thirds of his *Logic*—"would partly correspond to his *Transcendental Logic.*" More important yet is the corollary, stated two pages later: "The Objective Logic thus replaces old-style *metaphysics.* . . ."[18]

The difference from Kant is stated in the main part of the introduction: Kant's "Critical philosophy already turned *metaphysics* into *Logic,* but it, like subsequent idealism, gave the logical de-

[18] This "General Subdivision" was expanded in 1831, but the points here mentioned are equally emphatic in both versions: 1812, 2–4; 1841, 49–51.

terminations, as already mentioned, from fear of the object, an essentially subjective significance. . . ."[19] Kant assumed that there was a thing-in-itself to which the categories did not apply; in that sense, then, the categories were merely subjective. Hegel follows Fichte in having no use for the thing-in-itself, which is indeed inconsistent with Kant's main ideas. Thinghood or substance is itself a category; unity and plurality are categories; cause is yet another. To claim that these categories have no application to the thing-in-itself, which must nevertheless be assumed as a cause without which we should have no experiences, is manifestly self-contradictory. If these categories have application only to the objects of experience—and Kant produces powerful arguments in support of this position—then we have no grounds whatsoever for assuming anything beyond experience. But in that case we also have no grounds for considering the categories merely subjective. So far from merely telling us something about the structure of the human mind, they are part of the structure of all knowledge and of discourse on any subject whatsoever—whether that subject be knowledge and discourse, nature, ethics, art, religion, or philosophy. Therefore, the system of science—to recall the title Hegel originally gave the work to which the *Phenomenology* was meant as an introduction—should begin with the *Logic*.

43

When it comes to the actual contents of the *Logic,* it is easy to look at the table of contents and to copy it in the form of a chart, as some authors of studies of Hegel have done. But in the introduction Hegel says expressly:

". . . I point out that *the subdivisions and titles of the books, sections, and chapters indicated in this work,*[20] *as well as any explanations*[21] *connected with them,* have been made for the sake of a preliminary survey, and that they are really solely of historical value. They *do not belong to the contents and body of the science,* but are arrangements of external reflection, which has already run

19 1812, xv; 1841, 35.
20 1812: "in the following treatise on Logic."
21 1812: "remarks."

through the whole execution and therefore knows the sequence of the moments in advance and indicates them. . . ."[22]

Once again, as in the *Phenomenology,* Hegel first wrote each volume and then asked himself what precisely he had got and how it might be arranged neatly. He never set as much store by his triads or by the precise sequence as some of his expositors have done. In fact, in the *Encyclopedia* of 1817, the order differs somewhat from the *Logic* of 1812–16. In 1830 Hegel published a third, revised, and definitive edition of the *Encyclopedia,* but when he prepared a second and definitive edition of the *Logic* in 1831—he completed his work on the first volume—he did not make the order conform to that of the *Encyclopedia.* The precise sequence was, after all, as he had already said in 1812, not part of the "body of the science," any more than the neat disposition and headings.

What did matter was not any such progression from thesis to antithesis to synthesis, and hence to another antithesis, and so forth, as McTaggart claimed,[23] but a comprehensive analysis of categories and the demonstration that any two opposite categories are always both one-sided abstractions.

Hegel has been called an archrationalist and an essentialist, but his central purpose in the *Logic* is to demonstrate the inadequacy, the one-sidedness, the abstractness of our categories. Some are more abstract than others; hence some sort of sequential arrangement is possible; but this is not the main thesis or point of the book.

Only the somewhat cut-and-dried style of the *Encyclopedia,* which will be considered in due course, could give the impression that the table of contents structure was what mattered. The *Logic* belies it at every turn—quite especially the first volume in which the reader is introduced to the whole enterprise. But while the dehydrated summary of the "Logic" in the *Encyclopedia* was rendered into English, badly, in 1873 (the revised edition of 1892 was still bad),[24] no complete translation of the *Logic* itself appeared until 1929. When Stace's influential interpretation of Hegel appeared

---

[22] 1812, xxi; 1841, 39; Glockner's ed., IV, 52; Lasson's ed. (1923), 366. In the original only *historical* is emphasized.

[23] *Op. cit.,* §4 (cf. H 37).

[24] Moreover, much of the text Wallace chose to translate consists of "additions" of doubtful value which will be considered below (H 52). Wallace published an English version of the final part of the *Encyclopedia* in 1894; the middle part, containing the philosophy of nature, has never appeared in English.

(1924), his teacher, H. S. Macran, had published in English only approximately one ninth of the *Logic* (the first third of Part III).[25] But when a philosopher spends a large part of his life writing a three-volume work that eventually appears in installments over a period of five years, a discussion of the ideas in that work on the basis of a translation of a syllabus of roughly a hundred pages, designed for his students' use in connection with one of his lecture courses, is hardly the best we can do.

Concerning the charge of essentialism, the following distinction from the introduction is relevant: "Considering *education and the relation of the individual to Logic,* I finally remark that this science, like grammar, appears in two different perspectives or values. It is one thing for those who first approach it and the sciences, and quite another for those who return to it from them. Whoever begins to study grammar, finds in its forms and laws dry abstractions, accidental rules, altogether a lot of isolated determinations which manifest merely the value and significance that lie in their immediate meaning; at first, knowledge recognizes nothing else in them. Whoever, on the other hand, masters a language, and at the same time knows other languages with which to compare it, will find that the spirit and culture of a people reveal themselves to him in the grammar of its language; the same rules and forms now have a full, living value. Through the grammar he can recognize the expression of the spirit, the Logic.

"Thus, whoever approaches science, at first finds in the Logic an isolated system of abstractions that, limited to itself, does not reach over into other fields of knowledge or other sciences. On the contrary, compared with the riches of a notion of the world, with the content of the other sciences, which seems real, and compared with the promise of absolute science to uncover the *essence* of these riches, the *inner nature* of the spirit and the world, the *truth*,[26] this science, in its abstract form and in the colorless, cold simplicity of its pure determinations, rather has the appearance that it could do anything rather than keep this promise, and it seems to confront these riches without any content. The first acquaintance with Logic limits its significance to Logic itself; its content is considered merely an iso-

[25] *Hegel's Doctrine of Formal Logic, being a translation of the first section of the Subjective Logic* (1912).
[26] "the truth" was added in the 2d edition. There are a few more *very* minor stylistic changes that do not affect the sense.

lated concern with the determinations of thought, while other scientific concerns lie *beside* it as separate materials with a content of their own. . . .

"In this way, Logic must indeed be learned to begin with, as something one understands and admits but in which scope, depth, and further significance are missed to begin with. It is only out of the deeper knowledge of the other sciences that Logic rises for the subjective spirit as something that is not merely general in an abstract way but as the general which includes the riches of the particular—even as the same ethical maxim in the mouth of a youth who understands it quite rightly does not have the significance and scope it has in the spirit of a man who has had much experience of life. . . ."[27]

44

The first antinomy discussed in the *Logic* is not that of being and nothing, which forms the subject of the first chapter, but that of the immediate and the mediated, which is introduced at the beginning of the section "With what must the beginning of science be made?"

"The beginning of philosophy must either be something *mediated* or something *immediate;* and it is easy to show that it could be neither the one nor the other."[28] This is not some slight bit of cleverness, offered in passing. This antinomy closely parallels Kant's first antinomy, which assumes that the world must either have a beginning in time or not have a beginning in time, and then shows that both the "thesis" and the "antithesis" can be shown to be impossible. Kant assumed that this must be due to the illicit application of categories to the world as a whole and concluded that this corroborated his claim that our knowledge is perforce limited to experience. Hegel shows that the antinomy does not depend on the application of categories to the world as a whole; he points to a parallel antinomy when the question is merely one about the beginning of science, or philosophy; and he finds that the fault lies in the nature of our categories. He sums up the last point when he says

---

[27] 1812, xxv–xxvii; 1841, 42–44.
[28] 1812, 7; 1841, 55. The beginning of this section differs in the two editions, but this sentence does not.

on the next page "that there is nothing, nothing in the heavens or in nature or in the spirit or anywhere, which does not contain both immediacy and mediation; so these two determinations are seen to be *undivided* and *indivisible* [*ungetrennt und untrennbar*], and this opposition something vain [*ein Nichtiges*]."[29]

Nothing, in other words, is absolutely immediate (*unmittelbar*) in the sense that it is in no way mediated; and nothing is mediated (*vermittelt*) in the absolute sense that it is in no sense immediate. If, for example, I know "immediately" that the answer to the question "What is 5 plus 12?" is "17," my knowledge is, for all that, mediated by a process of learning back in my childhood. And, on the other hand, a picture that was not on the canvas "immediately" but got there through the mediation of many hours of work can still be seen all at once, at a glance, immediately.

What seems trivial logic-chopping, utterly academic, and remote from the concrete content of other sciences is in fact relevant to hundreds of disputes that fill thousands of articles and books as well as many oral discussions. Again and again, people, including scholars, take such categories as those just discussed in an absolute sense and hack away at each other instead of realizing the vanity, or nullity, of the dispute.

A few pages later, still in the same section, Hegel applies his point to "being" and says: "Further, what begins *is* already; but just as much, it *is not* yet. The two opposites, being and not-being, thus are found in it in immediate union; or it is their *undifferentiated unity*.

"The analysis of the beginning would thus furnish the Concept of the unity of being and not-being. . . . This Concept could be considered the first, purest, i.e., most abstract, definition of the absolute—which it would be in fact if the form of definitions and the name of the absolute mattered at all."[30]

[29] 1841, 56; not in the first edition.
[30] 1812, 13; 1841, 64. The phrase "i.e., most abstract" was added in 1831.

45

The first book of the *Logic* is called "The Doctrine of Being" and the first chapter is subdivided as follows:

FIRST SECTION: QUALITY[31]

First Chapter: Being

A. Being

B. Nothing

C. Becoming
  1. Unity of being and nothing

       Note 1: The opposition of being and nothing in our notions

       Note 2: Inadequacy of the expression: unity, identity of being and nothing[32]

       Note 3: On isolating these abstractions[33]

       Note 4: Incomprehensibility of beginning[34]

  2. Moments of becoming

  3. Sublimation of becoming

       Note: The expression: *Aufheben*

When we turn to consider the contents of the next two chapters, we find that the differences between the original edition of 1812 and the revised version are so great that it will be best to present the two versions on facing pages to facilitate comparisons.

[31] 1812: DETERMINATENESS (QUALITY)
[32] 1812: Being and nothing, each taken for itself
[33] 1812: Other relations [*Verhältnisse*] in the relation [*Beziehung*] of being and nothing
[34] 1812: The ordinary dialectic against becoming and against coming to be and passing away

These pages, which "cover" about 130 pages of text, should be compared with the breakdown of the same section in the so-called Lesser Logic, in the *Encyclopedia*. Here it is, in full:

A. Quality
    a. Being
    b. Existence
    c. Being for itself

That is it, in all three editions of the *Encyclopedia*.

The *Encyclopedia* text on this section comprises less than a dozen pages, even in the third edition. The *Encyclopedia* is a syllabus that invites yet further reduction to a chart. But Hegel's *Logic* is a work of an altogether different character, as even these three pages of the table of contents may suggest.

The *Logic* is indeed a marvel of organization, and the use of "Notes" is altogether ingenious. This device allows Hegel to anticipate objections, to elaborate, and to digress, while at the same time presenting an outline that is extraordinarily neat with its repeated triadic pattern. The structure is clear and pleases the eye in its astounding simplicity; but scope, profundity, and the riches of an unusually comprehensive mind are never sacrificed to it. Whatever seems worth saying, is said—if necessary, in a Note.

FIRST EDITION: 1812

Second Chapter: Existence [*Das Dasein*]

A. Existence as such
   1. Existence in general
   2. Reality [*Realität*]
      a. Being other
      b. Being for another and being in itself
      c. Reality
         Note: Ordinary meaning of reality
   3. Something

B. Determinateness
   1. Limit
   2. Determinateness
      a. Determination
      b. Condition [*Beschaffenheit*]
      c. Quality
         Note: Ordinary meaning of quality
   3. Change [*Veränderung*]
      a. Change of condition
      b. Ought and barrier
         Note: You ought to because you can
      c. Negation

C. (Qualitative) Infinity
   1. Finitude and infinity
   2. Reciprocal determination of the finite and the infinite
   3. Return of the infinite into itself
      Note: Ordinary juxtaposition of the finite and infinite

REVISED VERSION

Second Chapter: Existence [*Das Dasein*]

A. Existence as such
   a. Existence in general
   b. Quality
      Note: Reality and negation
   c. Something

B. Finitude
   a. Something and something other
   b. Determination, condition [*Beschaffenheit*], and limit
   c. Finitude
         The immediacy of finitude
         The barrier and the ought
         Note: The ought
      Transition of the finite into the infinite

C. Infinity
   a. The infinite in general
   b. Reciprocal determination of the finite and the infinite
   c. Affirmative infinity

The transition
         Note 1: Infinite progress
         Note 2: Idealism

FIRST EDITION: 1812

Third Chapter: Being for itself [*Das Fürsichsein*]

A. Being for itself as such
  1. Being for itself in general
  2. The moments of being for itself
     a. Its being in itself
     b. Being for one [*Für eines seyn*]
     Note: *Was für einer?*
     c. Ideality
  3. Becoming of the one

B. The one [*Das Eins*]
  1. The one and the void
     Note: Atomism
  2. Many ones (repulsion)
     Note: Multiplicity of monads
  3. Mutual repulsion

C. Attraction
  1. A one [*Ein Eins*]
  2. Balance [*Gleichgewicht*] of attraction and repulsion
     Note: The Kantian construction of matter out of the
            force of attraction and repulsion
  3. Transition to quantity

REVISED VERSION

Third Chapter: Being for itself [*Das Fürsichsein*]

A. Being for itself as such
   a. Existence and being for itself
   b. Being for one [*Sein-für-Eines*]
      Note: The expression: *Was für eines?*
   c. One

B. One and many
   a. The one in itself
   b. The one and the void
      Note: Atomism
   c. Many ones. Repulsion
      Note: Leibnizian monad

C. Repulsion and attraction
   a. Exclusion of the one
      Note: Principle of the unity of the one and the many
   b. The one one of attraction
   c. The relation of repulsion and attraction
      Note: The Kantian construction of matter out of the force of attraction and repulsion

Can Hegel's many triads be construed as so many theses, antitheses, and syntheses, even if he himself did not choose to do this? Let us look at them, beginning with the first three chapters: Existence (Chapter 2) is hardly the antithesis of Being (Chapter 1), and Being for itself (Chapter 3) is not their synthesis.

Nor will this construction work when we consider the A, B, and C of the third chapter, or their further subdivisions. The story is the same when we turn back to the second chapter: finitude is certainly not the antithesis of existence as such, and infinity cannot well be construed as their synthesis. Again, the subdivisions, too, do not lend themselves to that kind of dialectic.

The sole possible exception comes in the first chapter: the first triad of the book, that of being, nothing, and becoming, seems to substantiate the myth; though even here the further breakdown of the discussion of becoming will not fit, and even the mere headings of Notes 2 and 3 suggest the shallowness of the traditional misrepresentation.

It is tempting to suggest that those who cling to the legend of thesis, antithesis, and synthesis have obviously never got beyond the first triad, and have not even read the Notes that explain what it is all about. While this is unquestionably true in the majority of cases, the way a legend spreads is, of course, different. It is not true that everyone, or almost everyone, who believes in it has come to believe it on his own, by drawing a false conclusion from, say, the first triad. People are taught the legend before they have read any Hegel—or any Nietzsche, or the four Gospels—and when they finally look at some of the books themselves, few indeed read these books straight through, with an open mind. In fact, doing that with a really unprejudiced mind, discounting everything one has been taught for years, is so difficult that it borders on the impossible.

Typically, people read a little here and there, are delighted when they find what fits in with their preconceptions, and actually assume that they have now found for themselves what they had merely assumed previously. What does not readily fit is usually discounted as being due to one's imperfect knowledge. After all, everybody knows—well, what precisely? The truth of the legend.

46

Still, we should consider the first triad in some detail. We find that the text down to Note 1 takes up a mere two pages, even with the three big, space-consuming headings: Being, Nothing, and Becoming. But the four Notes take up twenty pages in the first edition, almost thirty in the second.

Here is what Hegel has to say about "being":

"Being, pure being—without all further determination. In its undetermined immediacy it is equal only to itself, and is not even unequal to something else, has no difference within it, nor toward the outside. Any determination or content that would be differentiated in it, or by which it would be posited as differentiated from something else, would mean that we no longer held fast to it in its purity. It is pure undeterminateness and emptiness.—There is *nothing* in it to be intuited, if one can here speak of intuition; or it is only this pure, empty intuition itself. Just as little is there anything in it to be thought, or it is just as much only this empty thinking. Being, the undetermined and immediate, is indeed *nothing,* and not more nor less than nothing."

After this comes the equally brief discussion of "nothing":

"Nothing, pure nothing; it is simple equality with itself, complete emptiness, lack of all determination and content; non-differentiation in itself.—Insofar as intuition or thinking can be mentioned here, it is considered a difference whether something or *nothing* is intuited or thought. To intuit or think nothing thus has a meaning[35]; both are differentiated, so there *is* (exists) nothing in our intuition or thought[35]; or rather it is the empty intuition or thinking itself; and the same empty intuition or thinking as pure being.—Nothing is thus the same determination, or rather lack of determination, and thus altogether the same as pure *being."*

Now comes "C. Becoming. 1. Unity of being and nothing"; and this is equally brief:

"Pure being and pure nothing are thus the same. What is truth is neither being nor nothing, but rather that being has passed over—

[35] The phrase between the two figures was slightly different in the first edition.

not that it is passing over—into nothing, and nothing into being. But just as much is truth not their non-differentiation but rather[36] that they are *not the same,*[36] that they are *absolutely different,* but just as much undivided and indivisible, and that *each* immediately *disappears in its opposite.* Their truth is thus this *movement* of the immediate disappearance of one in the other; *becoming;* a movement in which both are differentiated, but by a difference that has just as immediately dissolved."

Even this initial brief account is very different from the usual versions of Hegel's claim and fits our remarks about Hegel's approach to the categories. But if Hegel had stopped this discussion at this point in order to hurry on to the next triad, and hence to another, and yet another, we might still feel that he *was* somewhat oracular and had perhaps put something over on his audience. But now come the four Notes, all designed to elucidate what Hegel meant and what he did not mean.

It will suffice to quote some of the highlights. This discussion cannot serve as a substitute for reading Hegel's *Logic;* it is meant to clear away misconceptions and impediments and to show *how* the book is to be read.

We begin with Note 1:

"*Nothing* is usually opposed to *something;* but something is already a determinate being which is different from other somethings; thus the nothing that is opposed to something, the nothing of something, is also a determinate nothing. But here 'nothing' is to be taken in its undetermined simplicity.[37]—If it should be considered more correct that instead of nothing, *not-being* should be opposed to being, considering the result there would be no objection to this. . . . But what matters first is not the form of opposition . . . but rather the abstract, immediate negation, nothing purely for itself, the negation devoid of relation—what, if you wish, could also be expressed by the mere: *not.* . . .

"If the result that being and nothing is the same attracts attention, taken by itself, or seems paradoxical, there is no need to heed that particularly. . . . It would not be difficult to demonstrate this unity of being and nothing in every example, in *every* actuality or

[36] The phrase between the two figures is not found in the first edition.
[37] The remainder of this paragraph was added in 1831.

thought.[38] One must say the same thing that was said above about immediacy and mediation . . . about *being* and *nothing: that nowhere in the heavens and on earth is there anything that does not contain in itself both being and nothing.* To be sure, since here one speaks of *a something* and *what is actual,* these determinations are no longer present in the complete untruth in which they are as being and nothing, but in a further determination; and they are taken, e.g., as the *positive* and the *negative.* . . .

"One cannot try to meet all the confusions into which the ordinary consciousness enters, confronted with such a logical proposition, in every possible way; for they are inexhaustible. Only a few can be mentioned. One reason for such confusions—one among others—is that consciousness carries into such an abstract logical proposition[39] notions of a concrete something, forgetting that here one is not speaking of that but only of the pure abstractions of being and nothing, and that we must stick to these alone.

"Being and nothing is the same; *therefore* it is the same whether I am or am not, whether this house is or is not, whether these hundred dollars are part of my fortune or not.[40]—This inference or application of the proposition changes the meaning of the proposition completely. The proposition contains the pure abstractions of being and nothing; but the application makes of them a determinate being and a determinate nothing. But of a determinate being, as noted, one is not speaking at this point."[41]

The example of the hundred dollars leads Hegel to discuss Kant's analysis of the ontological proof of God's existence at some length, and this in turn leads to the remark[42] "that man should raise himself to this abstract generality in his mind, so that in fact it becomes a matter of indifference to him whether the hundred dollars . . . are or are not, just as it is indifferent to him whether he is or is not . . . *si fractus illabatur orbis, impavidum ferient ruinae,* a Roman

---

[38] The remainder of this paragraph was added in 1831.
[39] 1812: the paragraph was different up to this point, as follows: "The confusion into which the ordinary consciousness enters, confronted with such a logical proposition, is due to the fact that it carries into it . . ."
[40] Only a browser could mistake this for Hegel's own view.
[41] 1812, 23–26; 1841, 74–77.
[42] Only in the revised edition.

said,[43] and a Christian should maintain such indifference even more."

The second Note is shorter than the first; and we shall excerpt it too:

"Another reason may be cited which is conducive to the aversion against the proposition about being and nothing. This reason is that the expression of the result . . . in the proposition, *being and nothing is one and the same,* is imperfect. The accent is placed preferably on the *one and the same,* as one would generally do in a proposition in which only the predicate proclaims what the subject is. The meaning therefore seems to be that the difference is denied, although it appears immediately in the proposition itself; for it pronounces the *two* determinations, being and nothing, and contains them as differentiated. . . . Insofar as the proposition, *being and nothing is the same,* pronounces the identity of these determinations, while also containing both as differentiated, it contradicts itself and dissolves itself. If we stick to this, a proposition is here posited which, on closer examination, contains the movement to disappear through itself. But in this way what happens to it is precisely what is supposed to constitute its true content; namely, *becoming.*

". . . The sentence in the form of a *proposition* is not felicitous for the expression of speculative truths; acquaintance with this circumstance would help to do away with many misunderstandings of speculative truths."[44]

This last point had been made by Hegel at some length in the preface to the *Phenomenology,* and is discussed in the commentary, where something is also said about his reiteration of this point in the *Encyclopedia* (II.1.25). It is one of the central points of Hegel's philosophy and as relevant to the comprehension of his *Logic* as it is to the *Phenomenology.*

The point of the *Logic* is not to flout the law of contradiction, to confound common sense, and to climb, by means of some Indian rope trick, over theses, antitheses, and syntheses, out of sight, to the absolute. What Hegel offers is a critique of our categories, an attempt to show how one-sided and abstract they are, and a work that should destroy uncritical reliance on unexamined concepts and dog-

---

[43] Horace, *Odes.* III.3,7: "Even if the sky fell, broken, the ruins would slay an intrepid man." Freud also loved this quotation.
[44] 1841, 83 f. In the first edition this Note is altogether different.

matic insistence on propositions that invite contradiction. Far from taking a delight in contradictions and paradoxes, Hegel tries to show how these are inevitable unless we carefully analyze our terms and recognize what a proposition can and cannot do.

47

The prose of the *Logic* is worlds removed from the prose of Heidegger, both in *Being and Time* and in *What is Metaphysics,* which revolves around "the nothing"; and Hegel's thought is, too. The distinction between being [*das Sein*] and beings [*Seiendes*] is common to both but comes from Aristotle.[45] What Heidegger does with being and nothing is not merely different from what Hegel did with them; it is based on a total and unfortunate neglect of Hegel's discussion of these terms.

Heidegger begins *Being and Time* (1927) as a great quest for being, which allegedly has been covered up by beings. From the start, being is given the mystique of something long lost that we must seek; and human existence is then studied as one mode of being—the mode we as human beings know best—in the hope that through such a study we might gain some inkling of what being is. The suggestion throughout is that knowing something of human existence is relatively paltry; such knowledge is scarcely worth while; a philosopher should not bother with it—and Heidegger himself assuredly would not stoop so low—if it were not for the hope that we might acquire at least a little knowledge of being, which is held to be far bigger and better.

In Heidegger's later writings being has acquired such a sacred aura that talk of Heidegger's *Seinsmystik* (his mysticism of being) has long been a commonplace. He is on the way toward being; a

---

[45] Cf. Ros. 287 f: Many readers resisted Hegel's *Logik* "because they did not want to think the very beginning, the Concept of being as such [*des Seins als solchen*], but always looked behind this absolute abstraction for a particular substance, a being [*ein Sein*]. Being [*Das Sein*] was right away supposed to be something, a being [ein *Etwas*, ein *Seiendes*] . . . he had formed his German designations after *Greek* models in *Plato* and *Aristotle;* for *being-for-itself, being other, being-in-and-for-itself, being identical with oneself* all accord with ancient Greek usage, except that this was often much bolder still, as Aristotle's *to ti ēn einai* [the what it is to be that thing, or "essence"] and *entelecheia* show, as is well known."

vision of being is not vouchsafed to our generation; our time is one in which being has been forgotten, and being has forgotten us; all one can hope to do is to start in the direction of being and perhaps take a few steps.

In *What is Metaphysics?* (published two years after *Being and Time* and well before the later writings just referred to) Heidegger discussed the revelation of the nothing in the experience of anxiety. What are we afraid of when we experience *Angst*—as opposed to fear, which is fear of something particular? Nothing! In this lecture, often reprinted with a subsequently added postscript and an introduction added still later, Heidegger created a great mystique around the nothing, which was criticized by Rudolf Carnap as a semantic confusion.[46]

The point that must be stressed in our context is that such writings are *not* excrescences of Hegel's spirit, but, on the contrary, examples of the sort of thing Hegel hoped to prevent henceforth by means of his discussion of being and nothing. He tried to strip them of their aura. He discussed them as the poorest and most abstract categories and found it understandable and fitting that Parmenides, so near the beginning of Western philosophy, should have extolled being.[47] Any attempt to go back to Parmenides in modern times and to extol being in any comparable manner would have struck Hegel as utterly perverse and as evidence that anyone proposing to do such a thing had not profited from over two thousand years of philosophical thought—which Heidegger, to be sure, has renounced as an egregious fall from grace.

This historical digression is doubly pertinent because it shows how Hegel's *Logic* is indeed, as he himself suggested, abstract and isolated only for those who come to it for the first time, ignorant—to recall Hegel's own image—of other languages and sciences. For those who have lived with his ideas for a while, and who have studied other things, too, the relevance of his discussions becomes obvious. And the alleged essentialist who, a new generation supposes, ought to hang his head in shame when confronted with the existentialists of the twentieth century, is quite able to hold his own. In fact, Hegel might say, quoting the title of one of his essays: *Who* thinks abstractly?

[46] Cf. WK 351, 432, and 438.
[47] First page of Note I: 1841, 74; Glockner's ed., IV, 89.

48

In the *Logic,* as in the *Phenomenology,* Hegel is the philosopher of abundance in the same sense that one might call Shakespeare's poetry the poetry of abundance. For the second time he tries to write a book with a limited aim, and this time he actually begins by apologizing for its unavoidable abstractness; and for the second time the work transcends his limited intentions, reaches out to embrace ever so much more, and in the end anticipates his system.

The idea of Hegel as a desiccated professor who eked out a book at a time by ceaselessly applying a mechanical method—a thinker who did not really have very much to say because, after all, he had never had a concrete experience in his life—founders on the *Logic* as it does on the *Phenomenology.* Not counting the various prefaces, introductions, and essays in the beginning, the first volume alone contains thirty-three "Notes"[48]; the second has sixteen; and the last, which differs completely from the first two, as we shall see in a moment, only two. In the text, these Notes have no titles, except for the word *Anmerkung;* in the table of contents, most of them have a title indicating their approximate content, but some of them do not. Certainly, most of them were not written on set topics that were planned in advance for those particular places; and the great majority of the titles in the table of contents represent afterthoughts. The *Logic* is the work of a man who has a vast number of things to say, and who asks himself *afterwards* how best to arrange what he has said in an orderly fashion.

A man once called on a professor to ask permission to audit his seminar. He was working on a book, he said, and felt that the seminar would be of great help to him. To substantiate the impression he wished to make, he opened his brief case and produced two enormous spring binders. Opened, they revealed perhaps a thousand pages, each blank except for one or two lines. "Critique of Nicolai Hartmann," said a typical page. "What are you going to say by way of criticizing him?" asked the professor. "I don't know yet," replied the man, who was twice the professor's age; "that's why I want to take your seminar."

[48] 1812: twenty-eight, one of them not included in the table of contents.

Hegel was close to the opposite extreme, much nearer to Nietzsche than to this poor "author." But instead of beginning in his late twenties, or at least at thirty when he first came to Jena, to publish something like a book a year containing his current thoughts, he kept accumulating material and ideas and then faced the terrible problem of finally writing an orderly book. If his mind had not been so crowded with ideas that urgently pressed on him, he might have written more ordinary volumes. But as soon as the dike was broken and he began to write the *Phenomenology,* and later the *Logic,* everything threatened to rush in.

What exactly does the *Logic* contain? We have reproduced the "contents" of the first section, *Quality.* The second is called *Quantity,* and on the second page of it a "Note" (without title) begins. Then there are the usual three chapters, with their usual A, B, C, and with "Notes" on various subjects, including "Kantian antinomy of indivisibility and the infinite divisibility of time, space, matter"; "Modes of calculation in arithmetic. Kantian synthetic propositions *a priori* of intuition"; "Kant's application of the determination of degree to the being of the soul"; "The high opinion of progress *ad infinitum";* Kant's antinomy of the finitude and infinity of the world; the mathematical infinite; and the differential calculus.

The third section is called *Measure,* and there is the usual triadic division and subdivision, and as usual the triads cannot be construed as theses, antitheses, syntheses. A long excursus on elective affinities deserves special mention, as Goethe's novel with that title had appeared in 1809.

The second volume of the *Objective Logic,* the so-called *Doctrine of Essence,* is organized as follows. Some omissions are clearly indicated; but by simply omitting all the "Notes" one would falsify the tenor and dissemble the richness of the volume.

FIRST SECTION: ESSENCE AS REFLECTION IN ITSELF

First Chapter: Semblance [*Der Schein*]

A. The essential and unessential

B. Semblance

C. Reflection [subdivided further]

Second Chapter: . . . the determinations of reflection

Note: The determinations of reflections in the form of propositions [or, principles]

A. Identity [followed by 2 Notes]

Note 2: First original law of thought, the principle of identity

B. Difference [3 subdivisions and 2 Notes]

C. Contradiction

Note 1: Unity of the positive and the negative

Note 2: The principle of the excluded middle

Note 3: The principle of contradiction

Third Chapter: The ground [*Grund*]

Note: The principle of [sufficient] reason [*Grund*]

A. The absolute ground

a. Form and essence

b. Form and matter

c. Form and content

B. The determinate ground [3 subdivisions and 2 Notes]

C. The condition [*Bedingung*]

SECOND SECTION: APPEARANCE [*Die Erscheinung*]

First Chapter: Existence [*Die Existenz*]

A. The thing and its attributes

    a. Thing-in-itself and existence

    b. Attribute

      Note: The thing-in-itself of transcendental idealism

    c. The reciprocity of things

B. The thing's consisting of matter

C. The dissolution of the thing [followed by a Note]

Second Chapter: Appearance [3 subparts]

Third Chapter: The essential relation

A. The relation of the whole and the parts

    Note: Infinite divisibility

B. The relation of force and its expression [3 subparts]

C. Relation of the internal and external

    Note: Immediate identity of the internal and external

THIRD SECTION: ACTUALITY [*Die Wirklichkeit*]

First Chapter: The absolute [3 subparts]
    Note: Spinozistic and Leibnizian philosophy

Second Chapter: Actuality

A. The accidental, or formal actuality, possibility, and necessity

B. Relative necessity or real actuality, possibility, and necessity

C. Absolute necessity

Third Chapter: The absolute relation

A. Relation of substantiality

B. Relation of causality [3 subparts]

C. Reciprocity

There is one problem of translation that ought to be mentioned, though it fortunately does not have to be solved here. The second chapter of the *Logic* is entitled *Das Dasein,* rendered above as "Existence," and the first chapter of the "Second Section: Appearance" of the *Doctrine of Essence* is entitled *Die Existenz.* In a complete translation of the work one would obviously have to find two different English terms. The trouble is that there is no English equivalent for *Dasein,* which in German is a common and entirely untechnical term, by no means as cumbersome as "being-there." In English, "he is there" is as plain as *er ist da;* but "being-there" as a noun has quite a different ring.

These pages should fulfill several functions. First, they ought to give the reader some idea of the range of topics in the *Objective Logic.* Second, they should show where one can find Hegel's discussions of any number of crucial terms. Third, they should enable the reader to see for himself whether the procession of the categories is governed by the three-step of thesis-antithesis-synthesis. And finally, they show how many of the headings are plainly afterthoughts. The First Chapter is called "Semblance," and so is the second of its three parts. Similarly, the Second Section is called "Appearance," and so is the second of its three chapters. The point is not to blame Hegel on that score but rather to show that he meant what he said when he disparaged all "the subdivisions and titles of the books, sections, and chapters" (first quotation in H 43).

49

The last part of Hegel's *Logic* is in important respects a different kind of work from the first two. That is why Hegel himself did not divide the work as a whole into three parts but rather into two volumes, subdividing the first volume—the *Objective Logic*—into two parts. So far we have confined our attention to these: they are the part of the *Logic* that was meant to replace traditional metaphysics.

The *Subjective Logic,* though subtitled "The Doctrine of the Concept," was meant to treat the traditional subject matter of logic. It contains only two Notes, and it will suffice if we give the barest outline.

FIRST SECTION: SUBJECTIVITY

First Chapter: The Concept [3 subparts]

Second Chapter: The proposition

   A. The proposition of existence [*Dasein;* 3 subparts]

   B. The proposition of reflection [3 subparts]

   C. The proposition of necessity [3 subparts]

   D. The proposition of the Concept [3 subparts]

Third Chapter: The inference

   A. The inference of existence [*Dasein;* 4 subparts; Note]

   B. The inference of reflection

   C. The inference of necessity

SECOND SECTION: OBJECTIVITY

First Chapter: Mechanism [3 subparts, 2 subdivided further]

Second Chapter: Chemism [3 subparts]

Third Chapter: Teleology [3 subparts]

THIRD SECTION: THE IDEA

First Chapter: Life [3 subparts]

Second Chapter: The idea of knowledge

   A. The idea of the true

      a. Analytical knowledge

      b. Synthetic knowledge

         1. The definition

         2. The subdivision

         3. The axiom

   B. The idea of the good

Third Chapter: The absolute idea [no further subdivision]

Very little needs to be said about this volume. In the second chapter, which for once is divided into four parts, A, B, C, D, Hegel covers the traditional table of judgments: positive, negative, and infinite; singular, particular, and universal; categorical, hypothetical, and disjunctive; assertorial, problematic, and apodictic.

In the third chapter, under A he takes up the traditional four figures; under B the inferences of totality, induction, and analogy; under C, the categorical, hypothetical, and disjunctive inference.

None of this is really of a kind with the *Objective Logic,* and Hegel himself made plain that it was not. The point requires emphasis only because it shows how misguided all attempts are to construe the *Logic* as a relentless ascent from "being" to "the absolute." What makes this popular legend doubly silly is the fact that "the absolute" appears not at all at the pinnacle, but in the second part of the *Objective Logic* (i.e., in the second of the three volumes), and not even at the pinnacle of that but at the *beginning* of its third section, surmounted, of all things, by "actuality" (hardly in keeping with the tag of "essentialism").

There is no relentless ascent; there is rather an attempt to organize an excess of material. After traditional metaphysics has been replaced by an *Objective Logic,* which deliberately follows the precedent set by Kant's Transcendental Logic, the subject matter of traditional logic still requires a niche in the system—and is given one, rather oddly, *above* the analysis of the categories which has supplanted metaphysics. Hegelian metaphysics comes at the bottom, traditional logic above it. We simply have to discard the popular misrepresentations and all considerations of tops and bottoms. The analysis of the categories comes first because all subsequent discourse, including logic, involves them. Traditional logic is a way of manipulating such categories.

Some other subjects still remained to be taken care of before the philosophy of nature: they are put into the second of the three sections. By calling the first, which covers traditional logic, "Subjectivity," and this one "Objectivity," a semblance of symmetry is created; and one must concede that the whole arrangement looks very neat. Alas, it looks too neat. The poor man who was struggling to impose some order on excess and abundance created such an imposing appearance of neatness that readers who saw little but the table of contents assumed that the relentless progress upwards of which they had been told was plainly there, with "Objectivity" the plain antithesis of "Subjectivity," as if these two headings were not the most palpable afterthoughts.

It should at least have struck such non-readers that while the "Subjective" Logic came above the "Objective" Logic, here "Objectivity" comes above "Subjectivity." Hegel's emphatic disclaimer about all these headings (H 43) wants to be taken at face value. It would perhaps be excessively irreverent to say that there still had to be a "third section" which naturally became the place for any leftovers—much as a speaker, groping for a conclusion after an unusually long talk, looks for a few high-sounding and noble words that will make a good ending. So Hegel brings in life and knowledge, the true and the good—but suddenly, almost unaccountably, stops with "B. The idea of the good" and does *not* round it off with "C. The idea of the beautiful." There is no "C" this time, and the beautiful is left out of the *Logic*.

This omission is the beauty spot on the otherwise too-perfect complexion of the work. It seems deliberate, a touch of spite, an indication that the author was not a slave to triads. In any case, in the *Encyclopedia* "The Idea" is still subdivided into "Life," "Knowledge" (this heading represents a very slight change from "The idea of knowledge"), and "The absolute idea"; but "Knowledge" is not broken down into the true and the good, as in the *Logic,* but into "knowing" and "willing."

50

The four volumes—or two books—which unquestionably constitute Hegel's most original contributions were written by him between the ages of thirty-five and forty-five when he was lonely and far from successful. Other philosophers, his own age or even a little younger, had obtained chairs and fame, while he had no influence whatsoever. When the first book came out, he was editing a small newspaper; when the second came out in three installments, he was earning his living as the headmaster of a secondary school.

How obviously miscast he was in that role was summed up best by Clemens Brentano, the famous romantic, in a letter to a friend. One may well doubt the truth of his remark, but there is no denying that it is at least well invented: "In Nürnberg I found the honest, wooden Hegel as the principal of the Gymnasium; he read the Edda and Nibelungen, and to be able to enjoy them he translated them, as he was reading, into Greek."[49]

[49] Joseph von Görres, *Gesammelte Briefe,* II (1874), 75; quoted in Fischer, 2d ed. (1911), 1209.

Hegel was indeed as far as ever from the romantics' aspirations to glorify the German past and the Catholic Middle Ages, aspirations with which Brentano was prominently associated. Hegel was no patriot; he had no real home; he did not belong anywhere. He put his heart into the books he was writing—and into a sentence that he wrote into a *Stammbuch* where it lay buried until it was published in 1960:[50]

> "Not curiosity, not vanity, not the consideration of expediency, not duty and conscientiousness, but an unquenchable, unhappy thirst that brooks no compromise leads us to truth.
>
> Nürnberg, Sep. 30, 1809   Written to remember
>   HEGEL, Prof. & Principal."

[50] B IV, 67.

CHAPTER V

The System

51

In Heidelberg, where he went as a professor at the age of forty-six, Hegel faced new problems. The most urgent perhaps was that professors were expected to use "compendia" in connection with their courses at German universities, and though he had by then published four remarkable volumes, they certainly were not "Compendia." A "compendium" is "an abridgement of a larger work or treatise, giving the sense and substance within smaller compass; an epitome, a summary."[1] Hegel's works were at the opposite extreme.

To understand his predicament, it will be helpful to see briefly what Kant had done: "As a basis for his lectures he used the compendia of Meier, Baumgarten, Achenwall, and Eberhard. The use of such textbooks . . . was then quite general at German universities, and the professors at Königsberg were even specifically admonished in this regard by an edict of the minister von Zedlitz [to whom Kant dedicated his *Critique of Pure Reason* in 1781], dated October 16, 1778: 'The worst compendium is certainly better than none, and if the professors possess so much wisdom, they may criticize their author as much as they can; but lecturing about *dictata* simply has to be abolished.' . . . Even in the eighties and nineties he [Kant] still followed his 'author' at least externally—to be sure, more often to contradict than to agree."[2]

Immediately before his lectures, Kant often made notes in the compendia he used, referring to their paragraphs and problems, and

[1] *The Shorter Oxford English Dictionary.*
[2] Kant's *Gesammelte Schriften*, Akademieausgabe, XIV (1911), xxi.

then used these notes as he lectured; other notes were probably put down right after the lectures when his comments were still fresh in his mind (*ibid.*).

At Jena Hegel had kept announcing the forthcoming publication of a book that he hoped to use in connection with his courses; but no such book ever appeared while he lectured at Jena, and so he had lectured about *dictata*. He had carried over this form of instruction into the Gymnasium at Nürnberg. On the basis of his notes, he had dictated short passages to his students and then elaborated them in his lectures; and some students had written down his elaborations and given them to him for correction. Rosenkranz discovered a bundle of these notes when he visited Hegel's widow in Berlin. The ordering of the sheets presented a problem, and so did the many corrections and additions in the margins; but he carefully edited this material, and in 1840 it was published in volume XVIII of the master's collected works, under the title *Philosophische Propädeutik:* two hundred eight consecutively numbered paragraphs, not including the four-page introduction, covering roughly two hundred pages.

One recalls Brentano's lovely story (H 50) and realizes that Hegel would have gone out of his mind teaching philosophy in this demented fashion, had he not been able to write the *Logic* on the side. Or we might say, conversely, that he worked at the Gymnasium on the side, to earn a living while he was writing his *Logic*.

Having written four volumes that seemed to him to carry philosophy in a really significant way beyond Kant—not to speak of Meier, Achenwall, and Eberhard—Hegel, arrived at Heidelberg, did not feel like wasting time on the criticism of authors of no account. Unable to put his own ideas into book form, he had begun his career at the beginning of the century by dealing polemically with Krug and Schulze; now he had no wish to return to that level or, worse yet, to the compendia that were available. So he began by once again lecturing *ex dictatis;* but on the side he dashed off a compendium of his own, which was published in 1817. He had begun lecturing late in the fall of 1816.

The compendium was called *Encyklopädie der philosophischen Wissenschaften im Grundrisse: Zum Gebrauch seiner Vorlesungen:* "Encyclopedia of the Philosophical Sciences in Outline Form, for Use in Connection with his Lectures." The book begins: "The need to place in my students' hands a textbook for my philosophical lectures is the proximate cause for my letting this survey of the whole scope of philosophy appear sooner than I should have thought of doing otherwise."

He had been planning to write a system of philosophy even before he arrived in Jena, in January 1801; the *Phenomenology* had been intended as the introduction, the *Logic* as the first part; but now nothing on that scale would do at all. What was needed in a hurry was a compendium, and that is exactly what the *Encyclopedia* was. On 288 uncrowded pages, it presented in 477 consecutively numbered paragraphs, first, comprising not quite half of the book, an abridgment of the *Logic,* and then an abridgment of his as-yet-unwritten, or at least unpublished, philosophy of nature and philosophy of spirit. He had notes enough for those two parts, but to work them up into a book that could stand side by side with his previous volumes would have taken years. By quickly writing an immensely terse compendium, Hegel could point to a text whatever he might lecture on, and there was never any danger that the text made the lectures dispensable. This was the origin of the book that contained Hegel's famous system.

52

This book exists in four different forms, in German. We have considered the original edition. Ten years later, in 1827, Hegel published a second edition. He added a thirty-page preface, greatly expanded the introduction, let the *Vorbegriff* grow to more than four times its original size by finding a place in it for his remarkable discussion of dogmatic metaphysics, empiricism and skepticism, Kant's critical philosophy, and intuitionism, rewrote and expanded the rest of the book, too, and wound up with a work over twice the length of the original compendium. Still, there were more paragraphs than pages, showing at a glance that most of the paragraphs were less than a page in length. The compendium style was maintained, and title and subtitle remained unchanged; indeed, the purpose of the publication was plainly still the same.

The third edition (1830) is basically very similar to the second, though there now are three prefaces, 577 paragraphs instead of 574, and a few more pages as well. On close examination, however, one discovers literally thousands of changes. Even in his approach to this most cut-and-dried of his books, Hegel until right before his death was not by any means a man who had stopped thinking and rethinking.

In fact, every lecture tended to be a tortuous performance because Hegel was not content to repeat what he had written, or what he had said in previous years. The manner in which he lectured is highly relevant to the fourth and most influential edition of the *Encyclopedia*. It is also relevant to the influential posthumous edition of the *Philosophy of Right* (originally published in compendium form in 1821), and to the famous lectures on the philosophy of history, of art, of religion, and on the history of philosophy, all of which were published only after Hegel's death.

When the *Encyclopedia* appeared in the collected works—and the same is also true of the *Philosophy of Right*—the editors supplemented Hegel's terse paragraphs with what they called, and clearly marked as, *Zusätze* (additions). These additions were based on their lecture notes, or on the notes taken by fellow students. With these additions, the *Encyclopedia* took up three fat volumes— over sixteen hundred pages—and what had begun as a slim compendium to meet Hegel's needs as a lecturer had now grown into an imposing system.[3]

Even in the third edition, the abridgment of the *Logic* had been roughly as long as the original *Logic* down to the end of the first chapter. It was perfectly clear that anyone interested in Hegel's *Logic* had to turn to the work by that name, while the abridgment was, as the subtitle plainly indicated, "for use in connection with his lectures." Now, in the posthumous edition, the abridgment of the *Logic* grew into a whole big book, and it came to look as if one could take one's pick between the earlier big *Logic* or the later, perhaps more definitive, "Lesser Logic."

Until 1929, as mentioned above, the *Logic* was never rendered into English, complete; but a volume *called The Logic of Hegel* (Wallace's translation of the "Lesser Logic") went through two editions in the nineteenth century—and Wallace did not even mark the additions as clearly as the German editors had done. He merely used slightly smaller print. Since Hegel himself had made a typographical distinction between the main portion of each sec-

---

[3] The three volumes, each edited by a different man, appeared in 1840, 1842, and 1845. Bolland's huge one-volume edition (1906) reprints this text with added footnotes of his own.

tion and the notes[4] elaborating many of these, and Wallace ignores *this* distinction altogether, the additions in his text are often mistaken for part of Hegel's text.[5] Wallace further confounded confusion by not only misnaming his book, *The Logic of Hegel,* but by actually making a two-volume work of it, the first volume being taken up by his own *Prolegomena,* of which the less said, the better.

That the additions contain some nice phrases and examples, and that they are often clearer than the crabbed paragraphs they follow, there is no denying. If they had not been published as additions but rather in a separate volume, under some such title as "The Wit and Wisdom of Hegel, in Quotations from his Lectures," they would not be as problematic as they are. What is wrong with any heavy reliance on them comes under two headings.

First, it might seem that the students' procedure was entirely legitimate. After all, "Hegel's procedure was to read the text of a paragraph either entirely or one section at a time, then freely adding his comments. (The so-called notes which form part of many paragraphs, usually were not read out loud . . .)"[6] Yet the printed additions do not for the most part contain Hegel's comments on the paragraphs after which they are printed.

Until 1827 the lectures were based on the first edition of the *Encyclopedia,* and the editors had a lot of material that was based on these lectures and did not readily fit into the radically revised third edition into which they inserted the additions. From 1827 until 1830 the lectures were based on the second edition. In the summer of 1830 Hegel was able for the first time to use the third edition, and in November 1831 he died.

Hegel still lectured on the first part of the 1830 *Encyclopedia* both in the summer of 1830 and again in the summer of 1831, and

[4] T. M. Knox, in his translation of Hegel's *Philosophy of Right* calls them "Remarks." He includes the additions—together, at the end of the volume: an admirable solution.

[5] J. Loewenberg, in his *Hegel Selections,* in his own translation from what he calls Hegel's "Philosophy of Law," runs Hegel's text and Gans's additions into each other to form one continuous essay—and occasionally mistranslates. (For the most influential mistranslation, see WK 98.) Moreover, parts of Hegel's system are represented by selections from the *Propädeutik,* and Baillie's version of the preface to the *Phenomenology* is reprinted intact, without any attempt to correct the most obvious slips (necessarily even from Baillie's first edition, as the revised second edition appeared only after the *Hegel Selections*).

[6] F. Nicolin and Otto Pöggeler in their introduction to their critical edition of the *Enzyklopädie* of 1830 (1959), xxxi. Cf. text for note [4] above.

on the philosophy of nature (the second part of the book) in the
summer of 1830[7]; but the mass of the additions, even for these two
parts of the *Encyclopedia,* does not come from these final lectures.
In the case of the philosophy of nature, most of the material in the
additions is taken from Hegel's Jena lectures, delivered before he
had published the *Phenomenology,* over twenty-five years before he
published the book in which these additions are embedded.[8]

The editors did not indicate from which year their additions came,
and in many an addition they amalgamated notes based on lectures
given a great many years apart.[9] This does not merely mean that
many additions do not represent any single train of thought; it also
means that the editors had to supply all sorts of transitions, in their
own words, and that, in order to effect some unity of style, they
had to change what Hegel had said—or rather what he had said
according to the lecture notes of students.[10]

This brings us to the second reason for regarding the additions
with some suspicion. We have to consider Hegel's manner of lecturing. This is not merely of biographical interest, or of importance
only for the proper estimate of the additions; it is also crucial for
any estimate of the nine volumes of his lectures on the philosophy
of history, aesthetics, philosophy of religion, and history of philosophy.[11]

All of these lecture cycles have been translated into English, al-

---

[7] See Hoffmeister's "Übersicht über Hegels Berliner Vorlesungen" in his
critical edition of *Berliner Schriften: 1818–1831* (1956), 743–49.
[8] Ros. 193.
[9] "Altogether, the editors have worked together, without making any distinctions, lectures of all academic years, and Michelet actually used for the
philosophy of nature also Hegel's Jena drafts for his system.—Moreover,
the editors permitted themselves the most variegated changes, for stylistic
reasons, even in the printed text of the *Encyclopedia,* especially in the second
and third parts. The first section of the philosophy of spirit alone, which
comprises 105 paragraphs . . . , contains over 150 such editorial changes
which, not infrequently, change the meaning of the original text." Nicolin
and Pöggeler, *op. cit.,* xlv.
[10] Leopold von Henning, for example, says frankly in his editorial preface
to the first volume of the *Encyclopedia* (the one known in English as *The
Logic of Hegel,* translated by Wallace): "Whenever the . . . material was
insufficient, the editor did not hesitate . . . to complete from his own memory
the explanations that seemed necessary." Particularly in the early parts, he
admits, he did a lot of this.
[11] In the original German collected works (reproduced photomechanically
in Glockner's *Jubiläumsausgabe*), these four cycles comprise, respectively,
one, three, two, and three volumes. The English version of the *Philosophy
of Fine Arts* takes up four volumes; Lasson's critical edition of the Philosophy
of History, also four.

though many of Hegel's own writings have not been translated, and some of these lecture cycles are much better known than the *Phenomenology* and the *Logic*. The lectures on the philosophy of history are almost certainly Hegel's best known "work," in English as well as in German. Before we turn to consider Hegel as a lecturer, it should be noted emphatically that the reservations already stated in this section apply to the lectures as well—in fact, even more so. Here, too, the early editors amalgamated notes taken many years apart, and welded into a single sequence thoughts that had never formed any such sequence.

Even more than in the case of the additions, a consecutive narrative was wanted, and therefore even greater liberties had to be taken. Lest all this sound as if the editors had been unscrupulous, it should be kept in mind that the standards of modern philology developed considerably during the nineteenth and twentieth centuries. To the early editors it seemed important to let others share every worthy remark from the master's lips, and if good ideas, formulations, and examples were to be found in every single set of lecture notes, they considered it imperative to use them all. They did not want a vast historical-critical edition that might take decades to prepare and would then repose in a few large libraries to be consulted only by specialists. They wanted to make everything as readable, straight through, as possible. So a single narrative had to be created in every case, not volumes in which one could compare how the lectures changed every time Hegel offered them.

What these men fashioned was readable, and it created an image of Hegel that, with slight variations, stood for a century. Their editions were referred to by the readers of Kierkegaard's and Marx's polemics against Hegel; their editions were the only ones available when Hegel went into eclipse in Germany around the middle of the nineteenth century; and their editions were used by the English translators and interpreters of Hegel, as well as the British Idealists.

In the twentieth century, Lasson began the slow work of exhuming the true Hegel by publishing critical editions; Hoffmeister took over from him; and after he, too, died, a number of others continued a job that, sixty years after Lasson began, is nowhere near completion. But unlike most other enterprises of a similar scope, this one has had the immense good fortune of having a publisher—Felix Meiner—who has made each volume available separately, as far as possible at prices that students can afford. While some of the critical editions have by now gone through several revised editions, making citations a ticklish matter, these volumes, particularly the latest editions available, must be the basis for all responsible work on Hegel.[12]

The prefaces to the more recent critical editions and the lists of variant readings at the end of some of the volumes contain many examples of the liberties the original nineteenth-century editors took, introducing changes even into texts that Hegel himself had published, from his early articles and the *Phenomenology* down to the last edition of the *Encyclopedia* and some of his *Berliner Schriften*. For intellectual history this is a point of some interest when one considers, for example, how polemics against the editing of Nietzsche's works have failed to distinguish between the outright forgeries his sister introduced into some of his letters (even into the manuscripts; but generally only to publish as addressed to herself what had in fact been written to others) and the sort of thing that Hegel's editors did, too. While it is reasonable to ask for philologically sound editions, it is often utterly unreasonable[13] to malign the motives and the good character of those who have not employed the very highest standards, which are sometimes as difficult to put into practice as they are rare. Certainly, Hegel's lectures pose a very great problem for any editor.

53

As a lecturer Hegel was, to begin with, wholly unprepossessing. A brief description has already been given at the beginning of section 24; but that refers to the young Hegel at Jena. A long de-

[12] The prices, of course, have gone up, and few students can afford the *Berliner Schriften* and the invaluable four volumes of *Briefe*. When it comes to the books Hegel himself published, direct reference to the first editions sometimes shows things that even the critical editions do not indicate; and the more than 3600 differences of some importance between the second edition of the *Encyclopedia* (1827), which has never been reprinted, and the third of 1830 have never been listed in print. For the figure of 3600, see Nicolin and Pöggeler, *op. cit.*, xlviii. They also point out that even Hoffmeister's edition of 1949 was marred by approximately seventy errors that changed the meaning, including *Theorie* instead of *Theologie* and *psychologischen* instead of *physiologischen*.

[13] Cf. E. F. Podach, *Friedrich Nietzsches Werke des Zusammenbruchs* (1961), who is extremely harsh on earlier editors, and my article on "Nietzsche in the Light of His Suppressed Manuscripts" in *Journal of the History of Philosophy*, Oct. 1964.

scription, by H. G. Hotho, who also edited the three volumes of Hegel's lectures on aesthetics, will be found near the end of D: it shows how Hotho was put off at first, and how he then came to appreciate Hegel's style, even to the point of writing about it in a rather rhapsodical vein. Hotho's own style seems badly dated, but anyone interested in any of Hegel's lecture cycles ought to read his lengthy account—and then ask himself whether it is borne out by the nine volumes that are generally accepted as the substance of Hegel's lectures.

There can be no doubt whatsoever about the answer; or about the fact that Hotho's little-known description is essentially true to life, while the lectures we read were never delivered in any such form by Hegel. Snippets of Hotho's account have been quoted by Fischer and Glockner,[14] but the full account, to be found only in Hotho's long-forgotten little book *Vorstudien für Leben und Kunst* (1835) is practically unknown.

In his preface (also 1835) to Hegel's *Aesthetik,* Hotho explains how he has tried to turn forbidding notes into a well-written book. Lasson, in the preface to his own critical edition of the same lectures (1931), takes a rather different view of the matter. He prefers the raw materials to the "lightness, smoothness, and elegance" which Hotho missed and tried to introduce on his own. "How high-handed Hotho's procedure was is shown by the mere fact that he divides the whole work into three parts while Hegel himself in his synopsis expressly indicates a division into two parts, one general and one specific. . . . While Hegel declares in the opening words of his lectures that he excludes the beauty of nature from his aesthetics, Hotho offers an extensive chapter on the beauty of nature," which he composes of relevant passages cut out of their original contexts.

Of one of Hegel's lecture cycles two very different editions appeared within ten years of Hegel's death: *The Philosophy of History.* In the preface to the second edition (1840), Karl Hegel, the philosopher's son, explained that Eduard Gans, the original editor who had died in 1839, had based his text on the lectures given in 1830–31. This had been the last time Hegel gave the course, but Karl Hegel found the versions of 1822–23 and 1824–25 much more to his liking because they seemed to him to have a freshness that got lost in later years. Although his father had changed the course considerably every time he gave it, Karl Hegel inserted his favorite

[14] Fischer, I, 214–16; Glockner, I, 440–42.

passages from the two earlier versions in Gans's text, here and there.

All this was in keeping with the spirit of an age in which a mediocre Danish sculptor, Bertel Thorwaldsen (1770–1844), had been commissioned to restore the magnificent archaic Greek sculptures found in Aegina before they were placed on exhibit in Munich: "Their restoration was somewhat drastic, the ancient parts being cut away to allow of additions in marble."[15] One did not feel that the weathered torsos were infinitely more beautiful in the state in which they were found than after their "completion." Around 1900 Arthur Evans still perpetrated similar horrors on the frescoes of Knossos in Crete, commissioning a Swiss painter of less distinction than Thorwaldsen to complete the fragments, instead of having him execute Evans' ideas on a museum wall. In the case of Hegel, it might be supposed that the editors, unlike Thorwaldsen and Evans, did no irreparable damage; but a great many manuscripts they used are no longer extant.

Before we take leave of Karl Hegel, however, we should quote him on one point on which he clearly gives expression to his father's spirit: "For those who identify the rigor of thought with a formal schematism and even turn this polemically against another mode of doing philosophy, it may still be remarked that Hegel clung so little to the subdivisions he had once made that he changed them every time he gave a course. . . . The sureness of thought and the certainty of truth can be liberal in such matters, as is life itself; and the formal understanding that takes offense at this only shows that it still lacks any essential grasp of the philosophic idea and of life" (19).

These words are well taken as a prophetic warning against the charts in some books on Hegel that present his subdivisions as the core of his dialectical philosophy. And while no art historian of repute would base his discussion of archaic Greek sculpture on Thorwaldsen's additions, philosophers of repute do not hesitate to base dicta about Hegel on his editors' additions, on their reconstructions of his lectures, and on their tables of contents and arrangements.

To return to Hegel's style as a lecturer, this was explained by Rosenkranz (16 f.) substantially as Hotho had explained it nine years earlier, but Rosenkranz stated the main point briefly:

[15] *Encyclopaedia Britannica*, 11th ed., I, 252, under "Aegina." The article on Thorwaldsen, XXVI, 882, is also relevant.

"For those who can master the external presentation because they are finished with the subject, there is no inhibition between the inward and its expression. Their feeling, imagination, and thought are simultaneously communicated in their speech. For Hegel, even if he had put the speech on paper beforehand, there always remained a residue in this process. He always produced the content anew and therefore could always be only relatively finished, even for the moment. This struggle with the presentation to find the definitive, penetrating expression that would leave nothing behind; this incessant search; this wealth of possibilities made more difficult for him as the years passed—the richer his education became, the more many-sided his thought, and the greater his position—not only speaking in general but also writing; and one cannot find anything more hacked to pieces, more crossed out, more constantly rewritten than one of Hegel's drafts for a letter from the Berlin period."

Lecturing was not Hegel's forte. He obviously found it a harrowing experience, and so did his listeners. At Heidelberg he never became a major attraction. He had arrived there ahead of his family, and on October 29, 1816, wrote his wife:

"Yesterday I began my lectures, but the number of the students is not as splendid as represented and pretended. I was, if not perplexed and impatient, surprised not to find things as I had been led to expect. For *one* course I had only 4 listeners. But Paulus consoled me that he, too, had lectured for a mere 4 or 5. . . . The first semester when one first comes here one has to be satisfied to have a chance to get oneself across. The students must first warm up to one. . . ."

Before he left Heidelberg, he had over twenty in one course, over thirty in another. But the audience for his eloquent first lecture at Heidelberg, October 28, 1816—introducing his course on the history of philosophy, from which we shall quote when we reach that part of his system[16]—evidently comprised about ten listeners, if that many.

For the initial impact of his lectures at Berlin we can again cite Rosenkranz (320):

"But as great as the expectations of Solger, the ministry, and many people in Berlin had been concerning Hegel's effectiveness,

[16] EGP 1–17. This lecture was written out by Hegel in advance and could be published on the basis of his own manuscript. Quotation in H 67.

his appearance here, too, was soundless, without pomp and ado, and it was only gradually that he penetrated to the point of irresistibility. On November 22, 1818, Solger wrote Tieck: 'I was curious what kind of an impression the good Hegel would make here. Nobody speaks of him, for he is quiet and industrious. If the most stupid imitator had come here—the kind they would love to have here—they would make a terrific noise and the students would be sent into his courses for the salvation of their souls.' "

The main two reasons for Hegel's eventual success as a lecturer, to the point where he often, though by no means always, had over a hundred students in a course and once, just once, two hundred—when he lectured "On the Proofs of God's Existence" in the summer of 1829—are perfectly plain. First, word got around by and by that he was Germany's greatest living philosopher. Secondly, those who stuck with him became convinced that he was profound.

54

To begin with the first point, this was surely true. No German philosopher since Kant, with the exception of Nietzsche, who had not been born at that time, is in the same class. Schelling was still living, but had long disappeared from public view and had ceased to contribute to the development of philosophy, and Schopenhauer did not become famous until the middle of the century.

Schopenhauer's *magnum opus,* the original one-volume edition of *The World as Will and Representation,* had fallen stillborn from the press in 1819, without attracting any attention. On the last day of that year he applied to the philosophical faculty at Berlin and asked to be included in the next catalogue (*Vorlesungsverzeichnis*), with a course of six lecture hours weekly on "the whole of philosophy"—and that before he had fulfilled the usual requirements for habilitation. He left it to the faculty to fix the time, but added: "the most suitable time is presumably whenever Herr Prof. Hegel gives his biggest course [*sein Hauptcollegium*]."

The dean, while specifically commenting on Schopenhauer's "no mean presumption and extraordinary vanity" favored approval of the request, provided the requirements were fulfilled before he actually began to lecture. Hegel went along with this; other professors did not. One protested against inclusion of the announcement in the catalogue before the requirements were fulfilled, while another wrote: "I confess that the exceptionally great arrogance of Herrn S. does not incline me very much to declare myself in favor of any special exceptions on his behalf by action of the faculty"—and several others subscribed to that.

Nevertheless, the government representative looked favorably on Schopenhauer's request, the dean so informed Schopenhauer, and the young man came to Berlin to confer with Hegel on the title of his test lecture (*Probevorlesung*). March 18, 1820, he wrote the dean that he had asked Hegel the day before for permission to lecture on a subject he himself had chosen, namely on four kinds of causes. "Herr Prof. Hegel very graciously granted his approval with the greatest readiness. . . ."

It is indeed "unmistakable that Hegel placed no obstacles of any kind in Schopenhauer's way," as Hoffmeister puts it.[17] He also says: "In the whole decade from 1820 to 1831 we do not find anything more miserable regarding the lecturing by *Privatdozenten* of philosophy than the total failure of Schopenhauer." He never completed a course. After his initial approach, he was absent from Berlin for many years, then in the spring of 1826 asked permission to lecture again. He again chose the time when Hegel lectured, but not a single student showed up to hear him. The next semester he did not lecture because only one student came; after that, because only three appeared; after that, because only two came. The next three times—the topic always being the same "Foundations of Philosophy, comprehending Dianoology and Logic"—nobody came; in the summer of 1830, three students; the following winter again nobody; and then Schopenhauer left again. Later he published a famous diatribe against "University Philosophy," and again and again poured out venom against Hegel in bitter polemics.

Ritter, one of Schleiermacher's disciples, offered a course on ancient philosophy at the same hour at which Hegel lectured on philosophy of nature, in the summer of 1828, and Ritter had eighty-four students, while Hegel had sixty-eight. Other *Privatdozenten*, whether followers or opponents of Hegel, generally were content to start with a few students and after a while averaged between

---

[17] *Berliner Schriften*, 589. The account in the text is indebted to the section on Schopenhauer, 587–92, which is based on the documents.

fifteen and thirty. Hegel himself, as we have seen, once started with four. Although Schopenhauer liked to denounce him as a windbag, it seems clear that Hegel's more serious students soon gained the impression that while he lacked verbal facility, flamboyance, and showmanship—qualities that were not lacking in Schopenhauer's manner at that time—he was truly profound and amply repaid the effort it took to follow him.

55

Of course, the majority of those who came to listen to Hegel were not really serious about philosophy. As time went on, it became fashionable to hear him. Writing in 1844, Rosenkranz gave an interesting account of this phenomenon. This passage also furnishes an example, in the last sentence, of an objectionable use of the word "necessity." Hegel often misused the word in the same way; but this solecism, though by no means innocuous philosophically, is really a commonplace in German scholarly prose down to our time.

"Hegel's main effect on Berlin, philosophically, was that he really took the people to school and with naïve rigidity taught them his system. The previously described character of Berlin favored this *discipline* [*Zucht*], as Hegel himself liked to call it, to an extraordinary degree, since the Berliners have an immense potential and hunger for education but are as yet not very creative on their own. Thus they practically ask to be dominated and tolerate it gladly if only one does it with esprit [*geistreich*] and knows how to give them nourishment. Thus it was a great good fortune for the cheerful city that the Schleiermacher element with its versatile mobility was opposed by the Hegel element with its solid, neatly inclusive systematic approach and its insistence on method. But for Hegel and his school, too, it was a great favor of fortune that Schleiermacher's erudition, spirit, wit, renown, and popular strength did not allow it to shoot up too rapidly and continually created problems for it. Or rather, what we call good fortune was, viewed from a higher vantage point, the necessity [!] of the German spirit to place the classical representative of northeastern education in an immediate relationship with that of the southwest in order to introduce in this way a more profound and all-sided reconciliation of the German spirit with itself" (327).

No love was lost between Hegel and Schleiermacher. In his early article on "Faith and Knowledge" (1802), Hegel had called the author of *Reden über die Religion* (1799), without mentioning his name, a "virtuoso of edification and enthusiasm." Now they were colleagues in Berlin. The only two letters they ever exchanged date from November 1819 and are translated in D. Schleiermacher had a great reputation at that time, but today is largely forgotten, except by theologians. Others remember him mainly for saying that "The essence of religion consists in the feeling of an absolute dependence." Hegel's comment deserves to be remembered too: "Then the dog would be the best Christian." A *Privatdozent* at Berlin, von Keyserlingk, "wrote a philosophy of religion in 1824 and gave lectures on it, expressly against this remark, which Schleiermacher's friends and disciples . . . never forgave Hegel."[18]

And what were Hegel's own disciples like? Rosenkranz distinguished "three groups: the level-headed, the effusive, and the empty.

"The first comprised the quiet but profound minds who absorbed the new philosophy with lasting seriousness and then proceeded from it gradually, without any noise, to cultivate particular fields of scholarship.

"The second group, the effusive ones, were less scientific and more poetic. Hegel's conception of world history, his philosophy of art, the peculiarly poetic expressions that frequently break through his dialectic . . . all this delighted them. Their imagination received new materials from him. . . . As time went on, such encomia became so heated and intense that Hegel was venerated, not indistinctly, as a philosophical savior of the world.

"The majority of the disciples, of course, was constituted by the group of the empty who were especially fit to teach again quickly what they had learned fast . . ." (382).

Rosenkranz also thought that Hegel himself "gradually got used to the notion that for speculative education salvation could indeed be found only within his philosophy" (381). Perhaps there was

[18] Ros. 346. The relationship of Hegel and Schleiermacher is discussed 325 f.; cf. also D 1819 and the Appendix to Fischer, 2d ed., 1216–18 (1216–23 deal with "Hegel's position in the scholarly world in Berlin").

Hegel's remark is found in his preface to Hinrichs's *Die Religion* . . . (1822), *Berliner Schriften* (1956), 74: "If a man's religion were founded merely on a feeling, this would indeed have no further determination beyond being the *feeling of his dependence,* and then the dog would be the best Christian, for he has this feeling most intensely and lives most in it."

what Hegel liked to call a *Wechselwirkung:* their faith kindled his, and then his strengthened theirs.

Hegel had arrived; he was successful at long last; he was more famous than any other philosopher had been in Hegel's lifetime, save only Kant. In the preface to the *Phenomenology* he had argued that the time had come for what he proposed to do; and near the end he had stated his conviction "that it is of the nature of truth to prevail when its time has come." Now that his own philosophy, ignored and neglected at first, had prevailed against all odds, and he certainly could not charge its success to his literary brilliance or his fiery lectures, he must have considered this a most significant corroboration of its truth.

For all that, he retained a sense of perspective and distinguished between what was significant and presumably superior to the ideas of other contemporary philosophers, and details that were, no doubt, faulty. It was in that spirit, for example, that he kept revising his *Encyclopedia* until a year before his death. And his modesty about details is probably best illustrated by his letter to Daub, a colleague at Heidelberg who had offered his help in connection with the second edition of the *Encyclopedia*. Since the publisher was in Heidelberg, Hegel wrote Daub from Berlin, August 15, 1826:

"Finally, most revered friend, I am able to begin today or tomorrow with the mailing of the manuscript of the second edition of my *Encyclopedia*. I inform you of this, grateful for your gracious offer to take over in friendship the correction of the proofs. As much as I am obligated to you for this, I also have a bad conscience in view of the condition of the manuscript: I may have relied too much on you; for it is really such that it demands an attentive printer; so you may have more trouble than I could decently expect you to go to. But I did try to mark the changes, insertions, etc., very carefully and definitely. Moreover, I give you complete freedom wherever you encounter obscurity, incomprehensibility, also repetitions, to correct, delete, and improve entirely as you see fit. . . ."

Some of his disciples, of course, would never have dreamed of speaking of "obscurity, incomprehensibility," or even of lesser faults. But such are disciples in all ages: "What he said and how he did it was considered definitive by many and unqualifiedly worthy of applause and imitation. Even those were not lacking who sought to copy his gestures and speech."[19]

[19] Ros. 357.

56

Let us now consider the system. Hegel had decided long ago that it was to have three parts: Logic, philosophy of nature, and philosophy of spirit. Now it was obviously *not* the examination of the categories in the *Logic* that gradually led him to the point where it became plain that, once you entrust yourself to the inexorable dialectic, you are driven all the way from being to the absolute idea, which then irresistibly releases itself into nature, so that the philosophy of nature has to come next. Nor was it through years of study of the philosophy of nature that Hegel eventually came to see how the animal organism gives birth to its antithesis, the spirit, so that philosophy of the spirit must come third. Something like this fantastic construction is presupposed in many a discussion of Hegel. But what happened is obviously quite different.

Philosophy existed and even flourished before Hegel took it up. By the time he decided to contribute to it, several distinct branches of philosophy were well established. There was, for example, metaphysics, discussed by Kant in his Transcendental Logic, in the first *Critique*. There was moral and political philosophy, and recently some remarkable essays had been written on history; especially by Kant and Lessing, Herder and Schiller. Kant had also written on aesthetics; so had others. Kant and Fichte had written on religion, and Hegel himself was particularly interested in that. And then there was the philosophy of nature, cultivated especially by Schelling and, a little later, by his followers, too. There might be yet other fields: anthropology, on which Kant had published a book; psychology; perhaps also the history of philosophy, which certainly merited serious study.

The question confronting a man who thought that the time had come for philosophy to become systematic, and who wanted to construct a system, was how to order these various fields of inquiry. The point was plainly that as long as one pursues now one problem, and then another—as long, in short, as one philosophizes haphazardly—one is not likely to reap one's full benefits. By bringing to bear the results of one inquiry upon another, and by checking each against each, one was ever so much more likely to reach the truth. Indeed, if one were to hit the truth in any other fashion, it would be scarcely more than an accident. The only scientific procedure was to be systematic and to cover the whole field, branch by branch. (There is no need here to go into further detail about that because Hegel discusses the matter at length in his preface to the *Phenomenology*.)[20]

The word "system" was, one might say, in the air. Fichte had called his ethic *System der Sittenlehre* (1798). Schelling had published his *System des transcendentalen Idealismus* two years later. Hegel might have said of either, as he did so many times in his critique of Kant's ethic in the *Phenomenology*, in another context: "but he is not really serious about it." They had spoken of "system" without making a really rigorous and comprehensive attempt to construct a system in such a way that it would be clear where anything they had written had its place in the system.

This, then, was what Hegel resolved to do; this was his aim when he came to Jena; this was the enterprise to which the *Phenomenology* was intended as an introduction. His reasons for making his *Logic* the first part of the system have been considered in the previous chapter (H 42): the categories, which are basic to all discourse, are to be examined first.

Once one considers "philosophy of spirit" as one major part of the whole, it is clear that most of the rest of philosophy can be fitted into that: certainly, moral and political philosophy as well as philosophy of history; also aesthetics, philosophy of religion, the history of philosophy, and indeed even anthropology and psychology. What, then, remains? The philosophy of nature. This would be the proper place for discussing space and time and saying something about inorganic and organic nature. The decision was never seriously in doubt: this would, of course, come *before* the philosophy of spirit; the philosophy of nature would end with some remarks about animals, and the philosophy of the (human) spirit would come after that. The system, however, was not conceived as a ladder but as a circle, and charts that mechanically copy the table of contents are therefore misleading. The following figure shows what Hegel meant:

[20] For a comparison of Hegel's view with Nietzsche's ("the will to a system is a lack of integrity" and is "in a philosopher, morally speaking, a subtle corruption, a disease of the character; amorally speaking, his will to appear more stupid than he is") see my *Nietzsche* (1950), 58–73; Meridian ed., 65–80. There I have also gone into the merits of both positions.

Although many interpreters have simply ignored this, Hegel insisted repeatedly that the spirit is "the circle that returns into itself, that presupposes its beginning and reaches it only in the end," as he put it near the end of the *Phenomenology*.[21] In the preliminary essay in the *Logic*, "With what must the beginning of science be made?" Hegel said: "What is essential for science is not so much that something purely immediate should constitute the beginning but rather that the whole of it is a circle in which the first also becomes the last, and the last also the first. . . . The line of scientific progress thus becomes *a circle*."[22] And two pages before the end of the *Logic* we are reminded again that science is a circle, indeed "a circle of circles."[23]

Our diagram is obviously greatly oversimplified. The subdivisions of the Logic and the philosophy of nature have been omitted altogether to avoid confusion. Those of the Logic have in any case been presented in the last chapter. As a result, the philosophy of spirit occupies much more than one third of the whole system— which is as it should be. Proportionately, subjective spirit looms far too large in our diagram; absolute spirit not nearly large enough.

[21] Lasson's edition, 516; Baillie's, 801: about half a dozen pages from the end.
[22] 1841, 61; Glockner, IV, 75.
[23] Müller, 296, presents a diagram of the system as a circle of circles; but this is, not surprisingly, confusing and not very helpful.

57

Discussing the system in detail, we can skip the Logic, which was considered at length in the last chapter. Hegel's philosophy of nature is unquestionably much less interesting and important than either the Logic or his philosophy of spirit, and few interpreters have had much to say in its favor. Findlay is very much an exception when he speaks of Hegel's "brilliant and informed *Philosophy of Nature*" (75). Undoubtedly, Hegel was very well informed for a philosopher in the early nineteenth century, but Findlay does nothing to show that this small section of the *Encyclopedia*—and this is all his philosophy of nature comes to—repays close study today. Here is the basic structure:

I. Mechanics
   A. Space and time
   B. Matter and motion
   C. Absolute mechanics

II. Physics
   A. The physics of general individuality
   B. The physics of particular individuality
   C. The physics of total individuality

III. Organics
   A. Geological nature
   B. Vegetable nature
   C. The animal organism

The discussion of space and time—especially that of time—is obviously of considerable philosophic interest; much of the rest is not. In the first edition, incidentally, the first two parts of the philosophy of nature were somewhat different, as follows:

    I. Mathematics (not subdivided further)
    II. Physics of the Inorganic
       A. Mechanics (not subdivided)
       B. Elementary physics
          a. Elementary bodies
          b. Elements
          c. Elementary process
       C. Individual physics
          a. Form (*Gestalt*)
          b. Particularization of bodies
          c. Process of isolation (*Vereinzelung*)

In the second edition this disposition was replaced by the arrangement that was then kept in the third edition. Plainly, no "necessary" progression from stage to stage is suggested—at least not in any ordinary sense of "necessary." What is wanted is a sensible arrangement of the topics that Hegel, living in a particular period of history, considered it "necessary" to cover.

Exactly the same consideration applies to the realm of subjective spirit. Hegel may well have begun with the triad of art, religion, and philosophy, which somehow belonged together and deserved, if anything did, to be called absolute spirit. The realm of morals and ethics seemed to him to form a comparable unit with political philosophy and law; and this sphere belonged "before" absolute spirit as the social basis and context that made possible the development of absolute spirit. A third realm was needed to round out the philosophy of spirit. What might belong in that?

Anthropology, on which Kant had published a book in 1798 (second, revised edition in 1800), had been left out so far and might well be placed between the philosophy of nature and the higher regions of the philosophy of spirit; and psychology suggested itself readily enough for a place in this same realm, which Hegel decided to call subjective spirit, to distinguish it from spirit objectified in human institutions which he called objective spirit. (In the *Logic,* Subjective Logic had come after Objective Logic; but here subjective spirit comes before objective spirit.)

One embarrassment remained: subjective spirit still had only two subdivisions, anthropology and psychology. Where could a third science be found? Perhaps more obviously here than anywhere else, Hegel resorted to an *ad hoc* solution: phenomenology. This would have been a good solution if what he himself had done in his *Phenomenology of the Spirit* could really have found a fitting place at this point; but it certainly could not.

The *Phenomenology* had been conceived as an introduction to the system that was even then to consist of Logic, philosophy of nature, and philosophy of spirit. It was meant to be a ladder from sense-certainty to the philosophical point of view of the system. This introduction could not be plausibly placed between anthropology and psychology, as an intermediate sphere of subjective spirit. The added fact that the *Phenomenology* had absorbed, in the process of writing, ever so much that had originally been intended for the philosophy of objective spirit and the philosophy of absolute spirit, to employ Hegel's later terminology, need not be considered crucial: Hegel could now say that his book, *The Phenomenology of the Spirit,* had actually contained more than phenomenology in the stricter sense.

In fact, he did say something like this in the second and third editions of the *Encyclopedia* (§25)—but not in connection with his inclusion of phenomenology in the realm of subjective spirit; rather in embarrassment over the fact that in §§26–78 he proposed once again to consider a variety of philosophical attitudes. His words deserve to be quoted here because, so far from allaying the difficulty about the subsequent inclusion of phenomenology where it plainly does not belong, they really underline this difficulty:

"In my *Phenomenology of the Spirit,* which was therefore designated on publication as the first part of the System of Science, I took the way of beginning with the first and simplest appearance of the spirit, *the immediate consciousness,* developing its dialectic up to the standpoint of philosophical science, whose necessity is demonstrated by this progression. But to this end one could not stop with the formal aspect of mere consciousness; for the standpoint of philosophical knowledge is at the same time the most contentful and concrete. Thus emerging as a result, it also presupposed the concrete forms of consciousness, such as, e.g., morals, *Sittlichkeit,* art, religion. The development of the *contents,* of the objects of characteristic parts of philosophical science, therefore falls at the same time within this development of consciousness, which at first seems to be limited merely to the form. . . . The presentation thus becomes more complicated, and what belongs to the concrete parts is partly already included in this introduction."

The dozen pages that are devoted to "phenomenology" in the *Encyclopedia* are certainly not an acceptable compendium of *The Phenomenology of the Spirit,* which corresponds rather to the *Encyclopedia* as a whole: it represents a first, not altogether premeditated, attempt to organize the whole material in a somewhat different way. And the *Encyclopedia* §§26–78 correspond to some extent to the preface to the *Phenomenology.* This part of the preliminaries of the book has already been referred to above (H 19 and 42).

One consideration may seem to invalidate part of what has been said here: the content of subjective spirit differs from edition to edition, especially from the first to the second. This is its breakdown in 1817:

A. The soul

   a. Natural determination of the soul

   b. Opposition of the soul to its substantiality

   c. Actuality of the soul

B. Consciousness

   a. Consciousness as such

   b. Self-consciousness

   c. Reason

C. Spirit

   a. Theoretical spirit

      1. Feeling 2. Notion 3. Thinking[24]

   b. Practical spirit

      1. Practical feeling 2. Drive and inclination

      3. Happiness

At first glance it might seem as if in 1817 Hegel had not yet thought in terms of anthropology, phenomenology, and psychology.

[24] These subdivisions with Arabic numbers do not reappear in the text, and in the table of contents the "3" has dropped out before *Denken.*

But in fact he said even then in the first paragraph of the section on subjective spirit (§307): "Thus subjective spirit is (a) immediate, the spirit of nature—the subject of what is usually called anthropology,[25] or the soul; (b) spirit as the identical reflection in itself and in other things, relation or particularization—consciousness, the subject of the phenomenology of the spirit; (c) spirit being for itself or spirit as subject—the subject of what is generally called psychology."

In the second edition, we find this breakdown:

A. Anthropology
    a. Natural soul b. Dreaming soul c. Actual soul
B. Phenomenology
    a. Consciousness as such. b. Self-consciousness
    c. Reason
C. Psychology
    a. Theoretical spirit
    b. Practical spirit
        a. Practical feeling *β.* Drives *γ.* Arbitrary will and happiness

The third edition is close to the second; yet the disposition is not the same:

A. Anthropology
    a. Natural soul b. *Feeling* soul c. Actual soul
B. Phenomenology *of the Spirit*
    a. *Consciousness* b. Self-consciousness c. Reason
C. Psychology
    a. Theoretical spirit b. Practical spirit c. *Free spirit*

The departures from the previous edition, published only three years before, have been emphasized here; of course, they were not italicized in 1830. It will also be noted that the further breakdown of

25 Misprinted in the 1st ed. as "Athropologie." Hegel's very profuse italics in this paragraph have been ignored here.

"practical spirit" was omitted. Above all, psychology was saved from having only two subheadings: a third was found, barely in time, only a year before Hegel's death.

It would be silly to regard all these changes as evidence of continuing great philosophical discoveries, as if new necessities had kept swimming into view. It is almost equally misleading to present the 1830 version as "The Philosophy of Hegel," as Stace does, and to give the impression that it is all based on dialectical deduction. Findlay even informs his readers that the *Encyclopedia* was published in 1816 (false in any case) and never takes any notice of the fact that there are three different editions published by Hegel himself.[26]

The central point of our philological excursus is, of course, to show how Hegel himself handled his system: not as so much necessary truth, deduced once and for all in its inexorable sequence, but rather as a very neat and sensible way of arranging the parts of philosophy—not even the neatest and most sensible possible, but only the best he could do in time to meet the printer's deadline. There was always every presumption that the new edition would feature some improvements.

58

Apart from the Logic, only the philosophy of objective spirit and the philosophy of absolute spirit were of surpassing interest to Hegel. To the former he devoted a whole book, *The Philosophy of Right* (1821); to the latter, three cycles of lectures which occupy eight volumes in the posthumous edition of the works.

Hegel's treatment of objective spirit in the two later editions of the *Encyclopedia* is in fact an abridgment of *The Philosophy of Right*. The three main divisions are the same in the first edition; only the breakdown of *Sittlichkeit* is different. In 1817 the triadic subdivision of that is still quite forced, though it looks neat enough in the table of contents where we read: 1. The individual nation (*Volk*); 2. international law (*Aeusseres Staatsrecht*); and 3. general world history.

[26] Findlay is in error about the publication dates of three of Hegel's four books.

Once again, these headings are not found in the text but only in the table of contents, and they palpably represent afterthoughts. They are followed by page numbers, and it turns out that the first five pages of the section on *Sittlichkeit* (§§430–441) precede subheading ⚹1 which covers a single paragraph of less than eight lines (§442). Subheading ⚹2 covers less than a page and a half (§§443–447), and ⚹3 just about a page and a half (§§448–52). In other words, the neat triadic breakdown applies to a little less than the second half of this section.

In the second and the third editions something went wrong in the numbering of the subdivisions of objective spirit, both in the table of contents and in the text. In both 1827 and 1830, "A. *Das Recht*" (either Right or Law in this context) is divided into (a) property, (b) contract, and (c) right as such against wrong. The subdivisions of "B. *Moralität*" are also the same in both editions, but in 1827 they begin inconsistently with Greek alpha, beta, and gamma: (a) purpose, (b) intention and welfare, (c) good and evil.

In "C. *Sittlichkeit*" something went wrong in both editions. The initial subdivision is again the same in both, but in 1830 the headings are introduced inconsistently with AA., BB., and CC., instead of a., b., and c. There are no further subparts in 1830. In 1827 there were, and under (b) they are introduced with a.a., b.b., and c.c.; but under (c) with Greek alpha, beta, and gamma. It seems highly probable that even in the arrangement of objective spirit, on which Hegel had by then published an important book, he kept changing his mind about the disposition and in the process made so many alterations that he himself lost track.

Anyway, the edition of 1827 follows *The Philosophy of Right* in subdividing *Sittlichkeit* as follows:

    a. Family
    b. Civic society
       a.a. The system of needs
       b.b. The administration of law
       c.c. Police and corporation
    c. State
       α. Internal law
       β. International law
       γ. World history

In both of the last two editions of the *Encyclopedia,* the philosophy of history is assigned a niche at the end of objective spirit. By no stretch of the imagination is it, however often this has been asserted, "the culmination of the Hegelian system."[27] It is more nearly a stepchild, being the only major area to which Hegel devoted a cycle of lectures that was not accorded a chapter in the system, and that did not even appear in the table of contents of the last edition of the *Encyclopedia.*

This does not mean that between 1827 and 1830 Hegel had come to consider the philosophy of history less important or interesting; he merely tried to simplify the Contents by omitting almost all subheadings below a, b, and c, the sole exception being made in favor of "identity," "difference," and "ground" in the Logic. In fact, in 1827 world history rated less than eight pages; in 1830, almost twenty. The final paragraph alone (§552) grew from less than two pages to over twelve. But what we get is not an abridgment of Hegel's lectures on the philosophy of history, but a lengthy excursus on *"the relation of state and religion."*

One reason for this curious state of affairs was probably that Hegel had already abridged his philosophy of history in the concluding paragraphs (§§341–60) of his *Philosophy of Right.* In any case, he consistently included it in the realm of objective spirit, below art, religion, and philosophy, which comprise absolute spirit. The "history" of his philosophy of history was the history of states, what we might call political history; therefore he always subsumed it under "The State," at the end of objective spirit.

A little philological work has shown us the pointlessness of the persistent preoccupation of some scholars with Hegel's more difficult "transitions" from one "stage" to the next. But at the point we have now reached the transition is by all means significant. And it is not at all difficult to grasp.

History is not the culmination of Hegel's system; neither is the

---

[27] For example, Robert S. Hartman, in his edition of *Reason in History,* (1953, p. xxiii). This is an unreliable translation, not of *Die Vernunft in der Geschichte,* as edited by either Lasson or Hoffmeister, but rather of the second nineteenth-century edition, which was superseded by *Die Vernunft in der Geschichte.* Into this old version the editor has fitted excerpts from Lasson's text—not in the places where Lasson who knew Hegel from beginning to end, put them, but in places the editor considered suitable, though his translation and long introduction show that for all his virtues he is certainly not a Hegel scholar.

state. Hegel's relatively high estimate of the state depends on his belief that the development of art, religion, and philosophy, and their cultivation, depend on the state. Given the state, which provides the framework for the development of a culture, the continuity of cultural traditions, of language, education, and techniques, as well as the necessary security, an individual can occasionally form himself in solitude; but Hegel himself remarks that even if this should be the rule, it would not show that the state was altogether dispensable.[28]

The pinnacle of Hegel's system is absolute spirit; and within that, philosophy. This is what any reader of the *Phenomenology* would expect, and Hegel had made up his mind on that point long before he published his first book. But if there is any pinnacle at all, is not the system a ladder rather than a circle?

The work that represents philosophy in the system is the cycle of lectures on the history of philosophy, which ends with the present state of philosophy—with what Hegel has done by way of still further developing the work of Kant, Fichte, and Schelling. In other words, it ends with Hegel's system, which begins with the Logic. Thus the system is indeed a "circle that returns into itself," "a circle in which the first also becomes the last, and the last also the first."[29]

Where one starts in this system should not matter, as long as one proceeds until one has closed the circle. Thus one could, for example, begin with the philosophy of nature, go on from there to the philosophy of spirit, which ends with the history of philosophy, and hence to the Logic. And if, on having closed the circle, one should go all the way around a second time, one would get even more out of one's journey.

Why, then, does Hegel worry at the beginning of his *Logic,* "With what must the beginning of science be made?" There, the question is where to begin the *Logic.* And the point is that it is better to begin with the poorest and most abstract category, being, than to begin with the most concrete and complex. Moreover, it would obviously be foolish to begin one's journey somewhere in the middle of the Logic, closing the circle only after having gone through all the other parts of the system, thus separating pages that belong closely together by taking up all the other parts of the system in between.

[28] Hegel's philosophy of the state will be discussed more fully in H 63.
[29] See footnotes 21 and 22 above.

Indeed, two starting points seem superior to the others: the *Logic*, with which Hegel begins in the *Encyclopedia*, or—better perhaps— the history of philosophy.

There is no need here to go through the system, bit by bit. The *Logic*, in its full form, is much more lucid than is usually supposed, and there is no dearth of books about it. Hegel's philosophy of nature is not that important, nor is his treatment of subjective spirit. Hegel's book on objective spirit, *The Philosophy of Right*, is available in a good English translation by T. M. Knox, which is philologically sound and supported by a wealth of informed notes. In a companion volume, Knox has also made available Hegel's minor *Political Writings*, to which Z. A. Pelczynski has contributed a long and scholarly introductory essay. Moreover, Herbert Marcuse has dealt with this phase of Hegel's thought in his remarkable book on *Reason and Revolution: Hegel and the Rise of Social Theory;* and there is also Sidney Hook's *From Hegel to Marx*. In addition we have some excellent articles in this area by T. M. Knox and Shlomo Avineri (see the Bibliography) and, in German, Rosenzweig's fine two volumes on *Hegel und der Staat*.[30]

There is no need to lengthen the present book by including a summary of their conclusions; suffice it to say that these fit in very well with the reinterpretation here attempted. And Hegel's conception of the state and its relation to freedom will be considered briefly in the next chapter (H 63 and 64).

On Hegel's lectures on aesthetics and philosophy of religion, interesting monographs might and should be written. In any case, these two cycles of lectures offer no insurmountable difficulties to the interested reader, either in the original or in English translation. But the same is not true of the lectures on the philosophy of history and the history of philosophy.

While the present reinterpretation of Hegel need not be capped with a play-by-play summary or interpretation of any of these works, it seems well to conclude this account of Hegel's thought with some remarks about Hegel on history; for on this subject there is still some need of reinterpretation.

[30] Cf. also WK Chapter 7.

CHAPTER VI

Hegel on History

59

The basic structure of Hegel's philosophy of history furnishes another striking corroboration of our reinterpretation: nobody could possibly construe it in terms of thesis, antithesis, and synthesis, although there are, as usual, three stages. At first, in the ancient Orient, only *one,* the ruler, is free. The second stage is reached in classical antiquity where *some* are free, but not yet the slaves. The third stage is reached in the modern world with the recognition that *all* men are free, or—as Hegel also puts it, and we have these ideas not only in students' lecture notes but also in his own manuscript— "man as man is free."[1]

In another passage, also available in Hegel's own manuscript, he explains this more fully:

"Of world history . . . it may be said that it is the account of the spirit, how it works to attain the *knowledge* of what it is *in itself.* The *Oriental* peoples do not know that the spirit, or man as such, is free in himself. Because they do not know it, they are not free. They only know that *one* is free; but for that very reason such freedom is merely arbitrariness, savagery, dimness of passion, or at times a gentleness, a tameness of passion which is also a mere accident of nature or arbitrariness. This *one* is therefore only a despot, not a free man, a human being.

"Only in the *Greeks* did the consciousness of freedom arise, and therefore they were free; but they, as well as the Romans, knew

[1] VG 156. References to *Die Vernunft in der Geschichte,* ed. Hoffmeister, are followed by an L if they do not refer to Hegel's own manuscript.

only that *some* are free, not man as such. Plato and Aristotle did not know this; therefore the Greeks did not only have slaves, and their lives and the subsistence of their beautiful freedom were tied to this, but their own freedom, too, was partly only an accidental, undeveloped, ephemeral and limited flower, partly at the same time a harsh servitude of man, of what is humane.

"Only the *Germanic* nations[2] attained the consciousness, in Christianity, that man as man is free, that the freedom of the spirit constitutes his most distinctive nature. This consciousness arose first in religion, in the inmost region of the spirit; but to build this principle also into the affairs of this world, this was a further task whose solution and execution demands the long and hard work of education. With the acceptance of the Christian religion, slavery, e.g., did not stop immediately; even less did freedom immediately become dominant in states, or were governments and constitutions organized rationally and founded on the principle of freedom. This *application* of the principle to worldly affairs, the penetration and permeation [*Durchbildung*] of the worldly condition by it, that is the long process which constitutes history itself" (VG 61 f.).

That history is the story of the development of human freedom, is the central idea of Hegel's philosophy of history. This is its heart, and all the rest receives its blood from it.

60

Hegel speaks of reason in history, and his twentieth-century editors—first, Lasson and, following him, Hoffmeister—have taken the liberty of calling the volume containing the critical edition of the introductory lectures on the philosophy of history *Die Vernunft in der Geschichte* (Reason in History). Yet Hegel never claims that history has been rational in every detail. On the contrary, its abundant irrationality is so plain that it requires no special philo-sophical effort to see it. What does call for the exertions of a philosopher is to find some reason in history. It is pertinent to recall Hegel's early essay on "The Positivity of the Christian Religion"

2 The term *die germanischen Nationen* obviously refers to the Protestant nations of northern Europe and cannot by any stretch of the imagination be taken to mean merely "the Germans"; yet this is a point where Hegel has been mistranslated and misrepresented again and again.

and his decision, in 1800, to view the past in a different perspective, with the faith that what so many millions have died for was "not bare nonsense or immorality" (H 12).

There is a moving passage, again in Hegel's own manuscript, that suggests that he no longer found it easy to talk or write about the wretched side of history. The prose is complex, but the thought is perfectly clear:

"When we consider this spectacle of the passions; when the consequences of their violence and the folly that accompanies not only them but even, and indeed pre-eminently, good intentions and legitimate aims, come before our eyes—the ills, the evil, the destruction of the most flourishing realms that the human spirit has created; when we behold individuals with the deepest sympathy for their indescribable misery—then we can only end up with sadness over this transitoriness and, insofar as this destruction is not only a work of nature but of the will of men, even more with moral sadness, with the indignation of the good spirit, if there be any in us, over such a spectacle. We can raise such events, without any rhetorical exaggeration, merely by putting together all the misfortune that the most glorious peoples and states as well as individual virtues or innocence have suffered, into the most horrible portrait, and thus intensify our feeling into the most profound and helpless sadness which cannot be balanced by any conciliatory result. . . . But even as we contemplate history as this slaughter bench on which the happiness of peoples, the wisdom of states, and the virtue of individuals have been sacrificed, our thoughts cannot avoid the question *for whom, for what final aim* these monstrous sacrifices have been made" (VG 79 f.).

The explicit mention of innocence is noteworthy. Hegel does not believe that suffering proves guilt. Recalling how a former fellow student at Tübingen later related that the young Hegel had "found special pleasure in the Book of Job on account of its unruly natural language" (H 3), one wonders whether it was only the language that attracted him. Hegel's letter to Knebel, written in December 1810 (translated in D) comes to mind, too: So far from closing his eyes to the misery of humanity, Hegel needed his work, his philosophy, to cope with it. He tried to show himself and others that the indubitably monstrous sufferings recorded throughout history had not been altogether for *nothing*. There is something we can show in return for all this, though it cannot balance the misery: while even Plato and Aristotle, not to speak of the sages of India, had not known that man as such was free, this was now widely recognized, though it might still take considerable time before such freedom would be fully actualized.

In Hegel's mature work the emphasis is almost the opposite of the Book of Job, and also far from Nietzsche and some of the existentialists. Mostly, he stresses the goal rather than the sacrifices, the growing recognition of freedom rather than the slowness of its implementation, and reason rather than unreason.

If we ask why, two reasons offer themselves. They are supplementary. First, as Goethe said: "The greatest men always are attached to their century by some weakness."[3] Or we might express the same point by likening Hegel in one respect to his "world-historical individuals," whom we shall have to consider in a moment: he, too, knew "for what the time had come."[4] Either way, his distribution of emphasis reveals him as a man of the nineteenth century, not of the twentieth—not necessarily a child of the nineteenth century, but perhaps rather one of those who helped to mold its distinctive temper.

As we follow Hegel's development, we may also venture a psychological explanation, which is in no way incompatible with the first point. Human misery was perfectly obvious to him. His closest friend, Hölderlin, had become insane, and now this most lovable human being, by far the most gifted poet of his generation, vegetated mutely toward his long delayed death. Hegel's only sister lived on the verge of madness and was deeply despondent. His only brother had been killed in the Napoleonic wars. His mother had died when he was barely thirteen. It did not seem manly to Hegel to dwell on that aspect of life. But it was never far from the surface and found expression in, for example, his writings and lectures on tragedy and his immense admiration for Sophocles and Shakespeare. On the rare occasions when it finds more direct expression, as in the passage we have cited that ends with the image of the slaughter bench, one gets the feeling that he did not altogether trust himself to speak of these matters.

The popular view of Hegel as an "optimist" is certainly mis-

---

[3] *Elective Affinities* (1809); *Maximen und Reflexionen*, ⁂49.
[4] VG 97 L: *was an der Zeit, was notwendig ist.* Cf. Nohl 143, cited at the beginning of section 12, above: what is there said to be "a need of our time" is precisely what is at stake here.

leading. He never shared the view that gained ground in the later nineteenth century, and beyond that until 1914, that happiness had grown throughout history, and that ultimate happiness was around the corner. Nor did he believe that gradually so much had been learned from history that at long last tragedy was avoidable. On these points he expressed himself with vigor:

"What experience and history teach is this: peoples and governments have never learned anything from history and acted according to what one might have learned from it" (VG 19 L).

"History is not the soil of happiness. The times of happiness are empty leaves in it" (VG 92 L).

It would not go too far to call his vision of history tragic. The themes represented here by a few quotations are pursued throughout and recur again and again.[5] Hegel is still far from the type of the "Alexandrian" scholar of the later nineteenth century, whom the young Nietzsche derides in his first books. He is much closer to Nietzsche himself; say, to Zarathustra's "I have long ceased to be concerned with happiness; I am concerned with my work." Hegel says of the world-historical individuals: "It is not happiness they choose, but toil, struggle, work for their purpose."[6] That Hegel personally felt the same way appears from his two letters to his bride in the summer of 1811 (D): indeed, immediately upon becoming engaged he hurt her feelings by questioning whether "happiness is part of the destiny of my life."

Hegel is also close to Nietzsche when he says that *"nothing great in the world has been accomplished without passion"* (85). Or when he attacks envy (100 ff. L). Indeed, part of this attack deserves a place here:

"What schoolmaster has not demonstrated to his class that Alexander the Great and Julius Caesar were driven by such passions and were therefore immoral men? From which it immediately follows that he, the schoolmaster, is a more excellent human being than they, because he does not possess such passions, which he can prove, for he has not conquered Asia, nor vanquished Darius and Porus. He lives comfortably, to be sure, but he also lets live. . . . For a valet there are no heroes, says a familiar proverb. I have added—and Goethe repeated this two years later—not be-

---

[5] For example, 34 f. L, 72 L, and 100 L.
[6] VG 100 L; cf. 93 L. The *Zarathustra* quotation comes from the first chapter of Part IV.

cause there are no heroes but because he is a valet.[7] . . . Homer's
Thersites who reproaches the kings is a stock figure of all ages.
Blows, i.e., a beating with a solid stick, he does not receive in all
ages, as he did in Homer's; but his cnvy . . . is the thorn he
carries in his flesh[8]; and the undying worm that gnaws him[9] is the
torment that his excellent intentions and reproofs remain without
any success in the world" (102 f. L).

What is perhaps most like Nietzsche and Sartre is Hegel's constantly repeated insistence that "the organic individual produces
himself: it makes of itself what it is implicitly; thus the spirit, too,
is only that which it makes of itself, and it makes of itself what it
is implicitly."[10] This is almost a definition of spirit: "Spirit is this,
that it produces itself, makes itself into what it is" (74). Compare
this with Sartre's: "Man is nothing else but that which he makes
of himself. That is the first principle of existentialism."[11] Of course,
Sartre applies emphatically to each individual what Hegel had more
often said of spirit and of peoples, and Sartre does not stress as
Hegel does—but this is a mere truism in any case—that potentially
one was all along what one makes of oneself explicitly. Where they
really differ is in Sartre's suggestion that we could have chosen to
make something utterly different of ourselves—a point Hegel does
not discuss.

On a related point, however, Sartre's moral is also Hegel's.
Sartre presents this as the distinctive doctrine of existentialism:
"Man . . . is therefore nothing else but the sum of his actions. . . .
For the existentialist, there is no love apart from the deeds of
love; . . . there is no genius other than that which is expressed
in works of art. The genius of Proust is the totality of the works of
Proust. . . . In life, a man commits himself, draws his own portrait, and there is nothing but that portrait. No doubt, this thought
may seem comfortless to one who has not made a success of his
life."[12]

Hegel says in a similar vein—and only Descartes, Husserl, and
Heidegger are mentioned more often in Sartre's *Being and Noth-*

---

[7] *Phenomenology*, about 5 pages before the end of "VI. Spirit": Lasson's ed.,
430; Glockner's ed., 510; Baillie's, 673. Goethe, *Elective Affinities*.
[8] Alludes to II Corinthians 12:7.
[9] Alludes to Mark 9:44, 46, 48.
[10] VG 151; cf. 54 L, 58 L, 67 L, 72 f. L. Cf. also C II.1.8.
[11] "Existentialism is a Humanism," in *Existentialism from Dostoevsky to
Sartre*, ed. Kaufmann, 291.
[12] *Ibid.*, 300.

ingness than Hegel—"What man is, is his deed, is the series of his deeds, is that into which he has made himself. Thus the spirit is essentially energy and one cannot, in regard to it, abstract from appearance" (114 L). Elsewhere, Hegel notes "that often a difference is made between what a man is internally and his deeds. In history this is untrue; the series of his deeds is the man himself. . . . The truth is that the external is not different from the internal."[13]

61

From Hegel's own point of view, however, all this is incidental to the central point that history relates the development of freedom. And when in the following passage he contrasts youth and maturity, we know by now that he is not merely comparing his own wisdom with his students' lack of it but also, and perhaps mainly, his hard-won insight with the views of his own youth:

"It is easier to see the faults of individuals, states, and the governance of the world than to see what they contain of truth. For as long as one is negative and reproaches, one stands nobly, with a lofty mien, above the subject, without having penetrated into it and grasped it and what is positive in it. Certainly, the reproach may be well founded; only what is faulty is much easier to find than what is substantial (e.g., in works of art) . . . . It is the sign of the greatest superficiality to find what is bad everywhere and to see nothing of the affirmative and genuine. Age generally makes milder; youth is always dissatisfied; that is due to the maturity of judgment in age which does not merely, from disinterestedness, put up with the bad, too, but which has also been taught more profoundly by the seriousness of life and been led to the substantial and solid aspect of the matter . . .

"Thus the insight to which philosophy should help us is that the actual world is as it ought to be . . . God rules the world; the content of his government, the execution of his plan, is world

[13] VG 66 L; cf. also 100 L. Hegel also anticipates Spengler both in stressing the organic unity of all the aspects of a culture (121 L, with an appropriate bow to Montesquieu), and in pushing the organic metaphor still much further: "The spirit of a people is a natural individual; as such, it flourishes, is strong, declines, and dies" (67 L). On the following page this point is developed further, in language at points quite close to Spengler's.

history; to grasp this is the task of the philosophy of world history, and its presupposition is that the ideal accomplishes itself, that only what accords with the idea has actuality. Before the pure light of this divine idea, which is no mere ideal, the semblance that the world is a mad, foolish happening disappears. . . . What is ordinarily called actuality is considered something rotten by philosophy; it may well seem, but it is not actual in and for itself. This insight contains what one might call the comfort against the notion of absolute misfortune, of the madness of what has happened. Comfort, however, is merely a substitute for some ill that ought not to have happened, and is at home in the finite. Thus philosophy is not a comfort; it is more, it reconciles, it transfigures the actual, which seems unjust, into the rational . . ."[14]

Until we reach "the insight . . . that the actual world is as it ought to be," all one can say against Hegel is that he generalizes too much. Whether the positive or the negative is easier to see, and which it is more important to point out, depends greatly on the historical context. After the polemics of the Enlightenment, and after he himself had written his fragments on folk religion and "The Positivity of the Christian Religion," Hegel might well feel, as he put it in 1800, that "the horrible blabbering in this vein with its endless extent and inward emptiness has become too boring and has altogether lost interest—so much so that it would rather be a need of our time to hear . . . the opposite" (H 12). In another time and place, the horrible blabbering in quite a different vein might make it a need of the time to hear some pungent criticism.

The second half of the long quotation is open to even graver objections. Here Hegel goes against the spirit of not only his early fragments but also the preface to the *Phenomenology,* where he had announced that "philosophy, however, must beware of wishing to be edifying" (I.2.9). Then he had felt that philosophers must not "aim at *edification* and replace the pastor"[15]; now he seems to be doing just that. In these lectures "God" comes to his lips easily and frequently, and philosophy is invoked frankly to offer more than comfort, to reconcile us to the horrors of life and history, and to transfigure the actual—by what looks like a verbal trick.

In any ordinary sense of these words, Hegel himself does not

14 VG 77 f. L. Cf. 29 ff. L, 42 L, 48, 52 L.
15 Jena "aphorism" ⅗66, *Dok.* 371; Ros. 552.

believe that "the actual world is as it ought to be." This dictum
depends on calling actual only what "accords with the idea." What
is ordinarily called actual (*wirklich*) is admittedly "rotten"—but
simply not called actual "by philosophy." Is it really an "insight"
that reconciles Hegel to the terrors of history, or merely the
redefinition of "actual"?

First of all, it should be noted that Hegel's definition is not
offered *ad hoc* at this point. It goes back to the famous preface to
the *Philosophy of Right,* to the discussion of this category in the
Logic, and beyond that to the *Phenomenology.* Beyond that, it goes
back to Aristotle and Plato. Plato had taught that only perfect
justice and goodness, perfect circles and squares—or in other words,
only what he called the Forms—were actual; everything in the
world of experience that participates imperfectly in these Forms is
not actual but mere appearance. Aristotle had abandoned the belief
in otherworldly Forms, had found the Forms *in* things, as entelechies
which strive toward actuality through development. Hegel does not
believe that a pattern of a perfect state is laid up in the heavens, to
echo Plato's famous remark in the *Republic* (592); he does
believe, however, that there is a Concept of the state that existing
states actualize more or less—and then suggests in places that
those states that are not states in the highest normative sense of
that word are not actual.

While it makes perfectly good sense to say of a badly drawn
circle that it is not actually a circle, seeing that the definition of a
circle is generally and precisely understood, it would involve stretching a point, more often than not, to say that a poorly instituted
state is not actually a state. But to go still further and say that it is
not actual is surely utterly misleading. And if Hegel's comfort and
reconciliation to misfortune and madness depended solely on this
redefinition of terms, his philosophy of history would be far worse
than it is.

62

The following quotations, all from *Die Vernunft in der Geschichte,* explain the major points of Hegel's approach. The first
requires comment: "The philosophical approach to history has no
other intention than to eliminate the incidental" (29 L). *Das Zufäll-*

ige would usually be translated as "the accidental," but "incidental" is equally legitimate and in this case much clearer. All historiography involves the distinction between what really matters and what is merely incidental. (Hegel creates confusion by not keeping this contrast distinct from that between the accidental and the necessary.) No historian can relate everything. Historiography always requires selection—indeed, selection of a very few events out of an indefinite number. The historian who would relate the whole of world history in one volume, or for that matter in three or four volumes, must be even more selective. And he might as well be clear about his principle of selection. What nations shall he include? What individuals shall he mention by name?

This is the problem Hegel faces in his lectures. The same problem confronts not only those bold enough to write a history of the world but also teachers who offer some such survey either in one course or in a sequence of several courses. Should one discuss Bulgarian history at some length? Or Athens? And should Barbarossa be mentioned? And Charlemagne?

The standard solution is surely this: one leads up to one's own society. One includes what seems "necessary" for the development of this society, and one omits what is irrelevant. A German will discuss both Barbarossa and Charlemagne, a British teacher, pressed for time, probably the latter but not the former. Both will mention Caesar, Alexander, and Athens; neither will spend any time on Bulgaria. Whether they will say frankly what their principle of selection has been and call attention to its subjectivity, is doubtful. They are more likely to say that this *is* world history. And perhaps they will add, as most American secondary school teachers do, that their own society is the freest society that has ever existed—without the least inclination to compare it with any contemporary societies that might possibly claim to have achieved at least as much, if not somewhat more, freedom. Comparisons with earlier societies that were less free are almost inevitable; and if the teacher is British or American, Magna Charta will be presented as a milestone. In sum, in almost all American secondary schools history is taught as the gradual growth of freedom, specifically in the development of the teacher's and students' own society.

It has often been suggested that it was ridiculous of Hegel to present Prussia as the culmination of the development of freedom, but to this one may offer two brief replies. First, the point depends

wholly on comparing different societies *in the 1820s,* as there is no
suggestion whatsoever in Hegel's lectures that history will not go
on; on the contrary. And at that time it would have been less
ridiculous to single out Prussia than, say, the United States in which
there was a large slave population.

Secondly, Hegel does *not* present Prussia as the culmination of
the historical process, and his construction of world history does
not depend on any such implicit assumption. That Germany was,
during Hegel's lifetime, in the forefront of Western civilization
seems undeniable; but Hegel does not say that Germany represents
the pinnacle of the historical process. He merely believes, and
wants to show, that for all its many ups and downs there has been
a slow and painful development to the point where it is widely
admitted, certainly in the Protestant North of Europe, that all men
as such are free. And he understands world history as the gradual
development of this recognition.

Armed with this insight, he tells his students that there has been
reason in history; that all has not been in vain; that one must
approach the study of history with this faith; but that for him it is
no mere faith but "a result with which I am acquainted because
I am already acquainted with the whole" (30).

"But we have to take history as it is; we must proceed historically,
empirically" (30). That does not mean that one even *could* approach history without any prior ideas in one's head. "Even the
ordinary and mediocre historian, who may believe and pretend
that his attitude is only receptive . . . brings along his categories
and sees the data through them." And now comes the famous
epigram: "The world looks rational to those who look at it rationally" (31). The other way around: "If one approaches the world
only with subjectivity, then one will find it as one is constituted
oneself; everywhere, one will know everything better and see how
it should have been done, how things should have happened"
(32 L).

People say that it is presumption to try to understand Providence,
but "When theology itself has been reduced to such despair, then
one has to seek refuge in philosophy if one wants to know God."
It is "a tradition that God's wisdom is to be recognized in nature";
how much more, then, should it be discoverable in human history,
considering that this, much more than nature, is the realm of the
spirit (42 L). "The time must finally have come to comprehend

this rich product of creative reason—world history. . . . Our approach is to that extent a theodicy, a justification of God, which Leibniz still attempted metaphysically" (48).

Considering these "edifying" remarks in the context both of these lectures and of Hegel's other writings, it seems unquestionable that they are mere frills. At the University of Berlin, where he gave these lectures, he was the colleague of Schleiermacher, in whom he had early recognized a "virtuoso of edification" (H 55), and whether he liked it or not, they were rivals. Hegel did not disdain this contest and sprinkled these lectures on the philosophy of history with polemical remarks, suggesting that he had to defend God and divine Providence against the theologians.

The way had been pointed not only by Lessing's and Kant's essays on history, with their explicit references to Providence, but also by Schiller's celebrated line, in the poem "Resignation": *Die Weltgeschichte ist das Weltgericht* (world history is the world's last judgment). For Hegel this can only mean: This is the only *Weltgericht* there will be; there is no judgment beyond this. Schopenhauer, an avowed atheist, also adopted Schiller's line, but in a different spirit:

"If one wants to know what men, considered morally, are worth on the whole and in general, one should contemplate their fate, on the whole and in general. This is need, wretchedness, misery, torment, and death. Eternal justice rules: if they were not, on the whole, worth nothing, their fate, taken on the whole, would not be so sad. In this sense we can say: the world itself is the world's last judgment."[16]

This is surely the wisdom of Job's friends, albeit without God. Hegel, though he speaks of God, is less moralistic and in this respect more remote from popular theism. His "theodicy" finds much less justice in the world than Schopenhauer does: in effect, it does not acquit God of the charge of cruelty and injustice, it merely calls our attention to extenuating circumstances. There is *some* reason in the madness of history, and the suffering is not *wholly* pointless.

Hegel's view is similar to Einstein's formulation, carved over a fireplace in Fine Hall, at Princeton University: *Raffiniert ist der Herr Gott, aber boshaft ist er nicht,* which has been translated: "God's sly, but he ain't mean." One might also render it, less

---

[16] *Welt als Wille und Vorstellung,* I, §63.

irreverently: "God is subtle but not malevolent." And, of course, he is not omnipotent. That is Hegel's point, too—a point that is as easily demythologized in his case as in Einstein's. The great physicist knows from his results that there is some reason in nature, and in his further researches he proceeds on the assumption that more regularities amenable to mathematical formulation are to be found.

They are not easy to discover; they do not meet the eye; they are exceedingly subtle. But the world has not been abandoned to mere accident.[17] Even as the physicist might say with Hegel, "The world looks rational to those who look at it rationally," Hegel could say with Einstein, "God is subtle but not malevolent."

For the subtlety, Hegel coins a famous term: "One can call it the *cunning of reason* that it lets the passions do its work, while that through which it translates itself into existence loses and suffers harm."[18] The point does not depend on this non-theological anthropomorphism; in Hegel's own manuscript it is stated a little earlier in these lectures in admirably straightforward form: "in world history the actions of men also produce results quite different from their purposes" (88).

Hegel himself goes on to give the example of a man who sets fire to another man's house and, unintentionally, causes a huge conflagration. Moreover, his action may also lead to his punishment. "The only point to stick to in this example is that in the immediate action we may find more than lay in the will and consciousness of the agent" (89). Similarly, the importance of world-historical individuals is not reducible to their purposes. At times, they may well have been driven largely by ambition and other passions; but they also produced results they did not intend and, however far this may have been from their consciousness, they contributed in the long run to the development of freedom in the modern world.

World-historical individuals are not mysterious entities either: they are simply those individuals who belong in a world history of moderate size. Some very admirable kings, not to mention non-political figures, may safely be omitted from any such highly con-

[17] Einstein's formulation should not be construed as solemn theology, and Professor V. Bargmann recalls how Einstein said to him: *"Manchmal glaube ich, er ist doch boshaft, weil er uns an der Nase herumführt"* (Sometimes I believe he is malevolent after all because he leads us around by the nose). [18] VG 105 L. For a more comprehensive quotation of this passage see C III.3.28.

densed account—and really have to be left out—while some others, whose moral character is not necessarily any better, have had world-historical consequences and therefore have to be included. And the same goes for world-historical peoples.

Not being an envious Thersites, Hegel went further than necessary in the opposite direction and became rhapsodical (97 ff.), but these passages we have only in his students' notes, and in that lecture he may have got carried away a bit. What he says fits *some* of these individuals very well—for example, Pericles among those Hegel knew, Lincoln among those he did not—but also makes sense when applied to Alexander and Caesar.

63

Studying Hegel's philosophy of history, one should keep in mind that for him history is not everything but merely occupies one niche in his system. There are other points of view, and in one passage in these lectures Hegel poses the same contrast that Kierkegaard later presented in a famous passage of his *Concluding Unscientific Postscript*[19]:

"When, e.g., we see a man kneel and pray before an idol, and this content is reprehensible from the point of view of reason, we can nevertheless cling to his feeling that is alive in his prayer, and can say that this feeling has the same value as that of the Christian who worships the semblance [*Abglanz*] of truth, and as that of the philosopher who immerses himself in eternal truth with his thinking reason. Only the objects are different; but the subjective feeling is one and the same" (51 L).

Hegel, to be sure, goes on to point out that feeling is not everything, and "when we confront the fight of the Greeks against the Persians, . . . we are quite conscious of what interests us; namely, to see the Greeks liberated from barbarism" (52 L). In history we are concerned with the objective results of actions, not with merely subjective feelings. Indeed, the feelings of the men at Marathon hardly concern the historian, and the feelings of those who fought in battles that were not destined to become world-historical are ignored altogether.

[19] Princeton University Press 1944, 179 f.

"When we thus put up with seeing the individualities, their purposes and the satisfaction of these, sacrificed, while their happiness is abandoned to the realm of the forces of nature and thus to accident, and we consider the individuals altogether under the category of means, there is nevertheless one side to them which we refuse to consider only from this point of view, even in relation to what is highest [presumably, freedom]; for there is something that is emphatically not subordinate, something in them that is by its own nature eternal, divine. This is *Moralität, Sittlichkeit,* religiosity" (106).

Moreover, human beings "participate in this rational purpose and are thereby ends in themselves—ends in themselves, not only formally . . . individuals are also ends in themselves according to the contents of the purpose"[20]—for the freedom that is at stake in history is, after all, *human* freedom.

Once more Hegel returns to the non-historical point of view: "The religiosity, the *Sittlichkeit* of a limited life—of a shepherd, a peasant—in its concentrated inwardness and its limitation to a few and wholly simple conditions of life has infinite value, and the same value as the religiosity and *Sittlichkeit* of well-developed knowledge and an existence rich in the scope of relations and actions. This internal center, this simple region of the right of subjective freedom, the hearth of willing, deciding, and doing, the abstract content of conscience, that in which guilt and value of the individual, his eternal judgment, is enclosed, remains untouched and outside the loud noise of world history—outside not only external and temporal changes but even those which are involved in the absolute necessity of the Concept of freedom" (109).

In the margin of his manuscript, Hegel noted at this point: "*Sittlichkeit* in its true form—in the state." While this idea is developed more fully in the *Philosophy of Right,* it is also repeatedly discussed in these lectures, and in any case it deserves some account in this book.

The good state combines "with its general purpose the private interests of the citizens" (86). "It is the actuality in which the individual has and enjoys his freedom" (111 L). "All that man is he owes to the state; . . . All value man has, all spiritual actuality, he has through the state alone" (111 L). "It is the absolute in-

---

[20] VG 106. Where our omission of three and a half lines begins, Hegel had written in the margin of his manuscript: "see Kant."

terest of reason that this ethical whole should exist; and this interest of reason constitutes the right and merit of the heroes who established states" (112 L). "Only on this soil, i.e., in the state, can art and religion exist. . . . In world history one can discuss only peoples who have formed a state. . . . Indeed, all great men have formed themselves in solitude, but only by working for themselves upon what the state had already created" (113 L). "Thus the state is the more precisely defined object of world history in which freedom gains objective existence" (115 L). "An Athenian citizen did, as it were, from instinct what was his share. . . . *Sittlichkeit* is duty . . . second nature, as it has rightly been called; for the first nature of man is his immediate animal being" (115 f. L).

At this point, we can leave behind lecture notes and revert to Hegel's manuscript in which he takes note of "the direct opposite of our Concept that the state is the actualization of freedom, namely the view that man is free by nature. . . . That man is free by nature is quite right in the sense that he is free according to the Concept of man, but thus only according to his destiny,[21] i.e., only *in himself.*" To be sure, people have assumed a state of nature, but hardly as a historical condition that could actually be encountered somewhere. "Conditions of savagery one can indeed find, but they are seen to be tied to passions of brutality and acts of violence and at the same time, however undeveloped, to social institutions, which are supposed to limit freedom" (116).

The state is important in Hegel's philosophy because it is, he argues, the actualization of freedom, and because it alone makes possible the further development of spirit—the realm of absolute spirit. Hence the hyperbolic dictum that all of man's spiritual actuality and value depend on the state: Hegel refers specifically to the moral-ethical dimension and to art, religion, and philosophy; but beyond that he considers the state as the hearth of all that raises man above the brutality of beasts.

He opposes the view that man is free by nature, while the state curtails this freedom. Without the state, freedom remains merely man's destiny; without the state, freedom is not actual. A hundred and forty years later he might have pointed to the collapse of the

[21] *Bestimmung* could also be rendered as "determination" or even as "definition." In the title of Fichte's famous book, it has been rendered still differently: *The Vocation of Man.*

state in the Congo, not by way of suggesting, contrary to the facts, that the state that broke down had been good and had actualized the freedom of those living in it—plainly it had been bad by Hegel's standards—but only to show that such a collapse and the sudden removal of the restraints associated with a state does not mean freedom. To ensure freedom, maintain security, and make possible the development of art and philosophy, a good state is wanted.

"In order to . . . establish justice, insure domestic tranquility, provide for the common defense, promote the general welfare, and *secure the blessings of liberty*," those who framed and ratified the Constitution of the United States of America did not find it expedient or at all possible to replace British rule with anarchy, a return to nature, and the abolition of all states and all restraints; they established a state. That men who revere their constitution and learn this preamble by heart as children should find Hegel's association of the state with freedom perverse and talk as if it were self-evident that the state merely abridges our natural freedom is a triumph of thoughtlessness, which illustrates the bankruptcy of any common sense that prides itself on spurning philosophy.

64

It is interesting to note that most of the passages that have given offense come from the students' notes, not from Hegel's manuscript; this also applies to the following remarks. They take up Hegel's old polemic against Kant's moral philosophy as lacking content, and find *Sittlichkeit* in the concrete life of a community.

"When one wants to act, one must not only will the good, but one must know whether this or that is the good. But what content is good or not good, right or wrong, that is given for the usual cases of private life in the laws and customs of a state. There is no great difficulty about knowing that.

". . . The morality of the individual then consists in fulfilling the duties of his station; and these are easy to know: what these duties are is determined by one's station. . . . To investigate what might be one's duty [or: what duty might be] is unnecessary rumination; in the inclination to look upon the moral as something difficult, one might sooner recognize the hankering to get rid of one's duties. Every individual has his *station* and knows what rightful, honest activity means . . ." (94 L).

As examples of the "usual cases," Hegel gives the conduct of children toward their parents, or the situation in which one man owes another a sum of money. "There is nothing difficult here. The soil of duty is civic life"; and the individual must assimilate the customs (*Sitten*) and the *Sittlichkeit*—or the mores and morality —of his people.[22]

Here Hegel sketches in a few bold strokes what in *The Lonely Crowd* is described at immense length as "tradition-directedness." Insofar as he himself accepts this orientation, one is led to reflect that times have changed, and situations have multiplied in which even in ordinary life it is no longer easy to know one's duty.

Confronted with Kierkegaard's great crux, what Abraham was to do when God asked him to sacrifice his beloved son, many sensitive and thoughtful people may still agree with Kant's forceful reply, published forty-five years before *Fear and Trembling* (1843) in *The Quarrel among the Faculties:* "Abraham would have had to answer this supposedly divine voice: 'That I ought not to kill my good son, that is wholly certain; but that you, who appear to me, are God, of that I am not certain and never can become certain even if it should resound from the (visible) heavens.' "[23]

Kierkegaard's book, however, became timely when millions found themselves in situations where they felt uncertain, as a matter of fact—even if Kant was quite right that they ought not to have felt uncertain—whether they should or should not report their parents to the government, and how they should conduct themselves toward their Jewish or non-conformist neighbors, or toward people who had been publicly branded as Communists, or who had taken the Fifth Amendment, or toward Negroes. When is civil disobedience permissible? When is it a duty?

Hegel did not suppose that tradition-directed *Sittlichkeit* was the alpha and omega of moral philosophy. Loving tragedy as he did, he could not have thought so; and the philosophy of history was one place to take note of the limitations of such an ethic.

"In the course of history, the preservation of a people, a state,

[22] VG 95 L; cf. 67 L, as well as the idea in the preface to the *Phenomenology* that the individual must assimilate the work of the world spirit.
[23] Original ed., 1798, 102 f. (the third footnote in the section entitled *"Friedens-Abschluss und Beilegung des Streits der Fakultäten"*).

and the preservation of the ordered spheres of its life, is one essential moment. . . . The other moment, however, is that the stable persistence of the spirit of a people, as it is, is broken because it is exhausted and overworked; that world history, the world spirit proceeds. . . . But this is tied to a demotion, demolition, destruction of the preceding mode of actuality. . . . It is precisely here that the great collisions occur between the prevalent, recognized duties, laws, and rights and, on the other hand, possibilities which are opposed to this system . . ." (96 f. L).

In times of transition, the old mores no longer offer certainty, and the ethical world is rent by tragic collisions. It seems obvious that what Hegel still considered largely irrelevant to the lives of his listeners is of immediate and vital concern to young people who, partly for that reason, feel attracted to existentialism. While British moral philosophy, even after World War II, still proceeds on Hegel's assumption that in the usual cases there is no great difficulty about knowing what is right or good, Sartre has followed Kierkegaard in concentrating on the exceptional cases, those that are not ordinary, more interesting, and by no means so easy to resolve. And since World War II, the extraordinary is no longer exceptional.

In his lectures Hegel mentions two figures who are associated with great collisions: Socrates and Antigone. "The Greeks in their period of flowering, in their cheerful *Sittlichkeit,* did not have the Concept of general freedom . . . or *Moralität,* or conscience. *Moralität,* what the spirit's return into itself is, reflection, the spirit's search for refuge in itself, was lacking; that began only with *Socrates*" (71 L). In a similar vein, Hegel said later in these lectures: "Socrates is celebrated as a teacher of morality, but we should rather call him the *inventor* of *Moralität.*"[24] As the champion of a new principle, he was a world-historical figure who eventually triumphed posthumously; but he was also a tragic figure[25] who was put to death.

Antigone, on the other hand, stood for time-honored *Sittlichkeit,* opposing a tyrant. "Sophocles' Antigone says: the divine commandments are not of yesterday, or of today; nay, they live without end, and nobody could say whence they came. The laws of

[24] Glockner's ed., XI, 350.
[25] *History of Philosophy,* Glockner's ed., XVIII, 119.

Sittlichkeit are not accidental but the rational itself" (112 L). Here there is no reference to Antigone's martyrdom; but elsewhere, of course, Hegel spoke of it many times, by no means only in the *Phenomenology* (H 30).

This is as good a transition as any from history to the realm of absolute spirit: Hegel's repeated praise of Sophocles' *Antigone,* though all of these passages come from his lectures on the realms of absolute spirit, may help to round out his view of the state. Had he been the statist and totalitarian he has been called, how could he possibly have so loved this play, which is a song of songs on civil disobedience?

Hegel called this tragedy "one of the most sublime and in every respect most excellent works of art of all time" and the "absolute example of tragedy."[26] And he also spoke of "the heavenly Antigone, the most glorious figure ever to have appeared on earth."[27]

To understand Hegel on history, one should keep in mind the over-all structure of his system; and as this example shows, some awareness of what he says in his lectures on the three realms of absolute spirit dispels at one blow many misconceptions about his philosophy of history and of the state. There is no ambiguity, no metaphysical jargon, no uncertainty about that last brief quotation: it is as good a clue as any to what Hegel meant and did not mean when he spoke of the state.

In yet another way this praise of "the heavenly Antigone" is of immense interest: the phrasing makes it almost impossible not to think of Jesus, and to note that Antigone is here placed above him.

65

Hegel's treatment of Christianity in his last years has often been misunderstood. Among religions, he considers it supreme insofar as it seems to him to come closest to the truth comprehended ultimately in his philosophy. His references to Judaism and Islam reveal no sympathetic understanding and are patently unjust; like almost all other writers on these religions throughout the period of the En-

[26] *Aesthetik,* II, Glockner's ed., XIII, 51; and *Philosophy of Religion,* II, Glockner's ed., XVI, 133. Cf. also the passage cited from *Aesthetik,* XIV, 556, in H 13.
[27] *History of Philosophy,* II, Glockner's ed., XVIII, 114.

lightenment and the nineteenth century, he compares Judaism and Christianity only to affirm the superiority of the latter.[28]

In its relation to philosophy, however, religion, including even Christianity, is as a child compared to a man: it is an anticipation in less developed form of what finds mature expression in philosophy. In the very lectures on history that we have been considering, Hegel compares the three realms of absolute spirit (124 f. L). He considers religion first, then proceeds:

"The second form of the union of the objective and subjective in the spirit is *art:* it steps more into actuality and sensuousness than religion; at its most dignified it has to present, not the spirit of God but the form of the god, and what is divine and spiritual in general. The divine is to be presented to intuition by it.

"But the true does not only reach notions and feelings, as in religion, or intuition, as in art, but also the thinking spirit. Thus we come to the third form of union—*philosophy*. This is in the manner indicated the highest, freest, and wisest form."

In philosophy, mythical notions (*Vorstellungen*) and subjective feeling (*Gefühl*), as well as intuition (*Anschauung*), are transcended at last by genuine comprehension. When Hegel avails himself of Christian categories, he never implies acceptance of the Christian faith in the supernatural, in miracles, or in the incarnation and resurrection; he merely finds the Christian myths more suggestive and appropriate anticipations of his philosophy than the myths of other religions. And occasionally he enjoyed the accents of edification, both as a device for showing his students that his own ideas were not as far-fetched and counter-intuitive as they might seem, and as a means of polemicizing a little against the theologians.

The reference to "the form of the god," in the passage just quoted about art, obviously refers primarily to Greek sculpture. "What is divine" emphatically includes Antigone and Goethe's Iphigenia (cf. H 7). Hegel never scruples to call *Sittlichkeit* divine, and says, for example: "The ethical [*das Sittliche*] is the divine of religion as action."[29]

Consider the way Hegel introduces the brief section on "Revealed Religion" in his *Encyclopedia*. At this point, not only Logic, philosophy of nature, and philosophy of subjective spirit lie behind us,

[28] For example, VG 58 L, 126 f. L, 133 L.
[29] *Aesthetik*, Glockner's ed., XII, 316.

but also objective spirit with its discussion of the state and the passing remarks on history. We are in the realm of absolute spirit, and the five pages on art now give way to five on "Revealed Religion." The paragraph begins in a manner that, taken out of context, would sound pious enough: once again Hegel insists on the importance of *knowing* God and attacks the theologians who make things shamefully easy for themselves by claiming "that man knows nothing of God." Against them, Hegel insists that it is the whole point of the doctrine of revelation that God is not envious but makes himself known. He sounds more orthodox than many theologians—and thus uses a device employed previously by David Hume in his *Dialogues*. But then comes the conclusion:

"To grasp in thought, correctly and definitely, what God is as spirit, that requires thorough speculation [Hegel's odd way of saying that it requires *philosophy;* i.e., not theology which he has derided in the immediately preceding sentence]. To begin with, this contains the following propositions: God is only God insofar as he knows himself; his knowing himself is, furthermore, a self-consciousness in man and man's knowledge *of* God that goes on to man's knowing himself *in* God" (§564).

What does this mean if not that God does not know himself until man knows him; and since "God is only God insofar as he knows himself," God comes into being only when man "knows" him. Findlay has therefore called Hegel "the philosopher . . . of liberal Humanism."[30] One may cavil at "liberal": the temperament of the mature Hegel was conservative rather than liberal. But his religious position may be safely characterized as a form of humanism.

Even as one does not call a man a stage in the development of the embryo, but the embryo a stage in the development of a man, Hegel does not call the force that eventually becomes spirit as man develops, say, a late stage in the evolution of some *élan vital;* rather he sometimes speaks of pre-human manifestations of this force as manifestations of spirit. In the narrower sense, we should not speak of spirit until we reach man; and therefore only the third part of the system is called "philosophy of spirit." The same

[30] *Hegel,* 354; cf. the argument for this conclusion on 342. While I do not agree with several of Findlay's points on 342, his non-supernatural interpretation is certainly right.

point is made in the lectures on history: "The realm of the spirit is
what is produced by man" (50 L). And in another passage Hegel
even says: "The *world spirit* is the spirit of the world as it explicates itself in the human consciousness" (60 L).[31]

This should have caused no misunderstanding, had it not been
for Hegel's occasional references to God. His choice of the word
"spirit" had been very heavily influenced by the religious connotations of this term. What *was* he to call the force whose manifestations he wished to trace mainly in the ethical sphere, in history,
in art, in religion, and in philosophy, but of which it would also
make sense to speak when discussing nature? "Spirit" served admirably and at one blow connected Hegel's thought not only with
the Christian tradition but also with the decidedly un-Christian,
humanistic poetry of Goethe, Schiller, and Hölderlin: their verse
was full of references to *Geist,* not always, though usually, in the
singular. Moreover, *Geist* also retained the meaning of the etymologically related "gist"; for example, when Mephistopheles, instruct-
ing a young student, drops the "pedantic tone" and says: "The spirit
of medicine is easy to know" (line 2011).

Geist, like the Latin *spiritus,* Greek *pneuma,* and Hebrew *ruach*
(and unlike *mind, nous,* and *logos*) also means breath and wind,
is essentially a moving force and the essence of life. Etymologically,
it is also related to "yeast" and "geyser," and conceptually it is
associated with the notion of a ferment and an eruptive force.[32]
Still, one can also speak, as Goethe had done derisively in *Faust*—
in the Fragment published in 1790—of "the spirit of the times."
Faust's lines to Wagner bear quoting because they show what possibilities the use of this term opens:

> What spirit of the times you call,
>   Is but the scholars' spirit after all,
>   In which times past are now reflected. (577 ff.)

Once having chosen this eminently suggestive word, Hegel sometimes could not resist equating it with God, instead of saying clearly:

---

[31] Rosenkranz already noted that Hegel, when he spoke of the *Weltgeist,*
"did not mean God but mankind in its totality" (206).
[32] Cf. R. Hildebrandt's article on *Geist* in Grimm's *Deutsches Wörterbuch,*
reprinted separately, Halle, 1926, and the long footnote in my *Nietzsche*
(1950), 207, Meridian ed., 385.

in God I do not believe; spirit suffices me. Of course, there was
ample precedent for his occasional unorthodox use of "God." The
Greeks had made rather free with *theos* and *theoi,* and Hegel on
the gods in Homer is very good indeed and still worth reading,
both for those interested in the Greeks and for those interested in
Hegel's conception of God, gods, and the divine.[33] Aeschylus and
Sophocles, Plato and Aristotle had used such terms freely, too; and
Gilbert Murray remarks in his superb book on *Five Stages of Greek
Religion:* "A metaphysician might hold that their theology is far
deeper than that to which we are accustomed, since they seem not
to make any particular difference between *hoi theoi* [the gods] and
ho theos [god] or *to theion* [the divine, a term Hegel likes to use,
too]. They do not instinctively suppose that the human distinctions
between 'he' and 'it,' or between 'one' and 'many,' apply to the
divine."[34]

In addition to his beloved Greeks, Hegel saw before him the
example of Spinoza and, in his own time, the poetry of Goethe,
Schiller, and Hölderlin, who also liked to speak of gods and the
divine. So he, too, sometimes spoke of God and, more often, of the
divine; and because he occasionally took pleasure in insisting that
he was really closer to this or that Christian tradition than some of
the theologians of his time, he has sometimes been understood to
have been a Christian.

That he, in turn, became a precedent for theologians like Tillich
and Bultmann, is undeniable. But if one should consider the procedure of all three reprehensible, there are still important differences
in Hegel's favor. What he did very occasionally, *en passant,* by way
of being *geistreich,* they have made their full-time occupation. And
considering the whole weight and tenor of his work, he was ever
so much less likely to be misunderstood in his own time. Above all,
far from treating the latest philosophy as a remarkable anticipation
of Christianity, provided only that the latter were radically reinter-
preted on the basis of this philosophy, Hegel presented the very
opposite picture: in his system Christianity was treated as an anticipation in mythological form—on the level of vague notions and feelings—of truths articulated in philosophy.

The culmination of Hegel's philosophy is neither the philosophy

[33] *Aesthetik,* Glockner's ed., XII, especially 302 ff., and XIII, especially 60 ff.
[34] Anchor Books ed., 67.

of history nor that of religion but the history of philosophy. And to this we shall now turn. It is of very considerable interest but offers no immense difficulties and may therefore be discussed briefly.

66

Hegel's *History of Philosophy* begins with very remarkable introductory lectures, which we shall consider last. They are now available in German in a critical edition, in a volume of roughly three hundred pages, edited by Hoffmeister. For the rest we still have to rely on the three volumes of the nineteenth-century edition, reprinted without change under Glockner's editorship.

The apportionment of space is surprising but revealing: Chinese and Indian philosophy are allotted a little over 30 pages; Greek philosophy about 930 pages; medieval philosophy just over 100; and modern philosophy, from Bacon to Hegel, less than 430.

Greek philosophy up to Socrates: almost 300 pages. Socrates and the Socratics (Megarians, Cyrenaics, and Cynics): about 130 pages. Plato: about 130 pages. Aristotle: about 130 pages. "Dogmatism and Skepticism" (Stoics, Epicureans, New Academy, and Skeptics): about 165 pages. Neoplatonism (from Philo to Proclus and his successors): 94 pages.

Introduction to medieval philosophy: 21 pages. Arabic and Jewish philosophy: 11 pages. Scholasticism: 80 pages, including over 7 on Anselm, barely over 1 page on St. Thomas, and 5 on Occam. Renaissance philosophy, including Pomponatius, Ficinus, Bruno (20 pages), Vanini (6), and Petrus Ramus: about 40 pages.

In the last part, on modern philosophy, many philosophers are little more than mentioned. Those who receive detailed attention are: Bacon (18 pages), Jacob Böhme (32), Descartes (37), Spinoza (43), Malebranche (6), Locke (22), Hobbes (5), Leibniz (24), Wolff (8), Berkeley (5), Hume (7), Jacobi (16), Kant (60), Fichte (30), Krug (8 lines), Fries (3 lines), Schelling (38 pages), and "Result," which begins "The present standpoint of philosophy . . . ," (8 pages).

In sum: Almost two thirds of the history of Western philosophy is taken up by Greek philosophy. The pre-Socratics get three times as much space as all of medieval and Renaissance philosophy taken together. No single medieval philosopher really interested Hegel, and nothing in this whole period of one thousand years seemed as important to him as Anselm's ontological argument for the existence of God.

Giordano Bruno and Jacob Böhme would not receive comparable attention in modern histories of philosophy, nor would Neoplatonism get so much more attention than all British philosophers taken together. Kant gets half as much space as either Plato or Aristotle; the whole of "Recent German Philosophy," including Kant, a little more than either Plato or Aristotle alone.

It is a commonplace that one's judgment is most unreliable when one comes to the recent past and one's contemporaries, and it would not have been surprising if Hegel had left out some philosophers who now seem to be of the first rank. Thus John Passmore has said at the beginning of *A Hundred Years of Philosophy* (1957): "It is a salutary reflection that had I written this book in 1800 I should probably have dismissed Berkeley and Hume in a few lines, in order to concentrate my attention on Dugald Stewart —and that in 1850 the centre of my interest would have shifted to Sir William Hamilton" (7 f.). He also remarks that "Mill knew practically nothing of Hume" and that "interest in Hume dates back to the edition of his works by T. H. Green and T. H. Grose (1874); Berkeley . . . was little regarded as a philosopher until the publication of A. C. Fraser's edition (1871)" (11).

It is pleasing to find that Hegel gave Hume seven pages, and Berkeley five, to Dugald Stewart's page and a half. Between 1827 and 1829, Krug, whom the young Hegel had attacked (H 17), published his *Allgemeines Handwörterbuch der philosophischen Wissenschaften, nebst ihrer Literatur und Geschichte*,[35] in five volumes. He gave Stewart about a third of a page, Berkeley a little more than a page, and Hume more than three. Locke, too, he gave over three; Fichte got over three; and Hegel two, very unfriendly, of course.

It is not particularly surprising that both Krug and Hegel did better than Passmore thinks he himself would have done. One works in a tradition, and while British philosophy was not part of the mainstream of the German philosophical tradition in Hegel's day, and therefore received proportionately little attention, both Berkeley and Hume had been prominently mentioned by Kant and could not

[35] "General Cyclopedia of the Philosophical Sciences, together with their Literature and History."

be ignored. Through Kant they had gained a place in the tradition.

Hegel, of course, did not merely include Hume. He considered him the greatest representative of a major approach to philosophy —one of the four he selected for discussion in the preliminary part of the *Encyclopedia* (see H 19).

Even of England it is not true that interest in Berkeley and Hume "dates back" only to the 1870s, as Passmore suggests: In 1857 George Henry Lewes gave twenty pages each to Berkeley and to Hume, and none at all to Stewart, in *The Biographical History of Philosophy*.[36] Lewes, of course, had been to Germany; he had devoted one of his earliest essays to an appreciative account of Hegel's *Aesthetik;* and in 1855 he had published what is widely considered his major work, a *Life of Goethe*. And George Eliot (Mary Ann Evans), for whom he left his wife in 1854, had translated into English the major works of two of Hegel's leading disciples: D. F. Strauss's *Life of Jesus* (tr., 1846) and Ludwig Feuerbach's *Essence of Christianity* (tr., 1854).[37]

T. H. Green, to whose edition of Hume's works Passmore credits the origin of interest in Hume's philosophy, has been fittingly called "the most typical English representative of the school of thought called neo-Kantian, or neo-Hegelian."[38] It would seem that the British discovered Hume's philosophical significance by way of Kant and Hegel.

Hegel has sometimes been accused of reading his ideas into his predecessors. The essential generosity of his approach should not be overlooked. Instead of concentrating on the follies of his predecessors and then saying, as it were, "But I say unto you . . . ," Hegel makes no point of his own originality but tries to show how the labors of the great philosophers of the past add up. Hence he gives so much attention to the Neoplatonics, to Bruno, and to Böhme. Another man might have relied on public ignorance of works from which he had actually received much inspiration, in an effort, not necessarily entirely deliberate, to appear more original than he was in fact. Hegel goes to the opposite extreme. When he has found much that is good and helpful in a man, then he discusses him at length even if others might not deem him worthy of so much attention in a history of philosophy.

[36] Second edition, "much enlarged and thoroughly revised," 2 vols., New York, D. Appleton and Co., 549–68 and 569–88.
[37] For Strauss's and Feuerbach's attitudes toward Hegel, see D 1831 and 1840.
[38] *Encyclopaedia Britannica*, 11th edition.

His attitude is aptly summarized in one of his Berlin aphorisms (Ros. 556): "Once a man has reached the point where he no longer knows things better than others—that is, when it is a matter of total indifference to him that others have done things badly and he is only interested in what they have done right—then peace and affirmation have entered his mind."

It would be pointless here to discuss in detail Hegel's interpretation of his predecessors. To say that he was exceedingly well read and informed for his day would be a laughable understatement. His lectures on the subject established the history of philosophy as an area of central importance for students of philosophy: no great philosopher before him had given such lectures or insisted on his students' study of this subject. This part of his system thus represents one of Hegel's most noteworthy accomplishments, and as a contribution of truly revolutionary importance it forms a very fitting culmination for the system.

67

In conclusion, let us consider the introduction to these lectures. (The end has already been discussed in H 13). The first lecture Hegel gave as a professor at Heidelberg, October 28, 1816, was the introductory lecture of his course on the history of philosophy and survives in his manuscript. We shall begin with a remarkable passage from that:

"I hope I shall succeed in earning and gaining your confidence. To begin with, however, I may not claim anything except that you should bring along confidence in science and confidence in yourselves. The courage for truth, the faith in the power of the spirit, is the first condition of philosophy. Man, since he is spirit, may and should deem himself worthy of the highest; of the greatness and power of his spirit he cannot think grandly enough. And with this faith, nothing will be so coy or hard that it will not open up for him. The initially concealed and locked up essence of the universe has no strength to resist the courage to know; it must uncover its wealth and its depths before the eyes of such courage and let it enjoy them.

"The history of philosophy represents for us the gallery of the noble spirits who, by the boldness of their reason, penetrated into the nature of things, of man, and into the nature of God, unveiling its depth for us and through their work presenting to us the treasure of the highest knowledge. This treasure, of which we ourselves want to partake, constitutes philosophy in general; its genesis is what we shall learn to know and comprehend in these lectures" (5 f.).

Almost all of this passage was emphasized by Hegel himself in his manuscript. *This* is the introduction to the pinnacle of Hegel's philosophy. He did not introduce history, art, or religion in a remotely comparable tone.

When Hegel went to Berlin he rewrote the beginning and fashioned an altogether new manuscript for his first lectures, beginning October 24, 1820, and wrote what in print comes to over fifty pages. The following quotations come from this manuscript:

"Immediately we encounter the very common view of the history of philosophy that it has to narrate the *store of philosophical opinions* as they resulted and presented themselves in time. When people speak pleasantly, they call this material opinions; those who consider themselves able to express the matter with more thorough judgment call this history a *gallery* of follies, or at least of *aberrations* . . ." (25).

"One sees, on great matters . . . the greatest spirits *erred,* for they have been refuted by others" (26).

"What could be more useless than to get to know a series of mere opinions? what more boring? . . . An *opinion* is merely *mine* [*Eine Meinung ist mein:* an inspired pun that crystallizes an important point]. . . . Philosophy, however, contains no opinions; there are no philosophical opinions. . . . Philosophy is objective science of the truth. . . . *Truth, however, is one;* the instinct of reason has this insuperable feeling or faith. Thus only *one* philosophy can be the true one. And because they are so different, the others— one infers—must only be *errors*" (27).

"About this reflection one might say first of all that, however different philosophies are supposed to be, at least they have *this in common,* that they are *philosophy.* Whoever, therefore, studied or mastered any philosophy at all, if it really is a philosophy, would thus master some philosophy. This excuse and argument that clings merely to the difference I have compared elsewhere[39] with a (pe-

---

[39] *Encyclopedia* (1817), §8; (1827), §13. The point that follows has come to be widely associated with Gilbert Ryle's *Concept of Mind* (1949), as if it represented an entirely new insight. Ryle never said it did.

dantical) invalid whom his doctor advises to eat fruit and who is offered cherries or plums or grapes, but who will not take any . . . because none of these are *fruit* but merely cherries or plums or grapes" (28).

"But this proposition that truth is only *one,* is itself still abstract and formal. And what is most essential is to recognize that the one truth is not a merely *simple abstract* thought or proposition; rather it is something *concrete"* (29).

". . . The idea is essentially *concrete, the unity of differentiated determinations.* It is at this point that the knowledge of reason differs from the knowledge of the mere understanding, and it is the business of philosophy to show that the true, the idea, does not consist in empty generalities but in something general that is essentially particular and determinate. . . . Here the consciousness not yet trained in philosophy steps back and says that it does not *understand* this. That it does not understand this means first of all that it does not yet find this among its customary notions and convictions. . . . But to *understand* it and form some notion of it is easy. *Red,* e.g., is an abstract sensuous notion, and when ordinary consciousness speaks of red it is not of the opinion that it is dealing with anything abstract. But a rose that is red is a concrete red; it is a unity of leaves, of form, of color, of smell, something living and growing in which many such abstractions can be differentiated and isolated, and which can also be destroyed and torn, and which is nevertheless, in all the manifoldness it contains, *one* subject, *one* idea. Thus the pure abstract idea is essentially not something abstract, not empty simplicity like red, but a flower, something essentially concrete. Or to take an example from a determination of thought, the proposition 'A is A,' the principle of identity, is an entirely abstract simplicity. . . . But when I go on to the category of *ground* [*Grund*], this is already an essentially concrete determination. Ground, the grounds, what is essential in things is also that which is identical with itself and rests in itself; but ground is at the same time defined as something that goes out of itself to relate itself to something of which it is the ground. The simple Concept, therefore, contains not only what the ground is but also the other of which it is the ground; the cause contains also the effect. Something that was supposed to be a ground, taken without anything of which it is the ground, is no ground; just so, something that is supposed to be determined as a cause, but without effect. . . . This, then, is what it means to be concrete: to contain not only *one* immediate determination but also another.

"After having thus explained the nature of the concrete, I now add about its significance that the true . . . has the drive to *develop* itself. Only the living, that which is spirit, moves and stirs essentially, and develops. The idea, concrete in itself and developing, is thus an organic system, a totality which contains a *wealth of stages and moments.*

"Now philosophy is for itself the recognition of this development, and as thinking that comprehends, it is itself this thinking development. The further this development has reached, the more perfect is the philosophy" (30 ff.).

"Thus philosophy is system in the process of development" (33).

"Now I claim that the sequence of the systems of philosophy *in history* is *the same* as the *sequence in the logical derivation* of the conceptual determinations of the idea" (34).

It is time to stop and take stock. Hegel takes more seriously than any major philosopher before him the problem posed by the disagreement among the great philosophers. Leibniz had made a few scattered remarks about this problem; Aristotle, in the first book of his *Metaphysics,* had related the views of his predecessors and integrated them in his own system. Hegel discusses the problem at some length.

If philcsophy were as simple as a single abstract proposition, there would be no point, Hegel admits implicitly, in studying the history of philosophy. But philosophy is highly complex, much more like a flower or a living organism than like a simple quality, such as red, or such a proposition as the principle of identity. Since it is complex and alive, no simple proposition can exhaust it, and even a small collection of such propositions may do justice to only a few aspects of it. Indeed, the possibility arises that different collections of propositions—different philosophies, in other words—might be partially true, might supplement each other, and might therefore be worth studying one after the other. Not only might this be worth while; nobody who wants to do justice to the whole complex organism should dare to venture his own little collection of propositions without first studying the results of the cumulative labor of many centuries. The great philosophers of the past erred in not comprehending their own relation to their rivals in the most fruitful way; indeed they were wrong insofar as they considered their fellow workers merely as rivals; but for all that they were not a group of fools but "noble spirits" to whose boldness we owe treasures that no single lifetime would ever be sufficient for any one man to amass.

The last quotation may still seem surprising—and *would* be if the *Logic* had been written by Hegel before he had ever studied the history of philosophy. But though the manuscript we are now considering was begun in October 1820, Hegel had lectured on the history of philosophy as early as 1805, and the published version of the lectures draws heavily on the lectures given at Jena.[40] It has been noted previously that the sequence of the categories in the *Logic* was not determined by any strict necessity, logical or dialectical; that there was no relentless deduction from Concept to Concept; and that the whole structure of the work is much looser than is widely supposed. We now learn, in effect, that one guide for the sequence was a sidelong glance at the history of philosophy. But we may safely add that the statement quoted (from page 34) is something of an exaggeration—which is fortunate both for the *Logic* and for Hegel's *History of Philosophy*. Both are works of abundance in which the author faced the problem of organizing an excessive wealth of materials; he did not try wretchedly to eke out a whole volume by extrapolating from another work. When Hegel gave the course on the history of philosophy in 1829–30, he admitted, according to his students' notes, that there may be some differences; "but in the main points the sequence in the logical realm and in history must be *one*" (278).

One of the most important ideas he wants to establish in this way is no longer controversial: *"that the study of the history of philosophy is study of philosophy itself"* (35). In getting this firmly established, Hegel made a major contribution to intellectual history—and actually helped to create intellectual history as a field of scholarship.

As usual in Hegel, there are many passing points that are of interest. Here it will suffice to mention merely two or three. There is, for example, an interesting discussion of myth and its relation to truth (54 f.). Hegel equates *Dasein* (existence) with *In-der-Zeit-Sein* (being-in-time), a point that almost everybody considers original with Heidegger (37).

[40] "These [Jena] lectures on the history of philosophy he did not change greatly in his later courses in the versions that have also been printed; he merely elaborated them" (Ros. 201).

There is also a passage that reads like a deliberate polemic against Heidegger's many exegeses of the pre-Socratics[41]: Hegel insists "that the *beginning* is the *least formed, determinate,* and *developed* and is the poorest and *most abstract,* and the *first philosophy* is *the wholly general, indeterminate thought* and the *simplest,* while the *newest* philosophy is the most concrete and profound. One must know this lest one seek for more *behind the old* philosophies than they contain . . ." (66).

Even those who applaud the warning and approve of the examples Hegel goes on to give may take exception to his praise of "the newest philosophy," which sounds like self-praise. A few pages later Hegel repeats this praise, but immediately proceeds to explain it by saying that in this philosophy "everything that at first appears as something past, must be preserved and contained; it must itself be a mirror of the whole history."

We shall conclude our consideration of these introductory lectures with a quotation whose tone is markedly different from the exuberance of the passage with which we began:

"Every philosophy . . . *belongs to its time* and is biassed by its *limitations.* The individual is the son of his people, his world. He may put on airs as much as he pleases, he does not go beyond it . . ." (72).

68

Hegel saw what the times were ripe for, and he developed the historical approach to art, religion, and philosophy, to the whole realm of the spirit, to what in Germany are still called *Geisteswissenschaften.*[42] Under his influence, scholarship in the humanities flourished for over a century; indeed, much of his influence has become permanently embedded in Western civilization.

There is no history of philosophy written since his time that does

---

[41] On 73 f. there is another such passage: "When the most modern age is called upon to return to the standpoint of some ancient philosophy . . . to get out of all the complications of later times, such a return is not the spontaneous appearance of the first re-learning. . . ." And Hegel calls attention to the implicit authoritarianism of such an approach.

[42] Much of the discussion of the differences between natural sciences and *Geisteswissenschaften,* by Dilthey, Rickert, *et al.,* is an elaboration of, e.g., VG 70 L.

not bear the stamp of his spirit. Such German scholars as Erdmann, Zeller, and Kuno Fischer, as well as Windelband, stood directly in the main line of this influence, but others—even if they despise him, like Bertrand Russell in his *History of Western Philosophy*—are still following in his footsteps.

Hegel's influence has not been confined to the historiography of philosophy, or to the study of *Geisteswissenschaften*. Liberal Protestantism is unthinkable without it, and so are the British Idealism of F. H. Bradley, T. H. Green, and Bernard Bosanquet, the philosophies of Josiah Royce, Benedetto Croce, and R. G. Collingwood, and large parts of Sartre's *Being and Nothingness*.

Much intellectual history since Hegel's time is best understood as a series of revolts against Hegel's influence. It may be stretching a point to bring this under the heading of influence; but there are few men in history of whom such a statement could be made. In the end it matters little whether we call this some sort of influence or not: the significant fact is that without understanding Hegel one can comprehend relatively little of many movements since his time, while a study of his thought opens scores of doors.

The most obvious example, and by far the single most important one, is furnished by Marxism. Marx accepted a great deal from Hegel—especially what he took to be his dialectic, though he claimed that Hegel's idealism turned things upside down. As a matter of fact, Hegel's dialectic never was the rigorous method that Marx and his followers sought to make of it; and this we have tried to show in this book. By depriving it of its primary reference to ideas and applying it instead to modes of production, one cannot make the dialectic more precise; or materialism, "scientific." On the contrary, beliefs are at least *capable* of being literally contradicted and then subsumed in a higher synthesis, while any dialectic of modes of production or material circumstances is bound to be utterly lacking in rigor. The fact that Marxism further claims that the dialectic can be used to make predictions—Hegel never did and, on the contrary, insisted that philosophy must confine itself to the present and past—has led Marxism much further in the direction of pseudo-scientific rigor than Hegel himself ever went. But the fact that Marxism is in this respect intellectually indefensible obviously does not enable us to ignore it; and those who wish to comprehend it must study Hegel.

"One cannot completely comprehend Marx's *Capital*, and especially the first chapter, unless one has studied and comprehended the *whole* of Hegel's *Logic*. Consequently, after half a century not one of the Marxists has comprehended Marx." Thus wrote Lenin.[43]

William James polemicized against Hegel again and again, but hardly knew Hegel and really meant Royce who, ironically, was often less close to Hegel than James was. James's attack against the block universe, though aimed at Hegel, would have found an enthusiastic ally in Hegel. So, of course, would have James's "pragmatic" insistence that truth should make a difference in our lives, that philosophy is vision, and that the realm of faith and morals must not be severed from the realm of epistemology and metaphysics. In James it may have been partly an elective affinity rather than influence that drew him to Hegel's old paths. In his fellow pragmatist, John Dewey, it was clearly a direct influence; for Dewey, as is well known, began his philosophic career as a Hegelian.

In British philosophy, R. G. Collingwood was the last major representative of Hegel's direct influence. But the main drift of British philosophy, since G. E. Moore published his famous "Refutation of Idealism" in 1903, has been a revolt against Hegel's influence, specifically against McTaggart and the other British Idealists. Some of the excesses and the one-sidedness of this movement—features that constitute limitations though they certainly have not prevented a great many fine contributions—must be explained as an overreaction. Hegel's own conception of the development of philosophy helps us to comprehend these reactions against his impact.

A related movement requires a similar analysis: the so-called New Criticism. Here we have the same reaction against the historical school. The Hegelian as well as the Marxist approach is rejected in favor of close analysis, often with a deliberate disregard for historical context. What had been neglected tends to be made the alpha and omega.

Finally—there is no need for a more inclusive list here—there is existentialism. Even more than Marx, Kierkegaard saw himself in revolt against Hegel; unlike Marx, he was not clearly aware of how much he had taken from the man he fought. Through him, "dialectical" theology and neo-Orthodoxy are almost as incomprehensible without Hegel as is the liberal Protestantism they rose to attack.

---

[43] *Aus dem philosophischen Nachlass*, 99; quoted in Wilhelm R. Beyer, *Zwischen Phänomenologie und Logik: Hegel als Redakteur der Bamberger Zeitung* (1955), 226.

What makes Kierkegaard's revolt so interesting is that its influence has by no means been confined to religion. After the first World War, his protest against the Hegelian conception of philosophy as science found a hearing both among professional philosophers and in Western thought generally. When he penned his *Concluding Unscientific Postscript* in 1846, he was still "untimely": but, as Nietzsche remarked in *Ecce Homo*, "some are born posthumously."[44] A century later, "scientific" had come to mean to millions: shallow, mechanical, remote from the genuine problems of life. And Hegel was stigmatized as an "essentialist" and academician, a professor who constructed a system that bore no relation to his concrete existence, a philosopher who paid no heed to living experience. This book has sought to correct this impression.

Kierkegaard's attacks were not based on his own reading of Hegel and were usually as wide of the mark as his remarks about Goethe.[45] His image of Hegel was derived from the lectures of the old Schelling who had developed a profound resentment when Hegel's fame eclipsed his own. Any detailed analysis of this phase of the Schelling-Hegel relationship would lead us much too far afield: it belongs in a study of Schelling.[46] But the major documents are listed in chronological order in the Bibliography, under Schelling.

In brief, Schelling could not bear the thought that he himself was, as it were, a steppingstone between Fichte and Hegel, though he did not doubt that Fichte had been a steppingstone between Kant and himself; and he kept making two points. The first, which earned him Heinrich Heine's merciless mockery (D1835), was that Hegel had stolen his ideas. This won Schelling no respect at all. The second point, however, deeply impressed many Christians, including Kierkegaard: Hegel's philosophy, like Schelling's own youthful philosophy, had remained on the level of merely "negative philosophy," and the really significant advance remained to be made now, after Hegel's death; what was called for was a new "positive philosophy."

It was in this context that Schelling created the caricature of Hegel as a mere concept-monger. Indeed, Hegel had come after

[44] Chapter III, fourth sentence.
[45] Cf. Carl Roos's Danish study of *Kierkegaard og Goethe* (1955). Roos deals in detail with Kierkegaard as a reader and shows how completely he lacked objectivity and how heavily he was influenced by secondary sources.
[46] Cf. Fischer and Fuhrmans in the Bibliography and Schelling's letters in *Aus Schellings Leben*, III, pp. 63, 67, 95, 98, 142, 165.

the young Schelling, but the way Christian Wolff had come after the great Leibniz: "This empirical determination was removed instinctively, as it were, by one who came later and whom nature seemed to have predestined for a *new* Wolfianism, for our age: the *living* and *actual,* to which a former philosophy had attributed the quality of going over into its opposite (the subject) and then to return from this into itself, he replaced with the *logical Concept* to which he attributed, by means of the strangest fiction or hypostatization, a similar necessary self-movement. This last point was entirely *his own* invention and, as one might expect, admired by paltry minds . . ."[47]

Kierkegaard was soon disappointed by Schelling's lectures, which never lived up to the bold promises made in the beginning. Kierkegaard did not side with Schelling and had no interest in Schelling's historical position. But he did find Schelling's caricature of his erstwhile friend extremely useful as a theme one could develop and vary slightly when in need of a humorous contrast.

Through Kierkegaard, legions of twentieth-century readers who barely know Schelling's name have come to take for granted as historically accurate his spiteful caricature of Hegel. Many people assume that Hegel is the antipodes of existentialism. But the only major so-called existentialist who has shown as much interest in Hegel as Kierkegaard did is Sartre. He was actually sufficiently interested to read Hegel and has never made a secret of his immense debt to Hegel.[48]

On Hegel's influence on this man and movement or that, many a monograph can be and has been written. The point here is merely to suggest briefly how relevant Hegel is to twentieth-century concerns. No other nineteenth-century philosopher approaches him in this respect, with the sole exception of Nietzsche.

69

A brief contrast with Nietzsche may prove illuminating. Nietzsche came from a conservative background. By the time he was thirty-six

[47] *Vorrede* (preface) for Cousin's book on French and German philosophy (1834), p. xiv; see the Bibliography. Cf. also the passages referred to above in H 39, note [5].
[48] "Sartre learned to study Hegel in the classes of Kojève just before World War II" (Wilfred Desan, *The Marxism of Jean-Paul Sartre,* 1965, 52). See Biemel, Klaus Hartmann, and Kojève, in the Bibliography.

he had published eight small books, the last three more radical than his early essays, and during the next few years, before he collapsed at the age of forty-four, he published seven major works and completed three others that were published only later. Shortly before his collapse he also brought out "new editions" of several of his earlier books: he did not rewrite them but added brilliant prefaces and in one case a remarkable final chapter and an appendix of verse as well. His radicalism grew with the speed of his productivity. Like Van Gogh, he was driven to the breaking point in an incredible crescendo.

Hegel was most radical when he was young and never published his boldest essays. When he was thirty-six, he published his first major work, by far his most daring book. When he was forty-four he was in the midst of publishing his second major work. On the heels of that he published his system in syllabus form and then, in 1821, his last book, by all odds the least bold. During the final ten years of his life he did not attempt another book. First he wrote an unexciting preface for the book of one of his followers, then seven book reviews totaling about four hundred pages. In 1827 he published a thorough revision of his system, and three years later another revision, containing a very large number of very small changes. During the last year of his life he revised the first volume of his *Logic* and also made a great many minute and for the most part utterly unhelpful changes in the early pages of the preface to his *Phenomenology,* but died before finishing with the preface.

Saying that one prefers the late Nietzsche to the early Nietzsche, but the early Hegel to the later Hegel would sound highly subjective. But it is a fact that Hegel did his most original work before he went to Berlin and became a famous professor, that his inspiration gradually dried up, and that his growing conservatism went together with a lack of new ideas. His Berlin lectures contain many striking passages and have exerted an immense influence, but they drew heavily on his early notes, and the power to fashion his youthful visions into lasting works was gone. Hegel worked to the end and, far from being as self-satisfied as he has often been pictured, kept revising his lectures as well as his books. But his energies went into relatively insignificant changes, even if he did make thousands of them, and into unimportant reviews of less important books. Once more, Rosenkranz's testimony (16 f.) is to the point: "One cannot find anything more hacked to pieces, more crossed out, more constantly rewritten than one of Hegel's drafts for a letter from the Berlin period."

His early essays are bold both stylistically and in their radical critique of Christianity. In the *Phenomenology* and *Logic* the occasionally very striking prose keeps compromising with the author's notions of what is academically or "scientifically" respectable and solid, but the over-all conception of both projects is bold to the point of foolhardiness. In the *Encyclopedia* the format is cut and dried, but the attempt to offer so much in such a small compass is still anything but timid. Then, beginning about fourteen years before his death, Hegel dared no more.

The *Philosophy of Right* is not, as has been alleged, the work of a timeserver; neither is it a courageous book. The religious views of the later Hegel were remote from all forms of traditional Christianity, but he no longer heeded his own emphatic dictum that philosophy should beware of being edifying, and tried to show that he could be more inspiring, and sound more Christian, than Schleiermacher and other liberal theologians. He came to emphasize what his philosophy had in common with Christianity—what is heard gladly.

He had not always been a tired old man; he had known little peace until he was forty-five. The great battles of the Napoleonic era had never been far away. He had not found it easy to fit into the social structure of his time: while a great many mediocrities were appointed Professors of Philosophy, he was thirty-eight when he settled down to his first decent job—as headmaster of a boys' secondary school—and he was forty-six when he finally obtained an academic chair. (Nietzsche had been a professor for ten years when he retired in ill health at thirty-five.) When Hegel came to Berlin, he palpably enjoyed having finally found peace and security.

After his death, Hegel's works were edited by professors and other highly respectable men who had been his students. Yet his works were edited much more irresponsibly than Nietzsche's, although the editing of Nietzsche has long been considered a scandal. That four words and one erroneous quotation were left out of *The Antichrist* when it was published in 1895 has been cited as proof of the perversion of Nietzsche by his editors, while the fact that scores of changes were made by Hegel's editors, even in the books he himself had published, has excited no interest whatever, except among a very few Hegel scholars. That abundant "additions" of dubious character were interlarded in the posthumous editions of two of his four books is not considered a scandal, and these "additions" are quoted by the most reputable professors as Hegel's own words. Not one of Hegel's books is better known than "his" *Philosophy of History,* and inadequate translations of indefensible German texts keep being reissued with learned prefaces (cf. H 52 and 53).

It has often been said that Nietzsche was not really a philosopher because he had no system. Some German scholars still suppose that a philosopher without a system is like a square circle. This strange notion is largely due to Hegel's influence, although Hegel himself never denied the name of philosopher to anybody because he lacked a system. Nor are his own books as "scientific" as he would have liked them to be. As long as he was vigorous and original he was not rigorous and systematic, but a writer who thought and wrote in brief units. His span actually tended to be shorter than Nietzsche's: he did not write essays as long as Nietzsche's first five books or the three inquiries that constitute the *Genealogy of Morals* or *The Antichrist.* Even the famous system, which is the work of a professor older than Nietzsche was when he stopped writing, consists of hundreds of short aphorisms, averaging about half a small page in length in the original edition of 1817 and about one small page each in the final, third edition, including the "remarks" that amplify the pithy statements in the beginning. What is systematic is merely the arrangement.

What makes historical work so fascinating is that the realities one discovers are often, if not usually, so different from what everybody thinks he knows about the subject. Studying Hegel is no exception. An archaeologist may bring to light an unknown civilization. A philosopher who studies one of his predecessors cannot ask more than that he might verify Hegel's observation that what is familiar is not necessarily known: *Das Bekannte überhaupt ist darum, weil es bekannt ist, nicht erkannt* (C II.3.22). Under a portrait Hegel once wrote, "whoever knows me will recognize me here": *wer mich kennt, wird mich hier erkennen.* In another sense, these words might conclude this reinterpretation: may those who have long known of Hegel here come to know him; *wer ihn kennt, soll ihn hier erkennen.*

70

Others have seen him differently. To review their Hegel images would be subject matter enough for an interesting book. But let us go back once more to Schelling's triumph over Hegel in 1841 and see how Hegel's philosophy looked to the King of Prussia a little less than ten years after Hegel's death.

Even while Friedrich Wilhelm III was king, the crown prince felt drawn to Schelling: "In the forefront of his ideals stood the religious renewal and restoration of the church, while Schelling proclaimed the speculative renewal and restoration of positive religion, and promised to effect this in his Philosophy of Revelation."[49]

So the crown prince tried to bring Schelling to Berlin, as Hegel's successor. But this did not work out. In June 1840, his father died, and the crown prince ascended the throne as Friedrich Wilhelm IV. On August 1, 1840, Bunsen, close both to the new king and to Schelling, invited Schelling on behalf of the king.

"Schelling's call to Berlin was the declaration of war from above against the Hegelian philosophy. In the letter itself it was stated clearly against what enemy one wished to lead Schelling's intellectual power into the field. . . . It was against 'the dragon seed of the Hegelian pantheism'; thus the king himself had expressed it recently in a letter to Bunsen."[50]

For the Prussian king and the old Schelling, Hegel was the enemy of Christianity. For Kierkegaard, too, he was the philosopher who had dared to place philosophy above faith. For Marx he was a great genius who, however, had turned things upside down:

"He stands the world on its head and therefore also can dissolve all barriers in his head, while of course they endure for the bad sensibility, for the actual human being."[51]

"In direct opposition to German philosophy [i.e., Hegelianism], which descends from heaven to earth, we ascend from earth to

[49] Kuno Fischer, *Schellings Lebens, Werke and Lehre,* 2d rev. ed., Heidelberg, 1899, 236.
[50] *Ibid.,* 239.
[51] Marx and Engels, *Die Heilige Familie* in *Literarischer Nachlass,* II (1902), 304. This chapter was written by Marx, and page 304 refers expressly to the *Phenomenology.*

heaven. That is, we do not start from what people say, imagine, suppose, nor from said, imagined, supposed human beings, in order to arrive from there among human beings in the flesh; we start from actually working people, and from their actual life process we also present the development of the ideological reflexes and echoes of this life process. . . . Morality, religion, metaphysics, and other such ideology and forms of consciousness that correspond to them thus no longer retain the semblance of independence. They have no history, they have no development; instead, human beings who develop their material production and their material intercourse also change, along with this, which is their actuality, their thinking and the products of their thinking. It is not consciousness that determines life, but life that determines consciousness."[52]

On one point Marx and Kierkegaard were in agreement with the old Schelling who called Hegel's philosophy negative and called for a new positive philosophy. It is the point Schelling formulated in his *Philosophie der Mythologie* as he was making the transition to the *Philosophie der Offenbarung* (Revelation): "Negative philosophy may tell us in what blessedness consists, but it does not help us to achieve it."[53] Kierkegaard, in the Preface to his *Concluding Unscientific Postscript,* made the cornerstone of his approach his passionate concern about his infinite happiness, in the hereafter. Marx, in the last of his eleven "Theses Against Feuerbach," said: "The philosophers have merely *interpreted* the world differently; but what matters is to *change* it." They all wanted salvation.

In their different ways, Schelling and Kierkegaard were mainly preoccupied with themselves; Marx, who was not a Christian, with the salvation of others. The logic of Marx's philosophical arguments was not much better than Kierkegaard's, and certainly not generally superior to Hegel's: on the contrary, he was more abusive and infinitely less patient in his philosophical writings. But his impassioned interest in the salvation of wretched humanity made him the second Jew in history to be accepted by almost half the world as a messiah.

We are not tempted to contemplate Hegel's books as the Old Testament of Marxism—at least not the way a Christian fundamentalist looks at the Old Testament. Of course, if we prefer the Old Testament to the New and are used to studying the Old Testament

[52] Marx and Engels, *Deutsche Ideologie,* very near the beginning; *Volksausgabe* (1932), 15 f.
[53] *Werke* II, I, 567.

for its own sake, not as the background of a higher dispensation, then we may compare Hegel's writings to the Old Testament. He, too, offers us a world of riches of which too many people know only some dry genealogies and a few pious psalms.

The main effort of these chapters has been directed toward giving the reader some idea of the range, the depths, and the passion of Hegel. The point has not been to show that he was some one thing in particular, or that he should be considered above all as the proponent of some one great doctrine. Rather, Hegel was one of the few philosophers who in several of his books offered us a vision of the world, worked out in considerable detail. In this respect he belongs with Plato and Aristotle, Aquinas and Spinoza, Kant and Nietzsche.

As a human being, he seems more interesting than Aristotle and Kant; as a writer, he does not brook comparison with Plato and Nietzsche. Few will find their favorite philosopher in him. I, for one, do not. But there are not many who offer us so much.

CHAPTER VII:

Documentation, or Hegel's Development in Letters and Contemporary Reports

Hegel, Hölderlin, and Schelling called each other *Du:* they were fellow students at Tübingen. Hegel and Niethammer who became close friends a little later stuck always to the less familiar *Sie.* Reading Hegel's formal correspondence, especially that about his calls to Heidelberg and Berlin, one naturally wonders about the implications of his tone. In this connection it is relevant to consider Kant's dedication of his first book:[1]

"Dem Hochedelgebohrnen, Hochgelahrten und Hocherfahrnen Herrn, HERRN Johan Christoph Bohlius, Der Medizin Doctorn und zweyten ordentlichen Professorn auf der Academie zu Königsberg, wie auch Königlichen Leibmedico, meinem insonders Hochzuehrenden Gönner.

"Hochedelgebohrner Herr, Hochgelahrter und Hocherfahrner Herr Doctor, Insonders Hochzuehrender Gönner!"

(To the Highly and Nobly Born, Highly Learned and Highly Experienced . . . and second Full Professor . . . as well as His Majesty's Physician, my Patron, deserving of especially high reverence. . . .)

On the following three pages, *"Ew. Hochedelgebohrnen"* (Your Highly and Nobly Born Self) is repeated once in every sentence, and in the end all the forms of address are once more piled up on top of each other before Kant signs as "most obligated servant."

In 1781 Kant dedicated his masterpiece, the *Critique of Pure*

---

[1] *Gedanken von der wahren Schätzung der lebendigen Kräfte* . . . (Reflections on the True Estimate of the Living Forces . . .), Königsberg, 1746; but the dedication is dated April 22, 1747.

Reason, "To his Excellency, the Royal Minister of State, Freiherrn von Zedlitz" and signed the dedication as *"unterthäniggehorsamster Diener* Immanuel Kant" (most humbly obedient servant).

Naturally, the prose of the following letters sometimes strikes us as somewhat stilted. At other times it is rough in a different way: the writers evidently did not trouble to read their letters once more before mailing them; after all, they were not writing for publication. The long selection from Hotho's book presents different problems: Hotho was not much of a writer, and his book created no stir and was never reprinted.

None of this material is offered for its supposed stylistic excellence. On the contrary, in this respect these pages are often quite rough though here and there we do encounter passages that are brilliantly formulated or deeply moving. The principle of selection was to give a faithful image of Hegel. Indeed, this chapter may deliver the *coup de grâce* to the traditional misconception of Hegel and establish the reinterpretation attempted in the preceding chapters.

When Hegel's sister committed suicide, she left behind a letter addressed to Hegel's widow and dated January 7, 1832[2]:

". . . What I can bring together in my present sad physical and psychological state out of my brother's childhood, I will tell you: As a boy of 3 he was sent to the German school, and in his 5th year to the Latin school. At that age he already knew the first declension and the Latin words that go with it; for our blessed mother had taught him. She was, for those days, a woman of education and thus had considerable influence on his first studies. In all classes he received a prize every year because he was always among the top five; and from his 10th to his 18th year he was the first in his division in the Gymnasium. When he was 8, his teacher Löffler, who showed a great preference for him and contributed much to his later education, gave him Shakespeare's dramatic works, translated by Eschenburg, with a note: 'You do not understand them yet, but you will soon learn to understand them.' So this teacher already noticed the profundity that was latent in this boy; and I

[2] *Dok.* 392–94. This item is placed first because it concerns Hegel's childhood. Otherwise, the arrangement is chronological, following the dates of the letters and reports.

still remember well that it was *The Merry Wives of Windsor* to which he responded first. . . .

"In the year 1783, bilious dysentery [*Gallenruhr*] and bilious fever [*Gallenfieber*] raged in Stuttgart, and the latter attacked our father, our mother, Hegel, and me. Of the first three one did not know who would die first. Our mother became the victim. Hegel was so ill that he already had quinsy [*Bräune*], and everybody doubted that he would recover. He did get well but then got a big, nasty boil behind his ear and had to undergo a painful operation. I forgot to mention that in his 6th year he had pox [*Blattern*] in the worst way, so even the doctor thought he was lost, and he was blind several days. During his student years he had tertian fever [*Tertianfieber*] for a long time and on that account spent a few months at home where on his good days he read Greek tragedies, which were his favorite reading, and botany; as far as I know, he also visited the dissecting room in Tübingen. During his last years at the Gymnasium, physics was his favorite science. . . ."

Christiane also left a sheet of notes about her brother which came into his widow's possession:

". . . Pleasure in physics. Lacked all bodily agility. Must have been easy to get along with, for he always had many friends; loved to jump, but was utterly awkward in dancing lessons.

Fall 1788   Tübingen: was a gay but not dissolute student, loved to dance, enjoyed the society of women, preferred one now and then but never raised hopes for the future; as an M.A. still wanted to study law, was close to Schelling who was a few years younger. Pulpit delivery bad, not loud enough, faltering.

Fall 1793   Switzerland, more than three years, returned introverted, cheerful only in small and intimate gatherings.

Early 1797   to Frankfurt. . . ."

HÖLDERLIN *to* HEGEL: *July 10, 1794*

Dear brother!
    . . . Do write me a lot about what you think and do now, dear brother!
    My work now is rather concentrated. Kant and the Greeks are almost my only reading. . . .

                        Your [*Dein*] Hölderlin.

SCHELLING *to* HEGEL: *Tübingen, January 1795*

. . . Who would care to bury himself in the dust of antiquity
when the movement [*Gang*] of *his own* time lifts him up and carries him along from moment to moment. I live and breathe philosophy these days. Philosophy has not reached the end yet. Kant
has furnished the results; the premises are still lacking. And who
could understand results without premises?—A Kant, of course; but
what can the masses do with that? Fichte said, when he was here
the last time, that one must have the genius of Socrates to penetrate
Kant. I find it truer every day.—We have to go still further with
philosophy!—Kant has removed *everything*—but how should they
notice that? One has to smash it into small pieces before their eyes,
so they can't miss it! O these great Kantians that now abound everywhere! They stick to the letter and bless themselves that they still
see so much. I am firmly convinced that the old superstition not
only of positive but also of so-called natural religion has already
been combined in most heads with the letter of Kant's philosophy.
It is amusing to watch them pulling in the moral proof as on a
string. Before one knows what has happened, the *deus ex machina*
leaps out—the personal, individual being that sits in heaven
above!—

Fichte will raise philosophy to a height which will make even
most present-day Kantians dizzy. . . .

HEGEL *to* SCHELLING: *Late January 1795*

Mein Lieber!

. . . What you [*Du*] tell me of the theological-Kantian (*si diis
placet*) movement of philosophy in Tübingen is not surprising. Orthodoxy cannot be shattered as long as its profession is associated with
worldly advantages and woven through the whole state. This [worldly]
interest is too strong for it to be given up in the near future, and
it is effective even if those concerned are not clearly conscious of it.
Till then it will always have on its side the whole horde of thought-
less parrots and copycats—always as numerous as they are devoid
of all higher interests. When this horde reads something that runs

counter to their convictions (if one wants to honor their verbiage with this term) and of whose truth they have some inkling, they say, 'Yes, that seems to be true' and go to sleep—and in the morning one drinks one's coffee and pours it for others as if nothing had happened. . . .

. . . But I think it would be interesting to disturb the theologians as much as possible in their antlike industry as they amass Critical [i.e., Kantian] building materials to strengthen their Gothic temple; to make everything difficult for them, to whip them out of every nook and subterfuge till they found none any more and had to show their nakedness completely in the daylight. But among the building materials which they abduct from the Kantian stake to prevent the conflagration of dogmatics they surely also carry home live coals; these bring about the general spread of philosophical ideas.—

For the mischief of which you write and whose manner of inference I can therefore imagine, Fichte has unquestionably opened the door with his *Critique of All Revelation*. He himself made moderate use; but once his principles are firmly accepted, it will be impossible to set up any end or dike for theological logic. From the holiness of God he argues what God must do by virtue of his purely moral nature, etc., and has thus reintroduced the old manner of proof in dogmatics. It might be worth the trouble to elucidate this further.—

. . . One expression in your letter concerning the moral proof I do not quite understand: "which they know to handle in such a way that the individual, personal being leaps out" [see the preceding letter; the quotation is not exact]. Do you believe that we really cannot go that far? Farewell!

Let reason and freedom remain our watchword, and the invisible church our point of union.

H.

HÖLDERLIN *to* HEGEL: *Jena, January 26, 1795*

. . . I have spoken with Goethe. Brother! It is the most beautiful enjoyment of our life to find so much humanity fused with so much greatness. He conversed with me so gently and kindly that my heart really laughed and still laughs when I think of it. Herder was cordial, too, seized my hand, but seemed more like a man of the world, often spoke quite allegorically, as you know him, too. I expect to see him many more times. . . .

Fichte's speculative pages—*Grundlage der gesamten Wissenschaftslehre*—also his printed *Lectures on the Vocation of the Scholar* should interest you a lot. At first I suspected him very much of dogmatism. . . . His absolute ego (=Spinoza's Substance) contains all reality; it is everything, and outside it there is nothing. Thus there is no object for this absolute ego, for otherwise it would not contain all of reality; but a consciousness without object is not thinkable, and when I myself am this object, then I am necessarily limited as such, even if it should only be in time, and thus not absolute. Thus no consciousness is thinkable in the absolute ego; as the absolute ego, I have no consciousness, and insofar as I have no consciousness, I am (for myself) nothing; thus the absolute ego is (for me) nothing.

Thus I wrote down my own thoughts when I was still in Waltershausen where I read his first pages, immediately after reading Spinoza. . . .

SCHELLING *to* HEGEL: *Tübingen, February 4, 1795*

. . . Annoyed by the mischief of the theologians, I have often thought of having recourse to satire, reducing all dogmatics, with all the appendages of the darkest centuries, to practical grounds of faith; but I lacked the time, and God knows whether, if the satire had been *completed,* most readers wouldn't have taken it seriously, and I should have had the joy, secretly at least, of shining even as a young man as a philosophical light of the church.—The matter needs to be attacked seriously, and I shall look forward to seeing it begun by your hand, my friend.—Yet an answer to your question: whether I believe that with the moral proof we cannot reach a personal being? I confess that this question surprised me; I shouldn't have expected it from a friend of Lessing; but presumably you only asked to find out whether I had answered it *definitely for myself;* for you it has surely been decided long ago. For us, too, the orthodox concepts of God are no more.[3]—My answer is: We can go *beyond*

---

[3] An allusion to Lessing's words, reported by Jacobi in his book *On Spinoza's Doctrine.*

a personal being. I have meanwhile become a Spinozist!—Don't be amazed. You'll soon hear how.—For Spinoza, the world (the object as opposed to the subject) was—*everything;* for me this is true of the *ego.* The real difference between the Critical [Kantian] and the dogmatic philosophy seems to me to lie in the fact that the former starts from the absolute ego (not yet conditioned by any object), while the latter starts from the absolute subject or non-ego. The latter, pushed to its ultimate consequences, leads to Spinoza's system, the former to Kant's. Philosophy has got to start from the *unconditional.* The only question is what is unconditional, the ego or the non-ego. Once this question is decided, *everything* is decided.—For me the highest principle of all philosophy is the pure, absolute ego, i.e., the ego insofar as it is mere ego, not yet conditioned by objects but posited through *freedom.* The alpha and omega of all philosophy is freedom. . . .

HEGEL *to* SCHELLING: *Bern, April 16, 1795*

. . . To exhort you to elaborate your system in its entirety would be insulting because an activity that has seized on such an object requires no exhortation. From the Kantian system and its highest completion I expect a revolution in Germany which will start from principles that are already there and merely require to be worked over and to be applied to all our knowledge. An esoteric philosophy, to be sure, will always remain—the idea of God as the absolute ego will belong to that. . . .

. . . I am looking forward eagerly to the products of the Easter season: I am planning to study Fichte's *Wissenschaftslehre* this summer when I should have more leisure to develop some ideas which I have been hatching for a long time; but I lack the use of a library, though I need it very much. Schiller's [journal] *Horen,* two first pieces, have delighted me greatly; the essay on the aesthetic education of man is a masterpiece. Niethammer announced a philosophical journal earlier this year; did anything come of it? Hölderlin writes me often from Jena; he is full of enthusiasm for Fichte whom he credits with great intentions. How happy Kant must feel to see the fruits of his labors already in such worthy successors. The harvest will be magnificent one day. . . .

HEGEL *to* SCHELLING:
Tschugg near Bern, August 30, 1795

. . . I once was about to make clear to myself in an essay what it could mean to approach God . . . What I perceived obscurely and in an undeveloped way, your essay has explained to me in the most glorious and satisfying manner. . . .

Comments on your essay you cannot expect from me. I am merely an apprentice; I am trying to study Fichte's *Grundlage* [*der gesamten Wissenschaftslehre,* 1794]. Permit me one remark that occurred to me, just so you see my good will to comply with your request for comments. . . . You call the ego the only substance. If substance and accidents are corollaries, then it would seem to me that the concept of substance would not be applicable to the absolute ego—only to the empirical ego as it is encountered in self-consciousness. But that you do not speak of this ego (which unites the highest thesis and antithesis) seemed clear from the preceding paragraph. . . .

Regarding your disputation . . . I have found in it confirmation of a suspicion I have had for a long time: it might have turned out more honorably for us and for humanity if some—really any—heresy that was damned by church councils and symbols had developed into the public system of faith instead of the orthodox system's retaining the upper hand.

I am sorry for Fichte; beer glasses and patriotic swords have resisted the force of his spirit; perhaps he would have accomplished more if he had left them to their brutality and had only attempted to educate a quiet, select little group. But it surely is shameful— his and Schiller's treatment by would-be philosophers. My God, what pedants and slaves are among them! . . .

SCHELLING *to* HEGEL: *Leipzig, June 20, 1796*

. . . Permit me to tell you one more thing. You seem to be at present in a state of indecision and—judging from your last letter to me [which has been lost]—even depression [*Niedergeschlagenheit*], which is utterly unworthy of you. Phooey! A man of your powers must never allow such indecision to develop in him. Tear yourself away as soon as possible. If Frankfurt and Weimar should not work out, permit me to agree with you on a plan to get you out of your present situation. For you there must be means enough everywhere. You see, I count heavily on our friendship when I speak so frankly. Friends must have this right. Once more: your present situation is unworthy of your powers and claims.

From HEGEL'S *Diary of His Trip through the Bernese Alps, July/August 1796*[4]

We went the same evening to see the Staubbach. We had already seen it to some extent on the way, especially from the inn where, in spite of its proximity, it looked merely like an inconsiderable thread of water that did not at all repay the exertions and expenses of the day but rather seemed to confirm fully Herrn Meiner's judgment [in *Briefe über die Schweiz,* 1785]. In spite of these prejudices against it, and although it was beginning to get dark, we were still fully satisfied once we were very close to it and stood under it. Perhaps the fact that this was the first object of its kind on our trip contributed, while Herr Meiner, on the other hand, arrived there sated with great objects of nature. The height of the wall of rock from which it plunges down is great in itself; the Staubbach really is not. But the gracious, unconstrained, free, and playful descent of the water dust is only that much lovelier. Since one does not see a power, a great force, any *thought of the constraint, of the must of nature* remains *quite remote,* and the *life* that always dissolves, leaps apart, and is not united in *one* mass but *eternally moves on actively* [*ewig sich Fortregende und Tätige*] rather produces the *image of free play.* . . .

Today we saw these glaciers only at a distance of about half an hour, and there is nothing of interest in this sight. One can only call it *a new kind of seeing, but one that does not in any way give the spirit some further occupation,* except that one is struck at finding oneself in the greatest summer heat so close to masses of ice which, even at the depth where the heat ripens cherries, nuts, and grain, are not thawed to any considerable extent. Toward the bottom the ice is very dirty and in places completely covered with filth;

[4] Ros. 470 ff.; *Dok.* 223 f., 227, 231 f., 234 f., 236, 241 f.

and whoever has seen a broad filthy road, going downhill, on which the snow has begun to melt, can form a pretty fair idea of the sight of the lower part of the glaciers as it looks from a distance and will also admit that there is nothing either great or lovely about this sight. . . .

From here one enjoys a view of the falls as far as one can survey them, and this majestic spectacle certainly compensated us for the troubles of this uncomfortable day. Through a narrow ravine the water presses above, quite narrow, and then falls down vertically in much wider waves—in waves that continually draw the spectator's glances down with them and which one nevertheless can never fix, never follow, for their image, their form, dissolves every few moments and is replaced by another, and *in these falls one sees eternally the same image, and sees at the same time that it is never the same.* . . .

Meiner has quite rightly called attention to these falls, but a description cannot remotely take the place of seeing them for oneself, any more than a painting could. Confronted with a description, the imagination might more nearly paint the whole view for itself, if it already possessed similar images; but a painting, if it is not huge, must seem paltry and give only an inadequate notion. *The sensuous presence of the painting* does not permit the imagination to expand the object that is represented; it is seen the way it confronts the eye. We are still further prevented from expanding it because when we hold a painting in our hands or find it hung on a wall, the senses cannot help measuring it against our size and the size of the surrounding objects and thus finding it small. Such a painting would have to be brought so close to the eye that one would find it difficult to survey the whole, that one could not set it beside other objects, so that one lost every measure altogether. Moreover, even in the best painting the most attractive and essential feature of such a spectacle would be missing: *eternal life, the tremendous motion* [*Regsamkeit*] in it. A painting can offer only a part of the whole impression, namely the sameness of the image that it has to present in determinate outlines and parts; the other part of the impression, however, the eternal, inexorable alteration of every part, the eternal dissolution of every wave, every foam, which always draws down our eyes with it, which does not permit us the same direction of our glances for as long as one third: all this power, all this life is wholly lost.

Completely soaked, we arrived in Meiringen at 1:30. The continual rain prevented us from seeing the lower part of the Reichenbach Falls. . . .

. . . *I doubt whether the most believing theologian would dare* to ascribe to *nature* itself in these mountains *the aim of expediency for man,* who has to steal from her with great exertion what little he can use, and even that is paltry; and he can never be sure whether in the course of his wretched thieveries, while robbing a handful of grass, he will not be smashed by rocks or avalanches; whether the pitiful work of his hands, his poor cottage and cow stable will not be shattered one night. In these bleak wildernesses, educated men might perhaps sooner have invented all other theories and sciences but hardly that part of *physico-theology* which proves to the pride of man how nature has spread out everything for his enjoyment and comfort—*a pride that at the same time characterizes our age* inasmuch as one sooner finds satisfaction in the notion that so much has been done for us by a strange being than one would find in the consciousness that it is man himself who has offered all these aims to nature. . . .

. . . Near dusk, we reached a stone house with a few rooms, in a bleak, sad stone wilderness that is as savage as the regions through which we had come for several hours. Neither eye nor imagination finds in these formless masses a single point on which the former might rest with pleasure or where the latter might find some occupation or something to play with. Only the mineralogist finds material to venture inadequate hypotheses about the revolution [*sic*] of these mountain ranges. *Reason* finds in the thought of the duration of these mountains or in the type of sublimity that one ascribes to them nothing to impress it or demand from it amazement and admiration. The sight of these eternally dead masses gave me nothing but the monotonous and at length boring notion: *that is how it is* [*es ist so*]. . . .

. . . Between the water and the village Steg, an isolated, tremendous rock lies in a meadow near the road, and it is understandable that the childish minds of these shepherd peoples have long been struck by its presence and have attached a *myth* to it. But as always, as also in the case of the Devil's Bridge, the Christian imagination has produced nothing but an *insipid legend.* . . .

HEGEL *to* HÖLDERLIN

ELEUSIS

For Hölderlin, August 1796

Around me and in me dwells calm—the never weary
care of bustling humanity sleeps, and they grant me
freedom and leisure—thanks be to you, O my
liberator, O night!—with a white wreath of mist
the moon is shrouding the uncertain border lines
of distant hills; the glistening streak
of yonder lake is twinkling kindly—
the day's dull noise makes memory seem distant,
as if years separated it from now;
your image, whom I love, confronts me,
and the delight of days that fled; but soon it yields
to sweeter hopes of seeing you again—
The scene I picture of the long desired fiery
embrace and of the questions after that, the scene
of the more secret search to find each other out
and see what in the friend's expression, bearing, outlook
changed since that time—the rapture of assurance:
the ancient covenant's loyalty still firmer, riper,
the covenant that no oath had ever sealed,
to live for free truth only—and peace with the law
that regulates opinion and men's feelings, never, never!
. . .

HÖLDERLIN *to* HEGEL: *Frankfurt, October 24, 1796*

Dearest Hegel!
    . . . The day before yesterday Herr Gogel comes to us quite
unexpectedly and tells me that he would be pleased if you were
still free and interested in this job. You would have to educate two
nice boys, 9 and 10, would be able to live quite unembarrassed in
his house, would—and this is not unimportant—have a room of
your own, with the boys next door, would be very satisfied with the

economic terms; but of him and his family I should not write too many good things because raised expectations are always ill satisfied; but if you would come you would find his house open every day.

Now the commentary. Less than 400 florins you would scarcely get. Your travel expenses would be paid, as mine were, and you can probably count on 10 carlins. For every *Messe*[5] you would receive a very considerable present. And you will get everything free, excepting only haircuts, shaves, and other such trifles. At table you will drink very good Rhine wine or French wine. You will live in a house that is one of the most beautiful in Frankfurt and stands on one of the most beautiful squares in Frankfurt, the Rossmarkt. . . .

Finally, *Lieber,* let me urge this on you, too: A man whose situation and character have undergone motley changes but who has remained loyal to you with his heart, memory, and spirit, and who will be your friend with greater warmth and devotion than ever and share with you every concern of life eagerly and frankly, and who lacks nothing for a beautiful situation except you—this man does not live at all far from you if you should come here.

Really, *Lieber,* I need you and believe that you will not find me useless either. . . .

HEGEL *to* HÖLDERLIN: *Bern, November 1796*

Dearest Hölderlin!
. . . So I follow your call without hesitation . . .

HEGEL *to* NANETTE ENDEL (ca. 1775–1841; lived in the house of Hegel's parents for some months in 1796/97. According to a letter by D. F. Strauss, cited in B I, 442, "Hegel had a youthful love affair with her which echoes through the letters he wrote from Frankfurt till it dies down to friendship." Strauss does not seem to have had any information outside the letters, and these are inconclusive regarding the closeness of their relationship, though Strauss may have been right): *Frankfurt, March 22, 1797*

[5] "Fair": i.e., twice a year, in the spring and in the fall.

. . . Here in Frankfurt I come a little closer to the world again. I go to the comedy at least once a week and recently saw the *Magic Flute* which was performed with nice costumes and set but bad voices. Tomorrow they'll have *Don Giovanni* to which I am greatly looking forward on account of the music. . . .

My brother asks me to pay his compliments to you . . .[6]

HEGEL *to* NANETTE ENDEL: *Frankfurt, July 2, 1797*

. . . Memories of those days spent in the country now keep driving me out of Frankfurt; and as there I sought to become reconciled to myself and to men in the arms of nature, I often flee from here to this faithful mother, seeking separation from men with whom I live in peace, to preserve myself from their influence under her aegis and to prevent any covenant with them. . . .

HEGEL *to* NANETTE ENDEL: *Frankfurt, May 25, 1798*

. . . My sister probably attended the wedding, and it probably was great fun. We, too, might have danced a lot there, as we did the night before I left: ever since, I have been turning in circles; haven't you had balls in Memmingen? I am very well disposed toward dances: there is nothing gayer in our gloomy times. . . .

GOETHE *to* SCHILLER: *Weimar, July 18, 1798*

. . . It seems to be an unfailing law of nature that every action is opposed by a negation. . . .

CHRISTIANE HEGEL *to* HEGEL: *Stuttgart, January 15, 1799*

Last night, barely before 12, our father died quietly and painlessly. I am unable to write you more. God help me!

Your Christiane

---

[6] "*. . . Ihnen recht viel Schönes in seinem Namen zu sagen . . .*" This is the sole reference to Hegel's brother in the four volumes of *Briefe*.

SCHELLING *to* HEGEL: *Leipzig, May 24, 1802*

To write you from Berlin was quite impossible. Even here a few things still delayed me, so I can return to Jena only tomorrow. I shall arrive toward evening with Mme. Schlegel.[7] Be so kind, in case the furniture and other stuff have not been moved into the house in response to your first request in Mme. Schlegel's name, to ask Mme. Niethammer as soon as possible after you get this letter . . .

SCHELLING *to* HEGEL: *Cannstadt, July 11, 1803*

. . . The saddest sight I saw during my stay here was—Hölderlin. Since his journey to France, where he went on the recommendation of Prof. Ströhlin with utterly false notions about what would be expected of him in his new job, and whence he immediately returned since apparently demands were made on him that he was partly incapable of fulfilling and partly could not reconcile with his sensitivity—since this fatal journey his spirit is completely shattered, and though he is still capable of some work, e.g., translations from the Greek, up to a certain point, he is otherwise in a state of complete apathy. The sight of him shook me: he neglects his appearance to the point of arousing disgust and though his speech does not so much suggest derangement, he has acquired all the outward manners of people who are in such a state.—In these parts there is no hope of recovery. I thought of asking you whether you would want to look after him if he should come to Jena; this appealed to him. He needs a quiet environment. . . .

In view of our friendship, it will interest you to know that my friend and I recently got married. She sends you warm regards. . . .

[7] Caroline, wife of A. W. Schlegel, who divorced him in 1803 to marry Schelling.

HEGEL *to* SCHELLING: *Jena, August 16, 1803*

Above all, let me congratulate you on your marriage. In decency I ought to send you at least a sonnet on the subject, but you are accustomed to be satisfied with my prose, and prose does not allow one in such cases to be more demonstrative than a handshake and embrace are. . . .

GOETHE *to* HEGEL: *Jena, November 27, 1803*

Would you please look over the accompanying essay and tell me sometime when we see each other what you think of it.
                                                Goethe

GOETHE *to* HEGEL: *Jena, December 15, 1803*

If you, *wertester*[8] *Herr Doktor,* would write a review of the accompanying essay, in the sense in which you talked to me about it the other day, this would accomplish a doubly pleasing end for me, as you would thereby join our critical institute and you would give further occasion for interesting conversations which I should like to repeat with you often.
                                                Goethe

SCHELLING *to* HEGEL: *Würzburg, July 14, 1804*

. . . About 4 weeks ago, Sinclair surprised me. It seemed to me that with his quickly collected, still Fichtean ideas he has moved pretty much into shallowness. He was on his way to Swabia to fetch Hölderlin from there, and then also returned with him. Hölderlin's condition is better than last year, but he is still visibly shattered. The decay of his mind finds complete expression in his transl. of

---

[8] "Dearest" or "worthiest."

Sophocles.[9] He told me that he had become librarian for the Count of Homburg and went there with S.

  Best wishes and answer soon

Your Schelling

HEGEL to NIETHAMMER: Jena, March 4, 1805

. . . Finally, all four decrees concerning my professorship have arrived; Fries is getting one together with me. . . .

You will have heard that Goethe was very dangerously and Schiller also very ill[10]; I could not remain behind such great examples and was out for two weeks, too. . . .

HEGEL *to* VOSS (1751–1826, author of the classical German translation of Homer, Professor at Jena from 1802, Professor at Heidelberg from 1805): *Final Draft, May 1805* (The letter is lost, but three drafts have survived.)

. . . You yourself know best that Jena has lost the interest it used to have . . .

What has been lost here now flourishes in Heidelberg, even more beautifully; and I have the hope that my science, philosophy, will enjoy a favorable reception there . . .

If I am to speak of that which I might be able to achieve in this science, after my first excursions which a fair judge [should consider] not so much as they are, being first attempts, but rather to see if they contain the germ from which something finished will develop; I have remained silent before the public for 3 years and given lectures on the whole science of philosophy—speculative philosophy, philosophy of nature, philosophy of spirit, natural law—and moreover [wish] that I might fill in a certain philosophical

---

[9] *Die Trauerspiele des Sophokles,* Frankfurt, 1804. This strange estimate was not unusual at the time; but it is arguable that Hölderlin's versions of *Antigone* and *Oedipus Tyrannus* surpass any translation available in English 160 years later, especially in poetic power, but also in the superbly felicitous rendering of many lines. Carl Orff has set both of them to music. See also Sinclair's letter of May 23, 1807, below.

[10] Schiller died May 9.

subject that as yet has not been filled in Heidelberg and lecture on aesthetics in the sense of a *cours de lit[t]érature*—an intention I have long had and should like to execute even more since I should hope to be fortunate enough to enjoy your support in it. I shall present the work this fall as a system of philosophy; I hope that at least this will emerge from it, that I am not concerned with the mischief of formalism which is practiced at present by ignorance, especially with the help of a terminology behind which it is hiding . . .

Luther has made the Bible speak German; you, Homer—the greatest present that can be given to a people; for a people is barbarous and does not consider the excellent things it knows as its own property until it gets to know them in its own language;— if you would forget these two examples, I should like to say of my aspirations that I shall try to teach philosophy to speak German. Once that is accomplished, it will be infinitely more difficult to give shallowness the appearance of profound speech. . . .

VOSS *to* HEGEL: *Heidelberg, August 24, 1805*

Your trusting, candid letter, my most esteemed *Herr Professor,* I should have liked to answer with more than mere good will. Geheimrat von Reizenstein to whom I showed it said immediately that, as welcome as such an application would have been to him earlier, the budget of the academy limits him to the most urgent requirements. There was some hope of new income for which I wanted to wait. Now it is clear to me that for now, until the necessary subjects are taken care of, there can be no thought of anything extraordinary.

May the genius of Germany bless your resolve to lead philosophy down again from the clouds to friendly intercourse with well-speaking humankind. . . .

HEGEL *to* NIETHAMMER: *Jena, August 6, 1806*

. . . Meanwhile you may have an opportunity to find out discreetly from his printer how many copies [of the *Phenomenology*] have been printed. Partly, his behavior has made me suspicious, partly certain because during the negotiations he reduced the number of copies from 1000 to 750, which meant a reduction of the honorarium, and this made me suspicious only after I found out that he has his own printing shop—a circumstance he had carefully kept secret although, in view of my demand that the book be printed here, it would have been the most essential objection. . . .

NIETHAMMER *to* HEGEL: *Bamberg, October 3, 1806*

. . . So the matter stands pretty well, and everything depends merely on this, that you do not fail to send me the manuscript at the right time. But on this point I have to remind you again and again not to offer Herrn G.[11] the least loophole, for I consider him wholly capable of insisting quite literally on my bond. . . . In any case, it will be necessary that you get a very detailed receipt from the post when you mail the last shipment, so we are covered against all querulousness and chicanery on the part of Herrn G. The last possible date for dispatching the final shipment (if it is to be here for sure October 18), is *Monday, October 13.* Don't by any means exceed this deadline. If you cannot completely finish your corrections by then, I know of almost no course than that you yourself come here, too, and complete your corrections in the manuscript alongside the corrections of the proofs.—Coming here, to be sure, will be made somewhat difficult by the movements of the armies; but it will not be impossible, and once you got here you might well have more quiet here than there . . .

Nh.

HEGEL *to* NIETHAMMER: *Jena, October 8, 1806*

. . . Here is half of the manuscript, Friday you will receive the other half; and then I shall have done what could be done on my side. If any part of this got lost, of course, I should hardly know what to do; I should hardly be able to reconstruct it, and then the work certainly could not appear this year. . . .

[11] Goebhardt, the publisher of the *Phenomenology.*

HEGEL *to* NIETHAMMER

Jena. Monday, October 13, 1806,
the day Jena was occupied by the French
and the Emperor Napoleon arrived in it.

What worry I must feel about the former batches of manuscript,
dispatched last Wednesday and Friday, you see from the date-
line. . . . The Emperor—this world soul[12]—I saw riding through
the city to a review of his troops; it is indeed a wonderful feeling
to see such an individual who, here concentrated in a single point,
sitting on a horse, reaches out over the world and dominates it. . . .

From the whole appearance of things I must doubt whether my
manuscript, dispatched Wednesday and Friday, arrived—my loss
would really be too great—my other acquaintances did not suffer
anything; should I be the only one? How much I wish that you
had forgone the cash payment of part of the sum and had not made
the deadline so strict. But since the mail left from here I had to risk
the dispatch. God knows with what a heavy heart I now risk this
one, yet I do not doubt that the mails circulate freely now behind
the armies. . . .

HEGEL *to* NIETHAMMER: *Jena, October 18, 1806*

. . . Coming to my problems now, I have asked Asverus about
the legal side. He declares most emphatically that such circumstances set aside all obligations. Monday the first mail, either by
coach or on horseback, goes out again; so I shall send the last
pages then, having carried them for days in my pocket along with a
letter written during the night of terror before the fire [which raged
October 13]. . . .

The money now due me should enable me entirely to get through
this winter without trouble. If, moreover, one of the manuscript
packages got lost, my presence here will be absolutely necessary. To

---

[12] *Den Kaiser—diese Weltseele—sah ich durch die Stadt zum Rekognoszieren
hinausreiten;* misquoted by Royce, p. 73, and not only by him: "Hegel . . .
said that he had met the *Weltgeist zu Pferde.*"

be sure, those fellows have mixed up my papers like lottery tickets, so it would take the greatest exertion to find the necessary notes. How eagerly I am awaiting the first news.—But one request I cannot avoid: to send me money; I am in the most urgent distress . . .

HEGEL *to* SCHELLING: *Jena, January 3, 1807*

. . . I had long hoped—even last Easter—to be able to send you something of my work—and this, too, was responsible for my silence—but now I finally anticipate the conclusion of the printing and shall be able to send it to you—but it is only the beginning, though voluminous enough for a beginning—this Easter. It will interest me especially if you will not disapprove of my thought and manner. . . .

SCHELLING *to* HEGEL: *Munich, January 11, 1807*

. . . I am full of suspense and expectation concerning your finally appearing work. What must result when *your* maturity still takes time to mature its fruits! I only wish you calm conditions and leisure for the execution of such solid and, as it were, timeless works. . . .

HEGEL *to* NIETHAMMER: *Jena, January 16, 1807*

Your last letter, *wertester Freund,* which I received, as a result of the recommendation on the address, Saturday morning instead of noon, I have repaid by sending Göbhardt the manuscript of the preface the very same day . . .

Soon, but not yet, I can wish the child a happy trip. Reading it for the last time on account of misprints, I often wished, of course, that I might be able to clear the ship here and there of ballast to make it fleeter.—In the second edition which is to follow *soon—si diis placet?!*[13]—everything shall become better; this comfort I shall commend to myself and others. . . .

13 "If it pleases the gods." The second edition appeared only after Hegel's death.

HEGEL *to* C. G. ZELLMANN (one of his best students at Jena, who died in 1808): *Jena, January 23, 1807*

. . . I was glad that you still think of me now that you are away; even more, that you are devoting this winter of solitude to the study of philosophy. Both are still united in any case: philosophy is something solitary . . . But you, too, show that you pay attention to the history of the day; and indeed nothing could show more convincingly how education triumphs over brutality, and the spirit over understanding devoid of spirit and over mere cleverness. Science alone is the theodicy: it keeps one both from looking at events with animal amazement, or ascribing them, more cleverly, to accidents of the moment or of the talents of one individual— as if the destinies of empires depended on an occupied or not occupied hill—and from lamenting the triumph of injustice and the defeat of right. . . .

Through the bath of its Revolution, the French nation has been liberated from many institutions which the human spirit had outgrown like baby shoes and which therefore weighed on it, as they still do on others, as fetters devoid of spirit; and the individual has taken off the fear of death and that life as usual which lacks all internal steadiness as soon as the scene is changed. This is what gives the French the great strength they are demonstrating against others. . . .

One hardly needs to fear anything for northern Germany from Catholicism. It would be interesting if the point of religion were raised; and in the end it might come to that. Fatherland, princes, constitution, *et al.*, do not seem to be the levers that could raise the German people; the question remains what might happen if religion were touched. Without a doubt, nothing deserves to be feared more than this. The leaders are separated from the people; both sides do not understand each other. What the former can accomplish, these days have pretty well shown us; and how the latter carry on when they act on their own, that you will have seen best at close quarters. . . .

HEGEL *to* NIETHAMMER: *Bamberg, April 7, 1807*

I write you, *hochgeschätzter*[14] *Freund,* for two reasons.

First, I did not tell you about the exact disposition of the copies [of the *Phenomenology*] which you were gracious enough to take along; so I want to do this now. Of the three copies with paper covers, one printed on vellum is for Goethe, that on writing paper for Geheimrat Voigt, the other one on vellum for you. Of the three unbound copies, please be gracious enough to send one to Frommann; time did not allow, as you know, taking care of binding or even paper covers. Further, I want to ask you to bring back the other two unbound copies; but I shall send an order for two copies for Frommann which Göbhardt will send me today. Be so good as to get one of these to Major von Knebel, the other to Seebeck . . .

HEGEL *to* SCHELLING: *Bamberg, May 1, 1807*

. . . What I wrote is finally finished; but with the distribution of copies to my friends the same unfortunate confusion is taking over that has affected the whole process of publishing and printing, and in part even the composition itself. For this reason you still have not received a copy from me; but I am still hoping that I shall get to the point where you will soon receive one. I am curious what you will say about the idea of this 1st Part, which is really the introduction—for I have not yet got beyond introducing, *in mediam rem.*—Getting into the details has damaged, as I feel, the synopsis of the whole; but the whole is by its nature such an interlocking hither and thither that, even if it had been formed better, it would still take me a lot of time before it would stand there clearer and more finished.—That single parts, too, would require a lot more work in many ways to be really mastered, I need not say as you will discover this for yourself only too clearly.—Regarding the greater deformity of the later parts, be considerate also because I finished the editing around midnight before the Battle of Jena.— In the preface you will not find that I have gone too far against the shallowness that does so much mischief especially with your forms,

14 "Most highly esteemed."

reducing your science to a bare formalism.—Moreover, I need not tell you that if you approve of some pages of the whole this will mean more to me than if others should be satisfied or dissatisfied with the whole. Nor do I know anyone from whom I should rather see something to introduce this essay to the public and a judgment for my own benefit. . . .

SINCLAIR (1775–1815, philosopher and poet, remembered chiefly as Hölderlin's and Hegel's friend) *to* HEGEL: *May 23, 1807*

Dearest friend!
. . . About Hölderlin I, too, do not know anything except that Prof. Autenrieth has him under treatment in Tübingen. With what success, I do not know. But in Seckendorf's *Taschenbuch* there are a few things by him, written in his present condition, which I nevertheless consider incomparable and which F. Schlegel and Tieck, with whom I discussed them last year, pronounced the highest achievements of their kind in the whole of modern poetry. . . .

KNEBEL (1744–1834, major, retired 1773, introduced Goethe to the Duke of Weimar in 1775) *to* HEGEL: *Jena, September 11, 1807*

. . . Now I should rather speak with you of your newest philosophy—if only I had read it already. Seebeck gave me the preface, and I admired your profound, thinking spirit. What I and, as it seems, also some other friends still wish is that you might have put down the subtle net of your thoughts, which in places shines forth in a very clear and lovely manner, so that it would be at times more accessible to the senses of our more stupid eyes. Truly, we consider you one of the first thinkers of our age; but we wish that you might have supported the spiritual force with more physical form. What I am saying here is perhaps audacious, perhaps not sufficiently supported with reasons; but you must forgive a poetic wish when I should like to see what is serious pulled over into the field of the beautiful—not necessarily exactly into a Lucretian didactic poem.[15]

[15] Knebel's translation of Lucretius appeared in 1821 and was reviewed by Goethe. . . .

SCHELLING *to* HEGEL: *Munich, November 2, 1807*

I am enclosing a lecture I gave some time ago. You will judge it, as occasional lectures that are designed for a larger public should be judged.

It has been long since you received a letter from me. In your last letter you promised me your book. After I got it, I wanted to read it before writing you again. But the manifold interruptions and distractions of this summer left me neither the time nor the leisure required for the study of such a work. So I have so far read only the preface. Inasmuch as you yourself mention its polemical part: having a just standard in my opinion of myself, I should have to think too little of myself to relate this polemic to myself. So it may and should strike, as you say in your letter to me, the abuse and babble of the imitators, although in this essay itself this distinction is not made. You can easily imagine how happy I should be to shake them off.—That about which we should really have different convictions or views, could be found and decided between us briefly and clearly without reconciliation; for, of course, everything can be reconciled, with one exception. So I confess that so far I do not comprehend the sense in which you oppose the *Concept* to intuition. Surely, you could not mean anything else by it than what you and I used to call Idea, whose nature it is to have one side from which it is Concept and one from which it is intuition.

Be so good to let Liebeskinds read your copy of my lecture, too. In view of the small edition which was printed of it, I have only one copy left; if I should locate another one, I should send it to them.

My very best wishes; write me soon again and remain well disposed toward

Your sincere friend Sch.[16]

HEGEL *to* KNEBEL: *Bamberg, November 21, 1807*[17]

. . . You were gracious enough to say some words of praise in your letter about the preface of my book (which, as I see, you

---

[16] This was the last of the twenty-five extant letters exchanged by Hegel and Schelling. For discussion of their so-called break, see H 39; cf. H 68 and 70.
[17] See the letters of April 7 and September 11, above.

borrowed, so that I am perplexed by what misfortune the copy intended for you did not reach you—but I presume that this, too, was probably incomplete and therefore perhaps not given to you). I wish I could have complied with your wish for greater clarity and comprehensibility; but this is precisely the aspect which is most difficult to attain and constitutes the mark of perfection, assuming that the content is solid, too.—For there are contents that bring clarity with them, like those with which I am mostly dealing at present [as editor of a newspaper]: that Prince X passes through here today, that His Majesty has hunted wild boar, etc. But though the communication of political news is so clear, it is nevertheless pretty much the case these days that neither writers nor readers understand more about these matters. I might therefore infer *per contrarium* that with my unclear style that much more is understood—which I wish I could hope but do not believe. But seriously: although abstract material does not permit that clarity of presentation which from the first *abord*[18] shows the subject matter finished and clear, and of which more concrete materials are capable, I find your reproach just and can counter only with the lament— if it is permitted to lament—that I am prevented by so-called fate from producing something by my work that would better satisfy men of insight and taste in my science, like you, my friend, and that might give me the satisfaction that I could say: for this I have lived! . . .

CAROLINE PAULUS (1767–1844, novelist and wife of Professor H. E. G. Paulus (1761–1851), the theologian, 1793–1803 at Jena, then Würzburg, 1807 *Schulrat* in Bamberg, 1808 in Nürnberg where Hegel succeeded him in 1810; after 1810, Professor at Heidelberg) *to* HEGEL: *Bamberg, January 1808*

. . . Today, he [her husband] is continually studying your *System of Science*[19]; but as yet I do not know whether he will be able to solve the philosophical riddles as easily as the theological ones. He just had his hair cut, and since he does nothing without a reason, I presume that this sudden haircut might have some relation to the study of your system [to keep him from tearing his hair?].

[18] Attack or approach.
[19] *The Phenomenology.*

SCHELLING *to* K. J. H. WINDISCHMANN (1775–1839; a
Catholic writer who had studied philosophy and medicine at Würzburg and practiced medicine before becoming Professor of Philosophy and History at Aschaffenburg in 1803. In 1818 he became
Professor of Philosophy at Bonn): *July 30, 1808*

. . . I am eager to see what you will make of Hegel. I want to
see how you have disentangled the braid. I hope you have not
approached it from the God-fearing side, though it would be very
wrong on the other hand to let him get away with the manner
in which he wants to make a general standard of what is in accord
with and granted to his individual nature.

HEGEL *to* NIETHAMMER: *Bamberg, October 28, 1808*

. . . Theoretical work, as I am becoming more convinced every
day, accomplishes more in the world than practical work; once the
realm of notions is revolutionized, actuality does not hold out. . . .

WINDISCHMANN: The First Review of *The Phenomenology*[20]

Whether we have completely understood Herrn Hegel, we leave
for him to judge. We have understood ourselves, but this is precisely
the author's most profound intention in his work. Regarding the
author's manner, however, we have often missed that necessity
which should strike us as we consider each moment in turn. His
manner is often harsh, dry, and more difficult to cope with than
the subject matter; nor is it rare for it, though this is easily comprehensible at the beginning of such a work, to move around the
subject uncertainly and hesitate anxiously before it finally hits it
squarely. The fruit is delectable enough: the shell will fall off by
itself as it grows ripe.

[20] *Jenaer Allgemeine Literatur Zeitung,* February 7–10, 1809; conclusion reprinted in Hoffmeister's edition of *Phänomenologie* (1952), xxxix. The bulk
of the review was taken up by a lengthy summary of the book.

WINDISCHMANN *to* HEGEL: *Aschaffenburg, April 27, 1810*

Verehrter Freund!

I believe I may address you this way because I really mean the
former [revered], and the latter [friend] may well be said when
one finds that one has long been at one in what matters most. . . .

For about two weeks now I am in one of the worst of mental
conditions, brought on by an almost apoplectic attack. Now my
situation, oppressive in any case, becomes a rock on my chest: a
profound hypochondria and almost semiparalysis has overcome me;
everything I have written and done nauseates me; least of all do
I wish that I had undertaken a work of which I shall yet speak to
you. . . .

The study of your *Syst. of Sci.* has convinced me that this work
will be considered one day, when the time of understanding has
come, as the basic book of the liberation of man, as the key to
that new gospel of which Lessing prophesied.[21] . . . I wanted to
say this loud and publicly and could only hint at it because acceptance of my *entire* review was declined . . . I therefore enclose
the remarks about the preface and the significance of the whole
work which I retained—the more so since in the latest philosophical
part of the *Heidelberger Jahrbücher,* p. 149, a Dr. Bachmann
whom I do not know refers to me so unjustly, suggesting that I
must have had my own good reasons for not saying anything about
the preface. . . .

The work at which I hinted above and which I cannot consider
without feelings of anxiety because it transcends my powers is . . .
an investigation about magic.[22]

HEGEL *to* WINDISCHMANN: *Nürnberg, May 27, 1810*

. . . I am eager to see your work on magic. I confess that I
should not dare to tackle this gloomy side and aspect of spiritual
nature or the natural spirit, and am doubly delighted that you will
partly illuminate this for us, partly take up again and rehabilitate

---

[21] §86; cf. H 13.
[22] In 1813 he published *Untersuchungen über Astrologie, Alchemie und Magie,*
with an appendix about the relation of the police to the occult arts.

much that has been neglected and despised.—But there is no work that requires health and a cheerful, evenly cheerful, disposition more than this. Be assured that your mental state which you describe to me is partly due to this work: this descent into dark regions where nothing shows itself to be firm, determinate, and secure, where splendors flash everywhere, but next to abysses . . . —where the beginning of every path breaks off again and runs into the indefinite, loses itself, and tears us out of our destiny and direction.—From my own experience I know this mood of the mind, or rather of reason, once it has entered with interest and its intimations into a chaos of appearances and, though inwardly sure of the goal, it has not yet come through, not yet into the clarity and detailed grasp of the whole. I have suffered a few years of this hypochondria, to the point of enervation. Indeed, every human being may well have such a turning point in life, the nocturnal point of the contraction of his nature through whose narrows he is pressed, fortified and assured to feel secure with himself and secure in the usual daily life; and if he has already rendered himself incapable of being satisfied with that, secure in an inner, nobler existence.—Continue with confidence; only science, which has led you into this labyrinth of the mind, is capable of leading you out and healing you.—If you find this possible, cast out all this stuff for a while; if you stayed away from it, you would then return to it with renewed strength and with greater power.

With my further work things move slowly in view of my present duties; they are only partially connected with it, but I do not abandon it altogether. How fortunate you are that no such external obligations wither your activities on behalf of your inmost interests. . . .

P.S. Forgive the lateness of this reply. Through an accident, the beginning which was written long ago, before I was interrupted, disappeared from my sight for a while.

HEGEL *to* KNEBEL: *Nürnberg, December 14, 1810*

 . . . Hereabouts we have many railings and scaffolds of dry wood to which we nail and crucify our scions; and we also tabulate all this, put on orderly Spanish boots,[23] witness, attest, certify, examine,

---

[23] Cf. Goethe's *Faust*, line 1913.

and stamp. Then, when what is good is not achieved, regardless of the fact that we always work so hard to achieve something, we do not comprehend why, in the face of so much that is better, we don't attain what is good, and that the fever of meliorism is not precisely supreme health.

Let that be as it may; merely give us the hope that you may perhaps visit us here before long. You will find that you have retained your old friends who often remember you with this wish—and besides, diversion in sufficient external variety. For a few months now, we have an actually very nice museum which has taken the place of the old harmony which, however, persists, too;—recently a Herr von Haller has shot himself through the head; Frau Senatorin von Strömer has carried the child of her unmarried daughter into the water and sits in the tower; in a few days a man who has committed incest with his daughter will be broken on the wheel, and the latter will be beheaded together with him because both also killed the child; other *Fräulein* are still pregnant; recently, the fourteen-year-old daughter of one of my acquaintances absconded with a comedian, and a few days later another girl followed him, too; now and then one finds dead females in the water; deaths by natural causes not included;—we have concerts at which we only miss a singer like your wife—comedy, as well, not to speak of organizations and disorganizations, which one often cannot tell apart;—in brief, as you can see, we, too, do not lack incidents and *quodlibet*.[24]

Meanwhile, until I have again the good fortune of seeing you in person, I ask you, along with best regards to your wife and your son, to remember me in friendship—and also beg you, when you have occasion to do so, to attest my most respectful devotion to Herrn Geheimen Rat v. Goethe (and Dr. Riemer), and now only have space enough to call myself

Your most devoted
Hegel.[25]

[24] Literally, what pleases.
[25] Müller quotes parts of this letter in his *Hegel*—not in the Nürnberg chapter where they belong but in the section on Hegel's newspaper editorship in Bamberg, to illustrate the nature of his work. Indeed, he introduces the quotation, saying: "Only the purest *Empirie* [empirical matter] can feed the curiosity of the public: '. . .'" (222). In this way the whole weight of Hegel's bitterness is dissipated, and a passage that illuminates his profound sense of the wretchedness of life is trivialized into a cliché about newspaper work.

An MARIE
den 13. Apr. 1811

Tritt mit mir auf Bergeshöhen,
  Reiss Dich von den Wolken los;
Lass uns hier im Aether stehen,
  In des Lichtes farbelosem Schoss.

. . .

Sieh den Altar hier auf Bergeshöhen,
  Auf dem Phönix in der Flamme stirbt,
Um in ew'ger Jugend aufzugehen,
  Die ihm seine Asche nur erwirbt.

Auf sich war gekehrt sein Sinnen,
  Hatte sich zu eigen es gespart,
Nun soll seines Daseins Punkt zerrinnen,
  Und der Schmerz des Opfers ward ihm hart.

Aber fühlend ein unendlich Streben,
  Treibt's ihn über sich hinaus;
Mag die irdische Natur erbeben,
  Führt er es in Flammen aus.

Fallt so, enge Binden, die uns scheiden,
  Nur ein Opfer ist des Herzens Lauf;
Mich zu Dir, zu mir Dich zu erweiten,
  Geh' in Feu'r, was uns vereinzelt, auf!

. . .

Tritt der Geist auf freie Bergeshöhen,
  Er behält vom Eignen nichts zurück;
Leb' ich, mich in Dir, Du Dich in mir zu sehen,
  So geniessen wir der Himmel Glück.

For MARIE (*Hegel's bride*)
April 13, 1811

Step with me on mountain heights,
  Tear yourself away from clouds;
Let us stand here in the ether,
  In light's lap devoid of color.

. . .

See the altar on the mountain heights
   On which Phoenix in the flames is dying
To be raised up in eternal youth
   Which his ashes only gain for him.

On himself his mind was turned,
   For his own possession he had saved it;
Now his own existence shall dissolve,
   And the sacrifice has brought him pain.

Infinite he feels a striving that
   Tears him up beyond himself;
Though the nature of this world should tremble,
   He wants fiery consummation.

Fall thus, narrow bonds that keep us separate,
   For the heart's course is a sacrifice;
Me to you, you into me expanding,
   Fire consume whatever keeps us single!

      . . .

When the spirit steps on mountain heights
   Nothing of its own does it hold back;
Living to see me in you and you in me,
   We enjoy the happiness of heavens.

HEGEL *to His Bride: Nürnberg, Summer 1811*

Dear Marie:

I have written to you in my thoughts almost all night long. It was not about this or that single matter between us that I was concerned in my thoughts, but it necessarily concerned the whole thought: will we make each other unhappy?—From the depths of my soul it shouted: this can, this shall, this may not be!—It will not be!

But what I have said to you long ago now comes to me as a result: marriage is essentially a religious bond; love needs to be supplemented by a higher moment than it is in itself and for itself alone. [The next sentence, comprising seven lines about the relation of being entirely happy to religion and the sense of duty is very difficult to construe and not unambiguous.] . . .

In front of me I have the draft for the lines which I added to your letter to my sister; but the addition to which you certainly attributed too much significance is not there. Still I remembered what occasioned the sense in which I added it when copying these lines. On the evening before, we had definitely talked about this or agreed that we wanted to call contentment what we felt sure of attaining together; and 'There is a *blessed* contentment which, considered without illusion, is more than everything one calls being happy.'—When I had written the words that I now have in front of me and whose sense is so dear to me, 'You see from this how happy I can be with her for all the rest of my life, and how happy the attainment of such love, for which I scarcely had any hope left in this world, is making me even now?'—I added, quasi as if, in the light of our conversation, my happy emotion and its expression had been too much: '*insofar* as happiness is part of the destiny of my life.' I do not think that this ought to have hurt you.— Further, I remind you, dear Marie, that you, too, have been taught by your deeper sense and the education of what is higher in you that in minds that are not superficial all feelings of happiness are tied to a feeling of melancholy. I remind you, moreover, that you promised me to heal any residue in my mind of unbelief in contentment; i.e., you were to reconcile my true inner nature with the way in which I am—too frequently—against what is actual and for what is actual. And that this point of view gives your destiny a higher side; that I credit you with the strength to do this; that this strength must lie in *our* love;—your love for me, my love for you —spoken of separately in this way—introduce a distinction that would separate *our* love; and love is only *ours,* only this unity, only this bond. Turn away from the reflection into this distinction, and let us cling firmly to this unity which alone can also be my strength and my new pleasure in life. Let this confidence lie at the bottom of everything, then everything will be truly good.

Ah, I could still write so much, also about my perhaps only hypochondriac pedantry in which I so insisted on the difference between contentment and happiness—which is again so useless— that I have sworn by myself to both you and me that your happiness shall be for me the dearest thing I have.—There is also much that only passes away, forgets itself, and becomes undone when one does not touch on it.

Still this: I have long doubted whether I ought to write you because everything one writes or says depends again on the explanation alone, or because I dreaded it since it is so dangerous once one has begun to explain. But I have overcome this fear, too, and hope everything from your mind as it receives this writing.

All the best until we see each other again today [!] without a shadow, *dear* Marie—only this I should like to be able still to tell you, what feeling, how much—my whole existence, as much as it is—lies for me in these words: *dear Marie.*

Your Wilhelm

HEGEL *to His Bride: Nürnberg, Summer 1811*

. . . I have hurt you with some of the things I said. This pains me. I have hurt you by seeming to condemn as principles of your way of thinking and acting moral views that I must condemn.— About this I now only say to you that on the one hand I condemn these views insofar as they cancel the difference between what the heart likes and duty, or rather eliminate the latter altogether and destroy morality. But just as much—and this is the main point between us—I beg you to believe me that I do not ascribe these views insofar as they have this consequence to *you,* not to your self, but that I look on them as lying only in your reflection without your thinking, knowing, and realizing them with their consequences—that they serve you to excuse others (to justify is something else—for what one can excuse in others one does not therefore consider to be permitted to oneself; but what one can justify is right for all, including ourselves).

Regarding myself and the manner of my explanation, do not forget that when I condemn maxims I lose sight too easily of the manner in which they are actual in the determinate individual— in this case, you—and they stand before my eyes in their generality, in their consequences and ramifications and applications of which you are not thinking—much less that all these were for you contained in them. Moreover, you know yourself that even though character and the maxims of insight are different, it still is not indifferent what maxims insight and judgment employ. But I know just as well that maxims, when they contradict the character, are still more indifferent in the female than they are in men.

Finally, you know that there are evil men who torment their wives only to have constant visual proof of their behavior, namely their patience and love. I do not believe that I am evil in this way; but if such a dear soul as you are ought never to be hurt, I might almost not regret how I hurt you, for I feel that the deeper insight that I have thus gained into your nature has further increased the intensity and thoroughness of my love. Therefore be comforted also by the realization that whatever in my replies may have been unloving and untender vanishes insofar as I feel and recognize you ever more deeply to be through and through lovable, loving, and full of love.

I must go to class. All the best—dearest, dearest, blessed and fair Marie.

Your Wilhelm

HEGEL *to* NIETHAMMER: *Nürnberg, July 19, 1812*

. . . Jacobi will probably return only the end of July; his gracious disposition toward me and the good reception I owe to you, and I esteem highly what I owe to you in this respect.

Schelling passed through here with his wife, as I heard afterwards, but stayed here only a few hours and, on account of some rheumatism, saw nobody. . . .

HEGEL *to* NIETHAMMER: *Nürnberg, October 23, 1812*

You have requested me to put down on paper my thoughts about lecturing on philosophy at Gymnasia, and to send them to you. . . .

One final note is still missing, which, however, I have not added because I am still at odds with myself about it; namely, that perhaps all philosophical instruction at Gymnasia might seem superfluous, and the study of the ancients is most suitable for Gymnasium students and, according to its substance, the true introduction to philosophy. . . .

Please extend to Herrn President Jacobi my congratulations on his retirement. Rest is the best possession on earth. If it had been accorded to me, too, I should invite him doubly to come to our city of rest.

Schelling has visited me here in friendship; *philosophica* we did not touch on. . . .

[FROM THE 14-PAGE ENCLOSURE:]

. . . According to my view of Logic, *Metaphysics* is altogether
included in it. For this I can cite Kant as a predecessor and
authority. His *Critique* reduces what had hitherto been metaphysical
to a consideration of understanding and reason. Logic can thus be
construed in Kant's sense as containing not only, as usual, so-called
general logic but also, connected with this and actually before it,
what he designated as *Transcendental* Logic; namely, as far as the
contents go, the doctrine of the *categories, concepts of reflection,* and
then the *concepts of reason.* . . . My Objective Logic will serve,
I hope, to purify science again and to present it in its true dignity.
Until it is known more, these Kantian distinctions already contain
the bare necessities or crude outlines.

. . . As for the *Kantian critique* of natural theology, that can be
taken up, as I have done, in the *doctrine of religion* . . . It is
interesting, partly to offer some knowledge of the so famous proofs
of the existence of God; partly, to acquaint students with the equally
famous Kantian critique of these proofs; partly, to criticize this critique in turn. . . .

Method

A. Generally, one distinguishes philosophical *system* with its
particular sciences from *philosophizing* itself. It is the modern mania,
especially in pedagogy, that one should not so much be instructed
in the *contents* of philosophy as one should *learn to philosophize
without contents;* that means approximately: one should travel, and
always travel, without becoming acquainted with cities, rivers,
countries, people, etc.

First, as one becomes acquainted with a city, and then comes
to a river, another city, etc., one learns in any case to travel; and
one does not merely learn it, one actually travels. Thus, as one
becomes acquainted with the contents of philosophy, one does not
only learn to philosophize, one already philosophizes in fact.[26] . . .

Secondly, philosophy contains the highest *reasonable thoughts*

[26] Cf. Hegel's Jena aphorism ※69: "Kant is cited, full of admiration, for
teaching *philosophizing,* not *philosophy;* as if somebody taught carpentry, but
not how to make a table, chair, door, cabinet, etc." (Ros. 552; *Dok.* 371).
This polemical remark is still eminently applicable to Jaspers, especially to his
Nietzsche: Einführung in das Verständnis seines Philosophierens (1936).

about the essential subjects, contains what is *general* and *true* in them. It is of great importance to become acquainted with this content, and to get these *thoughts into one's head.* The sad, merely formal attitude, the perennial search and knocking about without content, unsystematic arguing or speculating, makes for the emptiness of content, the emptiness of thought in people's heads—incompetence [dass sie *nichts können*]. . . .

Third. The procedure in getting acquainted with a philosophy that has content is none other than *learning.* Philosophy has to *be taught and learned,* just like any other science. The unfortunate *pruritus* [itch] of educating students to *think themselves* and *produce themselves* has overshadowed this truth—as if, when I learn what substance, cause, or whatever else is, *I* did not think *myself;* as if *I* did not *produce* these determinations myself in my thinking; as if they were thrown into it like *stones.* . . . As much as the study of philosophy involves doing something oneself, it is just as much a *learning* process—learning an *already extant, elaborate* science. This is a treasure, elaborated, formed content; this extant hereditary possession should be acquired by the individual,[27] i.e., *learned.* The teacher possesses it; he thinks it before them, the students think it after him [*er denkt ihn vor, die Schüler denken ihn nach*]. . . .

HEGEL:
Commencement Speech as Rektor of the Gymnasium at Nürnberg,
September 2, 1813[28]

The end of an academic year naturally prompts us, and higher authority requires us, to look back at such a conclusion upon what has been done and what has happened in the course of the year, and to consider the results of our annual exertions. The lapse of the years is mere duration *for the institution; for the teachers,* a repeated circle of their business; *for the pupils,* however, above all a progressive movement that raises them to a new stage every year.—Since the annual report that is printed contains what can be included in the history of our institution during the past year, few words are needed now.

27 The allusion to *Faust,* lines 682 f. is unmistakable. Cf. V–PG II.3.6.
28 *Werke* (1834), xvi; Glockner's ed., III.

For an institution it is in any case the greatest good fortune if it has no history but merely duration. *What is better kills what is good* is a meaningful proverb: it expresses that the striving for what is better, if it becomes a mania, does not permit the good to develop and mature. When laws and arrangements which ought to provide a firm foundation and support for what is changeable are themselves made changeable—where should that which is changeable in and for itself look for support? General arrangements, too, are of course involved in some progress, but such progress is slow; a single year is insignificant in this respect; changes in them are marked by great and rare epochs. If a government may claim the gratitude of its subjects for *improvements,* they must be just as appreciative of the *preservation* of expedient arrangements which are current. Thus our institution, too, has had no history in the past year; the familiar arrangements have remained the same, except for more detailed determinations in a few formal matters. . . .

HEGEL *to His Sister* CHRISTIANE: *Nürnberg, April 9, 1814*

Your condition, dear sister, which you describe in the letter we received yesterday moves me and my wife very profoundly. There can be no question what is to be done. If your attack of illness is such that a journey would be sufficient for your distraction and recovery, then visit us and return to your job when you are strong again. But if you are not capable of taking care of the duties of your position any more, then you are invited by us to move in with us forever, to live with us and to receive the care you need. You are welcome from our hearts. My wife expects a child this fall, and if you can help her some, your presence then will be doubly suitable. What arrangements we make for you for your stay, we can see once you are here; we can let you have your own little room— a little attic room (which can be heated, of course).

Above all, calm your mind. Your way and nature, as it seems, cannot acquiesce in the attitude of Frau von B. When you ask her openly what you should do or not do, she does not give you a proper reply, you write. You require friendly instruction or even orders and commands what to do and not to do.—I know that kind very well. The chief cause is that when one does not know how to give a correct reply and order, then one is really embarrassed when one is supposed to say what is to be done. Nothing is more annoying than questions about it; and what is most agreeable and even commendable and a cause of gratitude is when the other person does things according to her own judgment. You are even more in the position of having to decide on your own course of action because the children entrusted to you are not those of the woman but were brought into her marriage, and she therefore should not look upon you as merely her inferior. Advice and orders from others do not help much anyway since the execution of the order still depends on our own character. Your position was an office that you yourself have to take care of according to your own knowledge and conscience, and one acquires the contentment and confidence of others the more one has confidence in oneself and acts independently, thus showing others how one is a support for them.

The reward for what you do you should seek partly in the vocation which, owing to your economic circumstances, you had to fulfil so far, partly in the work itself—the physical and psychological development of the children entrusted to you.—These thoughts were occasioned by the way you touched in your letter upon your relation to Frau von B. Do not make this relationship as something external a major matter in your own mind; but rather the relation with the children and your own convenience.—But otherwise take your own counsel and the doctor's about what you should do for your own good. . . .

Meanwhile look upon my house as a place of refuge which is open to you and prepared to receive you any time. If you can and want to stay longer in your present situation, you are doing it of your own choice and can break off any moment and withdraw. I look forward with inner satisfaction to the moment when I can repay you something for the many things you have always done for me, and when you will find calm and contentment with me.—Write soon again about what develops and in any case before you commence the journey.

Your faithful brother Wilhelm

HEGEL to NIETHAMMER: Nürnberg, April 10, 1814

. . . The final main decision hasn't come yet.—Yesterday another victory, dated the 25th, arrived; and this is supposed to be the decision. But they have so often lied to us about this, always the

more gloriously the worse matters actually stood, that one still doesn't
know whether this victory doesn't mean that the Allies have merely
escaped some great destruction.—Our government has now exercised
the possession of its attained freedom and shown the world and its
own subjects the sovereignty that was slighted by the French yoke.
The French Emperor had not permitted smaller powers to have field
marshals (even his king of Holland had to retract). But now, after
such a total revolution of things, after such splendid victories, such
heavy burdens, and abundant blood, we have got one. Whether in
addition to this we are to receive yet other consequences of our
liberation and fruits of our burdens, we shall quietly wait to
see. . . .

HEGEL *to* NIETHAMMER: *Nürnberg, April 29, 1814*

. . . Great things have happened around us. It is a tremendous
spectacle to see an enormous genius destroy himself.—That is the
tragikōtaton[29] [the most tragic thing] there is. The whole mass
of mediocrity with its absolute leaden gravity keeps pressing in its
leaden way, without rest and reconciliation, until it finally brings
down what is higher—to its own level or lower. The turning point
of the whole, the reason why this mass has such power and survives
as the chorus, on top, is that the great individuality itself must
give them the right and thus destroy itself.

The whole revolution, incidentally, I had predicted, as I'll boast.
In my book (completed the night before the Battle of Jena) I say,
p. 547: "Absolute freedom (this is described before; it is the purely
abstract, formal freedom of the French republic which issued, as I
showed, from the Enlightenment) moves out of its self-destroying
actuality into *another country* (I was thinking of a *country*) of self-
conscious spirit where, in this inactuality, it is considered the truth
whose thought one relishes, insofar as *it is and remains a
thought*. . . ."

Of the floods of blessings which must follow these great events
as rain showers must follow lightning, the little brown stream of
coffee already flows with more taste and spirit out of the pot for
our likes, since we have been delivered from guzzling surrogates . . .

[29] Aristotle uses this superlative, with a masculine ending, of course, when he
calls Euripides "the most tragic of the poets" (*Poetics* 13).

CHRISTIANE *to* HEGEL (*Draft*): *November 1815*

. . . For all the love you have shown me and all the goodness I thank you from my heart. I have disturbed the order of your house and am sorry about that; but not the peace of your house, and that comforts me. My condition during the last days of my stay touched especially you to the heart; for that I thank you with my whole heart. . . .

HEGEL *to* FROMMANN (1765–1837, owned a bookstore in Jena and was Hegel's close friend and the godfather of Hegel's illegitimate son): *Nürnberg, April 14, 1816*

. . . You would surely include Munich in your trip in any case. Even this alone would make it worth while. Last fall I finally visited it for two weeks—fourteen extremely gay and cosy days among my friends there who for the most part are yours too, even now: Niethammer, the old Jacobi whom I love and revere very much and who is also full of love for my wife and me, Roth, the brother-in-law of the man who will bring you this letter, Schelling, etc. The art treasures of Munich make it one of the most excellent places in Germany. . . .

KARL DAUB (1765–1836, Professor of Theology at Heidelberg since 1795) *to* HEGEL: *Heidelberg, July 30, 1816*

Wohlgeborener Hochzuverehrender Herr Schulrat![30]
   In a letter received yesterday from Karlsruhe [capital of the state of Baden] I have been entrusted with the task, which gives me and your friends here the greatest pleasure, of asking you whether you are inclined to accept the position of a Professor of Philosophy at the university here. The salary consists of 1300 fl. in money, 6 malters of grain, and 9 malters of spelt. That is not much, of course, but unfortunately I know that at present no more can be authorized. So my hope for an affirmative reply to the above question would be quite feeble if I could not add on the basis of experiences made over a period of years by several of my colleagues as well as myself,

[30] "Well-born, much-to-be-revered Mr. School Superintendent!"

that when professors teach with industry and some acclaim the government by and by increases their salaries considerably and will continue to do so in future. But if you accepted this call, Heidelberg would have in you a philosopher, for the first time since the university was founded (Spinoza once was called here, but in vain, as you presumably know). Industry the philosopher brings along, and the philosopher whose name is Hegel brings along many other things as well, of which, to be sure, very few people here and everywhere have the slightest intimation so far, things that cannot be gained by mere industry. Acclaim will not be lacking once they finally get to hear a philosopher. Upon this, venerable sir, and upon the generosity of your concern for science and its reanimation (at the moment science at the German universities is as turned to stone or wood) my hopes are founded. I therefore write as if the two of us were old acquaintances. But I really do know you, too, and indeed not just from yesterday, nor only from the titles and prefaces of your works, and least of all merely from the reviews with which they have been soiled.[31] Will you hold the intimate tone with which I have begun against me? I am not worried about that and shall therefore continue in the same vein.

It is urgently desired that you should already be with us in the coming winter semester and that the lectures you wish to give should be announced in the catalogue that is to be printed in August. I therefore ask you to reply to the above question as soon as possible. For the expenses of moving here you will be authorized, as I have been instructed in writing, a reasonable *aversum* or, if you prefer, you will be reimbursed for your actual expenses. Concerning the payments to widow and orphans there is a decree of 1810 which affects all civil servants alike and is entirely satisfactory.

I am rushing to make sure that this letter gets into the mail today, and I beg you to excuse my extremely hurried writing.

If I live to see you as a member of the University of Heidelberg, which I love as a foster mother and shall love till the end of my life, a pure and refreshing ray of light will have fallen on my life.

With the sincerest respect, Your most devoted

Daub

Provost

[31] An allusion to what Hegel himself had said in the final section of his preface to the *Phenomenology*.

HEGEL *to* VON RAUMER (1781–1873, since 1811 Professor of History in Breslau, after 1819 Professor in Berlin): *Nürnberg, August 2, 1816*

In line with our conversation, I permit myself to submit to you my thoughts about the teaching of *philosophy at the universities.* . . .

. . . We therefore see on the one side *scientific attitudes* and sciences *without interest,* on the other side interest without *scientific attitudes.*

What we generally see presented at the universities and in publications are still some of the old sciences: logic, empirical psychology, natural law, perhaps also morals; for even those who are otherwise still clinging to what is old consider *metaphysics* dead. . . . Concerning the sciences that survive, especially logic, it almost seems that it is for the most part only tradition and the regard for the formal expediency of the training of the understanding that still keeps them alive; for the contents and the form differ too much from the idea of philosophy to which interest has shifted and the now accepted manner of philosophizing. . . .

The demand for detailed knowledge and the otherwise admitted truth that the whole can be truly grasped only by those who have worked through the parts, have not only been circumvented but have been rejected with the claim that the *definiteness* and *manifoldness* of *detailed knowledge* are *superfluous* for the idea, indeed *opposed* to it and *beneath* it. From this point of view, philosophy is as compendious as medicine, or at least therapy, was at the time of the Brownian system, according to which it could be mastered in half an hour. Perhaps you have met a philosopher who adheres to this *intensive* manner in Munich, in person. Franz Baader now and then publishes a few pages which are supposed to contain the whole essence of the whole of philosophy or of a special branch of it. Whoever publishes in this manner has the advantage that the public believes that he also masters the detailed execution of such general thoughts. But while still in Jena, I witnessed Friedrich Schlegel's appearance with his lectures on transcendental philosophy. In six weeks he had finished his course, though not exactly to the satisfaction of his listeners who had expected and paid for half a year. . . .

I have just finished the publication of my works on Logic and now must wait to see how the public will receive this approach.

But this much I believe I can accept as right, that the teaching of philosophy at the universities can accomplish what it should accomplish—*the acquiring of detailed knowledge*—only if it follows a *detailed methodical procedure* that comprehends and *brings order* into the details. Only in this form is this science, like any other, capable of being *learned*. Though the teacher may avoid this word, he must be conscious of the fact that this is his first and main concern. It has become a prejudice not only of philosophical study but also of pedagogy—and is even more fateful there—that *thinking for oneself* should be developed and exercised in the sense that, first, *the material is irrelevant* and as if, secondly, *learning were opposed to thinking for oneself.* . . . According to a common error, a thought is supposed to bear the stamp of what one has thought by oneself only if it deviates from the thoughts of other people, in regard to which the familiar saying usually comes up that what is new is not true, and what is true is not new.—Further, this has given rise to the craving that *everyone wants to have his own system,* and a thought is considered the more original and excellent the more absurd and crazy it is because in that way it proves best how peculiar and different from the thoughts of others it is.

Further, philosophy attains the capability of being learned by means of its definite detail insofar as it is only in this way that it becomes *clear* and *capable of being communicated* and of thus becoming *common property.* . . .

I have mentioned *edification,* which is often expected from philosophers. In my view, even when presented to youths, it should never be *edifying.* But it has to satisfy a related need on which I still want to touch briefly. Though recent times have revived the direction toward solid material, higher ideas, and religion, yet the form of feeling, fantasy, and confused Concepts is still unsatisfactory for all this, indeed more so than ever. To justify solid contents for insight, to grasp them in determinate thoughts and comprehend them, and thus to preserve them from murky deviations, this must be the job of philosophy. . . .

VON RAUMER *to* VON SCHUCKMANN (1755–1834; from 1810, Minister for Trade, Culture, and Education in Berlin; helped to found the university there; from 1814 to 1834 Minister of the Interior): *August 10, 1816*

During my stay in Nürnberg I visited Professor Hegel, was very kindly received by him, and spent several interesting evenings in many-sided conversations with him . . . we were interrupted. But to get a detailed picture of Hegel's views I asked him for a brief written synopsis. He promised it, kept his word, and I almost consider it a duty to send you his presentation, with the request to return it to me, so Your Excellency can see what you would have or not have if you secured Hegel. . . . His conversation is fluent and sensible, so I cannot believe that his lectures would lack these qualities.

To be sure, there is a false pathos, shouting, and roaring, little jokes, digressions, half-true comparisons, one-sided comparisons with the present, arrogant self-praise . . . and attracts masses of students. But this direction one should surely brake rather than promote. In this false sense Hegel certainly does not lecture well; whether he lectures well in the genuine sense, that surely depends in the end on the contents of his philosophy . . .

VON SCHUCKMANN *to* HEGEL: *Berlin, August 15, 1816*

From a letter of . . . Niebuhr the Ministry of the Interior learns that you wish to be employed at the university here. The chair for philosophy is indeed vacant, and in view of the reputation and respect which you have acquired through your philosophical works, the Ministry will be happy to consider you. But it believes that in the best interests of the institution as well as your own, one scruple should first be removed, and this should be frankly presented to you as an honest man for your examination and reply. In view of the fact that for quite a number of years now you have not given academic lectures, and before that also were not an academic teacher for long, the doubt has been raised from several sides whether you still completely command the ability to give vivid and incisive lectures on your science. As you will be convinced yourself, this is very necessary because now that the sorry commotion around the bread-and-butter studies is so notable everywhere, this science above all requires that the spirit of the young people should be stirred up by vivid lectures and thus led toward it. With full confidence in your own insight into the duties of a teacher of philosophy and the requirements of science, the Ministry therefore leaves it to you to examine yourself whether you consider yourself fit to satisfy fully the obligations you would have to undertake here, and will wait for your explanation before deciding anything further.

HEGEL *to* DAUB: *Nürnberg, August 20, 1816*

P.S. . . . There is indeed no science in which one is as lonely as one is lonely in philosophy, and I long from my heart for a livelier sphere of action. I can say this is the highest wish of my life. I also feel keenly how the lack of a lively give and take [*Wechselwirkung*] has had an unfavorable effect on my works so far.

But how is it with theology? Is not the contrast between your profound, philosophical view of it and that which is frequently considered theology just as glaring or still more hair-raising? My work will also give me the satisfaction that I shall have to consider it as a propaedeutic for your science. . . .

HEGEL *to* VON SCHUCKMANN: *Nürnberg, August 28, 1816*

Your Excellency's gracious letter of the 15th, received the 24th, I believe I must answer with the information that, since I had the honor of speaking with Herrn Staatsrat Niebuhr, I received such an agreeable offer from the Grand-Ducal Government of Baden, regarding the chair of philosophy at Heidelberg, that I could not fail to accept, and I dispatched my decisive letter several days before I received the gracious missive of Your Excellency, and thus regret that thereby I have already renounced the prospect of the wider field of action at the University of Berlin which the grace of Your Excellency opened before me. Although I therefore refrain from detailed comments about my experience in lecturing freely at the Gymnasium for the past 8 years, since my first shy attempts, and

I may consider this more advantageous for myself in this respect than even an academic chair, I only wish to add respectfully what a deep impression Your Excellency's gracious procedure has made on me, insofar as the scruples about my lecturing were presented to me for my own examination and reply, and what deeply felt and pure respect I feel on this account. I may still ask Your Honor to accept most graciously the expression of the deepest devotion and the most grateful reverence with which I have the honor to remain

Your Excellency's most obedient servant
Hegel at present Principal
and Professor at the Royal Bavarian
Gymnasium here.

ALTENSTEIN (1770–1840, helped to found the University of Berlin in 1810, and in 1817 became head of the new Ministry for Culture, Education, and Health) *to* HEGEL: *Berlin, December 26, 1817*

. . . Having taken over the direction of public education, I consider it one of my most important tasks to fill the chair for philosophy, vacant since the death of Professor Fichte, in a worthy manner. I hereby invite you to accept this teaching post at the royal university here . . . I do not overlook the obligations which may keep you in Heidelberg, yet you have still greater obligations to science for which you will here have a more extended and important sphere of influence. . . .

SCHLEIERMACHER *to* HEGEL: *Berlin, November 16, 1819*

Lest I forget one thing over another, *wertester Herr Kollege:* the deputy of the house of Hesse in Bordeaux is named Rebstock and lives at Alexanderplatz 4.

Moreover, I must really be very much obliged to you for immediately replying to the naughty word that the other day should not have escaped from my lips; for in that way you at least attenuated the sting which the violence that overcame me has left in me. I could wish that we might soon be able to continue the discussion at the point where it stood before these improper words were spoken. For I respect you far too much to be able not to wish that we might come to an understanding about a matter which in our present situation is of such great importance.

Schleiermacher

HEGEL *to* SCHLEIERMACHER (*Draft*)

I *thank* you, *wertester Herr Kollege,* first for the address of the wine shop contained in your note, received yesterday—and then for the remarks which, by removing a recent unpleasant occurrence between us, also takes care of the reply that issued from my excitement and leaves me only with a decided increase of my respect for you. It was, as you remark, the mutual importance of the matter that misled me into bringing about at that gathering a discussion whose continuation in an attempt to equalize our views could not be other than interesting.[32]

GOETHE *to* HEGEL: *Jena, October 7, 1820*

. . . With pleasure I hear from several sides that your exertions to train young men are bearing the finest fruit. It is surely much needed that in these strange times a doctrine should spread somewhere from some center on which a life can be based theoretically and practically. Hollow heads, of course, one cannot prevent from wallowing in vague notions and resounding bombast; but good heads are in a bad way, too: finding that the methods in which they have been entangled from their youth are false, they withdraw into themselves, become abstruse or transcendentalize.[33]

May your meritorious accomplishments, *mein Teuerster,*[34] for this world and for posterity [*Welt und Nachwelt*] be continually rewarded with the most beautiful effectiveness [*Wirkungen*].

Most faithfully,
Goethe

[32] These are the only extant letters exchanged by Hegel and Schleiermacher. Cf. H 55.
[33] *Transzendieren* really means transcend, and Goethe *could* mean: go beyond (this world and become otherworldly).
[34] "My most esteemed friend."

HEGEL *to* GOETHE: *Berlin, April 24, 1825*

. . . When I survey the course of my spiritual development, I see you everywhere woven into it and would like to call myself one of your sons; my inward nature received from you nourishment and strength to resist abstraction and set its course by your images as by signal fires. . . .

G. PARTHEY (1798–1872; philologist; had obtained his doctorate in Berlin in 1820): *Report of a Conversation with Goethe: August 28, 1827*[35]

. . . He immediately began a conversation, not about my travels, but inquired about Hegel's position in Berlin. I . . . replied as briefly as possible that Hegel personally enjoyed the highest respect, that the awkwardness of his lectures had at first frightened away many, but that people had soon been convinced that the confusion was on the surface only and that under the tough shell there lay the sweet kernel of an entirely finished philosophical edifice, amazing in its consistency. . . .

EDUARD GANS (1798–1839; one of Hegel's leading disciples, habilitated in Berlin in 1820; Associate Professor in 1825; Professor of Law in 1828; editor of the posthumous editions of Hegel's *Philosophy of Right* and *Philosophy of History*): *Report of a Conversation with Goethe: August 28, 1827*[36]

. . . He credited Hegel with a great deal of knowledge about nature and history, but he said he could not keep from asking whether his philosophical thoughts would not always have to be modified in accordance with the new discoveries that would always continue to be made; and wouldn't they thus lose their categorical character.

I replied that a philosophy certainly made no claim to being a thought press for all time; that it merely wants to represent its age,

[35] Goethe's seventy-eighth birthday. Printed in Goethe's *Gespräche*.
[36] See preceding footnote.

and that with the new steps that history and the discoveries it brought would make, philosophy was gladly prepared to change its types into fluid development. This modesty of the philosophical consciousness seemed to please Goethe . . .

SCHELLING *to His Wife, August 1829*

. . . Imagine, yesterday I sit in the bath when I hear a somewhat unpleasant, half familiar voice ask for me. Then the stranger mentioned his name: it was Hegel, from Berlin, who has come here with some relatives from Prag and is staying for a few days while passing through. In the afternoon he came the second time, very *empressé* and extremely friendly as if there were nothing between us. But since so far we have not had any scientific discussion, which I certainly shall not enter into, and he is moreover a very intelligent person, I have spent a few evening hours in very pleasant conversation with him. As yet I have not returned his visit; it is a little too far to the *Goldene Löwe*.

HEGEL *to His Wife, Karlsbad, September 3, 1829*

. . . Last evening I had a get-together with an old acquaintance— Schelling—who also came here alone, like myself, a few days ago in order to take, not like myself, the cure. He is very healthy and strong; using the waters is only a preservative for him.—We are both very pleased and are together as old cordial friends. This afternoon we took a walk together and then in the cafe we read about the capture of Adrianople, an official bulletin in the Austrian *Observer*, and we also spent the evening together . . .

GOETHE *to* ZELTER: *Weimar, August 13, 1831*

. . . *Nature does nothing in vain,* is an old Philistine slogan. Her workings are ever alive, superfluous, and squandering in order that the infinite may continually be present because nothing can abide.

With this I even believe I come close to Hegel's philosophy which, incidentally, attracts and repels me; may the genius be gracious unto all of us! . . .

MARIE HEGEL (the widow) *to* CHRISTIANE HEGEL (the sister), *after Hegel's death.*[37]

I shall get a hold on myself and tell you briefly how everything happened. My blessed beloved husband began to feel unwell Sunday morning, after he had had breakfast with us, quite cheerfully. He complained about a stomach ache and nausea. . . . Thursday he had begun his lectures with perfect strength and cheerfulness; Saturday he had given examinations; and for Sunday dinner had invited several good friends. I informed them and devoted myself entirely to his care. Fortunately, the doctor came instantly and prescribed something—but none of us found anything to worry about in his condition. His stomach ache was tolerable. He vomited, at first without gall, then with gall. That had happened to him several times before. He was extremely restless during the night. I sat beside his bed, covered him when he sat up in bed or threw himself around, although he repeatedly asked me in the kindest manner to go to bed and leave him alone with his unrest. His stomach ache was not violent 'but as wicked as a toothache; one simply can't keep lying down quietly.'—Monday morning he wanted to get up. We brought him into the adjoining living room, but he was so weak that on the way to the sofa he almost collapsed. I had his bed moved close by. We lifted him into the warmed bed. He complained only of weakness. All pain, all nausea was gone; so he said: 'Wish to God I had had only one such quiet hour last night!' He told me he needed rest and I should not admit any visitors. When I wanted to feel his pulse he took my hand, lovingly as if he wanted to say: Stop worrying.—The doctor came early in the morning and prescribed mustard plaster for the abdomen, like the day before (leeches I had applied the evening before) . . . . He rested quietly, always in the same warmth and perspiration, always fully conscious and, as it seemed to me, without worry about any danger. A second physician, Dr. Horn, was called in. Mustard plaster over the whole body, flannel cloths, dipped in camomile decoction, over that. All this did not disturb or upset him. At 3 o'clock he began to have chest cramps; after that another quiet sleep. But over the left half of his face moved an icy coldness. His hands turned blue and cold. We knelt

[37] Ros. 422 f.

by his bed and listened to his breath. He passed away in the sleep of the blessed!

Let me break off! Now you know everything. Weep with me, but also thank God with me for this painless, quiet, blessed end. And tell me, would you have recognized a single symptom of cholera in all this? Shuddering, I heard that the doctors, Medizinalrat Barez and Geheimrat Horn, had diagnosed it as such—as the type that, without external symptoms, destroys the inmost life in the most violent way. . . .

DAVID FRIEDRICH STRAUSS *to* CHRISTIAN MÄRKLIN: *Berlin, November 15, 1831.*[38]

To whom, dearest friend, should I write that Hegel is dead if not to you of whom I thought most, even when I could still hear and see Hegel? Of course, the newspapers may tell you about it before my letter reaches you; but you should and must hear it from me, too. I had hoped to be able to write you more cheerful things from Berlin. Imagine how I heard it. I had been unable to see Schleiermacher until this morning. Then he naturally asked me whether the cholera had not made me afraid to come. I replied that the news had become more reassuring all the time, and now it really seemed to be over. Yes, he said, but it still seized one great victim—Professor Hegel died last night of the cholera. Imagine this impression! The great Schleiermacher—at that moment he seemed insignificant to me when I measured him against this loss. Our conversation was at an end, and I left quickly. My first thought was: now you leave; what would you do in Berlin without Hegel? But soon I reconsidered and am staying now. After all, I did travel here, and though Hegel is dead, his spirit is not dead here. I am glad that I still heard and saw the great master before his end. I heard both of his courses: History of Philosophy and Philosophy of Right.

If one abstracts from all externalities, his delivery gave the impression of pure being-for-itself, not conscious of its being for others; i.e., it was much more a way of thinking aloud than speech directed to listeners. Hence the only half-loud voice, the unfinished sentences—just as they may suddenly arise in one's thoughts. At the same time, it was a thinking that might develop in a place where one

[38] From Strauss (1808–74), *Ausgewählte Briefe,* ed. Eduard Zeller, 1895.

is not altogether undisturbed; it moved in the most comfortable, most concrete forms and illustrations that derived higher significance only from their connection and their context. . . .

Last Thursday I visited him. When I mentioned my name and place of birth, he immediately said: Ah, a Württemberger! And he was cordially delighted. . . . When one saw and heard Hegel lecturing, he seemed so infinitely old, stooped, coughed, etc.; I found him ten years younger when I saw him in his room. Gray hair, to be sure, covered by the beret one knows from Binder's picture; a pale face, but not fallen in; bright blue eyes; and especially when he smiled one noticed the most beautiful white teeth, which gave a very agreeable impression. His manner, when I visited him, was entirely that of a nice old gentleman, and in the end he said I should visit him often and he would then introduce me to his wife, too.—Now he is to be buried tomorrow at 3 P.M. The consternation at the university is extraordinary: Henning, Marheineke, even Ritter do not lecture at all; Michelet came to the lectern practically in tears. . . .

GOETHE *to* ZELTER: *Weimar, January 27, 1832*[39]

. . . After this I may not say how much the backside of Hegel's medallion displeases me. One simply does not know what is meant. That as a human being and a poet I knew how to honor and adorn the cross, I have proved in my verses; but that a philosopher leads his students on a roundabout way through the primordial grounds and abysses of essence and non-essence [*Ur-und Ungründe des Wesens und Nicht-Wesens*] to this dry contignation, that does not suit me. That can be had more inexpensively and expressed better. . . .

[39] Cf. Karl Löwith, *Von Hegel bis Nietzsche*, Europa Verlag, Zürich and New York, 1941, p. 28: "In 1830 Hegel received from his students, for his sixtieth birthday, a medallion that showed on one side his image and on the other an allegorical representation: at the left, a male figure is seated, reading in a book; behind it is a column on which an owl is perched; at the right stands a woman holding a cross that is taller than she is; and between the two figures there is, turned toward the seated youth, a naked genius whose raised arm points toward the cross on the other side. The attributes, *owl* and *cross*, leave no doubt about the intended meaning: the central figure of the genius mediates between *philosophy* and *theology*. This medallion, still in the Goethe Collections, was given to Goethe by Zelter, at Hegel's request. Zelter remarked: 'The head is good and not unlike Hegel; but the reverse displeases me. Why should I love the cross even if I myself have to bear the cross?' . . ."

GOETHE *to* ZELTER: *Weimar, March 11, 1832*

. . . Fortunately, the character of your talent relies on tones, i.e., on the moment. Now, since a sequence of successive moments is always itself a kind of eternity, it was given to you to be ever constant in that which passes and thus to satisfy me as well as Hegel's spirit, insofar as I understand it, completely . . .[40]

H. G. HOTHO (1802–73): *1835*[41]

I shall never forget the first impression of his face. Livid and loose, all features drooped as dead. They reflected no destructive passion but the whole past of thinking that worked on silently, day and night. The agony of doubt, the ferment of relentless storms of thought did not seem to have tormented and tossed this forty-year long pondering, seeking, and finding. Only the restless urge to unfold the early germ of fortunately discovered truth ever more richly and profoundly, ever more strictly and irrefutably, had furrowed the forehead, the cheeks, and the mouth. . . . How worthy the whole head was, how nobly the nose was formed, as well as the high but slightly receding forehead and the calm chin. The nobility of loyalty and thorough probity in the greatest matters no less than the smallest, of the clear consciousness of having sought final satisfaction to the best of his ability in truth alone, was impressed eloquently on all features in the most individual manner. . . .

When I saw him again after a few days, lecturing, I was unable at first to find my way into either the manner of his delivery or the train of his thought. Exhausted, morose, he sat there as if collapsed into himself, his head bent down, and while speaking kept turning pages and searching in his long folio notebooks, forward and backward, high and low. His constant clearing of his throat and coughing interrupted any flow of speech. Every sentence stood alone and came out with effort, cut in pieces and jumbled. Every word, every syllable detached itself only reluctantly to receive a strangely thor-

[40] By finding eternity in the moment. Zelter was a composer. Goethe died March 22.
[41] Hotho, *Vorstudien für Leben und Kunst*, Stuttgart und Tübingen, Cotta, 1835. On Hegel: pp. 383–99.

ough emphasis from the metallic-empty voice with its broad Swabian dialect, as if each were the most important. Nevertheless, his whole appearance compelled such a profound respect, such a sense of worthiness, and was so attractive through the naïveté of the most overwhelming seriousness that, in spite of all my discomfort, and though I probably understood little of what was said, I found myself captivated forever. But as soon as ardor and perseverance had shortly accustomed me to this external aspect of the lectures, their inner merits became ever more vivid in my sight and became interwoven with these defects into a whole that carried the standard of its perfection in itself alone.

Eloquence that flows along smoothly presupposes that the speaker is finished with the subject inside and out and has it by heart, and formal skill has the ability to glide on garrulously and most graciously in what is half-baked and superficial. This man, however, had to raise up the most powerful thoughts from the deepest ground of things, and if they were to have a living effect then, although they had been pondered and worked over years before and ever again, they had to regenerate themselves in him in an ever living present. A more vivid representation of these difficulties and this immense trouble than was accomplished by the manner of his delivery would be unthinkable. . . . Wholly immersed in the subject alone, he seemed to develop it only out of itself and for its own sake, scarcely out of his own spirit for the sake of those listening; and yet it sprang from him alone, and an almost paternal care for clarity attenuated the rigid seriousness that might have repelled the acceptance of such troublesome thoughts.

He faltered even in the beginning, tried to go on, started once more, stopped again, spoke and pondered; the right word seemed to be missing forever, but then it scored most surely; it seemed common and yet inimitably fitting, unusual and yet the only one that was right. . . . Now one had grasped the clear meaning of a sentence and hoped most ardently to progress. In vain. Instead of moving forward, the thought kept revolving around the same point with similar words. But if one's wearied attention wandered and strayed a few minutes before it suddenly returned with a start to the lecture, it found itself punished by having been torn entirely out of the context. For slowly and deliberately, making use of seemingly insignificant links, some full thought had limited itself to the point of one-sidedness, had split itself into distinctions and involved itself in contradictions whose victorious solution eventually found the strength to compel the reunification of the most recalcitrant elements.

Thus always taking up again carefully what had gone before in order to develop out of it more profoundly in a different form what came later, . . . the most wonderful stream of thought twisted and pressed and struggled, now isolating something, now very comprehensively; occasionally hesitant, then by jerks sweeping along, it flowed forward irresistibly. But even those who could follow with their entire mind and understanding, without looking right or left, felt the strangest strain and anxiety. To what abysses was thought led down, torn asunder to what infinite opposites. Ever again, everything gained so far seemed lost and all exertion in vain, for even the highest power of knowledge seemed constrained to stand still silently at the limits of its competence. But precisely in these depths of the seemingly inscrutable, this tremendous spirit wallowed and wove in magnificently self-assured calm and composure. Only then the voice rose, the eyes flashed sharply over the assembly and shone in the quietly flaring fire of their splendor, profound with conviction, while he, never lacking a word, reached through all the heights and depths of the soul. What he pronounced in such moments was so clear and exhaustive, of such simple truthfulness, that everyone able to grasp it felt as if he had found and thought it himself; and all previous notions vanished so completely that no memory whatever remained of the dreamlike days in which these thoughts had not yet awakened one for this knowledge. . . .

When it came to religious notions, he fought with cutting weapons for the enlightened freedom of thoughtful conviction, although he was superior to almost everybody in his clear comprehension of the most orthodox dogmas. In politics, his moderate constitutional bent inclined toward the basic principles of the English constitution. A corporate basis he considered indispensable also in more general matters; the rights of primogeniture for peers and princes he defended in every respect; indeed, he showed an involuntary ceremonial respect even for the accidental superiorities of social rank, class, and wealth. And because on the whole it was his opinion that cabinet members and civil servants naturally had more insight, he *granted* the freedom of representatives and of the press to criticize and know better, without really being disposed to claim it as an unalienable civil liberty. Above all, however, all demagogical rabble-rousing was hateful to him; and when it opposed more reasonable conditions with unclear feelings and irresponsible ideas—that rowdyish German political heartmongering—it found its bitterest opponent in him. For it was his consistent demand that from youth on one should break the fortuitousness of one's own feelings, of subjective opinion, arbitrariness, and passion, and exchange them for a solid bent toward everything in life that is firm, lawful, and substantial. But nobody except Goethe professed so deeply not that morality which always obtains only partial successes but that genuine ethic which is able to bring feeling, senses, drives, wishes, and will into the perfect accord of habit and custom with what is necessary and rational. . . . But since this tendency developed in him at a time which had cultivated in the opposite way, also one-sidedly, only the most subjective freedom of conscience, of manner of action, and of conviction, he pushed back—to be sure, more in sentiment than in thought—the incontestable rights of modern personality. Thus he was the most loyal, loving husband, the most tenderly concerned, if strict, father; yet he demanded that marriage should be entered upon for the sake of marriage, not for that of the most intimate love of souls; sympathy, respect, and loyalty would then emerge by themselves and knit the most indissoluble bonds. This righteous attitude did not preclude an insight into the most manifold oscillations, contradictions, and oddities of contemporary souls; and even as he knew how to describe such internal conflicts and abysses, he also met them with enduring sympathy and consideration, if only some more substantial needs stirred through them. For whatever might work in the depths of the human soul and tear it never remained alien to his rich heart.

How else could his love of art have continued to grow even in his last years? Here, too, he was entirely at home, and with his universal synopsis he was able to penetrate all its fields, epochs, and works. Poetry, to be sure, was most easily accessible to him, but architecture, too, revealed her secrets to him, and sculpture he knew even better. He was born with an eye for painting, and in music his ear and spirit came to understand the masterpieces of every kind ever better. He was the first to give Oriental art its proper place . . . Greek sculpture, architecture, and poetry was for him the acme of all art which he admired as the attained and most beautifully actualized ideal. With the Middle Ages, on the other hand, prior to the time when one felt the need to model oneself on antiquity, he never was able to become really friendly. The external confusion and the withdrawn mind that, unconcerned, hands over the external form to the barbarism of accident; the diabolic and ugly, the tribulations and tortures that antagonize the eye, the whole uncancelled contradiction between the heart inside, deeply absorbed in religion but uneducated in the world, and its visible appearance always remained for him a stumbling block. . . .

He was an equally delightful companion at concerts and at the theater: cheerful, inclined to applaud, always loud and comfortable, jocose, and, if the occasion called for it, glad to put up even with mediocrity for the sake of good company. . . .

The more secluded his earlier years had been, crowded with work, the more he sought out company in his later years; and as if his own depth required as compensation the shallowness and triviality of others, he would for a time find the most ordinary people pleasant and agreeable; indeed, he even could develop a rare sort of benevolent preference for them. . . .

When Plato praises Socrates in the *Symposium* for completely preserving sobriety and measure in full enjoyment, while late at night all around him the others were sleeping, intoxicated, if they had not stolen away; and he alone remained awake to philosophize with Aristophanes and Agathon, passing a large goblet with wine until he had put them to rest, too, and then, at the cock's crow, went to the Lyceum and only in the evening of this new day retired, as usual—*he, too,* was of all men I have ever seen, the only one who placed before my eyes, to remain present and unforgettable, the gay image of the most cheerful capacity for life.

HEINRICH HEINE (1797–1856): *1835 and 1838*

I believe that the attempt to achieve an intellectual intuition of the absolute concludes Herr Schelling's philosophical career. Now a greater thinker appears who develops the philosophy of nature into a finished system . . . This is the great Hegel, the greatest philosopher Germany has produced since Leibniz. No question, he towers above Kant and Fichte. He is as sharp as the former and as vigorous

as the latter and in addition has a pervasive peace of soul, a
harmony of thought that we do not find in Kant and Fichte in
whom a more revolutionary spirit predominates. To compare this
man with Herr Joseph Schelling is simply impossible; for Hegel
was a man of character. And although, like Herr Schelling, he accorded the *status quo* in state and church some altogether too questionable justifications, this was after all done for a state that at least
in theory pays homage to the principle of progress and for a church
that considers the principle of free inquiry as the element in which
it lives; and he did not make any secret of it but was perfectly frank
about all his intentions. Herr Schelling, on the other hand, wiggles
like a worm in the antechambers of an absolutism that is practical
as well as theoretical . . .

He was pushed ignominiously from the throne of thought; Hegel,
his major-domo, took the crown from his head and shaved his hair,
and the displaced Schelling now lives like a miserable monk in
Munich . . . There I have seen him staggering around like a specter,
with his big pale eyes and his depressed, deadened face, a wretched
image of glory gone to the dogs. But Hegel had himself crowned
in Berlin, unfortunately also anointed a little, and henceforth dominated German philosophy.

. . . in Munich. There I once saw him [Schelling] and could
almost have cried over the wretched sight. And what he said was
easily most wretched of all, it was envious vituperation of Hegel
who had supplanted him. As a shoemaker speaks of another shoemaker whom he accuses of having stolen his leather to make boots
of it, I heard Herr Schelling, when I met him accidentally, speak
of Hegel who had "taken his ideas"; and "it is my ideas that he
has taken"; and again "my ideas" was the constant refrain of the
poor man. Truly, if the shoemaker Jacob Böhme spoke like a
philosopher, the philosopher Schelling now speaks like a shoemaker.

Nothing could be more ridiculous than the claim that one owns
ideas. Hegel, to be sure, used very many Schellingian ideas in his
philosophy; but Herr Schelling after all would never have been able
to make anything of these ideas. He always merely philosophized
but would never have been able to offer a philosophy. Moreover,
it seems safe to say that Herr Schelling took more from Spinoza
than Hegel ever took from *him*. Once Spinoza is liberated from

his rigid, old-Cartesian, mathematical form and rendered accessible to a larger public, it will perhaps be seen that he could complain of theft of ideas with more right than anybody else. All our present-day philosophers, perhaps often without knowing it, look through glasses ground by Baruch Spinoza.

. . . Hegel, the man who sailed around the world of the spirit and intrepidly advanced to the north pole of thought where one's brain freezes in the abstract ice.[42]

LUDWIG FEUERBACH (1804–72): *1840*[43]

I certainly do not belong among those for whom a Kant and Fichte, a Goethe and Lessing, a Goethe and Hegel have lived and worked in vain. Indeed, my relation to Hegel was more intimate and influential than that to any other spiritual ancestor; for I knew him personally, for two years I listened to him—listened attentively, entirely, enthusiastically. I did not know what I wanted or should do; so confused and divided was my mind when I came to Berlin. But I had listened to him for barely six months when my head and heart had been put right by him; I knew what I wanted and should do: not *theology* but *philosophy!* Not to drivel and rave but to learn. Not believe but think.

It was in him that I gained my consciousness of myself and the world. It was him that I then called my second father, even as I called Berlin my spiritual birthplace. He was the only man who made me feel and experience what a teacher is; the only one in whom

---

[42] The first selection comes from *Zur Geschichte der Religion und Philosophie in Deutschland* (1835, 2d ed., 1852) and is found roughly ten pages from the end. The last chapter is entitled *"Von Kant bis Hegel."*

The second selection comes from *Die romantische Schule* (1835), Book II, Section 3.

The last quotation is from *Der Schwabenspiegel* (1838) and found on the fourth page, or near that. Original: *der Geistesweltumsegler, der unerschrocken vorgedrungen bis zum Nordpol des Gedankens, wo einem das Gehirn einfriert im abstrakten Eis.*

Cf. also D 1854.

[43] From Karl Grün, *Ludwig Feuerbach in seinem Briefwechsel und Nach-lass . . .* , vol. I (1874), 387. *Aus dem Nachlass:* "Feuerbach's Relation to Hegel" (1840, with later additions) comprises pp. 387–401; but 388–401 deal with Hegel's philosophy, not with the man.

I found the meaning for this otherwise so empty word; and I felt deeply indebted and grateful to him. Strange that the cold inanimate thinker alone should have made me conscious of the intimacy of a student's relation to his teacher! My teacher was thus Hegel, and I his student; I do not deny it; rather I still own it today with gratitude and joy. And what we once have been certainly never vanishes from our essence, even if it should disappear from our consciousness.

KARL ROSENKRANZ (1805–79): *1844*

This budget he continued in his own hand until he died. From the calendar entries of the Berlin years we can see among other things how often he returned to the students the cash they had paid to hear his lectures. (Ros. 266)

FRANZ GRILLPARZER (1791–1872): *Selbstbiographie (1853)*[44]

He seemed to be one of Hegel's favorite students. After the initial formalities he asked me whether I did not want to call on the great philosopher. I answered him that I did not dare because I did not know the least thing about his work and system. Now he confided in me that he had come with Hegel's knowledge, as Hegel wished to make my acquaintance. So I went and repeated to the master what I had said to the disciple: the reason I had not visited him earlier was that in our parts we had only got to the old Kant, and hence his, Hegel's, system was entirely unknown to me. So much the better, replied the philosopher, rather oddly.[45] It seemed as if he had taken a special interest in my *Golden Fleece,* although we scarcely discussed it and altogether spoke about works of art only on a very general level. I found Hegel as agreeable, sensible, and conciliatory as I later found his system abstruse and repellent.

[44] *Sämtliche Werke: Historisch-kritische Gesamtausgabe,* ed. August Sauer, XVI (1925), 187 f. Grillparzer is generally considered the greatest Austrian dramatist. Cf. D 1855.
[45] *höchst wunderlich:* the poet was evidently very surprised; but see the next report and footnote 47.

HEINRICH HEINE: Confessions (*Geständnisse, 1854*)[46]

. . . The more or less secret leaders of the German communists are great logicians, and the strongest among them have come out of the Hegelian school and are, without a doubt, the most capable heads and the most energetic characters of contemporary Germany. These doctors of the revolution and their pitilessly resolute disciples are the only men in Germany with any life in them, and the future belongs to them. . . .

It was easy for me to prophesy which songs would be whistled and twittered one day in Germany, for I saw the birds hatched that later sounded the new tunes. I saw how Hegel, with his almost comically serious face, sat as a brooding hen on the fatal eggs, and I heard his cackling. To be honest, I rarely understood him, and it was only through subsequent reflection that I attained an understanding of his words. I believe he really did not want to be understood: hence his delivery, so full of clauses; hence perhaps also his preference for persons who he knew would not understand him and on whom he bestowed the honor of his familiar company that much more readily.[47] Thus everybody in Berlin was perplexed by the close relationship between the profound Hegel and the late Heinrich Beer, a brother of . . . Giacomo Meyerbeer. . . . Altogether, Hegel's conversation was always a kind of monologue, sighed forth by fits and starts in a toneless voice. The baroqueness of his expressions often startled me, and I remember many of them. One beautiful starry-skied evening, we two stood next to each other at a window, and I, a young man of twenty-two who had just eaten well and had good coffee, enthused about the stars and called them the abode of the blessed. But the master grumbled to himself: "The stars, hum! hum! the stars are only a gleaming leprosy in the sky." For God's sake, I

---

[46] *Sämmtliche Werke*, XIV (1862), 275–82. These passages are obviously different in kind from the other testimonies in this chapter, but they should not be read as merely illustrations of Heine's wit: they also record the poet's impression that Hegel was strongly opposed to Christianity and theism, and that he was, in contemporary parlance, a humanist. After Hegel's friendship with Hölderlin and his relationship to Goethe, his encounter with the young Heine deserves to be remembered, too.

[47] Cf. the penultimate paragraph of D 1835, D 1853, and D 1880. The point Heine makes is also made, without wit, by Karl Hegel and Eduard Gans (quoted in the Appendix to Fischer, 2d ed., p. 1234).

shouted, then there is no happy locality up there to reward virtue after death? But he, staring at me with his pale eyes, said cuttingly: "So you want to get a tip for having nursed your sick mother and for not having poisoned your dear brother?"—Saying that, he looked around anxiously, but he immediately seemed reassured when he saw that it was only Heinrich Beer, who had approached to invite him to play whist. . . .

I was young and proud, and it pleased my vanity when I learned from Hegel that it was not the dear God who lived in heaven that was God, as my grandmother supposed, but I myself here on earth. This foolish pride did not by any means have a corrupting influence on my feelings; rather it raised them to the level of heroism. At that time I put so much effort into generosity and self-sacrifice that I certainly outshone the most brilliant feats of those good Philistines of virtue who merely acted from a sense of duty and obeyed the moral laws. After all, I myself was now the living moral law and the source of all right and sanctions. I was primordial *Sittlichkeit,* immune against sin, I was incarnate purity; the most notorious Magdalens were purified by the cleansing and atoning power of the flames of my love, and stainless as lilies and blushing like chaste roses they emerged from the God's embraces with an altogether new virginity. These restorations of damaged maidenhoods, I confess, occasionally exhausted my strength. . . .

FRANZ GRILLPARZER: *Aus dem Nachlass, 1855*

HEGEL

Was mir an deinem System am besten gefällt?
Es ist so unverständlich wie die Welt.[48]
What feature makes your system eligible?
It is like the world itself: unintelligible.

[48] Literally: "What I like best about your system? It is as unintelligible as the world." Similar but less successful epigrams about Hegel are found in *Sämtliche Werke in zwanzig Bänden,* ed. August Sauer, Stuttgart, Cotta, III, 82, 123, 134, 143, 173, and 219. The above couplet comes from p. 197. Cf. D 1853.

KARL GUTZKOW (1811–78): *1870*[49]

Hegel's manner as a lecturer was quite the opposite of that of all the famous men described so far. He was still in full vigor and had no idea that a disease that was then still in Asia, the cholera, and a few slices of melon, eaten for dessert, would soon put an end to his life. Schleiermacher's unique manner was close to Hegel's in character, unless any such comparison should be ruled out because the great virtuosity of Schleiermacher's delivery was so unlike the lame, dragging lectures of Hegel, interrupted by eternal repetitions and irrelevant filler words. What they had in common was that both improvised, spinning, as it were, their lectures out of thought processes going on at that very moment before the eyes of the audience. The others offered finished results of prior meditations. Schleiermacher and Hegel renewed the thought process in order to gain this or that result. And Hegel did this like a spider that sits concealed in one corner of its net and tries to draw its threads ever farther out on the outside, but closer and closer together toward the inside. . . .

But to be truthful, I confess that in Hegel's lectures the Damascus miracle (in reverse, I might say: the conversion from a theological Paul to a philosophizing Saul), which I had experienced in the park in the winter, was repeated for me hourly. Every Hegelian demonstration had a practical perspective. At the end of a long, certainly extremely monotonous and dull avenue of concept splitting, one always saw some proposition of experience that was to be confirmed or some proposition of tradition that was to be overthrown. The logical process, being and becoming, in-itself and for-itself, were, to be sure, a kind of jugglery pursued to the point where our eyes get confused and only the lifting of the cup brings us back to our senses. When Hegel lifted the cup, something unexpected usually lay under it: something Goethe or Spinoza had said, a mystical passage from Tauler or Jacob Böhme, an etymology from Grimm, a political dictum by Montesquieu, or an historical event. One could not help being full of amazement and admiration. . . .

[49] *Lebensbilder* (1870), II (2d ed., 1874), 105 f., 110 f. Gutzkow wrote a philosophy of history (1836) but is remembered for his novels and plays.

JOHANN EDUARD ERDMANN (1805–92): *1880*[50]

. . . Into his old age he kept the habit of reading everything, pen in hand, whether he was reading a book or a newspaper. . . .

Like Kant, he did not like *symphilosophein;* but, also like Kant, he was fond of *confabulari* with those who he felt sure would not seduce him into the former; and in Berlin whist took the place of *taroc*.

WALT WHITMAN: *1881*[51]
ROAMING IN THOUGHT
(*After reading* HEGEL)

Roaming in thought over the Universe, I saw the little that is Good
    steadily hastening towards immortality,
And the vast all that is call'd Evil I saw hastening to merge itself
    and become lost and dead.

[50] From "Hegel" (pp. 254–74) in *Allgemeine Deutsche Biographie,* Leipzig, Duncker und Humblot, XI (1880), 255, 256. Erdmann was one of Hegel's students, later became Professor of Philosophy at Halle, and wrote an important history of philosophy (1866; the 3d edition was translated into English).

Symphilosophein, a Greek word that the German romantics liked, means to philosophize together; *confabulari* means to chat together.

[51] *Leaves of Grass:* By the Roadside.

CHAPTER VIII:

The Preface to the *Phenomenology:*
Translation with Commentary on Facing Pages

... it is not saying too much when I claim that anyone understands Hegel's philosophy if he completely masters the meaning of this preface. RUDOLF HAYM, *Hegel und seine Zeit* (1857), 215.

... the most important of all Hegel texts ... Whoever has understood the preface to the *Phenomenology* has understood Hegel.
HERMANN GLOCKNER, *Hegel,* vol. II (1940), xx, 419.

The Preface to the *Phenomenology* is one of the greatest philosophical undertakings of all times. ... HERBERT MARCUSE, *Reason and Revolution: Hegel and the Rise of Social Theory* (1941), 97.

The *Phenomenology* is preceded by a remarkable *Preface,* which is a literary as well as a philosophical masterpiece.
J. N. FINDLAY, *Hegel* (1958), 83.

The preface roars like a romantic symphony ... I compare it to a world-historical festival. ...
GUSTAV EMIL MÜLLER, *Hegel* (1959), 203.

The original text of Hegel's long preface is far from easy to understand. This fact poses problems for the translator which are alleviated but not solved by the addition of a commentary on facing pages. In all of my other translations, including those in the present volume, I have aimed at the greatest possible faithfulness, to the point of giving the reader some feeling for the author's style. The following translation takes greater liberties than I am wont to take, but is still faithful.

Where the meaning is in doubt, or two interpretations are possible, I have not considered it my task to make up Hegel's mind. Where he is ambiguous, I have tried to be. I have not knowingly changed his meaning.

As far as possible, his tone is preserved, too. The alternation between cumbersome sentences that go on much too long and powerful epigrams that spell temporary relief is one of the most striking characteristics of this preface. But for the most part Hegel's excessively long sentences had to be broken up a little. He relies heavily on pronouns, both personal and relative, and in German the gender usually makes clear to what they refer, even if the referent is found many lines back. In English, lacking the guide of gender, one often has to repeat the referent—and one frequently has to begin a new sentence. Moreover, Hegel begins many sentences with such locutions as "For how and what it would be suitable to say. . . ." Or: "Also because. . . ." Or: "As firm as. . . ."; "At the same time, when. . . ."; "Just as much. . . ."

That all this is exceedingly awkward, there is no denying; but in German it is not as unusual as it would be in English. It may be one of the lesser values of the many quotations from other writers in this volume that they remind us how awkwardly ever so many Germans wrote during this period—or *at least* during this period.

In sum: the translation is, I believe, easier to follow than the original. Occasionally, splendid lines have been liberated from the coils of incredibly long sentences. Moreover, Hegel's long paragraphs have been broken up; and this device, too, allows one to call a little more attention to some sentences by letting them conclude a paragraph.

In this connection, Hegel's letter to Hinrichs, April 7, 1821, is relevant: "Even this would make things easier if you made more notches in your paragraphs and broke them up into more sections: the five first pages are one paragraph; the six following ones, ditto; etc." Hegel's paragraphs had never been as long as those of his young disciple; and by 1821 Hegel had developed a manner of writing *very* short paragraphs, in compendium style. I have aimed at striking a reasonable medium.

Hegel's all too abundant italics are more confusing than helpful. In the *Phenomenology,* German editors do not reproduce them, nor do I.

In the commentary I have inserted relatively few references to my reinterpretation. Naturally, I believe that a reading of the complete reinterpretation would be a great help in understanding the text. Chapter III, which deals with *The Phenomenology of the Spirit,* is obviously most relevant, and even a glance at the table of contents will give some idea of the topics it treats. I should like to call special attention to section 34, on "Hegel's terminology."

Hegel's characteristic terms are by no means always his coinages. *Weltgeist* (world spirit), for example, had been used by Kant, Herder, and Mendelssohn before him, and is also encountered in Schelling's and Schopenhauer's works. Some other terms now widely associated with Hegel were introduced by Schiller in his essay "On the Aesthetic Education of Man" (H 7). *An und für sich* (in and for itself), *an sich* (in itself), and *für uns* (for us) occur together on page 37 of Fichte's *Sun-clear Report* (1801), and in the same book Fichte contrasts, in passing, *räsonnieren* (argumentative thinking) and philosophizing. It would be as silly to say that Hegel stole these terms from others as it would be to suppose that he made them up as he went along, in a deliberate effort to be quaint: the point is rather that much that may seem strange today was not so far-fetched at the time. Hegel used expressions that were then current and, as often as not, gave them a new twist.

In an aphorism of the Berlin period, Hegel said: "a great man condemns men to explicate him" (Ros. 555). For a commentator this is an appropriate motto, but Hegel was almost certainly not thinking of himself, and the motto is as apt for his preface as it is for my commentary: we are all condemned, as Hegel sees it, to try to comprehend what man has thought up to our time and to relive, in condensed form, the experiences of the world spirit. The preface that follows is of a piece with the conclusion of Hegel's introductory lectures on the philosophy of history: "The moments which the spirit seems to have left behind, it also possesses in its present depth. As it has run through its moments in history, it has to run through them in the present—in the Concept of itself" (VG 183 L).

The parallel to Freud should not be missed. Indeed, the first of these two sentences might well have been written by Freud, except that he would probably have said "soul," not "spirit." But the second sentence, too, is reminiscent of psychoanalysis: recapitulating our past is the price of freedom.

Hegel's own description of the *Phenomenology* appeared in the Jena cultural supplement not before publication, as was then customary for *Selbstanzeigen*,[1] but on October 28, 1807.

"Announcements of new books:

"Jos. Ant. Goebhardt's Bookstore, Bamberg and Würzburg, has published and sent to all good bookstores: G. W. F. Hegel's *System of Science*. Volume One, containing *The Phenomenology of the Spirit*. Large Octavo. 1807. Price: 6 fl.

"This volume deals with the *becoming of knowledge*. The phenomenology of the spirit is to replace psychological explanations as well as the more abstract discussions of the foundation of knowledge. It considers the *preparation* for science from a point of view, which makes it a new, an interesting, and the first science of philosophy. It includes the various *forms of the spirit* as stations on the way on which it becomes pure knowledge or absolute spirit. In the main parts of this science, which in turn are subdivided further, consideration is given to consciousness, self-consciousness, observing and acting reason, the spirit itself as ethical, educated, and moral spirit, and finally as religious in its different forms. The wealth of the appearances of the spirit, which at first glance seems chaotic, is brought into a scientific order which presents them according to their necessity in which the imperfect ones dissolve and pass over into higher ones which constitute their next truth. Their final truth they find at first in religion, then in science as the result of the whole.

"In the preface the author explains himself about what seems to him the need of philosophy in its present state; also about the presumption and mischief of the philosophic formulas that are currently degrading philosophy, and about what is altogether crucial in it and its study.

"A *second volume* will contain the system of *Logic* as speculative philosophy, and of the other two parts of philosophy, the *sciences* of *nature* and the *spirit*."

[1] The author's description of his book.

Hegel's own Table of Contents (1807)[2]

[2] Only the part covering the preface has been translated here. In the original
the headings are run on and not numbered.

TRANSLATION

1. Of scientific knowledge[1]

[I.1]

In the preface of a book it is customary to explain the author's aim, the reasons why he wrote the book, and what he takes to be its relationship to other treatments, earlier or contemporary, of the same subject. In the case of a philosophical work, however, such an explanation seems not only superfluous but, owing to the nature of the subject matter,[2] altogether improper and unsuited to the end in view. For what contents and tone would be appropriate for a preface to a philosophical work? Perhaps a historical statement concerning the tendency and point of view, the general contents and results of the work, an attempt to connect sundry claims and assertions about the truth? Philosophical truth cannot be presented in this manner.

Philosophy deals essentially with the general in which the particular is subsumed. Therefore it *seems,* more than in the case of other sciences, as if the aim or the final results gave expression to the subject matter itself, even as if they did entire justice to its very essence, while the way in which things are worked out in detail may seem to be unessential. Yet people do not suppose that the general idea of, say, the nature of anatomy—perhaps as the knowledge of the parts of the body, considered *qua* their lifeless existence—automatically furnishes us with the subject matter itself. Everybody realizes that, if we want possession of the contents of this science, we must also exert ourselves to master the particulars, the detail.

Moreover, such an aggregate of information really has no right to the name of science; and any discussion of its aim and other such generalities is usually no different from the manner in which the content—i.e., the nerves, the muscles, etc.—is discussed, too: in both cases, the manner is equally historical and void of Concepts.[3] In the case of philosophy, however, such an introductory discussion would be an oddity: for it would employ this same manner while demonstrating that this manner is incapable of grasping the truth.[4]

COMMENTARY

I. *Philosophy must become scientific*

1. Science is not the naked result

¹ In the first edition of 1807, the table of contents includes nineteen subheads under the preface. They are not numbered as in our text but run on, interrupted only by Roman numeral page numbers. In the text itself no divisions are indicated. These headings afford some insight into Hegel's intentions and are worth reproducing. In the text they are numbered consecutively and italicized. In Hegel's table of contents, the first heading is not assigned a page number but immediately followed by the second; yet it surely belongs at the outset.

In the first critical edition of the work (1907), the editor, Georg Lasson, divided the preface into four major parts, and each of these into three sections. In his text these are indicated respectively by Roman and Arabic numerals, and in his table of contents, which does not follow the original one at this point, these four Roman and twelve Arabic numbers are followed by titles he proposed. His disposition is plausible and helpful and therefore reproduced in the commentary, but our titles (in *italics*) and subtitles (in Roman letters) are not his. In sum, Hegel's own subheads appear in the texts, ours in the commentary, opposite the places (marked by numerals only) where they belong.

² "Subject matter": in German, *Sache*. This word can mean: thing, matter, concern. *Zur Sache!* can mean: to the subject; and *das gehört nicht zur Sache:* that is irrelevant. *Sachlich* can also mean: objective; and *bei der Sache sein:* to concentrate.

³ "historical and void of Concepts": in German, *historisch und begrifflos*. The only previous translation, Baillie's (1910, revised 1931; reprinted also in Scribner's *Hegel Selections*) has: "descriptive and superficial." Plainly, this is not what Hegel says. The ordinary meaning of *Begriff* is definitely concept. Because this is one of Hegel's most characteristic terms, and he associates more than its ordinary meaning with it, some nineteenth-century English

The very attempt to determine the relationship of a philosophical work to other efforts concerning the same subject, introduces an alien and irrelevant interest which obscures precisely
that which matters for the recognition of the truth. Opinion
considers the opposition of what is true and false quite rigid, and,
confronted with a philosophical system, it expects agreement or
contradiction. And in an explanation of such a system, opinion
still expects to find one or the other. It does not comprehend the
difference of the philosophical systems in terms of the progressive
development of the truth, but sees only the contradiction in this
difference. The bud disappears as the blossom bursts forth, and
one could say that the former is refuted by the latter. In the
same way, the fruit declares the blossom to be a false existence
of the plant, and the fruit supplants the blossom as the truth
of the plant. These forms do not only differ, they also displace
each other because they are incompatible. Their fluid[5] nature,
however, makes them, at the same time, elements of an organic
unity in which they not only do not conflict, but in which one
is as necessary as the other; and it is only this equal necessity
that constitutes the life of the whole.[6]

The opposition to a philosophical system, however, usually
does not understand itself in this way. And the consciousness
that is confronted with this opposition usually does not know
how to liberate it, or how to keep it free, from its one-sidedness.
Nor does it know how to penetrate this appearance of conten-
tion and mutual opposition in order to recognize elements which
are necessary to each other.

The demand for such explanations or confessions and the satisfaction of this demand are easily mistaken for a concern with
what is essential. Where could one hope for a better expression
of the core of a philosophical work than in its aims and results?
And how could these be determined better than by noting their
difference from that which the age generally produces in the
same sphere? But when this procedure is taken for more than
the beginning of knowledge, when it is mistaken for knowledge
itself, then we must indeed count it among the devices for by-
passing the real subject matter, while combining the semblance
of seriousness and exertion with a dispensation from both.

For the subject matter is not exhausted by any aim, but only
by the way in which things are worked out in detail; nor is
the result the actual whole, but only the result together with
its becoming. The aim, taken by itself, is a lifeless generality;
the tendency is a mere drift which still lacks actuality; and the

translators felt that a less ordinary term was called for and hit on
"notion." This word is utterly misleading as it suggests vagueness
and caprice, while Hegel takes pains to *attack* haziness and subjectivity, opposing to them "the seriousness of the Concept" (cf. [11]
below). He upholds rigorous and highly disciplined conceptual analysis. *Begriff* is closely related to *begreifen* (to comprehend)—an affinity that unfortunately cannot be recaptured in English—and Hegel
considers it the task of philosophy to comprehend and not merely
to feel and rhapsodize.

[4] The oddity here noted is indeed a striking characteristic of the preface that follows. (Cf. H 14, 24 f., and 37.)

[5] "fluid": this image is picked up again later in the preface: see II.3, note [35] below.

[6] This is one of the most interesting and fateful paragraphs in Hegel's writings. In Descartes, Hobbes, and Spinoza, in
Locke, Berkeley, and Hume, or in Kant we find no comparable
conception of philosophical disagreement or "the progressive development of the truth." Different philosophies, according to Hegel, are
not to be viewed as laid out next to each other in a spatial arrangement; they cannot be fully understood as long as their temporal
relationship is ignored. Studying a single system is like studying,
say, a blossom; the study of the whole plant and of living organisms
corresponds to the study of the development of philosophy to the
present time. Different philosophies represent different stages of
maturity.

Here, then, at the beginning of his first book, Hegel announces
the vision that led him about fifteen years later, as a professor at
the University of Berlin, to establish the history of philosophy as a
subject of central importance for students of philosophy—which it
had not been before. (But see H 67, n. [40].)

"Necessary" and "necessity" in the last sentence are questionable.
Hegel means that philosophies should not be understood as capri-
cious webs spun by wayward thinkers but as significant stages in the
development of thought. When a philosopher disagrees with his predecessors, we should not reject the lot because they cannot agree with
each other; rather we should ask how the later thinkers correct the
partiality of the former, and how each contributes to the gradual
refinement of knowledge. Hegel notwithstanding, this does not imply
any genuine necessity. Hegel often uses "necessary" quite illicitly
as the negation of "utterly arbitrary."

naked result is the corpse which has left the tendency behind.[7]

In the same way, the difference is really the limit of the subject matter: it indicates where the subject matter ceases, or it is what the subject matter is not. Such exertions concerning the aim, the results, the differences that may exist in this respect, or the critical judgments of aim and results, are therefore easier work than they may seem to be. For instead of dealing with the subject matter, such talk is always outside it; instead of abiding in the subject matter and forgetting itself in it, such knowledge always reaches out for something else and really remains preoccupied with itself instead of sticking to, and devoting itself to, the subject matter.[8]

To judge that which has contents and workmanship is the easiest thing; to grasp it is more difficult; and what is most difficult is to combine both by producing an account of it.[9]

How should education begin, and how the process of working oneself up out of the immediacy of the substance of life? The beginning will always have to be made by acquiring some cognizance of general principles and points of view and by working oneself up, first of all, to the idea[10] of the subject matter. No less, one must learn to support or refute it with reasons, to comprehend a concrete and copious fullness in terms of exact determinations, and to be able to offer accurate information and serious judgments. Then, however, this beginning of education will have to give way to the seriousness of life in its fullness which leads us into the experience of the subject matter itself. And when, in addition to all this, the seriousness of the Concept[11] descends into the depth of the subject matter, then such knowledge and judgment will always retain a proper place in discussion.

2. *The element of truth is the Concept, and its true form the scientific system*[12]

The true form in which truth exists can only be the scientific system of it. To contribute to this end, that philosophy might come closer to the form of science—the goal being that it might be able to relinquish the name of love of knowledge and be actual knowledge—that is what I have resolved to try. The *inner* necessity according to which knowledge is science is grounded in the nature of knowledge, and the only satisfactory explanation of this is to be found in the presentation of philosophy it-

⁷ Most English-speaking philosophers 150 years after this was written would agree with this paragraph. A student who remembers and reproduces the conclusions of his teacher, or of some great philosopher, but not the way in which things are worked out in detail, has only got hold of something lifeless: the spirit of philosophy has escaped him. What counts in philosophy is not the striking aim or claim, but the detail.

⁸ What is wanted is devotion. The philosopher, like a scientist, should devote himself to, and immerse himself in, his subject instead of trying to be interesting and different. Or as Hegel puts it later, what is wanted is "the seriousness of the Concept."

⁹ External criticism that simply condemns without any prior effort to comprehend is relatively easy and trivial. To really grasp a position and the arguments involved in it is more difficult. But a philosopher must combine grasp and critical evaluation: for until we rethink every step critically we cannot fully comprehend what led a writer to go on as he did; what problems led him to develop his views; and what prompted later thinkers to differ with him.

¹⁰ "idea": German, *Gedanke;* literally, "thought." Translated as "idea" at this point because this is more idiomatic here.

¹¹ "the seriousness of the Concept": *der Ernst des Begriffs* is one of Hegel's famous phrases. For *Begriff* see note ³ above. This term is rendered, throughout this translation, as Concept—with a capital C to signal that Hegel uses this word as a technical term. Here, for example, "the seriousness of conceptual analysis" would be a little more idiomatic.

Some of the preceding might strike readers with no predilection for philosophy as an invitation to pedantry. But consider the Philistine who reads the final speech of Goethe's *Faust,* in the fifth act of Part Two, and says: "I always knew that nothing good could come of boundless striving; one has to settle down to a job and do it well." He has got hold of a "naked result" or a "lifeless generality." Real comprehension depends on a grasp neither of the play without the last act, nor of the speech without the play, but of "the result together with its becoming." (Cf. Hegel's Jena aphorism ⅗45 in *Dok.*) In the case of a philosophic position, too, the "becoming" involves not only the detailed arguments but also "the seriousness of life in its fullness" (*Ernst des erfüllten Lebens*). Yet this, however necessary, is not enough for philosophy which self. The *external* necessity, however, can also be understood more generally, apart from the accidents of the author's person or his individual motivation; and so understood, it coincides with the inner necessity; only the form is different in accordance with the manner in which time exhibits the existence of its stages. To demonstrate that the time has come for the elevation of philosophy to a science[13]—this would be the only true justification of the attempts which have this aim. For this would show the necessity of this aim even while accomplishing it.

[I.2]

Truth can attain its true form only by becoming scientific, or, in other words, I claim that truth finds the element of its existence only in the Concept. I know that this view seems to contradict a notion[1] and its consequences that are as presumptuous as they are widely accepted in our time. Therefore some discussion of this contradiction seems hardly superfluous, although at this point it can only take the form of a mere assertion—just like the view against which it is aimed.

Others say that truth exists only in that, or rather as that, which is called now intuition,[2] now immediate knowledge of the absolute, religion, or being—not *at* the center of divine love but the being itself of this very center.[3] It follows that what is then demanded for the presentation of philosophy is the opposite of the form of the Concept. The absolute is supposed to be not comprehended[4] but felt and intuited; it is not its Concept that is meant to prevail and be proclaimed but its feeling and intuition.

3. *Present position of the spirit*

The appearance of such a demand should be considered in its more general context, and one should see what stage the self-conscious spirit occupies at present. Clearly, it has passed beyond the substantial life that it formerly led in the element of thought—beyond this immediacy of its faith, beyond the satisfaction and security of that certainty which consciousness possessed about its reconciliation with the essence and its general, internal as well as external, presence. The spirit has not only passed beyond all this into the other extreme of its insubstantial requires, "in addition to all this, the seriousness of the Concept."

[12] The page number assigned to this heading in the original edition (vii) is clearly mistaken (vi must be meant); vii would move it down one paragraph.

[13] Fichte already had spoken of his "exertions to elevate philosophy to a science," on the second page of his preface to *Sun-clear Report to the Public at Large about the True Nature of the Newest Philosophy: An attempt to compel the readers to understand* (Berlin, 1801). "The time has come for": *an der Zeit ist;* a common idiomatic expression that is ill rendered by Baillie's "the time process does raise philosophy . . ."

I.2. Inner necessity that philosophy become scientific

In keeping with the preceding paragraph, Hegel proceeds to discuss, first, the "inner necessity" and then (I.3) the "external necessity."

[1] "notion": *Vorstellung.* This German word is usually rendered, by translators of Kant and Schopenhauer, as either "representation" or "idea." The former is literally correct but often, as in the present context, exceedingly clumsy. "Idea," on the other hand, is often needed to render the German *Idee.* An examination of all occurrences of *Vorstellung* in this long preface shows that Hegel generally means to suggest something vague and distinctly less scientific than a Concept. "Notion" seems just right.

[2] "intuition": *Anschauung.* This translation seems firmly established in English translations of German philosophy; and according to the *Shorter Oxford English Dictionary,* "intuition" means in *"Mod. Philos.* The immediate apprehension of an object by the mind without the intervention of any reasoning process." This sense, which goes back to 1600, is exactly right here.

[3] Mid-twentieth-century readers may associate this view with Paul Tillich, without realizing that Tillich wrote his doctoral dissertation on Schelling and owes much to German romanticism. Lasson, in 1907, associated the views criticized here with "Jacobi, the romantics, Schlegel, and Schleiermacher."

[4] "comprehended": *begriffen.* "Concept": *Begriff.*

reflection in itself; it has also passed beyond that. Not only has it lost its essential life; it is also conscious of this loss and of the finitude that is its contents. The spirit is turning away from the husks[5] and, confessing that it is in trouble and cursing, it now demands from philosophy not so much self-knowledge as that philosophy should help the spirit to establish such substantiality and the solidity of being. Philosophy is asked to answer this need not by unlocking the locks of substance and raising it to the level of self-consciousness, nor by returning the chaotic consciousness to the order of thought and the simplicity of the Concept, but rather by confounding the distinctions of thought, by suppressing the discriminating Concept, and by establishing the *feeling* of the essence,[6] granting not so much insight as edification.

The beautiful, the holy, the eternal, religion, and love are the bait that is required to arouse the desire to bite. Not the Concept but ecstasy, not the coldly progressing necessity of the subject matter but fermenting enthusiasm is held to be the best attitude and guide to the spread-out riches of the substance.[7]

In line with such demands one exerts oneself almost zealously and angrily to tear men out of their absorption in the sensuous, the vulgar, the particular, and to raise their sights to the stars—as if, utterly forgetful of the divine, they were at the point of satisfying themselves with dust and water, like worms. Formerly they had a heaven, furnished with abundant riches of thoughts and images. The significance of all that is used to lie in the thread of light that tied it to the heavens; and following this thread, the eye, instead of abiding in the present, rose above that to the divine essence, to, if one may say so, a presence beyond. The eye of the spirit had to be directed forcibly to the things of this earth and kept there. Indeed, it took a long time to work that clarity which only the supernatural possessed into the must and confusion in which the sense[8] of this world lay imprisoned; it took a long time to make attention to the present as such—what was called, in one word, experience—interesting and valid.

Now the opposite need meets the eye: sense[8] seems to be so firmly rooted in what is worldly that it takes an equal force to raise it higher. The spirit appears so poor that, like a wanderer in the desert who languishes for a simple drink of water, it seems to crave for its refreshment merely the bare feeling of the divine in general. By that which suffices the spirit one can measure the extent of its loss.

⁵ "husks" (*Treber*) alludes to the parable of the prodigal son, Luke 15:16. Cf. Schiller, *On the Aesthetic Education of Man, in a Series of Letters* (1795): "Nature (sense) unifies everywhere, the understanding differentiates everywhere, but reason unifies again. Hence man, before he begins to philosophize, is closer to the truth than the philosopher who has not yet concluded his inquiry" (note to the 18th Letter). Hegel scorns those who, at the first differentiation when they find they are far from home, turn back instead of persevering, pushing on the inquiry, and comprehending the truth. In his opposition to *Schwärmerei,* the cult of feeling, and the inspirational philosophizing of the pious, Hegel does not pit reason against passion, or academic pedantry against deep experience; instead he questions the seriousness of the passion and the depth of the experience of the writers he criticizes: they run back home as soon as the going gets rough and hide their lack of strength in a mist of emotion.

⁶ "the *feeling* of the essence": *das Gefühl des Wesens.* Baillie: "the feeling of existence."

⁷ It is the beauty of Hegel's criticisms that, though directed against some of his contemporaries, they are no less applicable to many well-known writers in other ages.

⁸ "sense": the German in both places is *Sinn;* but Baillie has "sense" the first time and "mind and interest" the second, thus missing some of the contrast.

Hegel juxtaposes the otherworldliness of the past with the worldliness of the present.

Lasson has a note at the point where our ⁷ appears: "This description of the spiritual situation of the age corresponds to the section on the 'unhappy consciousness,'" later in the book. But the immediately preceding sentence (split into two sentences in our translation) does not necessarily imply any otherworldliness: it might be applied, for example, to Jaspers and Tillich. Only the passage beginning "Formerly they had . . ." invites comparison with the "unhappy consciousness" (see H 33). On the whole, Lasson is a very helpful guide.

This modest contentment in accepting, or stinginess in giving, is, however, improper for science. Whoever seeks mere edification, whoever desires to shroud the worldly multiplicity of his existence and of thought in a fog to attain the indeterminate enjoyment of this indeterminate divinity, may look out for himself where he can find this; he will easily find the means to impress himself with his enthusiasm and thus to puff himself up. Philosophy, however, must beware of wishing to be edifying.[9]

Least of all should such modest contentment which renounces science make claims that such ecstasy and dimness are something higher than science. Such prophetic talk supposes that it abides right in the center and in the depths, views the determinate (*the horos*) contemptuously,[10] and deliberately keeps its distance from the Concept and from necessity, associating them with reflection[11] that makes its home in the finite. But even as there is an empty breadth, there is also an empty depth; even as there is an extension of the substance that pours itself out into finite multiplicity without the strength to hold it together, there is also an intensity void of content—pure force without any spread—which is identical with superficiality. The strength of the spirit is only as great as its expression; its depth is only as deep as it dares to spread and lose itself in its explication.[12]

Moreover, when this substantial knowledge without Concept[13] pretends to have drowned the personality of the self in the essence and to philosophize in a true and holy manner, it really hides the truth from itself: for instead of devoting itself to the god, it is undone because it spurns measure and determination, and now the accidental contents, now personal arbitrariness will lord it.—As they abandon themselves to the untamed ferment of the substance,[14] they suppose that by shrouding self-consciousness and yielding up the understanding they become His beloved to whom God gives wisdom in sleep;[15] what they thus conceive and give birth to in sleep indeed are, naturally, dreams.

⁹ Hegel's polemic against mere "edification" and the wish to be "edifying" (*erbaulich*) brings to mind Kierkegaard's *Edifying Discourses*. Kierkegaard's many polemical references to Hegel are better known than the fact that Hegel published his critique of Kierkegaard six years before the latter was born. Kierkegaard's authorship of *Edifying Discourses* and *Concluding Unscientific Postscript* has to be understood against the background not only of Hegel's *Logic,* which is usually cited in this connection, but also of the *Phenomenology,* which is too often ignored by Kierkegaard's expositors.

¹⁰ Hegel here sides with Plato against those who despise the limit and the determinate instead of realizing that this is the element of reason. Like Plato, he is aware of the power of poetry and passion, but considers the definite and precise superior to the indefinite and amorphous.

¹¹ "reflection": *Reflexion.* The German and English words have the same double meaning.

¹² "empty depth": a splendid phrase, by no means applicable only to the romantics of whom Hegel was thinking primarily. The last sentence offers a superb formulation of one of Sartre's central ideas: "for the existentialist, there is no love apart from the deeds of love; . . . there is no genius other than that which is expressed in works of art. The genius of Proust is the totality of the works of Proust . . . In life, a man . . . draws his own portrait and there is nothing but that portrait. . . . 'You are nothing else but what you live.'" "Existentialism is a Humanism" in *Existentialism from Dostoevsky to Sartre,* ed. Walter Kaufmann, 300 f.

¹³ "this substantial knowledge without Concept": *dies begrifflose substantielle Wissen.* Baillie: "this unreflective emotional knowledge."

¹⁴ "of the substance": *der Substanz.* Baillie: "of sheer emotion."

¹⁵ An allusion to Psalms 127:2, which is often cited in German.

[I.3]

It is surely not difficult to see that our time is a time of birth and transition to a new period. The spirit has broken with what was hitherto the world of its existence and imagination and is about to[1] submerge all this in the past; it is at work giving itself a new form. To be sure, the spirit is never at rest but always engaged in[2] ever progressing motion. But just as in the case of a child the first breath it draws after long silent nourishment terminates the gradualness of the merely quantitative progression—a qualitative leap[3]—and now the child is born, so, too, the spirit that educates itself[4] matures slowly and quietly toward the new form, dissolving one particle of the edifice of its previous world after the other, while its tottering is suggested only by some symptoms here and there: frivolity as well as the boredom that open up in the establishment and the indeterminate apprehension of something unknown are harbingers of a forthcoming change. This gradual crumbling which did not alter the physiognomy of the whole is interrupted by the break of day that, like lightning, all at once reveals the edifice of the new world.[5]

Yet what is new here does not have perfect actuality any more than the newborn child; and it is essential not to overlook this.[6] The first emergence is only its immediacy or its Concept.[7] Even as a building is not finished when its foundation has been laid, the attained Concept of the whole is not the whole itself. When we wish to see an oak—the strength of its trunk, the spread of its branches, and the mass of its foliage—we are not satisfied when in its place we are shown an acorn. Thus science, the crown[8] of a world of the spirit, is not complete in its beginning. The beginning of the new spirit is the product of a far-reaching revolution in ever so many forms of culture and education;[9] it is the prize for an immensely tangled path and an equally immense amount of exertion and toil. It is the whole which has returned into itself from succession as well as extension,[10] the resultant simple Concept of it. But the actuality of this simple whole consists in this, that these forms which have become mere moments[11] now develop anew and give themselves form, but in their new element,[12] in the sense that has emerged.

I.3. External necessity that philosophy become scientific

¹ "imagination": *Vorstellens;* literally, representing. "is about to": *steht im Begriff;* a common idiom that means, is about to. Baillie: "is in the mind to."

² "engaged in": *ist . . . begriffen;* another idiom. At first glance, the relation of these two idioms to *Begriff* (Concept) seems quite fortuitous and void of any significance; but Hegel, like Plato and Aristotle, paid attention to such matters and probably found in these expressions some intimation at the level of ordinary language of his own conviction that the Concept is essentially dynamic.

³ "qualitative leap" has often been quoted from Hegel, and some Marxists have harped on the idea that great quantitative differences eventually become qualitative differences.

⁴ "the spirit that educates itself" or "that forms itself": *der sich bildende Geist. Bild* means picture or image; *bilden,* to shape or form, but also to educate. *Sich bilden,* the reflexive form, usually means to educate oneself; and *Bildung,* for which there is no entirely adequate translation, education. *Ungebildet* means uneducated, uncultured, uncouth, raw. *Bildungsroman* is the novel that relates the education of the hero; and ever since Goethe published *Wilhelm Meisters Lehrjahre* (1795/96) this genre has attracted many of the best German writers. In his *Lectures on Modern Idealism* (published posthumously in 1919), Royce considered it pretty well extinct (p. 140), but since then Thomas Mann and Hermann Hesse have returned to it again and again. The *Phenomenology of the Spirit* is the story of the *Bildung* of the spirit.

⁵ Throughout this paragraph Hegel alludes to the French Revolution; for example, "time of birth and transition," "frivolity" and "boredom," and the "gradual crumbling" that precedes a sudden break.

⁶ It is also essential to translate *Wirklichkeit* and *wirklich* as actuality and actual, not as reality and real. The baby is real enough, but if we think in terms of the contrast of potentiality and actuality we can say that "the newborn child" lacks "perfect actuality." Hegel's notorious equation of the actual and the rational is not a sanctification of the *status quo;* in his terminology, most states are not fully actual and rational.

4. *The principle is not the completion; against formalism*

While on the one hand the first appearance of the new world is only the whole shrouded in simplicity or its general basis, the wealth of its previous existence is, on the other hand, still present to consciousness in memory.[13] In the newly appearing form it misses the spread and the particularization of the contents; but even more it misses the cultivation[14] of the form whereby the distinctions are determined with certainty and ordered according to their firm relationships. Without this elaboration[14] science lacks universal intelligibility[15] and has the appearance of being an esoteric possession of a few individuals. An esoteric possession: for it is present only in its Concept—only its inside is there. Of a few individuals: for its inarticulate appearance makes its existence merely individual. Only what is completely determinate is at the same time exoteric, comprehensible, and capable of being learned and of thus becoming the property of all. The intelligible[15] form of science is the way to science which is offered to all and made equal for all; and to reach rational knowledge by means of the understanding[15] is the just demand of consciousness as it approaches science. For the understanding[15] is thinking, the pure ego; and the sensible[15] is the already familiar and that which science and the unscientific consciousness have in common—that whereby the latter can immediately enter science.

The science which is still close to its beginnings and thus has achieved neither completeness of detail nor perfection of form is open to reproach for this reason. But if such censure is aimed at the very essence of science it is as unjust as it would be to refuse to recognize the demand for such elaboration. This opposition seems to be the most important knot on which scientific education is working today, wearying itself without as yet properly understanding the situation. One side insists on the wealth of its material and its intelligibility; the other side spurns at least the latter and insists on immediate rationality and divinity. Even though the first party has been reduced to silence, whether by the power of truth alone or also by the impetuosity of the other party, and though they feel overwhelmed in respect to the fundamentals of the case, they still have not been satisfied regarding their demands: their demands are just but have not been fulfilled. Their silence is only half due to victory

⁷ "immediacy" (*Unmittelbarkeit*) means for Hegel quite literally that which has not been mediated or gone through an intermediate condition. Babies and acorns, of course, are the results of prior developments, but here they are not considered as results but as what is given in the beginning. When the Concept is attained that all men are free, equal, and brothers, a long development may still be required before liberty, equality, and fraternity are fully actualized. (Cf. H 44 and 59 f.)

⁸ In German the top of a tree is often called its crown.

⁹ "revolution in ever so many forms of culture and education": *Umwälzung von mannigfaltigen Bildungsformen.*

¹⁰ The "new spirit" is the product of a long Odyssey of the spirit or, more prosaically, of a journey through time and space, "succession as well as extension."

¹¹ "moments": *Momente.* Hegel frequently uses this term, and his primary meaning is rarely, if ever, instants. The *Shorter Oxford English Dictionary* defines: "One of the elements of a complex conceptual entity. (After Ger. use.) 1863"; and the supporting quotation speaks of "elements or moments." But there is a slight temporal connotation, reflected in one of the other definitions: "A definite stage or turning-point in a course of events 1666." Sometimes "stages" comes a little closer to Hegel's meaning than "elements" would.

¹² The "new element" is philosophy. What has developed must now be comprehended and developed all over again, in thought.

¹³ The partisans of "immediate knowledge" suffer from amnesia: what they claim to know immediately was in fact mediated by a long historical process. What seems self-evident now was not obvious in the past, and what seems simple is in fact the whole development "shrouded in simplicity." (Cf. H 44.)

¹⁴ *Ausbildung.*

¹⁵ "intelligibility": *Verständlichkeit;* "intelligible": *verständlich;* "understanding": *Verstand;* "the sensible": *das Verständige.*

The basic idea of section I.3 so far, and of this paragraph especially, is that the time has come for all men to demand equal access to philosophy; and to become common property philosophy must become scientific. To become exoteric and democratic, phi-

—half to the boredom and indifference which are usually the consequences of constantly excited expectations when the promises made are never fulfilled.[16]

Regarding the contents, the others certainly sometimes make it easy enough for themselves to have great spread. They drag a lot of material into their field, namely material that is already familiar and well ordered. And when they deal preferably with the queer and curious, they only seem that much more to have firm possession of the rest which knowledge has long taken care of in its way, as if their mastery of the unruly came in addition to all this. Thus they subject everything to the absolute idea which then appears to be recognized in everything and to have developed into a comprehensive science. But when this comprehensiveness is considered more closely, it becomes manifest that it was not attained insofar as one and the same principle differentiated itself into different forms, but it is rather the formless repetition of one and the same principle which is merely applied externally to different material and thus receives a dull semblance of differentiation. The idea, true enough by itself, remains in fact just where it was in the beginning as long as the development consists merely in such repetition of the same formula. When the knowing subject applies the one unmoved form to whatever is presented, and the material is externally dipped into this resting element, this is not, any more than arbitrary notions about the contents, the fulfillment of that which is in fact required—to wit, the wealth that wells forth out of itself and the self-differentiation of the forms. Rather it is a drab monochromatic formalism that gets to the differentiation of the material solely because this is long prepared and familiar.

Yet he[17] proclaims this monotony and abstract generality as the absolute; he assures us that any dissatisfaction with this is mere incapacity to master the absolute point of view and to abide there. Formerly, the mere possibility that one could also imagine something in another way was sufficient to refute a notion,[18] and this same bare possibility, the general thought, also had the full positive value of actual knowledge. Now here we find that all value is also ascribed to the general idea in this form of non-actuality, while the dissolution of the distinct and determinate—or rather the resolve, which is neither developed further nor self-justifying, to thrust the distinct and determinate into the abyss of emptiness—is presented as the speculative mode of study.

losophy must be available to every intelligent person who is willing
to shirk no effort—regardless of whether he belongs to some special group or clique, whether that be the romantic circle or a religious denomination. The time for special privilege is past.

On the face of it, it is ironical that this insistence on universal
intelligibility should appear in the preface to a work of legendary
difficulty which even professionals have the greatest trouble in understanding. And after all is said, this irony remains striking. But
it should be noted that Hegel's position does not commit him to
popularization. Science, including higher mathematics and advanced
physics, is exoteric and democratic in the sense here at stake; and
Hegel constantly insists that philosophy requires the most serious
exertion and hard work. Indeed, this is part of what he means
when he speaks of elevating philosophy to the level of a science.

[16] Confronted with such allusions, which turn up
throughout the *Phenomenology,* one always has to ask both whom
in particular Hegel had in mind and whether he succeeded in char-
acterizing recurrent and typical phenomena. Here, "one side" seems
to refer to representatives of the Enlightenment, and "the other
side" to some of the romantics. In 1807 the romantics were pre-
vailing, but Hegel found the demand for universal intelligibility
"just."

The final sentence is very probably directed particularly against
Friedrich Schlegel, one of the leading spirits of the early romantic
movement in Germany, who aroused great expectations with his
bold promises, but who is said to have disappointed his hearers
dismally when he came to the University of Jena. (Cf. Hegel's
letter of August 2, 1816, in D.) But Schlegel may have been the
mere occasion for Hegel's insight into this type of romanticism. "The
boredom and indifference which are usually the consequences of
constantly excited expectations when the promises made are never
fulfilled" could also be documented from the journals of one of
Schelling's students at the University of Berlin, a decade after Hegel's death. The student was Søren Kierkegaard.

The immediately following polemic ("Regarding the contents
. . .") has often been understood as a critique of the young Schelling. For a discussion of the question whether some of the polemics
in this preface were aimed at Schelling, see H 39; cf. also Hegel's
and Schelling's correspondence of 1807, translated in D.

[17] The German pronoun, *er,* could refer—and, no doubt,

To study anything as it is in the absolute here means merely that one says of it: to be sure, it has just been spoken of as something, but in the absolute, the A=A, there is nothing of the sort, for in the absolute everything is one. To pit this one piece of information, that in the absolute all is one, against all the distinctions of knowledge, both attained knowledge and the search and demand for knowledge—or to pass off one's absolute as the night in which, as one says, all cows are black—that is the naïveté of the emptiness of knowledge.[19]

Recent philosophy accuses and derogates formalism, and yet formalism has regenerated itself in its very midst. But though the inadequacy of formalism is familiar and felt, it will not disappear from science until the knowledge of absolute actuality has gained perfect clarity about its nature.[20]

Since the general notion, if it precedes an attempt to execute it, makes it easier to understand the latter, it may be helpful to offer some suggestions at this point. At the same time, this occasion may be used to eliminate a few forms whose customary acceptance constitutes an obstacle for philosophical knowledge.

does, strictly speaking—to "monochromatic formalism." But it is a little difficult to picture this drab formalism as proclaiming things and assuring us, and the German reader who has recognized the portrait of Schelling—or of his typical imitator—is bound to think of *him,* not of *it.*

[18] "imagine": *sich etwas . . . vorzustellen;* "notion": *Vorstellung.* Cf. I.2, note [1] above.

[19] Here are a few pertinent quotations from Schelling's *Bruno* (1802):

"In this absolute unity, however—because in it everything is, as has been shown, perfect and itself absolute—nothing is distinguishable from anything else, for things are distinguished only by their imperfections . . ." (p. 83).

". . . that which is not but which is the ground of existence, the primeval night, the mother of all things" (p. 124).

"He, however, would stray furthest from the idea of the absolute who would determine its nature, in order not to determine it as being, by the concept of activity" (p. 171).

In connection with the preceding pages, the following quotation, too, is relevant:

"And philosophy is necessarily, by its very nature, esoteric . . ." (p. 31). In Schelling's *Werke:* I, IV, pp. 232, 258, 278, 303.

The "A=A" occurs in Schelling's *Darstellung meines Systems der Philosophie* (1801), §§4 ff.

See also his "Aphorismen zur Einleitung in die Naturphilosophie" in *Jahrbücher der Medizin als Wissenschaft* (1806): "The absolute therefore can be expressed eternally only as absolute, altogether indivisible identity"; "God is the equally eternal night and the equally eternal day of things" (*Werke,* 1860, vol. VII; 1927, reprinted 1958, vol. IV; ❊65 and ❊102).

On the whole question whether Hegel's polemic was directed against Schelling see H 39 and D 1807.

[20] "its nature" probably refers to formalism but could also refer to "the knowledge." No doubt, clarity about the nature of both is important.

5. *The absolute is subject—*

[II.1]

According to my view, which must justify itself[1] by the presentation of the system, everything depends on this, that we comprehend and express the true not as substance but just as much as subject.[2] At the same time it should be noted that substantiality involves the generality or immediacy both of knowledge itself and of that which is being or immediacy *for* knowledge.[3]

Comprehending God as the one substance outraged the age in which this definition was proclaimed.[4] On the one hand, this was due to the instinctive recognition that self-consciousness was only drowned in it and not preserved; on the other hand, however, the opposite view which clings to thinking as thinking is generality as such and the same simplicity or undifferentiated, unmoved substantiality.[5] And when, thirdly, thinking unites with itself the being of the substance and comprehends immediacy or intuition as thinking, it still remains decisive whether this intellectual intuition does not fall back into inert simplicity and present actuality in a non-actual manner.[6]

6. *—and what this is*

The living substance is, further, that being which is in truth subject or—to say the same thing in other words—which is in truth actual only insofar as it is the movement of positing itself, or the mediation between a self and its development into something different. As subject, it is pure, simple negativity[7] and thus the bifurcation of the simple, that which produces its own double and opposition, a process that again negates this indifferent diversity and its opposite: only this sameness which reconstitutes itself, or the reflection into itself in being different—not an original unity as such, or an immediate unity as such—is the true. The true is its own becoming, the circle that presupposes its end as its aim and thus has it for its beginning—that which is actual only through its execution and end.[8]

Thus the life of God and divine knowledge may indeed be spoken of as love's playing with itself; yet this idea descends

II. *The idea of a phenomenology of the spirit*
1. The true not only substance but also subject

[1] In the second, posthumously published, edition "only" (*nur*) was inserted at this point; and subsequent editions have retained this stylistic horror. Since the beginning of the preface had been revised for a second edition by Hegel just before he died— the point to which he got will be indicated in this commentary— the change was presumably made by him; but if "only" is inserted, "must" should be changed to "can."

[2] "substance" here remotely resembles Aristotle's matter, and "subject" his form. The two terms allude, respectively, to Spinoza and Fichte, and it is relevant that Fichte had claimed at a time when Spinoza was still in ill repute as an atheist that at bottom there were only two types of philosophy: Spinoza's "Dogmatism" and Fichte's "Idealism."

[3] One of Hegel's central ideas: philosophy should deal neither with the modes of knowledge alone nor with the objects alone, but with both in their correlation. Where the absolute is conceived as an undifferentiated, unmediated substance, it will be claimed that the absolute is accessible only to immediate knowledge.

[4] Spinoza.

[5] According to Lasson, Kant is meant.

[6] Schelling.

[7] Cf. Spinoza's famous *"determinatio negatio est"* Letter 50; June 2, 1674.

[8] In this paragraph Hegel explains what he means by calling "the true" a "subject." A subject is that which is "actual only insofar as it is the movement of positing itself, or the mediation between a self and its development into something different" (*die Vermittlung des sich anders Werdens mit sich selbst*). These phrases do not merely designate features of being a subject but are introduced: "or—to say the same thing in other words . . ." (*oder was dasselbe heisst*). To elucidate Hegel's meaning it may help to recall the motto which the young Nietzsche derived from Pindar, Pyth. II. 73: *genoi hoios essi,* and which he formulated in his *Gay Science*

to the level of edification[9] and even insipidity when seriousness, pain, and the patience and work of the negative have no place in it. In itself[10] this life is indeed unstained sameness and unity with itself which is not serious about otherness, estrangement, and the overcoming of this estrangement. But this in-itself is abstract generality in which the nature of this life to be *for itself*,[10] and thus also the self-movement of the form, are ignored.

When the form is said to be the same as the essence, it is plainly a misunderstanding to suppose that knowledge can be satisfied with the in-itself or the essence while sparing itself concern with the form—as if the absolute principle or the absolute intuition made the explication of the former or the development of the latter dispensable. Precisely because the form is no less essential to the essence than the essence itself, the essence is to be comprehended and spoken of not merely as essence, i.e., as immediate substance or as the pure self-contemplation of the divine, but just as much as form—and in the whole wealth of the developed form. Only in that way is it comprehended and spoken of in its actuality.[11]

The true is the whole. But the whole is only the essence perfecting itself through its development. Of the absolute it should be said that it is essentially result, that it is only in the end what it is in truth; and precisely in this consists its nature: to be actual, subject, or that which becomes itself.[12]

Though it may seem contradictory that the absolute is to be comprehended essentially as result, it requires only a little reflection to clear up this semblance of contradiction. The beginning, the principle, or the absolute, as it is spoken of at first and immediately is merely the general. Just as when I say, "all animals," this phrase is not acceptable as a zoology, it is obvious that such words as the divine, absolute, eternal, etc., do not express what they contain. And only such words do indeed express the intuition as something immediate. Whatever is more than such a word, even the transition to a mere proposition, contains a becoming something other which must then be taken back, and is thus a mediation. This, however, is precisely what some people abhor, as if absolute knowledge had been abandoned as soon as one makes more of mediation than to say that it is nothing absolute and that it has no place in the absolute.[13]

This abhorrence, however, is really rooted in ignorance of the nature of both mediation and absolute knowledge. For mediation is nothing else than self-identity that moves itself; or it is reflection into itself, the moment of the ego which is for itself,

(§270): "You shall become who you are." Much later he subtitled his *Ecce Homo: How one becomes what one is.* What Hegel means by a subject is that which makes itself what it becomes. Cf. Hegel's own formulations in his introductory lectures on the philosophy of history: "Thus the organic individual produces itself: it makes of itself what it is implicitly [*an sich*]; thus the spirit, too, is only that which it makes of itself, and it makes of itself what it is implicitly" (VG 151). Also: "The spirit essentially acts; it makes of itself what it is implicitly—makes itself into its own deed, its own work" (67 L); and "The spirit is essentially the result of its own activity: its activity is transcending of immediacy, negating it, and returning into itself" (72 f. L). Cf. H 60 and [12] and [17] below.

[9] Cf. I.2.9.

[10] "In itself": *an sich.* Often, as in note [8] above, what is meant is implicitly or potentially, but here the meaning is almost the opposite: looked at superficially, without regard for its entelechy, or, as Hegel says, ignoring its inner nature. The meaning here accords with both ordinary usage and Kant's precedent (the thing in itself, *das Ding an sich*). *An sich,* like in itself, often means: taken by itself, apart from its relations to other matters, or, in effect, considered superficially. Hegel's usage of this key term of his philosophy is thus not consistent.

The term is often paired by Hegel with "for itself" (*für sich*) which is meant to suggest individuality or, more specifically, both separate being and self-conscious being. This pair of terms has been adopted and adapted by Sartre: *en soi* and *pour soi.*

[11] Schelling already had identified form and essence, but in the sense of an undifferentiated identity. Any contrast was due merely to the finite point of view. Hegel, on the other hand, insists that philosophy must not concern itself exclusively with the undifferentiated essence [*Wesen*], which he equates with the in-itself; it must also try to comprehend the forms in which this essence reveals itself and through which it develops.

[12] Cf. note [8] above; also I.1, note [6] on the proper approach to philosophy. Hegel's insistence that the absolute is subject as well as substance may at first seem less heretical than Spinoza's position; but here it becomes perfectly plain that Hegel's conception is no less heretical though in a different way.

[13] One might communicate immediate knowledge by exclaiming "God!" But as soon as we describe the content of knowledge

pure negativity or, reduced to its pure abstraction,[14] simple becoming. The ego or becoming in general—this mediation is on account of its simplicity precisely growing immediacy and the immediate itself.[15]

It is therefore a misapprehension about reason when reflection is excluded from the true instead of being comprehended as a positive moment of the absolute. It is reflection that makes the true a result while also sublimating[16] this opposition to its becoming; for this becoming is also quite simple and therefore not different from the form of the true which manifests itself in the result as something simple: rather it is precisely this return into simplicity.

While the embryo is surely in itself human, it still is not human for itself: human for itself is only the educated reason which has made itself that which it is in itself.[17] Only this is its actuality. But this result is itself simple immediacy[18]; for it is self-conscious freedom which rests in itself and has not laid opposition aside to let it lie there, but is reconciled to it.

What has been said here can also be expressed by saying that reason is purposive activity. The elevation of what is supposed to be nature above thinking, which is also misunderstood, and especially the banishment of external purposiveness, have brought the form of purpose in general into disrepute.[19] Yet even as Aristotle, too, defines nature as purposive activity, purpose is the immediate, that which is at rest, the unmoved mover; thus it is subject.[20] Its power to move, taken abstractly, is being-for-itself or pure negativity. The result is the same as the beginning only because the beginning is purpose. In other words, the actual is the same as its Concept only because the immediate, being purpose, contains the self or pure actuality in itself. The executed purpose or the actual as existent is movement and unfolded becoming; but precisely this unrest is the self. And it is like the immediacy and simplicity of the beginning because it is the result, that which has returned into itself—and that which has returned into itself is the self, and the self is the identity and simplicity that relates itself to itself.[21]

The need to represent the absolute as subject has employed the propositions: God is what is eternal, or the moral world order, or love, and so forth. In such propositions the true is only posited straightway as the subject, but it is not represented as the movement of that which reflects itself into itself. In a proposition of this kind one begins with the word God. This by itself is a senseless sound, a mere name; only the predicate in a sentence we differentiate and depart from immediacy: we name the one (the subject) and the other (the predicate) and then simultaneously cancel and preserve this differentiation when we mediate between the two and assert the predicate of the subject. The result is no longer an undifferentiated and immediate simplicity.

[14] These five words, absent from the first edition, were inserted by Hegel when he prepared a revised edition. Most of his other revisions were even slighter, and it is surely astonishing that he did not succeed at all in making his extraordinarily difficult preface clearer and more readable.

[15] Hegel again suggests that the mode of knowledge corresponds to its object: propositional knowledge does not involve a fall from grace in which the object is betrayed. The absolute itself is a differentiated unity—not an unstained essence but a subject that lives and becomes what it is.

[16] "sublimate" is here employed throughout to render *aufheben*. Further on in the *Phenomenology,* near the beginning of the discussion of perception (*Die Wahrnehmung*) Hegel explains: "*Das Aufheben* exhibits its true double meaning which we have observed in the negative: it negates and at the same time preserves." Cf. H 34 and 42.

[17] See note [10] above. This passage helps us to understand Hegel's terminology.

[18] A result, though mediated, can be perceived immediately, all at once, as a simple datum. Cf. H 44.

[19] Hegel is referring to Kant's critique of that external teleology which claims, for example, that it is the purpose of the cork to furnish stoppers for our bottles.

[20] In the first edition: ". . . that which is at rest and is mover or subject." The revision is Hegel's.

[21] Kierkegaard's *Sickness unto Death* begins (not counting the prefatory matter) with an extraordinarily difficult passage in which he argues at length that the self as a mere synthesis of the finite and infinite, body and soul, etc., is not yet a self, and that what really defines a self is its relation to itself. Much of his book is a catalogue of bad attitudes toward oneself: what he calls despair and what others might prefer to call attempts to escape from oneself or *mauvaise foi*. Some of Kierkegaard's expositors assume that the synthesis view of the self which Kierkegaard attacks is Hegel's—

says what he is and fills the name with content and meaning; the empty beginning becomes actual knowledge only in this end. For this reason, it is not clear why they do not speak merely of the eternal, of the moral world order, and so forth—or as the ancients did, of pure Concepts, such as being, the One, and so forth—in sum, only of that which supplies the meaning, without adding the senseless sound as well. But this word signifies that what is posited is not a being or essence or mere generality, but rather something reflected into itself—a subject. Yet at the same time this is only anticipated. The subject is accepted as a fixed point to which the predicates are affixed as to their support—by a movement which belongs to those who know of the subject and which is not supposed to belong to the fixed point—though only this [recognition][22] could represent the content as a subject. In the way in which the movement is here constituted, it could not belong to the point; but after this point has been presupposed it really cannot be constituted differently and is bound to be merely external. This anticipation that the absolute is subject is therefore not only not the actuality of this Concept but even makes this actuality impossible; for it posits a point at rest, while the actuality is self-movement.[23]

Among several implications of what has here been said, one may be singled out for special emphasis: it is only as science or system that knowledge is actual[24] and can be expounded. Further, any so-called basic proposition or principle of philosophy, if true, is also false simply insofar as it is merely[25] a basic proposition or principle.

usually they also assume, falsely, that Hegel constantly talks of theses, antitheses, and syntheses—but in fact the view which Kierkegaard offers as his own is taken straight from this paragraph of the *Phenomenology*.

Many of Kierkegaard's expositors assume further that his insistence on "subjective" truth must be contrasted with Hegel's supposed belief that religion is a matter of propositions. In the following paragraph Hegel discusses the inadequacy of propositions about God.

²² "this": namely, the recognition that the movement belongs to the supposedly fixed point. Hegel's sentence is elliptical, and he did not improve it when he made many other unhelpful revisions. Strictly speaking, his pronoun, *sie* (here rendered as "this" on account of its emphatic position—the German reads *durch sie aber wäre allein*) can refer back only to "a movement . . ."

²³ Although traditional theology anticipates Hegel's insight that the absolute is subject—or, speaking more idiomatically, that God resembles a self—the form of this anticipation is really incompatible with that which is anticipated. Traditional theology is not completely irrational; it has a premonition of the truth; but when this truth is disentangled from the web of traditional theology, the web is broken. Hegel argues that in theology "God" is treated as a subject at rest whose nature we all know even before we are informed that "God is love"; but in fact we do not know the absolute to begin with, and apart from the development of the concepts that are here offered as predicates God cannot be known and does not know himself. Cf. notes ¹² and ⁸ above.

²⁴ *dass das Wissen* (knowledge) *nur als Wissenschaft* (science) *oder als System wirklich ist . . .*

Hegel's idea of science is obviously very different from Nietzsche's or the logical positivists'. Nietzsche, the author of *The Gay Science* (*Fröhliche Wissenschaft*) stressed open-mindedness, freedom from moral and religious preconceptions, and bold experimentalism. Other philosophers have stressed close attention to empirical fact and the importance of the verifiability of claims. Hegel says "science or system" and opposes his view on the one hand to those who extol feeling and intuition while disparaging the articulateness of propositions, and on the other hand to those who place their trust in a few fundamental propositions or dogmas. What is needed, according to Hegel, is a systematic and comprehensive analysis of concepts.

²⁵ "insofar as it is merely": Hegel's revision of the first

It is therefore easy to refute it. The refutation consists in demonstrating its deficiency; and it is deficient because it is merely general or a principle—the mere beginning. If the refutation is thorough, it is taken and developed out of the principle itself—and not effected externally by opposite assurances and notions.[26] Thus it would really be the development of this principle and the completion of its deficiency, if only the refutation would not misunderstand itself by paying attention solely to its negative activity without also becoming conscious of its progress and results on their positive side.

The positive explication of the beginning is at the same time also, conversely, a negative treatment of it insofar as it is directed against the one-sided form of the beginning which is only immediate or purpose. Therefore it can also be taken for a refutation of that which constitutes the basis of the system; but it would be more correct to look upon it as a demonstration that the basis or the principle of the system is in fact only its beginning.

That the true is actual only as system, or that the substance is essentially subject, is expressed in the conception which speaks of the absolute as spirit.[27] This is the most sublime Concept, and it belongs to the modern age and its religion. The spiritual alone is the actual[28]; it is [i] the essence or being-in-itself; [ii] that which relates itself and is determinate, that which is other and for itself; and [iii] that which in this determinateness and being outside itself remains in itself—or, in other words, it is in and for itself.

This being-in-and-for-itself, however, it is first for us or in itself: it is the spiritual substance. Then it must also become this for itself and attain the knowledge of the spiritual and of itself as the spirit; i.e., it must become an object for itself, but just as immediately an object which is sublimated,[29] reflected into itself. It is for itself only for us, insofar as its spiritual content is generated by it itself. But insofar as it is for itself also for itself, this self-generation, the pure Concept is for it at the same time the objective element in which it has its existence; and in this way it is in its existence for itself an object reflected into itself.[30]

The spirit that, so developed, knows itself as spirit is science. Science is the actuality of the spirit and the realm that the spirit builds for itself in its own element.

edition which read "because it is . . ." This change is a slight improvement.

Hegel took up this polemic and developed it in his *Encyclopedia* (1817, §§14 ff.; 1827, §§28 ff.; and in definitive form in the 3d edition of 1830, §§26–36; indeed, the following sections down through 78 are of the utmost interest in connection with the preface to the *Phenomenology*). See, for example, the last sentence of §28 (1830): "One failed to inquire whether such predicates were in and for themselves something true, and whether the form of the judgment could be the form of truth." And the end of §31: "the judgment is through its form one-sided and insofar false."

²⁶ This commendation of internal criticism, though original, owes something to the practice of Fichte vis-à-vis Kant, and of Schelling vis-à-vis both: whatever one may think of their work—and Kant disowned Fichte; and Fichte, Schelling—these men tried to remedy deficiencies in their predecessors.

²⁷ In view of the following sentence, even Baillie has to write "Spirit" here, as indeed he has to again and again because "spirit" is so plainly right and "mind" impossible; and yet Baillie's translation bears the title *The Phenomenology of Mind,* and often he translates *Geist* as mind. Cf. H 34 and 65.

²⁸ See I.3, note ⁶ above, and cf. Hegel's famous dictum in the preface to the *Philosophy of Right* (1821): "What is rational, is actual; and what is actual, is rational." Some of Hegel's detractors have claimed that this view was improvised to please the King of Prussia, as Hegel was by then a professor at the University of Berlin, but here we find the same view expressed in almost the same words in 1807.

The Roman numerals in brackets are not found in any of the early editions and have been added to help the reader.

²⁹ See note ¹⁶ above. The first edition read: "an object which is mediated, i.e., sublimated . . ." Hegel's revision.

³⁰ "in itself" and "for itself": see note ¹⁰ above. "In and for itself": *an und für sich* is a common German idiom with a minimum of meaning, really little more than a slightly more elegant equivalent of the "ah" and "er" with which some people sprinkle public speeches. Hegel employs this phrase as a technical term and defines it, under [iii]. "For us or in itself": the embryo is human only in itself and for us, not yet for itself. The infant is "for itself only for us."

7. The element of knowledge

[II.2]

Pure self-recognition in absolute otherness, this ether as such, is the ground and basis of science or knowledge in general. The beginning of philosophy presupposes or demands that consciousness dwell in this element.[1] But this element itself receives its perfection and transparence only through the movement of its becoming. It is pure spirituality as[2] the general that has the manner of simple immediacy[3]; this simple, as it has existence as such, is the basis that is thinking and only in the spirit. Because this element, this immediacy of the spirit, is the very substance of the spirit, it is the transfigured essence and the reflection which itself is simple and immediacy as such for itself —being that is reflection into itself. Science on her part demands of self-consciousness[4] that it should have elevated itself into this ether to be able to live—and to live—with her and in her. Conversely, the individual has the right to demand that science should at least furnish him with the ladder to this standpoint[5]—and show him this standpoint within himself. His right is based on his absolute independence which he possesses in every form of his knowledge; for in all of them, whether they are recognized by science or not and regardless of their contents, the individual is the absolute form, i.e., he is the[6] immediate certainty of himself and, if this expression should be preferred, he is therefore unconditioned being. It is the standpoint of consciousness to know of objective things in opposition to itself, and to know of itself in opposition to them. Science considers this standpoint as the other—and precisely that through which consciousness knows itself to be[7] at home with itself is for science the loss of the spirit.[8] Conversely, the element of science is for consciousness a distant beyond in which consciousness no longer has possession of itself. Each of these two appears to the other as the perversion of truth. That the natural consciousness immediately entrusts itself to science is an attempt it makes, attracted by it knows not what, to walk for once also on its head.[9] The compulsion to adopt this unaccustomed position and to move in it amounts to the presumption that the natural consciousness should do itself violence in a manner as unexpected as it must seem unnecessary.

II.2: What is phenomenology?

[1] Confronted with the works of past philosophers, I should make their thought my own and criticize them by taking their ideas more seriously, if possible, than they themselves did. I must not remain at rest as if I witnessed a spectacle and let the ideas be presented to me while I sit back and watch their procession. I have to understand the other as a manifestation of what I myself am, too: spirit.

[2] "as": first edition had "or." Hegel made many small changes in this paragraph.

[3] The following half sentence was not in the first edition, and the next sentence originally read: "Because it is the immediacy of the spirit, because the substance is the spirit, it is the transfigured essence, the reflection which itself is simple or immediacy, being that is reflection into itself."

[4] First edition: *Die Wissenschaft von ihrer Seite verlangt vom Selbstbewusstsein* . . . Revised version: *Die Wissenschaft verlangt von ihrer Seite an das Selbstbewusstsein* . . . The meaning remains unchanged, the style is worsened.

[5] The ladder that leads from "Sense Certainty . . . and Opinion" (Chapter I) to "Absolute Knowledge" in the last chapter is the *Phenomenology*. The image of the ladder that leads into the ether may have been suggested by Jacob's dream in Genesis 28:12. Philosophers who have used a similar image include Sextus Empiricus and Wittgenstein, at the end of his *Tractatus*.
The following half sentence was not in the first edition, and the addition impairs the passage.

[6] "i.e., he is the": the first edition said instead, "or has."

[7] "knows itself to be": the first edition said, "is."

[8] Ordinary consciousness defines its own standpoint in opposition to the ideas of others and, as it were, feels at home when it says, "as for me, . . ." But this is a sub-philosophic view (Hegel now uses "science" as a synonym for "philosophy"): see note [1] above.

[9] This passage undoubtedly prompted Karl Marx's fa-

Whatever science may be in itself,[10] in relation to immediate self-consciousness it presents itself as something topsy-turvy. Or: because immediate self-consciousness[11] has the principle of its actuality in its certainty of itself, science bears the form of un-actuality for this immediate self-consciousness which seems to itself to stand outside science. Science must therefore join this element[12] to herself,[13] or rather she must show that and how it belongs to her. As long as she lacks such actuality, she is merely the content as[14] the in-itself, the purpose which is still only something inward—not yet spirit, only spiritual substance. This in-itself[15] has to express itself and become for itself; in other words, it[16] has to posit self-consciousness as one with it-self.

8. *The ascent into this is the Phenomenology of the Spirit*

This becoming of science in general or of knowledge is what this phenomenology of the spirit[17] represents. Knowledge in its initial form, or immediate spirit, is that which lacks spirit,[18] the consciousness of the senses. To become true knowledge, or to generate the element of science which is her pure Concept itself,[19] it has to work its way through a long journey.

This becoming, as it will[20] appear in its content and the forms that will[20] show themselves in it, will[20] not be anything like what one would at first associate with an introduction to science for the unscientific consciousness. It will also be quite different from a foundation of science. Above all, it will differ from that enthusiasm which, as shot from a pistol, begins immediately with absolute knowledge, having done with other standpoints simply by declaring that it will not deign to take notice of them.

mous remark that is usually misquoted as if he had boasted that he had stood Hegel on his head (even R. G. Collingwood, *The Idea of History*, p. 124, says "upside down"), as if that were anything to boast of. What Marx actually said in the preface to the second edition of *Das Kapital* (1873) was that Hegel's dialectic stands on its head (as if the spirit were fundamental) and must be stood right side up again.

"for once": *auch einmal*. Baillie's "all at once" must be due to his confusing this phrase with *auf einmal*. His "attempt, induced by some unknown influence, all at once to walk on its head" quite misses Hegel's sudden whimsey.

10 "in itself": *an ihr selbst*. A solecism often used by Hegel in place of *an sich* or *an sich selbst*. Usually, as here, the intended meaning is the same: taken by itself, apart from its relations.

11 The revised version says only "the same"; the first edition: "because immediate self-consciousness is the principle of actuality, science bears . . ."

12 First edition: *jenes Element;* revision: *solches Element.*

13 "herself": to insure clarity without excessive clumsiness it seemed best to use the feminine pronoun for science, as in German.

14 "the content as": missing in the first edition.

15 "This in-itself": first edition had *sie* (it) which could mean science or the spiritual substance.

16 "it" (first edition) later changed to "the same."

17 After "spirit" Hegel struck out several words of the first edition: "as the first part of the system of the same." "The same" means science. On the original title page, "System of Science, First Part" had preceded the present title.

18 After "spirit" Hegel deleted "or is."

19 "itself": missing in first edition. The following "it" was originally *er* and referred to the spirit; now it is *es* and *may* be meant to refer all the way back to the consciousness of the senses (*das sinnliche Bewusstsein*). Again the original text is impaired.

20 In the original edition this sentence was cast in the present tense. Regardless of its tense, this is surely one of the least controversial sentences in Hegel's works.

[II.3]

The task of leading the individual from his uneducated standpoint to knowledge had to be taken in its general sense, and the general individual, the self-conscious spirit,[1] had to be considered in its education.

As for the relation of the two: in the general individual every moment shows itself as it gains concrete form and its own shape. The particular individual is the incomplete spirit, a concrete form in whose whole existence one determination predominates,[2] while the others are present only in blurred features. In the spirit who stands on a higher level than another, the lower concrete existence has been reduced to an insignificant moment; what formerly was the matter itself has become a mere trace; its form is shrouded and become a simple shade.

Through this past the individual whose substance is the spirit that stands on a higher level passes in the same manner in which the student of a higher science goes once more through the preparatory knowledge that he has long mastered, to present the contents to his mind: he recalls these memories without being interested in them for their own sake or wishing to abide in them. The individual must also pass through the contents of the educational stages of the general spirit, but as forms that have long been outgrown by the spirit, as stages of a way that has been prepared and evened for him.[3] Thus we see that as far as information is concerned, what in former ages occupied the mature spirits of men has been reduced to information, exercises, and even games suitable for boyhood; and in the boy's pedagogical progress we recognize the history of the education of the world as if it had been traced in a silhouette.[4] This past existence is property that has already been acquired by the general spirit which constitutes the substance of the individual[5] and, by thus appearing to him externally, his inorganic nature.

In this respect, education, considered from the point of view of the individual, consists in his acquiring what is thus given to him; he must digest his inorganic nature and take possession of it for himself.[6] But from the point of view of the general spirit as the substance this means nothing else than that this should acquire self-consciousness and produce its becoming and reflection in itself.[7]

Science represents this educational movement both in its detail and necessity and also as that which has already been reduced to a moment and property of the spirit. The aim is the

II.3: Whose spirit? Individual or universal?

[1] Instead of "the self-conscious spirit" the first edition had *der Weltgeist,* the world spirit; "education": *Bildung.*

[2] The first edition had: "a concrete form whose whole existence is given over to . . ."

Each philosopher represents above all one principle, one attitude, one point of view; and insofar as any individual has his own outlook, one aspect predominates though other positions may be discernible in his views, if only in blurred features. Are all men on the same level, then? No, some are more advanced: their vision is more inclusive and incorporates the partial insights of those who remain on a lower level.

[3] This is Hegel's ontogenetic principle and his answer to the question whether he is concerned with the spirit of the individual or with the *Weltgeist:* even as the embryo has to recapitulate in abbreviated form the stages of organic evolution, the individual spirit must recapitulate in condensed form the *Bildung* of the human spirit.

[4] N.B.: "as far as information is concerned." Hegel has not changed his mind about what he wrote in an early fragment in which he scorned the remark "that today any small child knows more about God than the wisest pagan" and insisted on the importance of "consciousness gained through experience" (Nohl, 11; quoted at length and discussed in WK 132).

"silhouette": without any depth and greatly oversimplified.

[5] Instead of the following seven words the first edition had "or." The "which" in this sentence can refer only to the general spirit. "Inorganic nature" until it is consumed, absorbed, and digested, and thus becomes part of our spiritual organism.

[6] Cf. Goethe's *Faust,* lines 682 f.: "What from your fathers you received as heir, / Acquire if you would possess it." Hegel's choice of words is strikingly similar, and this quotation would furnish a fitting motto for his book; but Goethe's lines did not appear in *Faust: A Fragment* (1790) and were published only in 1808 when the whole of Part One came out, a year after the *Phenomenology.* The lines were written much earlier, and it is possible that Hegel had heard them somehow. The minute differences between the wordings of Hegel's sentence in the first and second edition do not affect this point.

spirit's insight into what constitutes knowledge. Impatience demands the impossible, namely the attainment of the aim without the means. First, the length of this way must be endured, for every moment is necessary.[8] Secondly, one must take time over every one, for each is itself an individual and entire form and is considered absolutely insofar as one considers its determinateness as something whole and concrete, or the whole in the individuality of this determination.[9]

Because the substance of the individual, because[10] the world spirit has had the patience to pass through these forms in the long expanse of time, taking upon itself the tremendous labor of world history[11] in which it imparted as much of its content to every form as that form was capable of holding, and because it could not attain consciousness about itself with less labor, therefore the individual cannot in the nature of the case[12] comprehend his own substance with less than this; and yet he has less trouble because this is already accomplished in itself: the content is by now the actuality reduced to a possibility, vanquished immediacy,[13] and the forms have been reduced to abbreviations and to the simple determinations of thought. Having already been thought, the content is the possession of the substance.[14] No longer must existence be transformed into the in-itself; only the in-itself—which is neither raw any more, nor immersed in existence, but rather something recalled—needs to be transmuted into the form of the for-itself. How this is to be done[15] must now be described in some detail.

9. *The transmutation of the notion and the familiar into thought*—[16]

What is no longer necessary at the point at which we are here taking up this movement[17] is the sublimation of existence. But what remains[18] and still requires a higher transformation is the notion of and familiarity with the forms. Existence, taken back into the substance, has merely been transposed immediately by this first negation into the element of the self. This possession which the self has acquired[19] thus still has the same character of uncomprehended immediacy and unmoved difference as does existence itself: all this is retained in the notion.

At the same time it is thus something familiar, something that the existing[20] spirit has mastered so that its activity and interest no longer abide in it. The activity that masters existence is itself only the movement[21] of the particular spirit which

⁷ This sentence read in the first edition: "But this means nothing else than that the general spirit or the substance should acquire self-consciousness or its becoming and reflection in itself." The general spirit or *Weltgeist,* it should be noted, acquires self-consciousness only through us. So far is Hegel from theism.

⁸ "necessary": see I.1, end of note ⁶ above.

⁹ Here Hegel does not only defend the length of the *Phenomenology;* he also insists on the dignity of every single stage, "for each is itself an individual and entire form."

¹⁰ After "because" the revised version inserts "even" (*sogar*), another impairment. In the original text we are reminded that the world spirit *is* the substance of the individual.

¹¹ The following clause, down to the comma, was not in the first edition.

¹² "in . . . case": not in the original edition, nor an improvement.

¹³ The remainder of this sentence was not in the first edition.

¹⁴ "substance": the first edition had "individual."

¹⁵ First edition: the parenthesis in the previous sentence and the period at the end were missing, and in place of "How . . . done" it had "which."

¹⁶ *Verwandlung des Vorgestellten und Bekannten in den Gedanken.* On *vorstellen* see I.2, note ¹ above. The German seems to equate the notion and the familiar; and what is meant is below the level of thought and, *a fortiori,* of the Concept.

The next heading is elliptical and presupposes this one.

¹⁷ First edition: "What of this movement is no longer necessary for the individual is . . ."

¹⁸ The next six words were not in the first edition.

¹⁹ Instead of the first seven words of this sentence the first edition had simply "it," which referred to existence.

²⁰ "existing": not in the first edition.

²¹ Instead of "is itself only the movement," the first edition had: "is the immediate or existing mediation and thus the movement only . . ."

Hegel's revision of the text had got only to the end of this paragraph when he died in 1831.

does not comprehend itself; but knowledge is directed against the notion that arises in this way, against this familiarity: knowledge is the activity of the general self and the interest of thinking.

What is familiar is not known simply because it is familiar.[22] It is the most common self-deception and deception of others to presuppose something as familiar when it comes to knowledge, and to accept this; but with all its talking back and forth such knowledge, without knowing what is happening to it, never gets anywhere. The subject and object, etc., God, nature, the understanding, the sensibility, etc., are presupposed as familiar and valid foundations without having been scrutinized, and they are accepted as fixed points of both departure and return.[23] They remain unmoved as one moves back and forth between them—and thus only on their surfaces. Thus apprehension and examination, too, consist merely in seeing whether everybody finds what has been said of them in his notion, too, whether it seems and is familiar to him that way or not.[24]

The analysis of a notion, as it used to be performed, was nothing else than the sublimation[25] of the form of its familiarity. Dissecting a notion into its original elements means going back to its moments which at least do not have the form of the notion encountered as a datum, constituting rather the immediate property of the self. To be sure, this analysis only reaches thoughts which are themselves familiar, fixed, and static determinations. But what is thus differentiated and unactual is itself an essential moment; for it is only because the concrete differentiates itself and makes itself what is unactual, that it is that which moves itself. The activity of differentiating is the strength and work of the understanding, which is the most astonishing and the greatest, or rather the absolute, power.[26]

The circle that rests closed in itself and, being substance, holds its moments, is the immediate and therefore not perplexing relation. But that the accidental as such, separated from its circumference, that the bounded which is actual only in its connection with others, should gain an existence of its own and separate freedom, this is the tremendous power of the negative; this is the energy of thought, of the pure ego.[27] Death, if we care to call this unactuality by this name, is what is most terrible, and to hold on to what is dead requires the greatest strength. That beauty[28] which lacks strength hates the understanding because it asks this of her and she cannot do it. But not the life that shrinks from death and keeps itself undefiled by devasta-

²² This is one of Hegel's best epigrams: *Das Bekannte überhaupt ist darum, weil es bekannt ist, nicht erkannt.* This is not a pun but a reminder that there are at least two kinds of knowledge which should not be confused: what is known by acquaintance and familiar (*bekannt*) is not necessarily known in the sense of being comprehended (*erkannt*). In one sense we know our acquaintances, in another we often don't. Hegel's power of expression is often considerable, but he very rarely manages to be so brief and concise.

²³ This is perhaps Hegel's most central criticism of other approaches to philosophy, developed at great length in his *Encyclopedia* (1830, §§26–78): they fail to analyze such key terms or Concepts as those enumerated here.

²⁴ "apprehension and examination": *Auffassen und Prüfen.* The former could mean "understanding," but here plainly refers to something vaguer. The latter cannot mean "proving" as Baillie renders it. As an extreme illustration of what Hegel here criticizes one may recall Dr. Johnson's famous claim that he could refute Berkeley's idealism simply by kicking a stone. Dr. Johnson appealed to a familiar experience and, without realizing that he presupposed anything controversial, did presuppose a particular interpretation of that experience. But Hegel's critique embraces all kinds of common sense philosophies as well as every scholasticism that stops short of a thorough analysis of the concepts it uses.

²⁵ Here cancellation is the dominant sense, but some degree of preservation is present, too.

²⁶ Analysis dissects the familiar form and brings to light elements or moments that were not given, not data, but are in a sense the creatures of the mind. Yet the moments which we discriminate and which seem unactual insofar as they have no separate existence in the world are essential to what is analyzed. Cf. II.1, notes ³ and ¹⁵ above. Hegel's encomium on man's analytical powers in the final sentence of this paragraph is striking.

²⁷ Analytic thought does not rest content with unperplexing, familiar, immediately given experiences, things, or concepts: it penetrates the surface (perhaps a three-dimensional image is a little easier to understand than Hegel's two-dimensional circle) and brings to light the bones, muscles, and organs—parts that never had a separate existence before and, in the case of paintings or ideas, even elements that are as much constituted as discovered by thought.

tion, but the life that endures, and preserves itself through, death is the life of the spirit.[29] Spirit gains its truth only by finding itself in absolute dismemberment.[30] This power it is not as the positive that looks away from the negative—as when we say of something, this is nothing or false, and then, finished with it, turn away from it to something else: the spirit is this power only by looking the negative in the face and abiding with it. This abiding is the magic force which converts the negative into being.

It is the same which above was called the subject which, by giving determinateness existence in its element, sublimates abstract immediacy—i.e., immediacy which barely *is*—and thus is true substance: that being or that immediacy which does not leave mediation outside itself but which is mediation itself.[31]

10. —and this into the Concept[16]

That notions become the property of pure self-consciousness, this elevation to generality is only one side and not yet the completed education.[32]—Study in antiquity differed from that current in modern times: it was nothing less than the thorough education of the natural consciousness. Testing itself against every separate part of its existence, and philosophizing about everything it encountered, it made itself into a generality that was active through and through.[33] In modern times, on the other hand, the individual finds the abstract form ready-made: the exertion of grasping it and appropriating it is rather more the unmediated production of the inward and the cut-off generation of the general than the emergence of the general out of the concrete and the multiplicity of existence.[34] The work cut out for us now, therefore, is less to purify the individual from the manner of immediacy and the senses while making it into a thinking and thought substance, than to attempt the opposite: to sublimate fixed, determinate thoughts and thus to actualize the general and infuse it with spirit. But it is far more difficult to make fixed thoughts fluid than sense existence.[35] The reason for this has been mentioned above: the substance and the element of existence of these determinations is the ego, the power of the negative, or pure actuality; but the element of the sense determinations is merely powerless, abstract immediacy, or being as such. Thoughts become fluid when pure thinking, this inner immediacy, recognizes itself as a moment,

^{28} *Die kraftlose Schönheit hasst den Verstand* . . . : Baillie's "Beauty, powerless and helpless, hates understanding" is grammatically possible but shows no comprehension of Hegel. Beauty which does *not* lack strength—say, the beauty of a late Rembrandt portrait—can abide analysis, which only brings to light more and more of its excellence.

^{29} Probably an allusion to the crucifixion and resurrection.

^{30} An allusion to Dionysus Zagreus who (this is the meaning of "Zagreus") was dismembered—but who is ever reborn. Conceivably, we should also feel reminded of Kant's dismemberment of the spirit in his three *Critiques*.

^{31} Hegel closely associates the following terms: negative, determinateness, subject, mediation, and understanding—and juxtaposes, on the other side, substance, immediate, and intuition. In the paragraph before this, Hegel proceeds from the understanding to dismemberment (*Zerrissenheit*), because the analytic understanding tears its objects apart; and thence to the negative, because the understanding negates and does away with the familiar form of that which it analyzes. The understanding eliminates immediacy and introduces determinations and mediation. Cf. the Schiller quotation in I.2, note ^{5} above. Mediation is required to make what is *bekannt* also *erkannt*. Analysis gives way to a higher immediacy: one might call it a mediated immediacy, but Hegel calls it "that immediacy which does not leave mediation outside itself but which is mediation itself."

^{32} Self-consciousness, by analysis, dissects subjective notions into universal elements; but this is not enough.

^{33} An allusion, above all, to Socrates and Plato.

^{34} An allusion to Kant and an implicit criticism of Kant's deduction of the categories in the *Critique of Pure Reason:* instead of painstakingly working his way up to Concepts, like the Greeks, Kant found his categories ready-made in the traditional classification of judgments. This discovery was "un-mediated" and sudden, the deduction "cut-off" and incomplete.

^{35} The task confronting Hegel, then, is no longer that which confronted Socrates and Plato; it no longer requires any great effort to raise those interested in philosophy to the level of contemplating Concepts. The task now is no longer to show that the content of sense experience is fluid, as the Greeks from Heraclitus or when pure self-certainty abstracts from itself—not by leaving itself out or setting itself aside, but by abandoning the fixity of its self-positing—both the fixity of the pure concreteness which characterizes the ego even in its opposition to differentiated content and the fixity of differentiations which, posited in the element of pure thinking, share in the unconditionality of the ego.[36] Through this movement the pure thoughts become Concepts and come to be what they are in truth: self-movements, circles, that which is their substance, spiritual entities.[37]

This movement of the pure entities constitutes the nature of what is scientific.[38] As far as the coherence of the contents is concerned, it means the necessity and elaboration of the contents into an organic whole. The way in which the Concept of knowledge is reached thus also becomes a necessary and complete becoming. Hence this preparation ceases to be a fortuitous bit of philosophizing that takes off from these or those objects, relationships, and thoughts of the imperfect consciousness, depending on fortuitous circumstances, nor does it seek to establish what is true by reasoning back and forth, inferring and drawing consequences from determinate thoughts. Rather this way will encompass, by virtue of the movement of the Concept, the complete worldliness of consciousness in its necessity.

Such a presentation constitutes the first part of science because the existence of the spirit is at first nothing else than the immediate or the beginning, but the beginning is not yet its return into itself. The element of immediate existence is therefore that which distinguishes this part of science from the others.[39]—The indication of this difference leads us into a discussion of a few fixed thoughts which usually crop up in this connection.

to Plato showed, but, as "is far more difficult, to make fixed thoughts fluid." See I.1, note [5] above, where this image ("fluid") was first mentioned. That Plato in his *Parmenides* had preceded Hegel on this road, too, is duly acknowledged by Hegel later in the preface.

[36] The concepts that Kant, for example (though he is not mentioned specifically), acccpted as fixed and rigid and final, as if they required no further analysis and were self-sufficient, must be analyzed painstakingly and will then be seen not to be self-sufficient but essentially interrelated; for example, reality, negation, causality, existence, substance, simple, finite and infinite, free and necessary. This is what Hegel attempted in his *Logic*. But a similar point may be made about Kant's moral philosophy: he treated the bifurcation of reason and inclination as something fixed and thought he offered a timeless analysis of human nature, though in fact he gave us an analysis of only one form of moral consciousness, one *Gestalt des Bewusstseins,* one manifestation of the spirit, one episode in the *Phenomenology of the Spirit*— that which Hegel calls *Moralität* and distinguishes from *Sittlichkeit*. Regarding Hegel's break with Kant over this point, see WK 154 ff.

[37] Only when such concepts—or as Hegel might say, thoughts—as have been enumerated in the previous note are analyzed and considered in their interrelations, only when their fixity gives way in this manner to fluidity, do they become worthy of being called Concepts (*Begriffe*).

[38] "what is scientific": rather, what Hegel calls scientific. Cf. II.1, note [24] above.

[39] "the first part of science": i.e., the *Phenomenology of the Spirit* which was published as *System of Science, First Part*. The other parts referred to are Hegel's Logic, his philosophy of nature, and his philosophy of spirit. The claims made for the *Phenomenology* in the preceding passage are open to question, and the claim of "necessity" is certainly untenable. Cf. I.1, note [6] above.

[III.1]

The immediate existence of the spirit, i.e., consciousness, contains the two moments of knowledge and the objectivity which is negative to knowledge.[1] It is in this element [of consciousness] that the spirit develops itself and explicates its moments which are therefore characterized by this opposition and, without exception, appear as forms of consciousness. The science of this way is the science of the experience made by consciousness:[2] the substance is studied insofar as it and its movement are objects of consciousness. Consciousness knows and comprehends nothing but what lies within its experience; for what is within that is only the spiritual substance—specifically, as the object of its self. The spirit, however, becomes an object, for the spirit is this movement of becoming something other for itself, i.e., an object for its self, and then to sublimate this otherhood.[3] And experience is the name we give to just this movement in which the immediate, the unexperienced, i.e., the abstract, whether of sensible being or of a bare, simple thought, becomes estranged and then returns to itself from estrangement, and is only then presented in its actuality and truth and becomes the property of consciousness.[4]

The non-identity we find in consciousness between the ego and the substance that is its object, is their difference, the negative in general. It can be considered as the defect of both, but is really their soul or that which moves them. Therefore some of the ancients comprehended the void as that which moves, seeing well that that which moves is the negative, but not yet that it is the self.

When the negative thus appears at first as the non-identity of the ego and its object, it is just as much the non-identity of the substance with itself. What seems to happen outside it, as an activity directed against it, is its own doing; and thus the substance shows that it is essentially subject. When it has shown this completely, the spirit has made its existence equal to its essence; it becomes an object for itself as it is, and the abstract element of immediacy and of the separation of knowledge and truth is overcome. Being is mediated absolutely; it is substantial content which is just as immediately property of the ego, self-like,[5] or Concept. With this the phenomenology of the spirit is concluded. What the spirit prepares for itself in this phenomenology is the element of knowledge. In this element

III. *Truth*

1. The forms of consciousness and truth

¹ "immediate": "Consciousness" is the topic of the first part of the *Phenomenology* which is then followed by "Self-Consciousness" and "Reason." Consciousness does not have the benefit of any previous analysis or reflection; it lacks mediation. The first of the three phases of consciousness that are considered in the first part is "Sense Certainty"—the most naïve type of consciousness. But even at this stage there is some differentiation or, as Hegel here puts it, there are two moments: "knowledge and the objectivity which is negative to knowledge." The odd phrase "negative to" echoes Fichte's contrast of the ego and the non-ego.

² Half of the book had been printed before the second half was written, before its whole conception was clear in Hegel's mind, and before the title "Phenomenology" had occurred to him. Although the preface was written only after the rest of the book was completed, even some of the bound copies of the first edition still include a half title as page 1, immediately after the preface which has Roman numeral page numbers: "First Part. Science of the Experience of Consciousness." This title, to which the sentence in the text alludes, was plainly conceived before Hegel decided on "Phenomenology of the Spirit." Haering, *Hegel,* vol. II, p. 485, notes "that it was only during, or perhaps even after the conclusion of, the printing that Hegel substituted for the previous half title (after the "Preface") . . . another, 'Science of the Phenomenology of the Spirit (without First Part!!)'; yet the latter was substituted only in some copies, and in some in addition to the former and in the wrong place . . ."

³ Although Baillie here uses "mind," this is one of scores of passages where only "spirit" makes good sense. Cf. II.1, note ²⁷ above. ". . . the spirit is this movement . . ." alludes to the Holy Spirit: God the Father becomes God the Son—he becomes something other for himself, an object for himself—but then this otherhood is canceled and yet preserved in the Holy Spirit. Spirit is that which is not static, nor unstained self-identity; on the contrary, it is of its very essence that it is dynamic, is development, is sublimated otherhood.

⁴ The given is experienced as something strange before it becomes, through the experience, the property of consciousness.

⁵ "self-like": *selbstisch;* a most unusual word.

the moments of the spirit spread themselves out in the form of simplicity which knows its object as itself. They no longer fall apart into the opposition of being and knowledge but abide in the simplicity of knowledge; they are now the true in the form of the true, and their difference is only the difference of content. Their movement which in this element organizes itself into a whole is Logic or speculative philosophy.

11. In what way the Phenomenology of the Spirit is negative or contains what is false[6]

The system of the experience of the spirit deals only with the appearance of the spirit. Hence the progression from this system to the science of the true that also has the form of the true seems to be merely negative. Therefore one might wish to be spared the negative as something false, and one might ask to be led to truth without delay: Why bother with the false?[7]

This demand, mentioned previously, that one should begin straightway with science, one has to answer here by considering quite generally the nature of the negative as something false. The conceptions people have about this are pre-eminent obstacles on the way to truth. This also provides an occasion for speaking of mathematical knowledge which unphilosophical knowledge considers the ideal that philosophy should strive to reach, though so far it has striven in vain.

True and false are among the determinate thoughts which are considered immobile separate essences, as if one stood here and the other there, without community, fixed and isolated. Against this view one must insist that truth is not a minted coin which can be given and pocketed ready-made.[8] Nor does something false exist any more than something evil exists. To be sure, the evil and the false are not as bad as the devil, for in the devil they are even made into a particular subject; as the false and evil they are merely something general but still have opposed individual essences.

The false (for only this has a place in our discussion) would be the other, the negative of the substance which, as the content of knowledge, is the true. But the substance is itself essentially the negative, partly as the differentiation and determination of the content, partly as simple discrimination, i.e., as self and knowledge in general. One can know something falsely. That something is known falsely means that knowledge is not identical with its substance. Yet precisely this non-identity is

⁶ Although our division of the preface into twelve sections, following Lasson, does not mark this point, a careful reader would notice that there is a significant break here, even if he did not know that Hegel's original table of contents provided a new heading. This is the end of the first half of the preface, not only in a purely quantitative sense. Hegel has now submitted the major contentions which distinguish his philosophy, and he has explained the purpose of the *Phenomenology* and its relation to his then still unwritten *Logic*.

⁷ Hegel now asks, in effect: Why shouldn't one start straightway with the *Logic* (as English and American students of Hegel have generally done)? In a way Hegel has already answered this question; for example, when he likened the *Phenomenology* to a ladder (II.2, note ⁵ above). Above when Hegel asks, "why bother with the false?" and goes on to say that we must now consider "the nature of the negative as something false," we may feel that this point, too, has long been taken care of; for example, in the fourth paragraph of the preface, where Hegel spoke of bud, blossom, and fruit. But Hegel proposes to return to this question now in order to treat it more systematically and to compare, if only briefly, mathematical, historical, and philosophic truth.

⁸ An allusion to Lessing's play *Nathan der Weise* (1779), the work quoted more often in Hegel's *theologische Jugendschriften*, written in the 1790s, than any other. In Act III, scene 5, Saladin asks Nathan to tell him which of the three religions, Islam, Judaism, and Christianity, is the true one, and to state his reasons. In a soliloquy in scene 6, Nathan exclaims:

> Truth. Truth!
> He wants it so—so ready-made [*so bar, so blank*], as if
> Truth were a coin!—Yes, if at least it were
> A very ancient coin that one must weigh!
> That still might pass. But such a modern coin,
> Made by a stamp, as one may simply lay
> And count upon a board, that it is not.
> Like cash into a bag, truth should be shoved
> Into the head?

In the next scene, when the sultan returns, Nathan tells him the parable of the three rings. (For an English translation see Kaufmann, *The Faith of a Heretic,* section 80.)

differentiation which is an essential moment. Out of this differentiation their identity comes, and this resulting identity is the truth. But it is not truth as if non-identity had been thrown away, like dross from pure metal—nor even as the tool is excluded from the finished vessel; rather non-identity is, as the negative, as the self, still immediately present in the true as such. Yet it does not follow that the false may be called a moment of the true, let alone a part of it. That in everything false there is something true—in this dictum both are treated like oil and water which are unmixable and united only externally. Precisely on account of the meaning associated with the moment of complete otherhood, such expressions must no longer be used where such otherhood is sublimated. Talk of the unity of subject and object, of the finite and the infinite, of being and thinking, etc., is misleading because object and subject, etc., signify that which they are outside their unity, and in the unity they are not meant in the sense suggested by such an expression. Just so, the false is no longer something false as a moment of truth.

Dogmatism as a style of thought in knowledge and in the study of philosophy is nothing else than the opinion that the true consists in a proposition that is a fixed result or that is known immediately.[9] To such questions as, when Caesar was born, or how many feet there were in a stadium, etc., a neat answer should be given, just as it is surely true that the square of the hypotenuse equals the sum of the squares of the other two sides of a right-angled triangle. But the nature of such so-called truths is different from the nature of philosophical truths.

12. *Historical and mathematical truth*

[III.2]

Regarding historical truths—to mention these briefly—insofar as their purely historical aspect is considered, it will be readily granted that they concern particular existence and the accidental and arbitrary side, the features that are not necessary.[1]

But even such bare truths as those adduced here as examples do not lack the movement of self-consciousness. To know one of them one must compare much, consult books, or inquire in some manner; and even where one might appeal to immediate intuition, such knowledge is held to have true value only when

It is indicative of the state of Hegel study in the English-speaking world that one of the most scholarly American historians of philosophy has praised Kierkegaard's "indirect protest against the Hegelian pretensions to serve up all truth in an objective, cut-and-dried way. He [Kierkegaard] contended strongly that truth is no finished product, which can be handed over the counter of philosophy, quite impersonally and effortlessly" (James Collins, *The Mind of Kierkegaard,* 1953, p. 39). Cf. the following note.

[9] Hegel's position is more radical than Kierkegaard's. Kierkegaard accepts some Christian dogmas as propositions that are fixed results and known immediately, to use Hegel's language— or, in Collins' words, he believes that truth "can be handed over the counter of philosophy, quite impersonally and effortlessly." But he insists that the truth of Christianity cannot be *absorbed* impersonally and effortlessly: though it can be *known* immediately, it requires not so much effort as grace to put it into practice, to be changed by it, and to become a Christian in the highest sense of that word. There is nothing particularly radical or novel or anti-Hegelian about this aspect of Kierkegaard's thought; this is traditional Christian preaching. But Hegel insists not merely that it is difficult to put the truth into practice: this he takes for granted and therefore does not stress. But he insists that philosophical truth cannot be *given* in a fixed proposition, like a coin; not only that it cannot be pocketed like that. Philosophical truth is not expressible in formulas that can be learned by heart and recited at pleasure. Cf. I.1, notes [6], [7], [9], [11]; I.2, notes [5], [9], [12]; II.1, notes [24], [25]; II.2, note [1]; II.3, notes [3], [4], [6], [28]; and note [8] above.

III.2. Historical and mathematical truths

[1] Hegel disposes of historical truths in three sentences. While what he says is remarkably unprofound, he at least makes perfectly plain that the still widely popular notion of Hegel's conception of history is utterly wrong: so far from believing that historical events are necessary and can be deduced *a priori,* Hegel says the very first time he mentions historical truths in his first book that they concern the "accidental and arbitrary." In this respect, he suggests, they differ from philosophical truths.

it is backed up by reasons, although it may be alleged that only the bare result matters.[2]

As for mathematical truths, it is even more obvious that one would not consider a man a geometer if he knew Euclid's theorems by *heart,* but without their proofs—without, as one might say by way of juxtaposition, also knowing them by *mind.*[3] In the same way, if a man by measuring many right-angled triangles acquired the knowledge that their sides have the well-known relation to each other, such knowledge would be considered unsatisfactory. Yet even in mathematical knowledge, the importance of the demonstration still does not have the significance and characteristic that it is a moment of the result itself; in the result the demonstration is over and has disappeared. As a result, to be sure, the theorem is something whose truth is apprehended. But this additional circumstance does not concern its content but only its relation to the subject; the movement of the mathematical demonstration does not belong to that which is the object but is an activity that remains external to the matter. Thus the nature of the right-angled triangle does not take itself apart after the manner of the construction that is required for the demonstration of the proposition that expresses the relations; the whole production of the result is a way and means of knowledge.

In philosophical knowledge, too, the becoming of the existence as existence is different from the becoming of the essence or inner nature of the matter. But in the first place philosophical knowledge contains both, while mathematical knowledge represents only the becoming of the existence, i.e., the emergence of the nature of the matter in knowledge.[4] Secondly, philosophical knowledge also unites these two separate movements. The internal genesis or becoming of the substance is undivided transition into the external or into existence, into being for another; and, conversely, the becoming of existence is a retreat into essence. In this way the movement is the double process and becoming of the whole: each posits the other simultaneously, and therefore each also has both as two aspects of itself. Together they constitute the whole by dissolving themselves and making themselves into its moments.

In mathematical knowledge, insight is an event that is external to the matter; it follows that the true matter is changed by it. The means, construction and demonstration, contain true propositions; but at the same time it must be said that the content is false.[5] In the above example, the triangle is dismem-

2   Although many teachers in secondary schools believe that research consists in looking up things in an encyclopedia, different encyclopedias frequently disagree even about such "bare truths" as when a great man was born or when a famous book was first published. Any serious student, therefore, must inquire, compare, and support his contentions with reasons. Indeed, one of the "bare truths . . . adduced here as examples" illustrates this point. The traditional date for Caesar's birth was 100 B.C., because Suetonius, Plutarch, and Appian said that he was in his fifty-sixth year when he was assassinated; but Theodor Mommsen, writing a few decades after Hegel's death, convinced most historians that Caesar was born in 102 B.C.

3   The German *auswendig*, literally external, means "by heart"; *inwendig*, which is much less common, means internal and is here used by Hegel for a play on words.

4   Hegel claims that mathematical demonstrations, at least of the kind he discusses, involve an epistemological process only, not also an ontological one, while in philosophy the two are inseparable. His terminology and his way of putting the point, so far from increasing precision and clarity, create wholly unnecessary difficulties. Hegel says—to translate the end of his sentence just a little more literally than we have done in the text: "But in the first place the philosophical knowledge contains both, while the mathematical represents only the becoming of the existence [*Dasein*], i.e., of the being of the nature of the matter in knowledge as such." The point is surely that in mathematical demonstrations, according to Hegel, we witness the development of knowledge about something, but not the development of that which is known: the demonstration remains external to the content of knowledge. And because it remains external to the content, it may be said that it does not penetrate the essence of, say, a triangle. But when Hegel distinguishes essence and existence (in the immediately preceding sentence he contrasts *Dasein* und *Wesen* most emphatically) and then goes on to say that mathematical demonstrations represent "only the becoming of the existence," he surely makes things unnecessarily difficult and confusing for the reader.

5   This is a rather impressionistic use of the word "false" (*falsch*).

bered and its parts are allotted to other figures which the construction brings into being alongside it. Only in the end one reconstitutes the triangle which really matters, but which during the procedure was lost from view and appeared only in pieces which belonged to other wholes.—Here, then, we also see the negativity of the content enter, which would just as much have to be called a falseness of the content as is the disappearance in the movement of the Concept of the thought that had been considered fixed.

The real defectiveness of mathematical knowledge, however, concerns both the knowledge itself and its content.—Regarding the knowledge, the first point is that the necessity of the construction is not apprehended. This does not issue from the Concept of the theorem; rather it is commanded, and one must blindly obey the command to draw precisely these lines instead of an indefinite number of others, not because one knows anything but merely in the good faith that this will turn out to be expedient for the conduct of the demonstration. Afterwards this expediency does indeed become manifest, but it is an external expediency because it manifests itself only after the demonstration.[6]

Just so, the demonstration follows a path that begins somewhere—one does not yet know in what relation to the result that is to be attained. As it proceeds, these determinations and relations are taken up while others are ignored, although one does not by any means see immediately according to what necessity. An external purpose rules this movement.

The evident certainty of this defective knowledge, of which mathematics is proud and of which it also boasts as against philosophy, rests solely on the poverty of its purpose and the defectiveness of its material and is therefore of a kind that philosophy must spurn.—Its purpose or Concept is magnitude. This is precisely the relation that is not essential and is void of Concept.[7] The movement of knowledge therefore proceeds on the surface, does not touch the matter itself, not the essence or the Concept, and is therefore not comprehension.

The material about which mathematics offers such a pleasing treasure of truths is space and the unit. Space is the existence into which the Concept writes its distinctions as into an empty, dead element in which they are equally immobile and lifeless. The actual is not something spatial the way it is considered in mathematics; with such unactuality as is exemplified by the things of mathematics neither concrete sense intuition nor phi-

6 Hermann Glockner, *Hegel,* vol. II (1940), p. 455, says: "I do not wish to inquire here whether Hegel's account stands up; I only wish to point out that his critique coincides, down to the details of the chosen example, with that of his later antipode, Arthur Schopenhauer." A footnote refers us to *The World as Will and Idea,* I, §15, and remarks that "there are several parallel passages," before Glockner proceeds: "Yet Hegel's critique of mathematical method differs from Schopenhauer's in one very significant respect. While the latter insists above all on 'pure intuition' and 'analytical method,' Hegel tries to make clear the one-sidedness or defectiveness of mathematical concept formation. . . ."

Here is a translation of parts of Schopenhauer's long §15: "We are convinced that intuition is the primary source of all evidence, and the immediate or mediated reference to it alone is absolute truth, and that the nearest way to it is always the safest because every mediation through Concepts exposes us to many deceptions. When with this conviction we turn to *mathematics,* as it was set up as a science by Euclid and has on the whole remained to this day, we cannot help finding the way it pursues strange—indeed, perverted [*verkehrt*] . . . instead of thus granting a thorough insight into the essence of the triangle, he sets up a few disjointed, arbitrarily chosen propositions about the triangle and offers a logical reason for them by way of a tortuous, logical proof. . . . Instead of an exhaustive knowledge of these spatial relations, one therefore receives merely a few . . . results from them and is in the position of a person to whom the various effects of a complex machine are shown, while their inner relation and the works are kept from him. That what Euclid demonstrates is indeed that way, one has to admit, compelled by the principle of contradiction: but *why* things are that way, one is not told. One therefore has almost the uncomfortable feeling that attends a sleight of hand; and in fact most Euclidean proofs are strikingly similar to that. Almost always truth enters through the backdoor. . . . Often, as in the Pythagorean theorem, lines are drawn, one knows not why: afterwards it appears that they were nooses that are unexpectedly tightened and captivate the assent of the student who now has to admit, amazed, what in its inner context remains totally incomprehensible for him—so much so that he can study all of Euclid without gaining any insight into the laws of losophy concerns itself. In such an unactual element there are only unactual truths, i.e., fixed, dead propositions: one can stop with any one of them; the following one starts anew for itself, and the first one does not move itself on to the next, nor does a necessary connection come about in this way through the nature of the matter.—Also, on account of this principle and element—and in this consists the formalism of the evident certainty of mathematics—knowledge proceeds along the line of equality. For what is dead and does not move itself does not attain the differentiation of its essence or the essential opposition and inequality; and therefore it also does not attain the transition from the opposed into the opposed, nor the qualitative, immanent movement, nor self-movement. For mathematics considers only magnitude which is the unessential difference.[7] Mathematics abstracts from the fact that it is the Concept that bifurcates[8] space into its dimensions and determines the relations of and in these. It does not consider, e.g., the relation of the line to the plane; and when it compares the diameter of the circle with the circumference it comes up against incommensurability, i.e., a relation of the Concept, something infinite that escapes mathematical determination.

Immanent or so-called pure mathematics also does not juxtapose time as time with space, as the second material for its consideration. Applied mathematics, to be sure, does treat of it as well as of movement and other actual things. But it takes the synthetic propositions, i.e., those about their relations which are determined by their Concept, from experience, and it merely applies its formulas to these assumptions. The so-called demonstrations of such propositions as those about the equilibrium of the lever, or the relation of space and time in the movement of a fall, etc., are often given and accepted as demonstrations; but this only demonstrates how great a need knowledge has of demonstrations: where it lacks anything more, it respects even the empty semblance of a demonstration and thus gains some satisfaction. A critique of these demonstrations[9] would be as remarkable as it would be instructive and might both cleanse mathematics of this false finery and show the limitations of mathematics and thus also the necessity of another kind of knowledge.

As for time, of which one should think that, juxtaposed with space, it would constitute the material of the other part of pure mathematics, it is the existing Concept itself.[10] The principle of magnitude, that difference void of Concept, and the principle of spatial relations; instead he would merely learn by heart a few of their results. This really empirical and unscientific knowledge is like that of a doctor who knows disease and remedy, but not their connection. . . . Just so, the Pythagorean theorem teaches us to know a *qualitas occulta* of the right-angled triangle: Euclid's stilted, really crafty proof leaves us when it comes to the why, and the accompanying familiar simple figure offers at a single glance far more insight into the matter . . . than that proof:

In the case of unequal sides, too, it must be possible to achieve such intuitive conviction; indeed this must be so in the case of every possible geometrical truth if only because its discovery always was prompted by such an intuitive necessity and the proof was thought out only afterwards . . ."

§15 comprises almost twenty pages; our quotations come from the first quarter, and some of our omissions are considerable. Extremely long sentences have been broken up in translation, no less than in Hegel's text. Schopenhauer, born February 22, 1788, was barely nineteen when the *Phenomenology* appeared in 1807. By the time *The World as Will and Idea* was published in 1819, he was very much aware of Hegel's philosophy, and until his death in 1860 he never tired of heaping outright abuse on Hegel in print. For his encounter with Hegel at Berlin, see H 54.

⁷ Quantitative differences, as opposed to qualitative ones, do not concern the essence of a thing: as soon as they do, we say that the difference is not merely quantitative.

⁸ Since space is usually taken to have three dimensions, "bifurcates" is a little odd; but Hegel says *entzweit*.

⁹ Lasson says in a footnote: "In the *Encyclopedia*, §267, Hegel illuminated the laws of gravitation more closely in this sense."

¹⁰ That time is the existing Concept itself (*der daseiende Begriff selbst*) is here thrown out *en passant* as an epigram split in two by a parenthesis twice as long as the epigram itself. Perhaps one should recall Plato's remark in the *Timaeus* (37) that time is "a moving image of eternity." Plato first introduces this haunting phrase and then says, a few lines later: "and this image

equality, that abstract and lifeless unity, are incapable of concerning themselves with this pure unrest of life and this absolute differentiation. This negativity, therefore, becomes the second material for this knowledge only in paralyzed form, namely as the unit; and this knowledge, being external to its content, reduces that which moves itself to mere material in which it then has an indifferent, external, lifeless content.

13.   The nature of philosophical truth and its method

[III.3]

Philosophy, on the other hand, considers not the inessential determination but the determination insofar as it is essential.[1] Not the abstract or unactual is its element and contents but the actual, that which posits itself and lives in itself, existence in its Concept.[2] It is the process that generates and runs through its moments, and this whole movement constitutes the positive and its truth. This truth, then, includes the negative as well—that which might be called the false if it could be considered as something from which one should abstract. The evanescent must, however, be considered essential—not in the determination of something fixed that is to be severed from the true and left lying outside it, one does not know where; nor does the true rest on the other side, dead and positive. The appearance is the coming to be and passing away that itself does not come to be or pass away; it is in itself and constitutes the actuality and the movement of the life of the truth.[3] The true is thus the bacchanalian whirl in which no member is not drunken; and because each, as soon as it detaches itself, dissolves immediately —the whirl is just as much transparent and simple repose.[4] In the court of justice of this movement, to be sure, the individual forms of the spirit endure no more than determinate thoughts do, yet they are just as much positive and necessary moments as they are negative and evanescent.—In the whole of the movement, considering it as repose, that which distinguishes itself in it and gives particular existence is preserved as something that remembers, and its existence is knowledge of itself even as this knowledge is just as immediately existence.[5]

It might seem necessary to devote a lengthy preamble to the

we call time." For Hegel, time is not an image of the Concept but the existing Concept itself. The Concept, as we have seen (especially in II.3, note [37]), is fluid by nature—it is of its very essence that it transcends fixity—and its existence, the existence of such fluidity, involves time. But the *obiter dictum* that time *is* "the existing Concept itself" illustrates Hegel's esprit rather better than "the elevation of philosophy to a science" (I.1, text for note [13]).

III.3. Philosophical truth

[1] In the first paragraph of III.2 we were told that historical truth is concerned with the accidental and arbitrary; for example, when Caesar was born. In the longer discussion of mathematical truths Hegel tried to show in various ways that the geometer does not reach the essence of the triangle, for example. Philosophy, on the other hand, concerns itself with the essence of what it studies. An example may help. While the historian of art or religion must occupy himself with accidental events that were not necessary, the philosopher of art or religion must ask about the essence of art or religion.

[2] When Hegel insists that the philosopher is concerned with the essence, he does not by any means concede that existence is of no concern to him. Any dichotomy of that sort between essence and existence would strike him as utterly subphilosophical. As he uses these terms, mathematics, so far from dealing with essences, deals with the abstract or unactual; and philosophy, which deals with what is essential, deals necessarily with the actual.

[3] The evanescent is essential: for this and what follows we have been prepared in the opening paragraphs of the preface in which Hegel eventually disparaged "the naked result."

[4] This very striking sentence is one of the most memorable and famous Hegel ever wrote. It is doubly noteworthy that, as published by him in 1807, it cannot be construed. And though he made dozens of changes, mostly minute, in the early pages of the preface, he evidently never noticed that this flamboyant dictum sorely needed another pronoun to make sense; at least he left no notation to

method of this movement or of science. But the Concept of this method is implicit in what has been said, and its real exposition belongs to the Logic, or rather constitutes the Logic. For the method is nothing else than the edifice of the whole, constructed in its pure essence. But the entire system of prevalent notions of philosophical method belongs to an extinct form of education.

If this should sound boastful or revolutionary, though I know that my tone is altogether different, it should be noted that the scientific finery furnished by mathematics—such as explanations, divisions, axioms, rows of theorems, their demonstrations, principles, and deductions and inferences from them—is at least according to current opinion quite outmoded. Even if the unfitness of these procedures is not yet clearly understood, one makes little or no use of them; and if one does not disapprove of them, at least they are not loved. And we must have the prejudice in favor of what is excellent that it will get itself used[6] and loved.

But it is not difficult to see that positing a proposition, adducing reasons for it, and in the same way refuting the opposite by giving reasons, cannot be the form in which truth appears. Truth is its own self-movement, while this is the method of knowledge that remains external to its material. It is peculiar to, and must be left to, mathematics which, as we have noted, has for its principle the relation of magnitude—a relation void of Concept—and for its material dead space and the equally dead unit. In a somewhat freer style, i.e., mixed more with the arbitrary and the accidental, this method may retain its place in ordinary life, in conversation, or in historical instruction which is aimed at curiosity more than at knowledge—and therefore perhaps also in a preface.[7] In ordinary life, consciousness has for its contents information, experiences, sense concretions, also thoughts, principles—altogether, what is considered as a datum or as a being or essence in fixed repose. Now consciousness follows this thread, now it interrupts the connection by freely and arbitrarily disposing of such contents, and altogether consciousness here treats and determines its contents from the outside. Things are led back to some certainty, even if that is only the feeling of the moment; and conviction is satisfied when it has reached a familiar point of rest.

While the necessity of the Concept banishes the looser gait of conversational arguments as well as the stiffer gait of scientific pomp, it has been pointed out above that their place must not be indicate which pronoun should be inserted. The first half sentence is inelegant enough with its double negative; the second half reads in the first edition: *und weil jedes, indem es sich absondert, ebenso unmittelbar auflöst,—ist er ebenso die durchsichtige und einfache Ruhe.* But *auflösen,* unlike "dissolve," is never intransitive. In the posthumous edition of 1832, the editor inserted *sich* before *auflöst:* "and because each, as it detaches itself, just as immediately dissolves (*itself*) . . ." Lasson, on the other hand, thought it made more sense to suppose that *er* had dropped out after *weil:* "because it (the whirl) dissolves each . . ." Hoffmeister went back to the reading of 1832; so do I. The difference in meaning seems negligible: what is interesting is the fact that Hegel himself did not do anything about this flaw in one of his most colorful and oft quoted sentences.

Royce knew enough German to be able, when he misquoted this dictum in his *Lectures on Modern Idealism,* 215 f., to do so in fluent German as well as English: "As Hegel boldly expressed the situation, in the metaphorical language of his early period, and of his *Phaenomenologie,* 'The truth is the Bacchanalian revel, wherein every one of the finite forms of the truth appears as an intoxicated illusion.' (*Die Wahrheit ist der Bacchantische Taumel, worin alle Gestalten trunken sind.*)" This is entirely characteristic of Royce's excessively free interpretation of Hegel (cf. H 29)—and of J. Loewenberg's editing (cf. H 52, n. [5]). Royce's *Lectures* were published posthumously, and Loewenberg said in his "Editor's Preface": "Written as they were for oral delivery the lectures required much revision; the editor hopes he has not used his pen too freely." One wonders why he did not catch this mistranslation and misquotation: after all, the reference to "illusion," of which there is no trace in Hegel, is as characteristic of Anglo-American Idealism as it is alien to the whole spirit of Hegel's work. But Loewenberg also failed to correct Royce's wrong dates, e.g., on pp. 101 and 142.

What Hegel means is plainly that the forms of consciousness that are examined in the *Phenomenology* are all unbalanced and a little ridiculous; they exist and can be illustrated from history; but they are evanescent—passing stages in the story of the spirit's *Bildung;* and as we recall that story and behold them all at once or singly—detached—as we turn the pages of the book, the whirl has lost its fury and appears as tranquil repose. Indeed, the second half-sentence, about dissolution and repose, is bound to be more obvious to taken by the unmethod of intimation[8] and enthusiasm and the arbitrariness of prophetic speech which despises not only this scientific pomp but scientific procedures quite generally.

14. *Against schematizing formalism*

Now that Kant, by instinct, has rediscovered triplicity, albeit still dead and still uncomprehended, and it has subsequently been raised to its absolute importance, and with it the true form in its true content has been presented and the Concept of science has emerged, it is equally obvious that we must not consider scientific that use of this form which reduces it to a lifeless schema,[9] really to a phantom,[10] and scientific organization to a table.[11]

In a general way this formalism has already been discussed above, but we now want to describe its manner in a little more detail. This formalism supposes it has comprehended and expressed the nature and life of a form when it merely ascribes to it as a predicate some determination of the schema; e.g., subjectivity or objectivity, or magnetism, electricity, etc., contraction or expansion, east or west, *et al.* This sort of thing can be multiplied *ad infinitum* because in this manner every determination or form can be used again as a form or moment of the schema when it comes to another, and each can gratefully perform the same service for another. But in this circle of reciprocity one never learns what the matter itself is—neither what the one nor what the other is. In this process one sometimes uses sense determinations from common intuition—but then these are supposed to mean something different from what they say—and sometimes one uses the pure determinations of thoughts, meaningful in themselves, such as subject, object, substance, cause, the general, etc.—but just as uncritically and without examination as in ordinary life and as strengths and weaknesses, expansion and contraction. This metaphysics, then, is as unscientific as these sense conceptions.

Instead of the inner life and the self-movement of its existence, such a simple determinateness is taken from intuition, which here means the knowledge of the senses, and expressed according to a superficial analogy, and then this external and empty application of a formula is called construction.—Such formalism is like any other. How dull would a mind have to be that could not learn in a quarter of an hour the theory that there are asthenic, sthenic, and indirectly asthenic diseases, and

Hegel's readers than the first. What requires emphasis is that he himself did not merely recollect in tranquillity but also had a sense of the Dionysian whirl.

⁵ An allusion to the end of the *Phenomenology.*

⁶ A polemical allusion to the last sentence of Spinoza's *Ethics:* "But everything excellent is as difficult as it is rare." Hegel has the faith that what is excellent prevails and gains currency— *dass es sich in den Gebrauch setze.*

⁷ As in I.1.4 above, Hegel casts aspersions on his own preface.

⁸ *Ahndung:* an allusion to Jakob Friedrich Fries, *Wissen, Glaube und Ahndung* (Knowledge, Faith, and Intimation), Jena, 1805. Fries, Hegel's contemporary at Jena, had become Professor of Philosophy at Heidelberg in 1806. When he accepted a chair at Jena in 1816, Hegel became his successor at Heidelberg.

In the twentieth century, Leonard Nelson founded a Neo-Friesian School. The conception of *Ahnung* (*Ahndung* is now wholly obsolete) was also revived by Rudolf Otto in his classic, *Das Heilige* (1917). In the English version, *The Idea of the Holy* (1923; often reprinted), *Ahnung* is rendered somewhat oddly as "divination."

⁹ *Schema.*

¹⁰ *Schemen.* The pun is lost in translation.

¹¹ Kant's rediscovery of triplicity: After offering his table of twelve categories in the *Critique of Pure Reason,* Kant added some remarks in the second edition (1787): "About this table of categories one can offer some neat observations [*artige Betrachtungen*] which might well have considerable consequences in regard to the scientific form of all knowledge of reason. . . . 2d Note: That everywhere the number of the categories in each class is the same, namely three, which also calls for reflection since elsewhere all division *a priori* by means of Concepts must be dichotomy. And on top of that [*Dazu kommt aber noch, dass*] the third category always emerges from the connection of the second with the first of its class. Thus totality is nothing else than plurality considered as unity; limitation nothing else than reality connected with negation; community is the causality of a substance in the determination of another, reciprocally; finally, necessity nothing else than the existence that is given by the possibility itself. . . ." (B 109–11; cf. *Prolegomena,* 1783, §39, footnote.)

Hegel speaks of a rediscovery because this sort of triplicity had equally many attempts at cures! And since such instruction was until quite recently considered sufficient, anybody but a dullard could in such a short span of time be transformed from a *routinier* into a theoretical physician.[12] The formalism of such philosophy of nature teaches, say, that the understanding is electricity, or that animals are nitrogen or equal the south or north, etc., or represent it—whether all this is expressed as nakedly as here or brewed up with a little more terminology. Confronted with such power that brings together what had seemed far apart, and with the violence that the calmly restful things of sense suffer from such connections while they thus receive the semblance of a Concept, though they are spared the main thing, namely to express the Concept itself or the significance of the notion of the senses—confronted with all this, inexperience may well be plunged into admiration and amazement, and it may even venerate in all this the signs of profound genius. Inexperience may also be delighted by the good cheer of such determinations, since they substitute something that can be intuited for the abstract Concept and thus make things more pleasing, and inexperience may even congratulate itself on its intimation of an affinity of souls with such glorious activity.[12]

The trick of such wisdom is learned as quickly as it is easy to master it; its repetition, once it is known, becomes as insufferable as the repetition of a sleight of hand one sees through. The instrument of this monotonous formalism is no more difficult to handle than a painter's palette on which there are only two colors, say, red and green, one if an historical piece is wanted, the other for landscapes.[13]

It would be difficult to decide what is greater—the smugness with which everything in the heavens, on earth, and beneath the earth is coated with such a broth of paint, or the conceit that is based on the supposed excellence of this panacea: each supports the other.[14] The product of this method of labeling everything in heaven and earth, all natural and spiritual forms, with a few determinations of the general schema, and thus pigeonholing everything, is nothing less than a sun-clear report[15] on the organism of the universe—namely a tabulation that is like a skeleton with little pieces of paper stuck all over it, or like the rows of closed, labeled jars in a spicer's stall. While it is as explicit as both of these, it is like them in other ways too: here, flesh and blood are removed from the bones; there, the also not living matter is concealed in jars; and in the report, the living essence of the matter is left out.[16]

played a great role in Neoplatonism, especially in Proclus (412–85). It was again raised to "absolute importance" by Fichte who made much of theses, antitheses, and syntheses. Glockner suggests that Hegel here means to lump Schelling with Fichte, including him in his encomium: "The few words in which Hegel expresses this high praise of Fichte and Schelling almost in passing are remarkable. For they show that the immediately following sharp attack on romantic philosophy of nature was indeed meant to be directed only against its excrescences but not against Schelling himself" (II, 460; a footnote refers to Hegel's letter to Schelling, May 1, 1807, but not to Schelling's reply: see D 1807 for both).

Another interpretation would reserve the praise for Fichte and the critique for Schelling. In that case, to be sure, Hegel's letter to Schelling was simply dishonest. But Hegel was not thinking so much in terms of personalities, and what he meant was almost certainly: After Kant, the triplicity on which he had remarked in passing and whose importance he suspected without comprehending it, was raised to absolute importance, first of all, but by no means only, in Fichte's *Doctrine of Science* (*Wissenschaftslehre*) in 1794. Schelling, too, shared in the development of this great insight. But both also reduced triplicity to a lifeless schema. The detailed attack that follows could hardly be directed only against Schelling's imitators. The point might be put best by saying that, as Hegel saw it, Schelling himself had not always retained the *niveau* of his own greatest contributions to philosophy: again and again he had fallen to the level of a mere Schellingian. See H 39.

What is much more interesting and important than these historical considerations, however, is that Hegel once again goes out of his way to attack the very views which posterity, ironically, came to associate with him. Ever since the mid-nineteenth century, Hegel himself has been ridiculed for allegedly holding the views which he mocks here.

[12] Hegel's long sentences have been broken up throughout. In that respect our translation is not faithful to the style of the original. By way of compensation, a few long sentences are indicated in this commentary; for example, the passage that runs from here to the end of this paragraph ("The formalism of such . . . glorious activity") forms a single sentence in the original.

[13] At its best—here, for example—Hegel's ridicule is easily as good as Kierkegaard's at its best.

This manner has been further perfected into monochromatic absolute painting: ashamed of the distinctions of the schema, one drowns them in the emptiness of the absolute because they belong to reflection, and the new product is then pure identity, formless white.[17] But this has been noted above. That monotony of the schema and its lifeless determinations and this absolute identity, and the transition from one to the other—all are equally dead understanding and equally external knowledge.

The excellent, however, not only cannot escape the fate of being thus deprived of life and spirit, of being flayed and then seeing its skin wrapped around lifeless knowledge and its vanity. Rather we can recognize even in this fate the power of the excellent over the hearts, even if not over minds; also the development toward the generality and determinateness of the form which constitutes its perfection and which alone makes it possible that this generality can be used in the service of superficiality.

Science may organize itself only through the life of the Concept; the determinateness which some would take externally from the schema to affix it to existence is in science the self-moving soul of the abundant content. The movement of beings is, first,[18] to become something other and thus to become their own immanent content; secondly,[19] they take back into themselves this unfolding or this existence of theirs, i.e., they make themselves into a mere moment and simplify themselves into determinateness. In the first[20] movement negativity consists in the differentiation and positing of existence; in the return into oneself it is the becoming of determinate simplicity. In this way, the content does not receive its determinateness from another, like a label; instead it determines itself and assigns itself its place as a moment of the whole. The tabular understanding keeps to itself the necessity and the Concept of the contents— that which constitutes the concreteness, the actuality, and the living movement of the matter that it arranges—or rather, the tabular understanding does not keep this to itself, it does not know this; for if it had this insight it would surely show it. It does not even know the need for it; otherwise it would stop schematizing, or at least know that this process produces no more than a table of contents: it gives only the table of contents; the content itself, however, it does not furnish.

Suppose even that the determinateness is, like magnetism, e.g., concrete in itself and actual: even then it is reduced to

¹⁴ The passage from this point to the end of this paragraph ("The product . . . is left out") forms a single sentence in the original.

¹⁵ This phrase alludes to Fichte's *Sun-clear Report to the Public at Large* . . . (see I.1, note ¹³ above). This mocking allusion helps to confirm our suggestion that Fichte as well as Schelling had been guilty, according to Hegel, of reducing triplicity to a lifeless schema.

¹⁶ One should here recall Mephistopheles' remarks about *Collegium Logicum* in *Faust* I, lines 1911–41. Hegel knew this scene as it had been included in *Faust: A Fragment* (1790). Readers of *Faust* who have been gulled by the Hegel legend have often associated this passage with Hegel (who was twenty in 1790). Actually, this scene was already part of the *Urfaust*, written before 1775, before Schelling was even born and before Fichte was thirteen and Hegel five.

> Days will be spent to let you know
> That what you once did at one blow,
> Like eating and drinking so easy and free,
> Can only be done with One, Two, Three. . . .
> The philosopher comes with analysis
> And proves it had to be like this:
> The first was so, the second so,
> And hence the third and fourth was so,
> And were not the first and the second here,
> Then the third and fourth could never appear. . . .
> Who would study and describe the living, starts
> By driving the spirit out of the parts:
> In the palm of his hand he holds all the sections,
> Lacks nothing, except the spirit's connections. . . .

¹⁷ This is surely an allusion to Schelling, and it harks back to the jibe about the night in which all cows are black, at the end of section I.3. Some relevant quotations from Schelling were adduced there, in note ¹⁹.

¹⁸ "first": *einesteils;* more literally: on the one hand.

¹⁹ "secondly": *anderenteils* or on the other hand.

²⁰ *In jener Bewegung:* in that movement. Glockner summarizes this sentence and the preceding one by saying: "Hegel describes the three-step: thesis, antithesis, synthesis" (II, 460). But according to Glockner's own four-volume *Hegel-Lexikon* (a very

something dead, as it is merely predicated of some other existence instead of being known as the immanent life of this existence, or as that which has its native and characteristic self-generation and presentation in this existence. The formal understanding leaves it to others to add this main point.

Instead of entering into the immanent content of the matter, it always looks over[21] the whole and stands above the individual existence of which it speaks, i.e., it simply overlooks it.[22] Scientific knowledge, however, demands precisely that we surrender to the life of the object or—and this is the same—that we confront and express its inner necessity.[23] Thus immersed in its object, scientific knowledge forgets that survey which is merely the reflection of knowledge out of the content into itself. But absorbed in the matter and following the movement of that, it returns to itself—but not until the abundance of the content, simplified into determinateness, returns into itself, reduces itself to one side of existence, and develops into its higher truth. Thus the simple whole that surveys itself emerges from the riches in which its reflection had seemed lost.

Because, as we put it above, the substance is in itself subject, all content is its own reflection in itself.[24] The subsistence or substance of an existence is self-identity; for its non-identity with itself would be its dissolution. But self-identity is pure abstraction; but this is thinking.[25] When I say quality, I say simple determinateness. By its quality an existence is different from another, or is existence; it is for itself, or it subsists through this simplicity with itself. But through this it is essentially thought. —In this the fact is comprehended that being is thinking; and this includes the insight that eludes the usual talk, void of Concept, of the identity of thinking and being.[26]

Inasmuch as the subsistence of existence is self-identity or pure abstraction, it is its own abstraction from itself, or it is itself its non-identity with itself and its dissolution—its own inwardness and return into itself—its becoming.[27] Insofar as this is the nature of beings, and beings have this nature for knowledge, knowledge is not an activity that handles its content as something strange—not reflection into itself, away from the content. Science is not that idealism that replaced the dogmatism of assertions with a dogmatism of assurances or a dogmatism of self-certainty. Rather, when knowledge sees the content return into its own inwardness, the activity of knowledge is both absorbed in the content, being its immanent self, and at the same time this knowledge has returned into itself, for it is pure self-elaborate and helpful index to his twenty-volume *Jubiläumsausgabe* of Hegel's works), thesis, antithesis, and synthesis are only once mentioned together by Hegel—disparagingly, in his lectures on the history of philosophy, toward the end of his critique of Kant. (Cf. WK 166–67, and Gustav E. Mueller's "The Hegel Legend of 'Thesis-Antithesis-Synthesis.'")

[21] "looks over": *übersieht.* The German word can mean both survey and also overlook in the sense of not seeing. The first meaning is intended here.

[22] "overlooks it": *sieht es gar nicht.* This can only mean: does not see it at all. I have tried to keep the pun in English.

[23] This harks back to I.1.8 above. At this point Hegel's conception of the ethos of scientific work is by no means remote from positivism or from Max Weber's classical statement in *Wissenschaft als Beruf* (1919; Scholarship as a Vocation). Hegel's influence may even have contributed to the fact that in 1919 *Wissenschaft* could still be used in this broad sense for scholarly work in general; and Weber, though far from being a Hegelian, was close to Hegel's spirit when he said: "'Personality' in the area of scholarship is restricted to those who serve exclusively the subject [*rein der Sache*]" (p. 13). What matters to Hegel is that the impetus that leads from point to point should not come from the arbitrary disposition of the writer but rather from the subject matter. A thorough analysis of one Concept, for example, should require that the analysis proceed to a second Concept, and in this way we should be led on and on by the "inner necessity" of the content. If the analysis should concentrate on the whole position, as it does in the *Phenomenology,* i.e., on the form of consciousness as well as the content, then we should still immerse ourselves in each position in turn, taking it more seriously than its actual proponents, and find that, thus pushed to its limits, it gives way to another position which must then be considered next.

[24] "In the following sentences," says Glockner (II, 461), "Hegel accomplishes the decisive, and as I see it extraordinarily problematic, *turn to Panlogism.*" This is Glockner's coinage, and what he means by *Panlogismus* is similar to what is more often called rationalism. See the next note.

[25] After the sentence cited in the previous note, Glockner quotes the two sentences between our [24] and [25] and comments:

identity in otherhood. Thus it is the cunning[28] that seems to abstain from activity while it looks on as determinateness and its concrete life suppose that they are pursuing their self-preservation and particular interests though in fact they are the converse, an activity that dissolves itself and makes itself a moment of the whole.

Above, we indicated the significance of the understanding with reference to the self-consciousness of substance; from what has now been said one can see its significance with reference to the determination of substance as having being. Existence is quality, self-identical determinateness or determinate simplicity, determinate thought; this is the understanding of existence. Thus it is *nous,* as Anaxagoras[29] was the first to recognize. Those who came after him comprehended the nature of existence more determinately as *eidos* or *idea,*[30] i.e., determinate generality, species. The expression "species" may seem too common and inferior for the Ideas, for the beautiful, holy, and eternal which are now in fashion. But in fact the Idea expresses no more, nor less, than the species. Yet in our day an expression that designates a Concept precisely is often spurned in favor of another term which, if only because it belongs to a foreign language, shrouds the Concept in a fog and thus sounds more edifying.

Precisely when existence is determined as species it is simple thought; the *nous,* the simplicity, is the substance. On account of its simplicity or self-identity it appears firm and enduring. But this self-identity is also negativity; therefore this firm existence passes over into its dissolution. The determinateness at first seems merely due to the fact that it is related to something else, and the movement seems imposed on it by an alien power; but what is contained in this simplicity of thinking is precisely that this determinateness is qualified by its own otherhood and is thus self-movement. For it is the thought that moves and differentiates itself, its own inwardness, the pure Concept. Thus reasonableness is a becoming, and as such becoming it is rationality.

In this nature of beings, to be their Concept in their being,[31] consists logical necessity. This alone is the rational and the rhythm of the organic whole; it is just as much the knowledge of the content as the content is Concept and essence—or it alone is what is speculative.

The concrete form, moving itself, makes itself into simple determinateness. Thus it raises itself to become logical form and attain its essential nature. Its concrete existence is nothing but this movement and is immediately logical existence. Therefore it

"It should be remarked that 'identity' is certainly a logical determination; yet it won't do to conceive something existing and self-identical as for that reason essentially 'thought-ful' ['*gedanklich*']. In that case one leaves out of consideration the moments of individual singularity and organic wholeness, or one logicizes them; i.e., one works merely with positing and opposition, position and negation."

[26] The third fragment of Parmenides of Elea (born about 510 B.C.) has often been interpreted as saying: "thinking and being are the same thing." Twentieth-century philologists have offered many other translations.

[27] The passage from here to the end of the paragraph forms a single sentence in the original.

[28] "the cunning": *die List*. This conception was later developed by Hegel and called *die List der Vernunft* (the cunning of reason): first, in his *Encyclopedia* (1817, §158; 3d edition, 1830, §209) and then in a famous passage in his introductory lectures on the philosophy of history: "The particular has its own interest in world history; it is something finite and as such must perish. It is the particular that wearies itself fighting against each other and a part of which is ruined. But precisely in the fight, in the destruction of the particular, the universal results. This is not disturbed. It is not the universal idea that incurs opposition and fight and danger: it keeps itself safe from attack and unharmed in the background, while sending the particular of passion into the fight to wear itself out. One can call it the cunning of reason that it lets the passions do its work, while that through which it translates itself into existence loses and suffers harm. . . . The individuals are sacrificed and surrendered. The idea pays the tribute of existence and transitoriness not out of itself but through the passions of individuals" (VG 105 L). Cf. H 62.

[29] The only other proper names mentioned so far in the preface are Aristotle's and Kant's; toward the end, Plato is mentioned, too. The reference to Anaxagoras (about 500–428/7) harks back to Aristotle's *Metaphysics* (A, end of 3, 984b): when Anaxagoras said "that reason was present—as in animals, so throughout nature—as the cause of order and of all arrangement, he seemed like a sober man in contrast with the random talk of his predecessors" (the W. D. Ross translation; *nous* is the Greek word he translated as reason).

is unnecessary to impose formalism externally on the concrete content: the content is in itself the transition into formalism which, however, ceases to be this external formalism because the form is the native development of the concrete content itself.

This nature of the scientific method—to be partly not separate from the content, and partly to determine its rhythm by itself—receives, as already mentioned, its proper exposition in speculative philosophy.[32]

What has here been said, to be sure, expresses the Concept, but cannot count for more than an anticipatory assurance. Its truth does not lie in this partly narrative exposition; therefore it also cannot be refuted by the opposed assurance that things are not so but otherwise, or by recalling and recounting conventional conceptions as if they were established and familiar truths, or by assurances of something newly dished up from the shrine of inward divine intuition.

A reception of this sort is usually the first reaction of knowledge to something unfamiliar: one wants to save one's freedom and one's own insight and authority from the alien one—for that which is now first encountered appears in this form. Also, one wants to remove the appearance, and the sort of shame that is supposed to lie in this, that something has been learned. Similarly, when the unfamiliar is accepted with applause, the reaction is motivated the same way and consists in what in another sphere would take the form of ultra-revolutionary speech and action.

[30] The reference here is to Plato.

[31] This clause sounds even far worse in German: *in seinem Sein sein Begriff zu sein*. Hegel's claim that "logical necessity . . . alone is . . . rational" seems highly implausible and objectionable. See I.1, note [6] above. What Hegel is driving at is explained to some extent in note [23] above.

[32] "speculative philosophy": Hegel's then still unwritten *Logic* is meant.

At this point there is another sudden shift in tone: the style becomes once again concrete, even earthy.

The final paragraph of this section (beginning "A reception of this sort . . .") seems close to Nietzsche and psychoanalysis. Here Hegel tries to uncover the hidden motives that underlie men's reactions to a new doctrine: one feels in danger of being overpowered and prepares to meet a form of aggression. Hegel suggests that even applause is an outlet for aggressive impulses—a kind of counterattack.

15. *The demands of the study of philosophy*

[IV.1]

What therefore matters in the study of science is taking upon oneself the exertion of the Concept.[1] What is wanted is attention to the Concept as such, to the simple determinations, e.g., of being in itself, being for itself, self-identity, etc.; for these are such pure self-movements which one might call souls if their Concept did not designate something higher.[2] To those accustomed to progress from notion to notion, being interrupted by the Concept seems just as bothersome as it does to formalistic thinking that argues back and forth in unactual thoughts.[3] The former custom should be called material thinking—an accidental consciousness that is merely absorbed in the material and therefore finds it hard to lift the self at the same time clear out of the material to be with itself.[4] The other type, argumentative thinking,[5] is, on the contrary, the freedom from the content and the vanity that looks down on it. This vanity is expected to exert itself, to give up this freedom and to immerse it in the content, instead of merely being the arbitrary moving principle of the content: the content should be made to move itself by virtue of its own nature, i.e., through the self as its own self, and then to contemplate this movement. One should not intrude into the immanent rhythm of the Concepts[6] either arbitrarily or with wisdom gained elsewhere: such restraint is itself an essential moment of attention to the Concept.

16. *Argumentative thinking in its negative attitude—*[7]

One should note the two ways in which the argumentative manner is opposed to the thinking that comprehends.[8]—First, such reasoning adopts a negative attitude against its content and knows how to refute and destroy it.[9] That things are otherwise—this insight is merely negative; it is a finality that does not proceed beyond to a new content. Rather, to gain a content again one has to find something somewhere else.[10] This is the reflection into the empty ego, the vanity of its knowledge.

This vanity, however, does not only express that this content is vain but also that this insight itself is vain; for this insight is the negative that does not see what is positive in itself. By never making its own negativity its content, such reflection is

IV. *Conclusion*
1. The exertion of the Concept

¹ "The exertion of the Concept" (*die Anstrengung des Begriffs*) is one of the odd but memorable phrases coined by Hegel. In German, too, it would be more idiomatic to speak of the exertion of conceptual thinking or conceptual analysis. But what Hegel means should be clear by now and has been commented on in several notes above.

² The close association of "pure self-movements" and "souls" may seem strange to modern readers if they are not familiar with Greek philosophy. But in Plato's *Laws,* Book X, soul is defined as the motion which can move itself (895 f.). For Hegel the Concept is even "higher" than the soul.

³ Analysis of Concepts is unwelcome both to those who are used to relying on mere notions (*Vorstellungen*)—readers who are glued, as it were, to visual aids and the comfortable vagueness of less rigorous ways of thinking—and to addicts of formalistic thinking. Hegel speaks of the latter as *dem formalen Denken, das in unwirklichen Gedanken hin und her räsonniert.* It is a kind of thinking that relies on abstractions ("unactual thoughts") which are never analyzed. Instead of devoting itself to an effort to comprehend Concepts, it juggles around abstractions.

⁴ Those who rely on notions are not aware of having a point of view: thinkers of this type forget to analyze the self and its position.

⁵ "argumentative thinking": *das Räsonnieren.*

⁶ This is the first time in the preface that we encounter Concepts (*Begriffe*) in the plural; and the plural occurs only twice after this. This is connected with the fact that Hegel associates the Concept not merely with particular concepts, though he does that, too, but also with a mode of thinking. In his usage the Concept stands for scientific philosophy, even as intuition stands for another approach which we might call romantic, notions for yet another which we might call popular, and argumentative thinking, which Hegel is about to discuss here, for a fourth type.

⁷ In the original table of contents from which this heading is taken, the page reference is LXXII, but the heading clearly

never in the matter but always beyond it; therefore it imagines that with its claim of emptiness it is always more advanced than a contentful insight. On the other hand, as shown above, in the thinking that comprehends the negative belongs to the content itself and is the positive both as the immanent movement and determination of the content and as the whole of this. Seen as a result, it is the determinate negative that comes out of this movement, and thus just as much a positive content.

But considering that such thinking has a content, whether it be of notions or of thoughts or of a mixture of both, it has another side that makes comprehension difficult for it. The strange nature of this second side is closely connected with the above-mentioned essence of the idea[11]—or rather expresses it as it appears as the movement which is thinking apprehension.[12]

17. —in its positive attitude; its subject

In its negative behavior, just discussed, argumentative thinking is itself the self into which the content returns; in its positive knowledge, on the other hand, the self is a represented subject[13] to which the content is related as an accident and predicate. This subject constitutes the basis to which the content is tied and on which the movement runs back and forth.

It is different with the thinking that comprehends. The Concept is the object's own self which presents itself as its becoming; thus it is not a subject at rest[14] that carries its attributes unmoved, but it is the Concept that moves itself and takes its determinations back into itself. In this movement the resting subject itself perishes:[15] it enters into the differences and the content and constitutes the determinateness, i.e., the differentiated content and its movement, instead of abiding outside it. The firm ground that argumentative reasoning found in the resting subject thus quakes, and only this movement itself becomes the object. The subject that fills its content ceases to go beyond that and cannot have any other predicates or attributes. The dispersion of the content, conversely, is bound under the self, and the content[16] is not something general that, free from the subject, could be assigned to several others.[17] The content is thus in fact no longer the predicate of the subject; rather it is the substance and the essence and Concept of that which is dis-belongs where we have placed it, i.e., at the very top of page LXXIII. This subtitle is continued in the next one, number 17: the connection is the same as between numbers 5 and 6, and again between 9 and 10 above.

[8] *das begreifende Denken:* see note [6] above; also I.1, note [3]. This is the type of thinking Hegel commends.

[9] According to Glockner (II, 464), "This is an allusion to Kant's doctrine of the unknowability of the thing in itself. Fichte already had recognized its untenability." This interpretation of Hegel's text is very questionable: the long attack on argumentative thinking is not aimed particularly at Kant, and one cannot discredit such thinking by suddenly associating it with, or blaming it for, Kant's doctrine of the unknowable thing in itself. Rather, Hegel characterizes a type of thought that argues against a rival position, "adopts a negative attitude" against that which it discusses "and knows how to refute and destroy it."

[10] Glockner comments (*ibid.*): "Besides Fichte one may here think also of Jacobi insofar as he replaced the content that was not accessible to reason with faith." Again, Hegel's point seems much more general: "argumentative thinking" completely rejects the position it attacks and then has to find a new content elsewhere.

The thinking that comprehends, as Hegel suggests in the next paragraph, is constructive in its criticism. This whole discussion should be compared with I.1, paragraphs 4 and 5, and *ibid.,* note [9].

[11] *Idee.*

[12] "thinking apprehension": *denkendes Auffassen.*

[13] *ein vorgestelltes Subjekt.*

[14] *Indem der Begriff das eigene Selbst des Gegenstandes ist, das sich als sein Werden darstellt, ist es nicht ein ruhendes Subjekt . . . :* "its becoming" (*sein Werden*) can refer to the self or to the object; but the following "it" (*es*) can refer only to the self.

The best commentary on all of this and a great deal of what follows is given by Hegel himself a few paragraphs later when he gives the example of the proposition: "God is being."

[15] For an illustration see the text for note [30] below.

[16] Reading: *er ist nicht . . . ,* i.e., the content is not . . . (Lasson's emendation, 1907, taken over by Hoffmeister in his editions). The original edition of 1807 read: *es ist nicht . . . ,* which would seem to mean that the self is not . . . In the *Werke,* in 1832

cussed.[18] It is of the nature of representational thinking[19] to follow the attributes or predicates and to go beyond them, quite rightly, too, because they are mere predicates and attributes; but because that which in a proposition has the form of a predicate is really the substance itself,[20] representational thinking is stopped in its advance. To represent it that way: it suffers a counterthrust.[21] Beginning with the subject, as if this remained the basis, it finds, because the predicate is really the substance,[20] that the subject has moved into the predicate and has thus been sublimated. Thus that which seemed to be predicate has become the whole and independent mass, and thinking can no longer stray freely but is brought to a stop by this gravity.[22]

Usually, the subject is first made the basis as the objective, fixed self, and the necessary movement to the multiplicity of the determinations or predicates proceeds from there. Here, however, this subject is replaced by the knowing ego itself which connects the predicates and becomes the subject that holds them. The first subject[23] enters into the determinations and is their soul; thus the second subject,[24] which knows, still finds in the predicate that with which it had wished to be done so it could return into itself; and instead of being in a position to function as the active element in the movement of the predicate—arguing back and forth whether this or that predicate would be suitable —the second subject is still preoccupied with the self of the content[25] and has to stay with that instead of being by itself.[26]

What has here been said can be expressed more formally: the nature of the judgment or proposition, which involves the distinction between subject and predicate, is destroyed by the speculative proposition;[27] and the identical proposition into which the former turns contains the counterthrust against this relation.[28]—This conflict between the form of a proposition[29] and the unity of the Concept that destroys it resembles the conflict between meter and accent in rhythm. Rhythm results from the floating center and unification of both. Thus, in the philosophical proposition, too, the identity of subject and predicate is not meant to destroy the difference between both that is expressed by the form of the proposition; rather their unity is meant to emerge as a harmony. The form of the proposition is the appearance of the determinate sense, or the accent that distinguishes its fulfillment; but that the predicate expresses the substance, and the subject itself falls into the general, that is the unity in which this accent fades away.

and 1841, in the only two posthumous editions before 1907, the original wording was kept.

[17] In the proposition, "God is being," which Hegel himself soon adduces as an example, being is not "something general that, free from the subject [i.e., God], could be assigned to several others."

[18] To stick to this example: being is no longer a mere predicate of the subject but said to be the substance, essence, and Concept of God.

[19] "representational thinking": *das vorstellende Denken;* a type of thinking that sticks to notions (*Vorstellungen*) instead of dealing with Concepts (*Begriffe*) like the thinking that comprehends (*das begreifende Denken*).

Heidegger contrasts representational thinking with the thinking that recalls (*das andenkende Denken*) and, unlike Hegel, seeks to move philosophy closer to poetry rather than science. (See "The Way Back into the Ground of Metaphysics," the introduction Heidegger added in 1949 to *What is Metaphysics?* in Kaufmann, *Existentialism from Dostoevsky to Sartre,* especially pp. 206 and 219.)

[20] For example, being in the proposition "God is being."

[21] *Gegenstoss:* Glockner (II, 465 f.) refers to "the important doctrine of the *counterthrust.*" He does not explain this doctrine; he merely quotes. But it seems misleading to speak of a *wichtige Lehre vom Gegenstoss.* These very abstract paragraphs may give the impression that Hegel is expounding a new and difficult doctrine, but as soon as he discusses examples a little later on, it appears that he is merely elaborating a point made earlier, in II.1: see the text following note [21], as well as notes [23] and [25] in the same section.

[22] The weight or gravity of "being" in the proposition "God is being" stops us, and we cannot simply go on to look for other predicates.

[23] "the first subject": the subject of the proposition; in our example, God.

[24] "the second subject": the student.

[25] That is, with the first subject, God.

[26] "by itself"—and ready to go on to other things.

[27] For example, "God is being." Immediately afterwards this is called an "identical proposition" because it identifies God with being.

Examples may help to explain this. In the proposition "God is being," the predicate is "being." It has substantial meaning in which the subject dissolves.[30] Being here is not meant to be a mere predicate but rather the essence, and God apparently ceases to be the firm subject, in spite of his position in the sentence.—Thinking here does not progress in the transition from the subject to the predicate: the subject gets lost, and thinking feels inhibited[31] and, missing the subject, is thrown back[32] to the thought of the subject. Or, because the predicate is expressed as itself a subject, as being, as the essence which exhausts the nature of the subject, thinking finds the subject immediately in the predicate; and now, instead of attaining in the predicate the free position to argue, it is still absorbed in the content—or at least the demand is present that it ought to be so absorbed.[33]

It is similar when one says: the actual is the general.[34] The actual as a subject vanishes in the predicate. The general is not meant to have merely the meaning of the predicate, as if the proposition were merely meant to say that the actual is general. Rather, the general is supposed to express the essence of the actual.—Thus thinking loses the firm objective ground it had in the subject whenever the predicate throws it back[35] to the subject, so that in the predicate it returns not to itself but to the subject of the content.

This unaccustomed inhibition[36] is the main source of the complaints about the unintelligibility of philosophical writings —at least from those who do not lack other educational prerequisites for understanding them. In what has here been said we find the reason for the specific reproach, which is often heard, that many passages have to be read several times before one can understand them. This is considered improper, and it is supposed that this reproach, if well founded, is final and unanswerable.—From the above it should be clear what this amounts to. The philosophical proposition, being a proposition, gives rise to the opinion that the relation of subject and predicate and the procedure of knowledge are as usual. But the philosophical content destroys this procedure and this opinion; one learns that what one supposed was not what one was supposed to suppose;[37] and this correction of one's opinion requires knowledge to return to the sentence and to reinterpret it.

One difficulty should be avoided: mixing up the speculative style with the argumentative style so that what is said of the subject sometimes has the meaning of its Concept, at other times

²⁸ The counterthrust, as we now see, is simply that what seemed to be a subject-predicate relation turns into a relation of identity, and this comes as something of a shock.

²⁹ Cf. II.1, notes ²³ and ²⁵.

³⁰ Cf. text for note ¹⁵ above.

³¹ "inhibited": *gehemmt.*

³² "thrown back": this is the counterthrust.

³³ Instead of being free to argue about this predicate and that, one is perplexed about the meaning of Concepts.

³⁴ The second example is not developed at length like the first, but it shows that the point of the first example does not depend in any way on its reference to God. To be sure, other propositions about God could be added as further examples: God is love, God is spirit, God is the ground of being. But "the actual is the general" does just as well, as Hegel tries to indicate briefly.

³⁵ This is, once again, the counterthrust.

³⁶ "inhibition": *Hemmen.* See text for note ³¹ above.

³⁷ *die Meinung erfährt, dass es anders gemeint ist, als sie meinte.* Baillie quite misses Hegel's touch of humor when he translates this: "The common view discovers that the statement is intended in another sense than it is thinking of . . ."

Now that Hegel has given examples, his meaning seems clear enough to require very little commentary.

only the meaning of its predicate or attribute.—One style interferes with the other, and only a philosophical exposition that strictly precluded the usual relation of the parts of a sentence would attain the goal of being really vivid.

Yet non-speculative thinking also has its valid rights that are ignored in the style of the speculative proposition. That the form of the proposition is sublimated should not merely happen immediately, through the mere content of the proposition.[38] Rather, this opposite movement must be expressed; it must not be a mere internal inhibition,[39] but the return of the Concept into itself must be represented expressly. This movement which takes the place of that which proof was once supposed to accomplish is the dialectical movement of the proposition itself.[40] This alone is the actually speculative, and only the expression of this is speculative exposition. As a proposition the speculative is merely internal inhibition[39] and the failure of the essence to return into itself. Therefore we often find that philosophical expositions refer us to this internal intuition[41] and thus spare themselves the presentation of the dialectical movement of the proposition, which we demanded.

The proposition should express what the true is, but essentially this is subject; as such it is merely the dialectical movement, this way that generates itself, leads itself on, and returns into itself.[42]—In non-speculative knowledge proof constitutes this side of expressed inwardness. But since dialectic has been separated from proof, the Concept of philosophical proof has been lost.[43]

Here it may be recalled that the dialectical movement also has propositions for its parts or elements; the difficulty shown here therefore appears to recur always and to be a feature of the matter itself.[44]—This is similar to the situation in ordinary proof where the reasons used require reasons in turn, and so forth ad infinitum. Yet this form of finding reasons and conditions is a feature of those proofs which differ from dialectical movement; it belongs to external knowledge. But the element of the dialectical movement is the pure Concept;[45] thus it has a content that is through and through subject in itself. Thus no content occurs that functions as an underlying subject and receives its meaning as a predicate; the proposition is immediately a merely empty form.[46]

Apart from the self that is intuited or represented by the senses, it is above all the name as name that designates the pure subject, the empty unit void of Concept. For this reason

³⁸ The goal mentioned at the end of the preceding paragraph cannot be attained after all by banishing from one's prose all but speculative propositions, such as "God is being," or "the actual is the general." In these two cases, and in others like them, the content of the proposition suggests that what looks like a subject-predicate relation is really meant to be a relation of identity.

³⁹ See text for note ³¹ above.

⁴⁰ The reader must not be left to gather from the content that what looks like a predicate is not supposed to be a predicate; but this appearance of the proposition must be cancelled expressly. And this denial of what seems to have been said, this contradiction of one proposition by the next, this qualification of an assertion by what follows it, is what Hegel now introduces as "the dialectical movement."

⁴¹ "internal intuition": the insight that attends the internal inhibition which has been mentioned a number of times.

⁴² The true, being subject, is not given all at once or immediately in the form of a proposition. It develops (see II.1, note ⁸ above) and has to be developed in a series of propositions. In other words, as Hegel has told us before, the form of the true cannot be a single proposition but only a whole system.

⁴³ The dialectical progression described in note ⁴⁰ above must replace proofs in philosophy. It is plainly not the same thing, and Hegel thus does not claim that in his *Phenomenology* and *Logic,* or in the philosophy of nature and the philosophy of spirit, he will prove his claims in any ordinary sense. He promises, in effect, to be rigorous, but in a somewhat novel way. Not entirely novel: soon Hegel will mention some ancient precedents.

⁴⁴ When propositions are employed to qualify propositions that went before, the same problem would seem to be inevitable at every turn.

⁴⁵ Once again, the Concept stands for a whole way of thinking. See note ⁶ above.

⁴⁶ See II.1, note ²⁵ above.

it may be expedient, e.g., to avoid the name "God" because this word is not immediately also a Concept but rather the proper name, the fixed repose of the underlying subject, while, e.g., being or the One, the particular, the subject, etc., also immediately suggest Concepts.[47]

Although speculative truths are formulated about this subject,[48] their content lacks the immanent Concept because it is present only as a subject at rest, and owing to this such truths easily acquire the form of mere edification.[49]—The habit of construing the speculative predicate on the model of a proposition and not as Concept and essence constitutes an obstacle that can be increased or diminished by the manner of the philosophic exposition.[50] In keeping with our insight into the nature of the speculative, the presentation should retain the dialectical form and include nothing except insofar as it is Concept and comprehended.

[IV.2]

There is another obstacle that is as serious as the argumentative manner. The study of philosophy is obstructed no less by a conceit that does not deign to argue: one supposes that one is in possession of established truths which do not require discussion but can be assumed as the basis of what follows; one feels free to pronounce them and to judge and condemn by appealing to them. At this point it is particularly necessary that philosophy should again be made a serious pursuit. Of all sciences, arts, skills, and crafts one is convinced that mastery requires a multiple effort of learning and exercise.[1] But when it comes to philosophy, quite another prejudice is prevalent today: although one grants that having eyes and fingers is not enough to enable everyone who is given leather and tools to make shoes, it is held that everybody can immediately philosophize and judge philosophy merely because he possesses the measure in his natural reason—as if one did not equally possess the measure for a shoe in one's foot.

It seems that the mastery of philosophy is found precisely in the lack of knowledge and study, as if philosophy ceased where these begin. Philosophy is often considered a merely formal knowledge, void of content, and the insight is sadly lacking that whatever content of knowledge or science is truth does not deserve this name unless it has been produced by philosophy. Let

[47] A proper name as the subject of a proposition creates the same presumption that would be created by a noun that designates an object of sense perception; namely, that we are confronted with a fixed "underlying subject" to which some predicate is attached. Therefore, propositions about God are misleading insofar as people construe "God" as a proper name. When the subject of a proposition is being, the One, the actual, identity, quantity, becoming, the idea, or anything at all that immediately suggests a Concept, this misunderstanding is likely to be avoided.

[48] "this subject": God.

[49] For example, "God is love" and "God is spirit" are edifying propositions rather than speculative propositions. To take twentieth-century examples, Tillich's "God is being-itself" and "God is the ground of being" are at least ambiguous in this respect, and their wide appeal certainly depends on their being interpreted as edifying and inspirational.

[50] A writer can go out of his way to cultivate the audience that construes his propositions as edifying; or he can take pains to point out that he does not wish to be read that way, and that what he means is different.

IV.2. There is no royal road to science

[1] Twenty years later, in the second edition of his *Encyclopedia* (1827, §5; unchanged in the 3d edition, 1830, §5) Hegel says very similarly: "This science [philosophy] is often treated with such contempt that even people who have taken no trouble with it express the conceit that they understand all by themselves [*von Haus aus;* literally, from home] what philosophy is all about and are able, simply on the basis of an ordinary education and especially of religious feelings, to philosophize and judge philosophy. One concedes that one has to study other sciences before one knows them, and that one is entitled to judge them only on the basis of such knowledge. One concedes that, to make a shoe, one must have learned this and it requires practice, although everybody possesses the measure for it in his foot and also his hands and in them the natural skill for the required task. Only for philosophy itself such study, learning, and trouble is not supposed to be necessary.—In recent times this comfortable opinion has received confirmation through the doctrine of immediate knowledge, knowledge by intuition."

the other sciences try to get somewhere by arguing without philosophy as much as they please: without it, they cannot contain life, spirit, or truth.

18. *Natural philosophizing as healthy common sense and as genius*

When it comes to real philosophy, the long path of education and the movement, as rich as it is profound, through which the spirit reaches knowledge are now considered dispensable, and the immediate revelation of the divine and a healthy common sense that has never troubled or educated itself with other knowledge or with philosophy proper are held to be just as good and as perfect a substitute as some claim chicory is for coffee.[2] It is not pleasant to remark that ignorance, indeed even crudeness that lacks form as much as taste and is incapable of concentrating thought on an abstract sentence, not to speak of the connection of several, assures us now that it is the freedom and tolerance of thought, now that it is nothing less than genius. As is well known, such genius, now the rage in philosophy, once raged no less in poetry; but when the products of such genius had any meaning at all, they were not poetry but trivial prose or, when they were more, mad oratory. Thus a supposedly natural philosophizing that considers itself too good for Concepts and thinks that this lack makes it an intuitive or visionary and poetical thinking, in fact brings to market arbitrary combinations of an imagination that has merely been disorganized by thought—fabrications that are neither flesh nor fish, neither poetry nor philosophy.[3]

Flowing along in the calmer bed of healthy common sense, natural philosophizing entertains us with a rhetoric of trivial truths. Reproached with the insignificance of all this, it assures us that meaning and fulfillment reside in its heart and must reside in other hearts, too—and one supposes that such references to the innocence of the heart, the purity of conscience, *et al.*, represent final matters which brook no objections or further demands. But the task was not to leave the best deep inside but to bring it to light out of these depths. To produce final truths of that sort was trouble one might easily have spared oneself, for it has long been easy to find them in the catechism, in popular proverbs, etc.[4]

It is not difficult to show how indeterminate and vague, or how misleading, such truths are, or even to show to consciousness how it also contains diametrically opposite truths.[5] As con-

² For once, one of Hegel's long sentences has not been broken up in translation; but many of his sentences are a great deal longer than this one. Hegel, incidentally, loved coffee and despised substitutes (cf., e.g., his letter of April 29, 1814, in D).

³ Here the great difference between Hegel and Heidegger, referred to above (IV.1, note ¹⁹), becomes quite explicit.

Toward the end of the preface, Hegel made some use of notes which Rosenkranz called "Aphorisms from the Jena Period" when he published them in 1844 near the end of his Hegel biography. The numbers I use for reference were assigned by Hoffmeister when he reprinted these notes under the same title in 1936 in *Dokumente zu Hegels Entwicklung*. The main examples will be cited below. At this point one of the aphorisms seems relevant although one cannot truly say that Hegel "used" it:

"The truth of science is a calm light that illuminates and delights everything, like the warmth in which everything simultaneously flourishes and explicates the internal treasures in the breadth of life. A *flash of inspiration* [*Gedankenblitz:* a common German word, comparable to "brain storm" and stylistically suggestive of aphorisms] is the Capaneus who . . . cannot attain enduring life" (⚹23).

Capaneus, one of the Seven against Thebes, defied Zeus who struck him dead with a lightning bolt.

⁴ The task of philosophy is not to compete with popular proverbs or religious wisdom but to supplant notions with Concepts, intuition with science.

⁵ Appeals to common sense can often be met by appealing to common sense on behalf of "diametrically opposite truths."

sciousness tries to extricate itself from this confusion it is likely to fall into new confusions[6] and may finally expostulate that as a matter of fact things are thus and thus while those supposed truths are sophistries. "Sophistries" is a slogan that common sense likes to use against educated reason, even as ignorance of philosophy likes to apply the expression "idle dreams" to philosophy.

Those who invoke feeling as their internal oracle are finished with anyone who does not agree: they have to own that they have nothing further to say to anyone who does not find and feel the same in his heart—in other words, they trample under foot the roots of humanity. For it is the nature of humanity to struggle for agreement with others, and humanity exists only in the accomplished community of consciousness. The anti-human, the animalic consists in remaining at the level of feeling and being able to communicate only through feelings.[7]

If someone asked for a royal road to science, no road could be more comfortable than this: to rely on healthy common sense and, in order to progress with the times and with philosophy, to read reviews of philosophic essays, at most the prefaces and first paragraphs; for the latter offer the general principles, which are all-important, and the former, in addition to a historical notice, also some judgment which, being a judgment, goes beyond what is judged.[8] This vulgar road can be taken in one's dressing gown; but the elevated feeling of the eternal, the holy, and the infinite struts about in a high priest's robes—on a road that[9] itself is immediate being at the core, the genius of profound and original ideas and lofty flashes of inspiration.[10] Yet even as such profundity still does not reveal the fount of essence, so, too, such rockets are not yet the empyrean.[11] True thoughts and scientific insight are to be won only through the work of the Concept. This alone can produce the generality of knowledge which is neither the common vagueness and paltriness of common sense, but educated and complete knowledge, nor the uncommon generality of the disposition of reason that has corrupted itself through laziness and the conceit of genius, but truth that has developed into its native form—and is thus capable of being owned by all self-conscious reason.

⁶ "new confusions": Hegel says "new ones" which could also mean "new truths," in which case, of course, "truths" would be meant ironically. In context the sense of the passage remains unaffected by this ambiguity.

⁷ Once again Hegel returns to a theme introduced early in the preface. Cf. I.3, especially note ¹⁵. But this paragraph near the end is singularly eloquent in its insistence that irrationalism, whether religious or romantic, destroys "the roots of humanity." In the twentieth century it has become fashionable to associate Kierkegaard and existentialism with humanity and to consider Hegel the archetype of the inhuman thinker. Hegel himself sees reason and exoteric scientific procedures as the ground of humanity and points out that those who spurn reason are driven also to spurn communication with those who do not feel what they feel.

⁸ In his commentary on Euclid (Book II, Chapter 4), Proclus reports how Pharaoh Ptolemy I wanted to study geometry without going through the thirteen parts of Euclid's book; he wanted a short cut. But Euclid replied: "There is no royal road to geometry."

This passage makes use of two of Hegel's posthumously published "Aphorisms": "The usual royal road in philosophy is to read the prefaces and reviews in order to get an approximate notion of the matter" (⨯52). "The last royal road for the student is to think for himself" (⨯53).

⁹ Here one might interpolate: does not lead to but . . .

¹⁰ *Gedankenblitze:* see note ³ above.

¹¹ Here Hegel uses "Aphorism" ⨯9: "Even as there was a language of genius in poetry, the present seems to be the *philosophical period of geniuses.* A little carbon, oxygen, nitrogen, and hydrogen kneaded together [*zusammengeknetet*] and stuck into a piece of paper on which others have written about polarity, etc., rockets shot into the air with a wooden pigtail of vanity, they suppose that they represent the empyrean. Thus Görres, Wagner, *et al.* The crudest empiricism [*Empirie*] with the formalism of materials and poles, embellished with analogies devoid of reason and boozy [*besoffenen*] flashes of inspiration."

19. Conclusion: the author's relation to the public

[IV.3]

I find the distinctive mark of science in the self-movement of the Concept but have to admit that the above-mentioned, as well as several other peripheral, features of the notions of our time about the nature and form of truth are different and indeed quite opposed to my view. It would therefore seem that an attempt to present the System of Science from this point of view is not likely to meet with a favorable reception. But[1] there are other considerations. Occasionally, e.g., the excellence of Plato's philosophy was supposed to be due to his scientifically worthless myths; but there have also been times, which are even called times of wild enthusiasm, when Artistotle's philosophy was esteemed for its speculative profundity and Plato's *Parmenides,* probably the greatest work of art of ancient dialectic, was considered the true disclosure and the positive expression of the divine life, and in spite of the frequent turbidity of the products of ecstasy, this misunderstood ecstasy was in fact supposed to be nothing less than the pure Concept. Furthermore, what has excellence in the philosophy of our time finds its own value in being scientific; and although others understand this differently, it is only through this scientific posture that it actually gains credit.[1] Therefore I can also hope that this attempt to vindicate science for the Concept and to present it in this, its proper, element may win acceptance through the inner truth of the matter.

We must have the conviction that it is of the nature of truth to prevail when its time has come, and that truth appears only when its time has come—and therefore never appears too early, nor ever finds that the public is not ready for it.[2] And the individual needs public acceptance to prove the truth of what is as yet his solitary concern; he needs to see how the conviction that is as yet particular becomes general. But at this point the public must often be distinguished from those who act as if they were its representatives and spokesmen. In some respects the public behaves differently from these people, even in the opposite way. When a philosophical essay is not found appealing, the public may good-naturedly ascribe the fault to itself, but the others,[3] sure of their competence, ascribe the sole fault

IV.3. The philosopher and the public

[1] The passage from the first [1] to the second [1] forms a single sentence in the original. Hegel's tribute to Plato's *Parmenides,* which is amplified in Hegel's lectures on the history of philosophy, is in the Neoplatonic tradition and indebted to Proclus.

[2] This is reminiscent of an earlier passage in the preface: see the text for III.3, note [6]. But the present formulation is more extreme, and its strikingly untragic conclusion is plainly untenable. Hegel's later conception of world-historical individuals, of which note [28] in III.3 above gives at least some idea, is not quite so objectionable. Hegel's supreme confidence in the passage to which the present note refers is obviously based on his own case: he has no doubt that the time has come for his type of philosophy. And although he was then, at the age of thirty-six, still very little known, and though the first review of the *Phenomenology* did not appear until almost two full years after the publication of the book, Hegel's confidence was astonishingly justified within much less than two decades—to repeat, in his own case.

[3] Those who pose as spokesmen.

to the author. In the public the effect is quieter than the activity of these dead men when they bury their dead.[4]

The general level of insight now is more educated, curiosity is wide awake, and judgments are made more quickly than formerly; so the feet of them which shall carry thee out are already at the door.[5] But from this we must often distinguish the slower effect which corrects the attention that was extorted by imposing assurances as well as disdainful reproaches: some writers find an audience only after a time, while others after a time have none any more.[6]

In our time general participation in the life of the spirit has been greatly strengthened, and every particular, as is fitting, counts for that much less. Moreover, this vast public clings to and demands its full extent and the wealth of its education; so the share of the total work of the spirit that can be assigned to the activity of any individual has to be small. Hence the individual—and this is in any case in keeping with the nature of science—should forget himself that much more. To be sure, he should become and do what he can; but less should be demanded of him, even as he must expect less of himself and demand less for himself.[7]

⁴ "Follow me; and let the dead bury their dead" (Matthew 8:22). The would-be spokesmen are spiritually as dead as most of the books they review and bury.

⁵ "The feet of them which have buried thy husband are at the door, and shall carry thee out" (Acts 5:9). Hegel assumes as he is writing in his study that there is no dearth of people outside who are ready to bury his book as soon as it is published.

⁶ In the original this whole paragraph forms a single sentence which ends: ". . . *und einem Teile eine Mitwelt erst in einiger Zeit gibt, während ein anderer nach dieser keine Nachwelt mehr hat.*" *Mitwelt,* literally "with-world," and *Nachwelt,* literally "after-world," are common nouns that mean, respectively, one's contemporaries and coming generations. More literally, then, Hegel says that some are given a with-world only after a time (the tragic possibilities implicit in this admission are not noted expressly), while others, after a time, have no after-world any more.

⁷ The final paragraph also forms a single sentence in the original. It spells out another implication of Hegel's insistence that philosophy should attain the level of a science. While he is confident that the time has come for what he has to offer and that his philosophy will, after a while, gain wide acceptance, he does not infer from this that he himself is important. A philosopher should forget his own person, devote himself to his subject matter, "and do what he can."

CHAPTER IX:

"Who Thinks Abstractly?"

In the nineteenth-century edition of Hegel's *Werke,* this article (*Wer denkt abstrakt?*) appears in volume XVII, 400–5. Rosenkranz discusses it briefly (355 f.) and says that it shows "how much Hegel . . . entered into the Berlin manner."

Glockner reprints it in his edition of the *Werke* in vol. XX (1930), which is entitled: *Vermischte Schriften aus der Berliner Zeit.*[1] He includes it among "four *feuilletons* that Hegel wrote for local papers during the later years of his Berlin period." But Glockner admits: "The exact place of publication is unfortunately unknown to me" (xix).

Hoffmeister, whose critical edition of Hegel's *Berliner Schriften: 1818–1831* (1956) is much more comprehensive than Glockner's (800 pages versus 550), does not include this article. In a footnote he says that it belongs to Hegel's "Jena period (1807/08)" (xiii). This is an uncharacteristic slip: at the beginning of 1807 Hegel went to Bamberg, in 1808 to Nürnberg; and in the first weeks of 1807, before he left Jena, he certainly lacked the time and peace of mind to write this article.

Of Glockner's "four *feuilletons*" Hoffmeister retains only one, and that is really a letter to a newspaper, protesting their review of a new play. Hoffmeister gives no reasons for dating this article so much earlier than Rosenkranz and Glockner did. Possibly, the disparaging remark about Kotzebue (a German playwright, 1761–1819) suggests a date before Kotzebue was stabbed to death by a German theology student. That the piece was written in Jena seems

[1] "Diverse Writings of the Berlin Period."

most unlikely: it is so very different from the articles—and the *Phenomenology*—that Hegel wrote during his harassed and unhappy years in that city. But Hoffmeister could be right that it was written in 1807 or 1808.

WHO THINKS ABSTRACTLY?

TRANSLATION

Think? Abstractly?—*Sauve qui peut!* Let those who can save themselves! Even now I can hear a traitor, bought by the enemy, exclaim these words, denouncing this essay because it will plainly deal with metaphysics. For *metaphysics* is a word, no less than *abstract,* and almost *thinking* as well, from which everybody more or less runs away as from a man who has caught the plague.

But the intention here really is not so wicked, as if the meaning of thinking and of abstract were to be explained here. There is nothing the beautiful world finds as intolerable as explanations. I, too, find it terrible when somebody begins to explain, for when worst comes to worst I understand everything myself. Here the explanation of thinking and abstract would in any case be entirely superfluous; for it is only because the beautiful world knows what it means to be abstract that it runs away. Just as one does not desire what one does not know, one also cannot hate it. Nor is it my intent to try craftily to reconcile the beautiful world with thinking or with the abstract as if, under the semblance of small talk, thinking and the abstract were to be put over till in the end they had found their way into society incognito, without having aroused any disgust; even as if they were to be adopted imperceptibly by society, or, as the Swabians say, *hereingezäunselt,* before the author of this complication suddenly exposed this strange guest, namely the abstract, whom the whole party had long treated and recognized under a different title as if he were a good old acquaintance. Such scenes of recognition which are meant to instruct the world against its will have the inexcusable fault that they simultaneously humiliate, and the wirepuller tries with his artifice to gain a little fame; but this humiliation and this vanity destroy the effect, for they push away again an instruction gained at such a price.

In any case, such a plan would be ruined from the start, for it would require that the crucial word of the riddle is not spoken at the outset. But this has already happened in the title. If this essay toyed with such craftiness, these words should not have been allowed to enter right in the beginning; but like the cabinet member in a comedy, they should have been required to walk around during the entire play in their overcoat, unbuttoning it only in the last scene, disclosing the flashing star of wisdom. The unbuttoning of the metaphysical overcoat would be less effective, to be sure, than the unbuttoning of the minister's: it would bring to light no more than a couple of words, and the best part of the joke ought to be that it is shown that society has long been in possession of the matter itself; so what they would gain in the end would be the mere name, while the minister's star signifies something real—a bag of money.

That everybody present should know what thinking is and what is abstract is presupposed in good society, and we certainly are in good society. The question is merely *who* thinks abstractly. The intent, as already mentioned, is not to reconcile society with these things, to expect it to deal with something difficult, to appeal to its conscience not frivolously to neglect such a matter that befits the rank and status of beings gifted with reason. Rather it is my intent to reconcile the beautiful world with itself, although it does not seem to have a bad conscience about this neglect; still, at least deep down, it has a certain respect for abstract thinking as something exalted, and it looks the other way not because it seems too lowly but because it appears too exalted, not because it seems too mean but rather too noble, or conversely because it seems an *Espèce,* something special; it seems something that does not lend one distinction in general society, like new clothes, but rather something that—like wretched clothes, or rich ones if they are decorated with precious stones in ancient mounts or embroidery that, be it ever so rich, has long become quasi-Chinese—excludes one from society or makes one ridiculous in it.

Who thinks abstractly? The uneducated, not the educated. Good society does not think abstractly because it is too easy, because it is too lowly (not referring to the external status)—not from an empty affectation of nobility that would place itself above that of which it is not capable, but on account of the inward inferiority of the matter.

The prejudice and respect for abstract thinking are so great that sensitive nostrils will begin to smell some satire or irony at this point;

but since they read the morning paper they know that there is a prize to be had for satires and that I should therefore sooner earn it by competing for it than give up here without further ado.

I have only to adduce examples for my proposition: everybody will grant that they confirm it. A murderer is led to the place of execution. For the common populace he is nothing but a murderer. Ladies perhaps remark that he is a strong, handsome, interesting man. The populace finds this remark terrible: What? A murderer handsome? How can one think so wickedly and call a murderer handsome; no doubt, you yourselves are something not much better! This is the corruption of morals that is prevalent in the upper classes, a priest may add, knowing the bottom of things and human hearts.

One who knows men traces the development of the criminal's mind: he finds in his history, in his education, a bad family relationship between his father and mother, some tremendous harshness after this human being had done some minor wrong, so he became embittered against the social order—a first reaction to this that in effect expelled him and henceforth did not make it possible for him to preserve himself except through crime.—There may be people who will say when they hear such things: he wants to excuse this murderer! After all I remember how in my youth I heard a mayor lament that writers of books were going too far and sought to extirpate Christianity and righteousness altogether; somebody had written a defense of suicide; terrible, really too terrible!—Further questions revealed that *The Sufferings of Werther* [by Goethe, 1774] were meant.

This is abstract thinking: to see nothing in the murderer except the abstract fact that he is a murderer, and to annul all other human essence in him with this simple quality.

It is quite different in refined, sentimental circles—in Leipzig. There they strewed and bound flowers on the wheel and on the criminal who was tied to it.—But this again is the opposite abstraction. The Christians may indeed trifle with Rosicrucianism, or rather cross-rosism, and wreathe roses around the cross. The cross is the gallows and wheel that have long been hallowed. It has lost its one-sided significance of being the instrument of dishonorable punishment and, on the contrary, suggests the notion of the highest pain and the deepest rejection together with the most joyous rapture and divine honor. The wheel in Leipzig, on the other hand, wreathed with violets and poppies, is a reconciliation à la Kotzebue, a kind of slovenly sociability between sentimentality and badness.

In quite a different manner I once heard a common old woman who worked in a hospital kill the abstraction of the murderer and bring him to life for honor. The severed head had been placed on the scaffold, and the sun was shining. How beautifully, she said, the sun of God's grace shines on Binder's head!—You are not worthy of having the sun shine on you, one says to a rascal with whom one is angry. This woman saw that the murderer's head was struck by the sunshine and thus was still worthy of it. She raised it from the punishment of the scaffold into the sunny grace of God, and instead of accomplishing the reconciliation with violets and sentimental vanity, saw him accepted in grace in the higher sun.

Old woman, your eggs are rotten! the maid says to the market woman. What? she replies, my eggs rotten? You may be rotten! You say that about my eggs? You? Did not lice eat your father on the highways? Didn't your mother run away with the French, and didn't your grandmother die in a public hospital? Let her get a whole shirt instead of that flimsy scarf; we know well where she got that scarf and her hats: if it were not for those officers, many wouldn't be decked out like that these days, and if their ladyships paid more attention to their households, many would be in jail right now. Let her mend the holes in her stockings!—In brief, she does not leave one whole thread on her. She thinks abstractly and subsumes the other woman—scarf, hat, shirt, etc., as well as her fingers and other parts of her, and her father and whole family, too—solely under the crime that she has found the eggs rotten. Everything about her is colored through and through by these rotten eggs, while those officers of which the market woman spoke—if, as one may seriously doubt, there is anything to that—may have got to see very different things.

To move from the maid to a servant, no servant is worse off than one who works for a man of low class and low income; and he is better off the nobler his master is. The common man again thinks more abstractly, he gives himself noble airs vis-à-vis the servant and relates himself to the other man merely as to a servant; he clings to this one predicate. The servant is best off among the French. The nobleman is familiar with his servant, the Frenchman is his friend. When they are alone, the servant does the talking: see Diderot's *Jacques et son maître;* the master does nothing but take snuff and see what time it is and lets the servant take care of everything else. The nobleman knows that the servant is not merely a servant, but also knows the latest city news, the girls, and harbors good suggestions; he asks him about these matters, and the servant may say what he knows about these questions. With a French master, the servant may not only do this; he may also broach a subject, have his own opinions and insist on them; and when the master wants something, it is not done with an order but he has to argue and convince the servant of his opinion and add a good word to make sure that this opinion retains the upper hand.

In the army we encounter the same difference. Among the Austrians a soldier may be beaten, he is canaille; for whatever has the passive right to be beaten is canaille. Thus the common soldier is for the officer this *abstractum* of a beatable subject with whom a gentleman who has a uniform and *port d'epée* must trouble himself—and that could drive one to make a pact with the devil.

Bibliography

I. HEGEL BIBLIOGRAPHIES

The best bibliographies are long dated:

1. Benedetto Croce, *Lebendiges und Totes in Hegels Philosophie, mit einer Hegel-Bibliographie: Deutsche, vom Verfasser vermehrte Übersetzung von* K. Büchler, Heidelberg, Carl Winter, 1909. "Abriss einer Hegelschen Bibliographie," pp. 177–228. There are separate sections listing 10 Italian translations of Hegel's writings, 6 French, 13 English, and 3 Spanish ones. The literature about Hegel includes 83 German works of a general nature, 30 on the *Logic,* and over 80 on other special topics; followed by 73 Italian items, 46 French, 74 English, and 14 in other languages: 400 items *about* Hegel, altogether.

2. Friedrich Ueberweg, *Grundriss der Geschichte der Philosophie: Vierter Teil: Die deutsche Philosophie des XIX. Jahrhunderts und der Gegenwart,* ed. T. K. Oesterreich, 13th ed. (unchanged reprint of the 12th ed. of 1923), Basel, Benno Schwabe & Co., 1951. Bibliography of Hegel's writings, pp. 77–80; of writings about Hegel, pp. 678–81.

3. *Hegel und die Hegelianer: Eine Bibliothek,* Dr. Hellersberg Antiquariat & Verlag, (Berlin-) Charlottenburg, Knesebeckstr. 20/21, n.d. This library included 20 items of biographical interest; 153 works "on Hegel's system"; 39 "on Hegel's Logic"; and 117 on other special areas. The most recent items in this library were published in 1927.

The following bibliography, while more up-to-date, is much less comprehensive than these three. It stresses (A) the German editions of Hegel's collected works, (B) the editions of his collected letters, (C) single works published by Hegel himself, and (D) posthumously published "works." Under C and D the major editions have been listed; also the most important English translations. But not all recent reprints or partial translations were deemed worthy of inclusion, and translations into other languages are not listed. The main point is to show the reader what Hegel wrote, how the major editions differ, and what is available in English.

The list of works *about* Hegel (Part III) is confined to works cited in this volume and a few other books and articles that, for one reason or another, are likely to be of special interest to readers of this volume.

Current Hegel literature is listed periodically in *Hegel Studien*, ed. F. Nicolin and Otto Pöggeler, Bonn, H. Bouvier & Co., vol. I, 1961, vol. II, 1963; more to be published. Vol. II, 424–41, offers a list of German, Austrian, and Swiss *dissertations on Hegel*, from 1842–1960, in chronological order. There were only 12 dissertations before 1900, never more than one a year, except for two in 1898; 1900–9: 18; 1910–19: 17; 1920–32: 47; 1933–45: 39; 1946–60: 54. Total: 187.

See also *Hegel-Archiv*, ed. Georg Lasson, vols. I–II, Leipzig, 1912–14, and *Hegelkongress, Verhandlungen*, ed. B. Wigersma, vols. I–III, 1931, 1932, 1934.

Articles in the *Studien* and *Archiv* are not listed below as there are too many of them.

II. HEGEL'S WRITINGS

A. Hegel's Collected Works

1. *Werke: Vollständige Ausgabe durch einen Verein von Freunden des Verewigten*, 18 vols. (actually 21 since the *Encyclopädie* appeared in vols. VI, VII.1, and VII.2, and the *Aesthetik* in vols. X.1, X.2, and X.3), Berlin, Duncker und Humblot, 1832–45, 2d ed., partly revised, 1840–47. Students' lecture notes were used to supplement the texts of the *Encyclopädie* and *Philosophie des Rechts*, section by section, in the form of additions (*Zusätze*), and whole "works" not written by Hegel were constructed from lecture notes: see D below. Four such cycles of lectures fill 9 vols.; the notes covering Hegel's philosophy courses in the Nürnberg Gymnasium, another; and the above-mentioned additions comprise the equivalent of over 2 vols. In sum, less than half of the *Werke* were written by Hegel, who published only 4 books and a few essays and articles, as well as some long book reviews: see C below. For Hegel's letters, see B below.

2. *Sämtliche Werke: Jubiläumsausgabe in 20 Bänden*, ed. Hermann Glockner; Stuttgart, Frommann, 1927–30. A photostatic reprint of A.1, without any corrections or critical apparatus, but rearranged in chronological order. Supplemented by a very useful 4-vol. *Hegel-Lexikon*, 1935–39; 2d rev. ed. in 2 vols., thin paper, 1957 (much of the work on the *Hegel-Lexikon* was done by Frau Dr. Marie Glockner), and by *Dokumente zu Hegels Entwicklung*, ed. Johannes Hoffmeister, 1936; both also Frommanns Verlag. This is the most widely accessible "complete" edition. But the letters included in A.1 (see B below) are omitted.

3. *Sämtliche Werke: Kritische Ausgabe,* begun by Georg Lasson, continued after his death (1932) by Johannes Hoffmeister, and after *his* death (1955) by several other editors; published by Felix Meiner, Hamburg. Since Lasson re-edited the *Encyclopädie* (1905) and the *Phänomenologie* (1907), the editions have gradually become more and more exacting philologically. The early volumes were conceived as separate single volumes within the framework of Meiner's Philosophische Bibliothek; by the 1920s the pages facing the title pages announced *Sämtliche Werke* and the announcements of other volumes in the back referred to a *kritische Gesamtausgabe.* Some works have by now been published in several different critical editions, the latest being generally the best, except that in a few instances valuable editorial prefaces have been deleted. This edition is still *incomplete.* For details see C and D below.

4. A new critical edition in larger format is projected. The plan calls for 35 volumes, including 4 volumes of correspondence and one index volume. Cf. Friedhelm Nicolin, "Die neue Hegel-Gesamtausgabe: Vorraussetzungen und Ziele" in *Hegel-Studien,* vol. I (1961), 295–313.

B. Letters

1. The first selection appeared in A.1, vol. XVII, 473–634.

2. This was superseded by A.1, vols. XIX.1 and XIX.2: *Briefe von und an Hegel,* ed. Karl Hegel; Leipzig, Duncker und Humblot, 1887.

3. This, too, was superseded by *Briefe von und an Hegel,* published as vols. XXVII–XXX of A.3: vol. I: 1785–1812 (1952), vol. II: 1813–22 (1953), vol. III: 1823–31 (1954)—all ed. by Johannes Hoffmeister. Vol. IV: *Nachträge, Dokumente, Personenregister* (1960), ed. Rolf Flechsig. All published by Felix Meiner, like A.3. I, 433–515, II, 371–508, III, 365–475, and IV, 139–78, comprise editorial notes, and IV, 179–327, an annotated index of persons. These four volumes are an invaluable contribution to Hegel scholarship.

C. Single Works Published by Hegel Himself

Asterisks mark Hegel's four major works. The references at the end of many entries, which are preceded by an H, are to the Sections or, if expressly indicated, the Chapters of the present work in which the item is discussed; but in this connection the Contents and Index should also be consulted.

1. *Vertrauliche Briefe über das vormalige staatsrechtliche Verhältnis des Waadtlandes (Pays de Vaud) zur Stadt Bern: Aus dem Französischen eines verstorbenen Schweizers.* Anonymously translated by Hegel, with preface and notes. Frankfurt [Jägersche Buchhandlung], 1798. Pp. 212. (H 11)

2. *Differenz des Fichte'schen und Schelling'schen Systems der Philosophie in Beziehung auf Reinhold's Beyträge zur leichtern Übersicht des Zustands der Philosophie zu Anfang des neunzehnten Jahrhunderts, 1 stes Heft.* Jena, in der akademischen Buchhandlung bei Seidler, 1801. Reprinted: A.1, vol. I; A.2, vol. I; and in *Erste Druckschriften,* ed. Georg Lasson, 1928. (H 14)

3. *Dissertatio philosophica de Orbitis Planetarum.* Jena, 1801. Reprinted: A.1, vol. XVI; A.2, vol. I; *Erste Druckschriften.* (H 15)

4. *Dissertationi Philosophicae de Orbitis Planetarum Praemissae Theses . . . Publice Defendet Die XXVII. Aug. a. MDCCCI.* Jena [1801]. Reprinted: *Erste Druckschriften.* (H 15)

5. "Über das Wesen der philosophischen Kritik überhaupt, und ihr Verhältnis zum gegenwärtigen Zustand der Philosophie insbesondere," *Kritisches Journal der Philosophie,* ed. Schelling and Hegel, I.1 (1802). Reprinted: A.1, vol. XVI; A.2, vol. I; *Erste Druckschriften.* (H 16)

6. "Wie der gemeine Menschenverstand die Philosophie nehme,— dargestellt an den Werken des Herrn Krug's," *Krit. Journal,* I.1 (1802). Reprinted like C.5. (H 17)

7. "Verhältnis des Skeptizismus zur Philosophie, Darstellung seiner Modifikationen, und Vergleichung des neuesten mit dem alten." *Krit. Journal,* I.2 (1802). Reprinted like C.5. (H 18)

7a. "Über das Verhältnis der Naturphilosophie zur Philosophie überhaupt." *Krit. Journal,* I.3 (1802). Reprinted A.1, vol. XVI. Claimed for Hegel by his early editors, but in fact written by Schelling.

8. "Glauben und Wissen oder die Reflexionsphilosophie der Subjectivität in der Vollständigkeit ihrer Formen, als Kantische, Jacobische, und Fichtesche Philosophie." *Krit. Journal,* II.1 (1802). Reprinted: A.1, vol. I; A.2, vol. I; *Erste Druckschriften.* (H 20)

9. "Über die wissenschaftlichen Behandlungsarten des Naturrechts, seine Stelle in der praktischen Philosophie und sein Verhältnis zu den positiven Rechtswissenschaften." *Krit. Journal,* II.2/3 (1802/3). Reprinted: A.1, vol. I; A.2, vol. I; and in *Schriften zur Politik und Rechtsphilosophie,* ed. Georg Lasson, 1913; 2d (almost identical) ed., 1923. (H 21)

10. Four short reviews in *Erlanger Literaturzeitung.*
    a. *Anfangsgründe der spekulativen Philosophie: Versuch eines Lehrbuchs* von Fried. Bouterwek (1800). Sept. 15 and 16, 1801. Reprinted in Lasson, *Beiträge zur Hegel-Forschung* (1909) and in *Erste Druckschriften,* 131–42.
    b. *Entwurf eines neuen Organons der Philosophie, oder Versuch über die Prinzipien der philosophischen Erkenntnis* von Wilh. Traug. Krug (1801). June 4, 1802. Reprinted twice by Lasson, like a. Pp. 159–60.

c. *Kurze wissenschaftliche Darlegung der Unhaltbarkeit—sowohl des transzend. ideal. Systems von Fichte, als auch des Systems der eiteln Grundlehre—und des kritischen Systems—usw.* von J. Fr. C. Werneburg (1800). *Versuchte, kurze, fassliche Vorschilderung der Allwissenschaftslehre, oder alleinigen sogenannten Philosophie und fasslichere Darstellung der Grundlosigkeit beider extrematischer Systeme des Idealismus und des Dogmatismus usw.* von D. J. Fr. C. Werneburg (1800). April 9, 1802. Reprinted twice by Lasson, like a. Pp. 212–14.

d. *Versuch einer gemeinfasslichen Deduktion des Rechtsbegriffs aus den höchsten Gründen des Wissens als Grundlage zu einem künftigen System der Philosophie des Rechts* von K. Fr. Wilh. Gerstäcker (1801). April 28, 1802. Reprinted twice by Lasson, like a. Pp. 214–19.

*11. *System der Wissenschaft: Erster Teil, die Phänomenologie des Geistes.* Bamberg und Würzburg, bei Joseph Anton Goebhardt, 1807. Reprinted: A.1, vol. II; A.2, vol. II; ed. Lasson, Leipzig, Verlag der Dürr'schen Buchhandlung, 1907; ed. G. J. P. J. Bolland, Leiden, 1907; ed. Hoffmeister, 1952.

NOTE: Just before his death, Hegel made minor revisions for a planned second edition but got only through the early pages of the preface. A.1 and A.2 embody the revisions; so does Lasson, but he lists the variants in the back. Kaufmann's commentary calls attention to interesting differences.

ENGLISH: *The Phenomenology of Mind,* tr. J. B. Baillie, 2 vols., London & New York, 1910; 2d rev. ed. in 1 vol., London, George Allen & Unwin, New York, The Macmillan Co., 1931. Preface, with commentary, tr. Walter Kaufmann: H Chapter VIII. (H Chapter III)

*12. *Wissenschaft der Logik. Erster Band: Die objective Logik.* Nürnberg, bey Johann Leonhard Schrag, 1812. *Erster Band: Die objective Logik. Zweytes Buch: Die Lehre vom Wesen. Ibid.,* 1813 (this date is generally given wrongly as 1812). *Zweiter Band: Die subjective Logik oder Lehre vom Begriff. Ibid.,* 1816. (This is the wording of the left page, omitted in part of the edition. The facing title page reads:) *Wissenschaft der subjectiven Logik oder die Lehre vom Begriff. Ibid.,* 1816. Reprinted: A.1, vols. III–V; A.2, vols. IV–V; ed. Lasson, 2 vols., 1923.

NOTE: Just before his death, Hegel made very considerable changes for a planned second edition and got through the 1812 volume. The rare original edition has never been reprinted or translated, nor does any edition list the variants. In Chapter IV, above, all citations are based on comparisons with the first edition, and interesting differences are duly noted. The volumes of 1813 and 1816 are not affected.

ENGLISH: *Science of Logic,* tr. W. H. Johnston and L. G. Struthers, 2 vols., London, Allen & Unwin, 1929. Partial tr. (of the last third only) by H. S. Macran: *Hegel's Doctrine of Formal Logic, being a translation of the first section of the Subjective Logic,* Oxford, Clarendon Press,

1912, and *Hegel's Logic of World and Idea, being a translation of the second and third parts of the Subjective Logic, ibid.*, 1929. (H Chapter IV)

*13. *Encyklopädie der philosophischen Wissenschaften im Grundrisse. Zum Gebrauch seiner Vorlesungen.* Heidelberg, in August Osswald's Universitätsbuchhandlung, 1817. Pp. xvi, 288. Second completely rev. ed., *ibid.*, 1827. Pp. xlii, 544. Third rev. ed., Heidelberg, Verwaltung des Osswaldischen Verlags (C. F. Winter), with the words "Im Vereins-Verlage" pasted over the old publisher's name, 1830. Pp. lviii, 600. Reprinted: 1st ed. in A.2, vol. VI; 2d ed.: *never;* 3d. ed.: ed. Rosenkranz, Berlin, 1845 and 1878, ed. Lasson, 1905 and 1911, superior critical ed. by Friedhelm Nicolin and Otto Pöggeler, 1959. Third ed., with extensive additions, based on students' lecture notes and marked as *Zusätze,* in 3 vols., in A.1, vols. VI, VII.1, VII.2; in A.2, vols. VIII–X; and in a single volume, ed. G. J. P. J. Bolland, with many editorial footnotes, Leiden, A. H. Adriani, 1906. Pp. lxxvi, 1072.

ENGLISH: Part I: *The Logic of Hegel,* tr. William Wallace, Oxford, Clarendon Press, 1874; 2d rev. ed., *ibid.*, 1892. Part II (Philosophy of Nature): *never.* Part III: *Hegel's Philosophy of Mind, ibid.*, 1894. *Encyclopedia of Philosophy, translated and annotated by* Gustav Emil Mueller, New York, Philosophical Library, 1959, contains an informed essay on Hegel (31 pp.) but, as the "Translator's Note" (7 pp.) explains, not really a translation. Here 25 lines are rendered in 3, there 71 in 10; §§230–59 of the Philosophy of Nature are dismissed in 11 lines; etc. Moreover, usually the edition of 1817 is paraphrased, often that of 1830, occasionally additions from the posthumous edition. (H Chapter V)

14. Two major reviews in *Heidelbergische Jahrbücher der Literatur.* The dates indicate when the reviews appeared.
    a. "Ueber Friedr. Heinr. Jacobi's *Werke: Erster Band.*" 1813. Reprinted: A.1, XVI, 203–18. This review is not by Hegel but by E. von Meyer.
    b. "Ueber Friedr. Heinr. Jacobi's *Werke: Dritter Band.*" 1817. Reprinted: A.1, XVII, 3–37; A.2, VI.
    c. "Beurteilung der im Druck erschienenen Verhandlungen in der Versammlung der Landstände des Königreichs Würtemberg im Jahre 1815 und 1816." 1817. Reprinted in A.1, XVI, 219–360; A.2, VI; *Schriften zur Politik und Rechtsphilosophie* (see C.9 above).

ENGLISH: partial translation of c. in *Hegel's Political Writings,* tr. T. M. Knox, with an introductory essay by Z. A. Pelczynski, Oxford, Clarendon Press, 1964.

*15. *Naturrecht und Staatswissenschaft im Grundrisse. Zum Gebrauch für seine Vorlesungen.* (Facing right page:) *Grundlinien der Philosophie des Rechts.* Berlin, 1821. In der Nicolaischen Buchhandlung. Reprinted:

A.1, vol. VIII; A.2, vol. VII; both with Eduard Gans's additions (*Zusätze*) based on Hegel's lectures. Lasson followed their example. Hoffmeister's ed. (1955) omits the additions but offers (pp. 299–430) Hegel's manuscript comments on his text in his own copy.

ENGLISH: *The Ethics of Hegel: Translated Selections from his "Rechtsphilosophie,"* tr. with an introduction by J. Macbride Sterrett, Boston, Ginn & Co., 1893; *Philosophy of Right,* tr. S. W. Dyde, London, George Bell & Sons, 1896; *Philosophy of Right,* tr. with notes by T. M. Knox, Oxford, Clarendon Press, 1942 (with Gans's additions in the back, pp. 224–97, and translator's notes, pp. 298–376). Knox's translation is by far the best.

16. *Vorrede.* In H. Fr. W. Hinrichs, *Die Religion im inneren Verhältnisse zur Wissenschaft.* Heidelberg, 1822, pp. i–xxviii. Reprinted: A.1, vol. XVII; A.2, vol. XX; *Berliner Schriften, 1818–1831,* ed. Hoffmeister, 1956.

17. Seven major book reviews in *Jahrbücher für wissenschaftliche Kritik,* all reprinted in A.1, vols. XVI and XVII; in A.2, vol. XX; and in *Berliner Schriften* (see C. 16). Each title is followed by the year of publication of the review and by the page numbers in *Berliner Schriften.*

   a. *Über die unter dem Namen Bhagavad-Gita bekannte Episode des Mahabharata von Wilhelm von Humboldt.* 1827. 85–154.

   b. *Solgers Nachgelassene Schriften und Briefwechsel.* 1828. 155–220.

   c. *Hamanns Schriften.* 1828. 221–94. Reprint in A.1 and A.2 was incomplete.

   d. *Aphorismen über Nichtwissen und absolutes Wissen im Verhältnis zur christlichen Glaubenserkenntnis: Ein Beitrag zum Verständnis der Philosophie unserer Zeit* von Carl Friedrich G[ösche]l. 1829. 295–329.

   e. *Über die Hegelsche Lehre oder: Absolutes Wissen und Moderner Pantheismus.* And: *Über Philosophie überhaupt und Hegels Enzyklopädie der philosophischen Wissenschaften insbesondere: Ein Beitrag zur Beurteilung der letztern* von Dr. K. E. Schubarth und Dr. L. Carganico. 1829. 330–402. Several other titles are listed at the head of this review but not discussed in it.

   f. *Der Idealrealismus. Erster Teil auch unter dem besonderen Titel: Der Idealrealismus als Metaphysik in die Stelle des Idealismus und Realismus gesetzt.* Von Dr. Alb. Leop. Jul. Ohlert. 1831. 403–21.

   g. *Über Grundlage, Gliederung und Zeitenfolge der Weltgeschichte: Drei Vorträge* von J. Görres. 1831. 422–47.

18. "Über die englische Reformbill." In *Allgemeine Preussische Staatszeitung,* 1831. Reprinted: A.1, vol. XVII; A.2, vol. XX; *Berliner Schriften.*

ENGLISH: tr. T. M. Knox in *Hegel's Political Writings* (see C.14.c above).

19. Very short pieces:
   a. "Wer denkt abstrakt?" Place of original publication unknown. Reprinted: A.1, vol. XVII; A.2, vol. XX. English: tr. Walter Kaufmann: H Chapter IX: see *ibid.* about the date.
   b. "Über Wallenstein." Originally published in *Schnellpost,* ed. Moritz Gottlieb Saphir (1795–1858); reprinted like 19.a. Hoffmeister, *Berliner Schriften,* p. xiii, claims that Glockner's inclusion of 19.a and b in *his* ed. of *Berliner Schriften* (i.e., A.2, vol. XX) was a mistake, and that this essay was written in Frankfurt in 1800. 2 pp.
   c. "Über Lessings Briefwechsel mit seiner Frau." Place of original publication unknown. Reprinted like 19.a. 4 pp.
   d. "Über die Bekehrten. (Antikritisches.)" *Berliner Schnellpost,* 1826; ♯8, 9; *Beiwagen zur Berliner Schnellpost,* ♯4. Dated January 11, 1826. Reprinted like 19.a, also in *Berliner Schriften,* ed. Hoffmeister, pp. 451–60.

D. Posthumously Published "Works"

1. *Hegels theologische Jugendschriften, nach den Handschriften der Kgl. Bibliothek in Berlin,* ed. Herman Nohl, Tübingen, Mohr (Paul Siebeck), 1907. A careful edition of some exceptionally interesting early essays and drafts, not intended for publication by Hegel: I. "Volksreligion und Christentum," II. "Das Leben Jesu," III. "Die Positivität der christlichen Religion," IV. "Der Geist des Christentums und sein Schicksal," V. "Systemfragment von 1800." Pp. xii, 405.

ENGLISH: *Early Theological Writings,* tr. T. M. Knox, with an introduction (66 pp.) and Fragments Translated by Richard Kroner, The University of Chicago Press, 1948. Paperback ed., unrev. but with the title: *On Christianity: Early Theological Writings by Friedrich Hegel,* New York, Harper Torchbooks, 1961. Items I and II have *not* been translated. (H 8–10, 12)

2. *Kritik der Verfassung Deutschlands, aus dem handschriftlichen Nachlass,* ed. Georg Mollat, Kassel, 1893. Reprinted: as a companion vol. to A.2, 1935. Critical ed.: *Die Verfassung Deutschlands,* in *Schriften zur Politik und Rechtsphilosophie,* ed. Lasson 1913, 2d ed., 1923.

ENGLISH: "The German Constitution," tr. T. M. Knox (on the basis of Lasson's 2d ed.), in *Hegel's Political Writings* (see C.14.c above). (H 21)

3. *System der Sittlichkeit, aus dem handschriftlichen Nachlass,* ed. Georg Mollat, Osterwieck, 1893. Critical ed. in *Schriften zur Politik und Rechtsphilosophie* (like D.2, above). (H 21)

4. *Jenenser Logik, Metaphysik und Naturphilosophie, aus dem Manuskript* ed. Lasson, 1923. Drafts for a system, antedating the *Phenomenology.*

5. *Jenenser Realphilosophie*, I: *Die Vorlesungen von 1803/04, aus dem Manuskript*, ed. Hoffmeister, 1932. Contains: "Hegels Naturphilosophie von 1803," pp. 1–191; "Hegels erste Philosophie des Geistes von 1803/ 04," pp. 193–241; fragments, pp. 243–70; and apparatus, pp. 271–84.

6. *Jenenser Realphilosophie*, II: *Die Vorlesungen von 1805/06, aus dem Manuskript*, ed. Hoffmeister, 1931. Contains: "Naturphilosophie," pp. 1–176; and "Geistesphilosophie," pp. 177–273.

7. *Nürnberger Schriften: Texte, Reden, Berichte und Gutachten zum Nürnberger Gymnasialunterricht: 1806–1816*, ed. Hoffmeister, 1938. Pp. xxxvi, 499. This volume supersedes *Philosophische Propädeutik*, ed. Rosenkranz, A.1, XVIII, 1840, pp. 205; also A.2, III: *Philosophische Propädeutik, Gymnasialreden und Gutachten über den Philosophieunterricht*, pp. 335; also "Fünf Gymnasial-Reden, gehalten zu Nürnberg" in A.1, XVI, 133–99.

ENGLISH: "Hegel's Propädeutik, translated, with commentary," by W. T. Harris, in *The Journal of Speculative Philosophy*, vols. III–IV.

8. *Berliner Schriften* (see C.16–19) also contains the texts of 4 speeches, 9 "Gutachten und Stellungnahmen," material from the files concerning 15 habilitations (including Schopenhauer's) and 8 doctorates, as well as 5 topics for prize essays, and 65 pages of excerpts and notes.

9. *Vorlesungen über die Philosophie der Geschichte*, ed. Eduard Gans, 1837; 2d rev. ed. by Karl Hegel, 1840; 3d ed. by Karl Hegel, 1843— all in A.1, IX; Karl Hegel's ed. reprinted: A.2, XI.

ENGLISH: *Lectures on the Philosophy of History*, tr. from the 3d German ed. by J. Sibree, 1858; often reprinted both in hard covers and in paperback.

Entirely new ed. in 4 vols., ed. Lasson, 1917–20. Vol. I: *Die Vernunft in der Geschichte: Einleitung in die Philosophie der Weltgeschichte*, 2d enlarged ed., 1920; 3d rev. ed., 1930; 4th ed., not rev., 1944; 5th rev. ed. by Hoffmeister, 1955, reprinted 1963. Vol. II: *Die orientalische Welt;* III: *Die griechische und römische Welt;* IV: *Die germanische Welt.* My discussion of vol. I is based on Hoffmeister's ed.

ENGLISH: *Untranslated. Reason in History*, tr. Robert S. Hartman, New York, Liberal Arts Press, 1953, is *not* a translation of *Die Vernunft in der Geschichte* but follows Karl Hegel's 2d ed. "with a few exceptions," interpolating in places of the editor's choosing some passages from Lasson's 1917 ed. It is thus not a translation of any one German book. The translations of "Selections from the Philosophy of History" in *The Philosophy of Hegel*, ed. Carl J. Friedrich, New York, Modern Library, are based partly on Lasson's 1920 ed., partly "upon Sibree's old translation which followed the German of Karl Hegel." (H 59–65)

10. *Vorlesungen über die Aesthetik*, ed. H. G. Hotho, A.1, X.1, X.2, X.3, 1835, 1837, 1838; 2d slightly rev. ed., 1842. Reprinted: A.2, XII–XIV.

ENGLISH: *The Philosophy of Fine Art*, tr. F. P. B. Osmaston, 4 vols., London, G. Bell & Sons, 1920.

Critical ed. (incomplete): *Erster Halbband: Einleitung und Erster Teil, 1. Abteilung: Die Idee und Das Ideal,* ed. Lasson, 1931.

11. *Vorlesungen über die Philosophie der Religion, nebst einer Schrift über die Beweise vom Dasein Gottes,* ed. Philipp Marheineke, A.1, XI–XII. Reprinted: ed. G. J. P. J. Bolland, Leiden, 1901; A.2, XV–XVI.
ENGLISH: *Lectures on the Philosophy of Religion, Together with a Work on the Proofs of the Existence of God,* tr. from the 2d German ed. by the Rev. E. B. Speirs, B.D., and J. Burdon Sanderson, 3 vols., London, Kegan Paul, Trench, Trübner, & Co., 1895.
Critical ed., *nach den vorhandenen Manuskripten vollständig neu herausgegeben von* Lasson: *Begriff der Religion,* 1925; *Die Naturreligion,* 1927; *Die Religion der geistigen Individualität,* 1927.

12. *Vorlesungen über die Geschichte der Philosophie,* ed. Karl Ludwig Michelet, A.1, XIII–XV. Reprinted: ed. G. J. P. J. Bolland, Leiden, 1908; A.2, XVII–XIX.
ENGLISH: *Lectures on the History of Philosophy,* tr. Elizabeth S. Haldane and Frances Simson, London, Kegan Paul, Trench, Trübner, & Co. 1892–96.
Critical ed. of the introductory lectures only: *Einleitung: System und Geschichte der Philosophie, vollständig neu nach den Quellen herausgegeben* von Hoffmeister, 1940, reprinted 1944 and 1959. In 1959 the title was changed to *Einleitung in die Geschichte der Philosophie,* and F. Nicolin substituted a few short *Vorbemerkungen* (ix–xvii) for Hoffmeister's interesting preface (i–xliv). (H 66–67)

III. WRITINGS ABOUT HEGEL

Avineri, Shlomo, "The Problem of War in Hegel's Thought" in *Journal of the History of Ideas,* 1961 (XXII.4), pp. 463–74.
————, "Hegel and Nationalism" in *The Review of Politics,* October 1962 (XXIV.4), pp. 461–84.
————, "Hegel's Views on Jewish Emancipation" in *Jewish Social Studies,* April 1963 (XXV.2), pp. 145–51.

Baillie, J. B., *The Origin and Significance of Hegel's Logic: A General Introduction to Hegel's System,* London & New York, 1901.

Barion, Jakob, *Hegel und die marxistische Staatslehre,* Bonn, 1963.

Bauer, Bruno (anonymous), *Die Posaune des jüngsten Gerichts wider Hegel, den Atheisten und Antichristen,* Leipzig, 1841.
————, *Hegels Lehre von Religion und Kunst,* Leipzig, 1842.

Bergmann, Frithjof, "Harmony and Reason: An Introduction to the Philosophy of Hegel," unpublished dissertation, Princeton, 1960.

————, "The Purpose of Hegel's System" in *Journal of the History of Philosophy,* 1964 (II.2), pp. 189–204.

Beyer, Wilhelm R., *Zwischen Phänomenologie und Logik: Hegel als Redakteur der Bamberger Zeitung*, Frankfurt, 1955.

Biemel, Walter, "Das Wesen der Dialektik bei Hegel und Sartre" in *Tijdschrift voor Philosophie*, 1958 (2), pp. 269–300.

Bloch, Ernst, *Subjekt-Objekt: Erläuterungen zu Hegel*, Berlin, 1951.

Bosanquet, Bernard, *A History of Aesthetic*, London, 1892; 2d ed., 1904; paperback ed. Meridian Books, 1957, pp. 334–62, 471–87.

Bradley, A. C., "Hegel's Theory of Tragedy" in *Oxford Lectures on Poetry*, London, 1909, pp. 69–95.

Carrit, E. F., "Discussion: Hegel and Prussianism" in *Philosophy*, April 1940, pp. 190–96; July 1940, pp. 315–17. See Knox, below.

Collingwood, R. G., *The Idea of History*, Oxford, 1946, pp. 113–26.

Croce, Benedetto, *Ciò che è vivo e ciò che è morto della filosofia di Hegel;* Bari, 1907. German tr.: see above, I.1. English: *What is Living and What is Dead of the Philosophy of Hegel,* tr. from the 3d Italian ed., 1912, by Douglas Ainslie, London, 1915.

Derbolav, Josef, "Die kritische Hegelrezeption des jungen Marx und das Problem der Emanzipation des Menschen" in *Studium Generale*, 1962 (XV.4), pp. 271–88.
——————, "Hegel und die Sprache" in *Sprache—Schlüssel zur Welt: Festschrift für Leo Weisgerber*, Düsseldorf, 1959, pp. 56–86.

Dilthey, Wilhelm, *Die Jugendgeschichte Hegels*, Berlin, 1906; reprinted in Dilthey's *Gesammelte Schriften*, IV, Leipzig & Berlin, 1921.

Easton, Lloyd D., "Alienation and History in the Early Marx" in *Philosophy and Phenomenological Research*, 1961 (XXII.2), pp. 193–205.
——————, "Hegelianism in Nineteenth-Century Ohio" in *Journal of the History of Ideas*, 1962 (XXIII.3), pp. 355–78.

Feuerbach, Ludwig, *Philosophie und Christenheit in Beziehung auf die der hegelschen Philosophie gemachten Vorwürfe der Unchristlichkeit*, Mannheim, 1839.

Findlay, J. N., *Hegel: A Re-examination*, London & New York, 1958; paperback reprint, Collier Books, 1962.

Fischer, Kuno, *Hegels Leben, Werke und Lehre*, 2 vols., Heidelberg, 1901; 2d ed., Heidelberg, 1911, with new appendix by Hugo Falkenheim and Georg Lasson.
——————, *Schellings Leben, Werke und Lehre*, 2d rev. ed., especially pp. 145 f., 208 ff., 215 ff., 829 f., Heidelberg, 1899.

Fleischmann, Eugène, *La philosophie politique de Hegel, sous forme d'un commentaire des Fondements de la philosophie du droit,* Paris, 1964.

Foster, Michael B., *The Political Philosophies of Plato and Hegel,* Oxford, 1935.

Franklin, Mitchell, "On Hegel's Theory of Alienation and Its Historic Force" in *Studies in Hegel* (Tulane Studies in Philosophy, vol. IX), New Orleans, 1960, pp. 50–100. The same volume contains shorter contributions by A. B. Brinkley, J. K. Feibleman, P. G. Morrison, A. J. Reck, R. C. Whittemore, and E. G. Ballard.

Friedrich, Carl J., "Introduction" in *The Philosophy of Hegel,* ed. Carl J. Friedrich, pp. xiii–lxiv, New York, Modern Library. See also under Travis, below.

Fuhrmans, Horst, "Schelling und Hegel: Ihre Entfremdung" in F. W. J. Schelling, *Briefe und Dokumente,* vol. I: 1775–1809, ed. Horst Fuhrmans, pp. 451–553, Bonn, 1962.

Garaudy, Roger, *Dieu est mort: Étude sur Hegel,* Paris, 1962.

Glockner, Hermann, *Hegel,* 2 vols., Stuttgart, 1929, 1940; I: *Die Voraussetzungen der Hegelschen Philosophie;* II: *Entwicklung und Schicksal der Hegelschen Philosophie.* 3d ed. with new preface, 1954.

Göschel, Karl Friedrich, *Hegel und seine Zeit. Mit Rücksicht auf Göthe,* Berlin, 1832. Cf. above, II.C.17.d.

Gray, J. Glenn, *Hegel's Hellenic Ideal,* New York, 1941.

Haering, Theodor, *Hegel: Sein Wollen und sein Werk: Eine chronologische Entwicklungsgeschichte der Gedanken und der Sprache Hegels,* 2 vols., Leipzig & Berlin, 1929, 1938.
————, "Die Entstehungsgeschichte der Phänomenologie des Geistes" in *Verhandlungen des dritten Hegelkongresses vom 19. bis 23. April 1933 in Rom:* Im Auftrag des Internationalen Hegelbundes, ed. B. Wigersma; Tübingen & Haarlem, 1934, pp. 118–38.

Harris, William T., *Hegel's Logic, A Book on the Genesis of the Categories of the Mind: A Critical Exposition,* Chicago, 1890, 2d ed., 1895. "A Selection of Books on Hegel's Philosophy for the English Reader" (pp. xxix–xxx) includes an itemized list of the many "Translations from Hegel's works" in *The Journal of Speculative Philosophy.*
————, *Hegel's First Principle: An Exposition of Comprehension and Idea (Begriff und Idee),* tr. from the German (from the *Philosophische Propädeutik*) and accompanied with an Introduction and Explanatory Notes, St. Louis, 1869.

Hartmann, Klaus, *Grundzüge der Ontologie Sartres in ihrem Verhältnis zu Hegels Logik,* Berlin, 1963.

Hartmann, Nicolai, *Hegel* (*Die Philosophie des deutschen Idealismus, II. Teil*), Berlin & Leipzig, 1929.

Haym, Rudolf, *Hegel und seine Zeit: Vorlesungen über Entstehung und Entwickelung, Wesen und Wert der Hegel'schen Philosophie*, Berlin, 1857; unchanged, photo-mechanical reprint, Hildesheim, 1962; 2d ed., incl. a letter from Haym to Rosenkranz (pp. 471–75) and Haym's essay "An Hegels 100. Geburtstag" (pp. 476–85), as well as Hans Rosenberg's "Zur Geschichte der Hegelauffassung" (pp. 510–50), Leipzig, 1927.

Heidegger, Martin, "Hegels Begriff der Erfahrung" in *Holzwege*, Frankfurt, 1952.

——————, "Hegel und die Griechen" in *Die Gegenwart der Griechen im neueren Denken: Festschrift für H. G. Gadamer*, pp. 43–57, Tübingen, 1960.

Herbart, Johann Friedrich, reviews of Hegel's *Philosophie des Rechts* in *Leipziger Literaturzeitung*, 1822, and of Hegel's *Enzyklopädie* of 1827 in *Hallesche Literaturzeitung*, 1831, both reprinted in Herbart's *Werke*, vol. XII (1852), pp. 419–35 and 664–86.

Hibben, John Grier, *Hegel's Logic: An Essay in Interpretation*, New York, 1902.

Hoffmeister, Johannes, *Goethe und der deutsche Idealismus: Eine Einführung zu Hegel's Realphilosophie*, Leipzig, 1932. (His introductions to his editions of Hegel's writings are also noteworthy; see Part II of this Bibliography, above.)

Hook, Sidney, *From Hegel to Marx: Studies in the Intellectual Development of Karl Marx*, New York, 1936; reprinted, New York, 1950. See also under Travis, below.

Hotho, H. G., *Vorstudien für Leben und Kunst*, Stuttgart & Tübingen, 1835.

Hyppolite, Jean, *Genèse et structure de la Phénoménologie de l'esprit de Hegel*, Paris, 1946.

——————, *Introduction à la philosophie de l'histoire de Hegel*, Paris, 1948.

——————, *Logique et existence: Essai sur la Logique de Hegel*, Paris, 1953.

——————, *Études sur Marx et Hegel*, Paris, 1955.

Iljin, Iwan, *Die Philosophie Hegels als kontemplative Gotteslehre*, Bern, 1946.

Jakowenko, Boris, "Hegel in Russland" in *Der Russische Gedanke: Internationale Zeitschrift*, 1931 (II.3), pp. 1–8, incl. "Kurze russische Hegel-Bibliographie," pp. 5–8.

James, William, "Hegel and His Method" in *A Pluralistic Universe,*
Lecture III, New York, London, Toronto, 1909; reprinted, 1943.

Kaufmann, Walter, *Nietzsche* (comparison of Hegel's and Nietzsche's
methods and views of systems in Ch. II, and of Hegel's concept of
Geist with Nietzsche's will to power in Ch. VIII), Princeton, 1950;
rev. paperback ed., Meridian Books, 1956.
————————, "The Hegel Myth and Its Method" and "Hegel's Early
Antitheological Phase" in *The Philosophical Review,* Oct. 1951 (LX.4)
and Jan. 1954 (LXIII.1). German tr. of the former, with a new
section, in *Zeitschrift für philosophische Forschung,* 1956 (X.2).
Both articles rev. and greatly enlarged in *From Shakespeare to Existentialism* (Chs. VII–VIII; Ch. IX: "Hegel: Contribution and Ca-
lamity"), Boston, 1959; British ed., entitled *The Owl and the Night-
ingale,* London, 1960; rev. paperback ed., Anchor Books, 1960.
————————, "Hegel" in *The Concise Encyclopedia of Western Philosophy
and Philosophers,* ed. J. O. Urmson, London & New York, 1960,
pp. 157–61.
————————, Critical Notice of J. N. Findlay's *Hegel* in *Mind,* April
1961 (LXX.278), pp. 264–69.

Kedney, John Steinfort, *Hegel's Aesthetics: A Critical Exposition,*
Chicago, 1885; 3d ed., 1897.

Knox, Israel, *The Aesthetic Theories of Kant, Hegel, and Schopenhauer,*
New York, 1936.

Knox, T. M., "Hegel and Prussianism" in *Philosophy,* January 1940, pp.
51–63, July 1940, pp. 313–14. See Carrit, above.

Kojève, Alexandre, *Introduction à la lecture de Hegel: Leçons sur la
Phénoménologie de l'esprit, professées de 1933 à 1939* . . . , *réunies
et publiées par* Raymond Queneau, Paris, 1947. Partial German tr.:
*Hegel: Eine Vergegenwärtigung seines Denkens: Kommentar zur
Phänomenologie des Geistes,* ed. Iring Fetscher, Stuttgart, 1958.

Kroner, Richard, *Von Kant bis Hegel,* 2 vols., Tübingen, 1921, 1924;
2d ed., 1961.
————————, "Introduction: Hegel's Philosophical Development" in
Hegel's *Early Theological Writings* (see II.D.1, above). Also articles in
Hegel Studien and *Hegel-Kongress, Verhandlungen;* see end of I above.

Krug, W. T., *Schelling und Hegel oder die Neueste Philosophie im
Vernichtungskriege mit sich selbst begriffen,* Leipzig, 1835.

Kupfer, Johannes, *Die Auffassung des Sokrates in Hegels Geschichts-
philosophie,* dissertation; Borna-Leipzig, 1927.

Lasson, Georg, *Hegel als Geschichtsphilosoph,* Leipzig, 1920. (His long
introductions to his editions of Hegel's writings are also noteworthy:
see Part II of this Bibliography.)

Levy, Heinrich, *Die Hegel-Renaissance in der deutschen Philosophie,* (Berlin-) Charlottenburg, 1927.

Litt, Theodor, *Hegel: Versuch einer kritischen Erneuerung,* Heidelberg, 1953.

Loewenberg, J., "The Exoteric Approach to Hegel's *Phenomenology of Mind"* and "The Comedy of Immediacy in Hegel's *Phenomenology of Mind"* in *Mind,* 1934 and 1935 (XLIII, XLIV).

——————, "Introduction" in *Hegel Selections,* ed. J. Loewenberg, pp. ix–xliii, New York, Chicago, Boston, 1929; reprinted in Scribner paperback.

Löwith, Karl, *Von Hegel bis Nietzsche,* Zürich & New York, 1941; English tr.: *From Hegel to Nietzsche,* tr. David E. Green, New York, 1964.

Lukács Georg, *Der junge Hegel Über die Beziehungen von Dialektik und Oekonomie,* Zürich & Wien, 1948; 2d ed. with new 4-page preface and title, *Der junge Hegel und die Probleme der kapitalistischen Gesellschaft,* different pagination, Berlin, 1954.

Mackintosh, R., *Hegel and Hegelianism,* Edinburgh, 1913.

McTaggart, J. M. E. M., *A Commentary on Hegel's Logic,* Cambridge, 1910.

——————, *Studies in Hegelian Cosmology,* Cambridge, 1918.

——————, *Studies in the Hegelian Dialectic,* Cambridge, 1896.

Marcuse, Herbert, *Reason and Revolution: Hegel and the Rise of Social Theory,* Oxford University Press, 1941; 2d ed., New York, 1955; Beacon paperback, 1960.

Marx, Karl, "Zur Kritik der Hegelschen Rechtsphilosophie" in *Deutsch-Französische Jahrbücher,* Paris, 1844, pp. 71–85; "Kritik des Hegelschen Staatsrechts (§§261–313)" and "Kritik der Hegelschen Dialektik und Philosophie überhaupt," published posthumously in Marx-Engels, *Historisch-Kritische Gesamtausgabe,* Abteilung I, vol. III (1932). All three essays have been reprinted; e.g., in Marx, *Frühe Schriften,* vol. I, Stuttgart, Cotta, 1962, pp. 488–505, 258–426, and 637–65. Most of this material is also included in Marx, *Die Frühschriften,* Stuttgart, Kröners Taschenausgabe, 1953. Different translations of the third essay by Martin Milligan in Marx, *Economic and Philosophic Manuscripts of 1844,* Moscow, Foreign Languages Publishing House, 1961, and by T. B. Bottomore in Erich Fromm, *Marx's Concept of Man,* New York, Ungar, 1961, and in Karl Marx, *Early Writings,* New York, McGraw-Hill, 1964, which also contains the first essay. The second essay, which is much longer, is not available in English.

Meulen, Jan van der, *Heidegger und Hegel oder Widerstreit und Widerspruch*, Meisenheim, 1953.

Moog, Willy, *Hegel und die Hegelsche Schule*, München, 1930.

Müller, Gustav Emil, *Hegel: Denkgeschichte eines Lebendigen*, Bern & München, 1959.

——————, "The Hegel Legend of 'Thesis-Antithesis-Synthesis' " in *Journal of the History of Ideas*, June 1958 (XIX.3). See also under Travis, below.

Mure, G. R. G., *An Introduction to Hegel*, Oxford, 1940.

——————, *A Study of Hegel's Logic*, Oxford, 1950.

Pelczynski, Z. A., "An Introductory Essay" in Hegel's *Political Writings*, pp. 5–137. See II.C.14.c., above.

Peperzak, Adrien, *Le jeune Hegel et la vision morale du monde*, La Haye, 1960.

Pöggeler, Otto, *Hegels Kritik der Romantik*, dissertation, Bonn, 1956. See also H 22, note 1.

Popper, Karl, *The Open Society and Its Enemies*, vol. II, London, 1945, Chapter 12; rev. ed., Princeton, 1950, pp. 223–73, 642–60. For a detailed critique, see Kaufmann, "The Hegel Myth and Its Method," above. In the 4th rev. ed., London, 1962, vol. II, pp. 393–95 explain that errors in the Hegel chapter have not been corrected.

Purpus, Wilhelm, *Zur Dialektik des Bewusstseins nach Hegel: Ein Beitrag zur Würdigung der Phänomenologie des Geistes*, Berlin, 1908.

——————, *Eduard von Hartmanns Kritik der dialektischen Methode Hegels, antikritisch gewürdigt*, Ansbach, 1911.

Radermacher, Hans, *Kierkegaards Hegelverständnis*, dissertation, Köln, 1958.

Rosenkranz, Karl, *Georg Wilhelm Friedrich Hegel's Leben*, Berlin, 1844.

——————, *Kritische Erläuterungen des Hegel'schen Systems*, Königsberg, 1840; Reprografischer Nachdruck, Hildesheim, 1963.

——————, *Hegel als deutscher Nationalphilosoph*, Leipzig, 1870. English: *Hegel as the National Philosopher of Germany*, tr. Geo. S. Hall, reprinted from *The Journal of Speculative Philosophy*, St. Louis, 1874.

Rosenzweig, Franz, *Hegel und der Staat*, 2 vols., *I: Lebensstationen* (1770–1806); *II: Weltepochen* (1806–1831), München & Berlin, 1920; reprinted Aalen, 1962.

Rotenstreich, Nathan, "Hegel's Image of Judaism" in *Jewish Social Studies*, 1953 (XV.1), pp. 33–52.

——————, "Man and the Estranged God (Hegel)" in *The Recurring Pattern: Studies in Anti-Judaism in Modern Thought*, London, 1963.

Royce, Josiah, "Hegel" in *The Spirit of Modern Philosophy: An Essay in the Form of Lectures,* pp. 190–227, Boston & New York, 1892.

——————, "Hegel's Terminology" in *Dictionary of Philosophy and Psychology,* ed. James Mark Baldwin, vol. I, pp. 454–65, New York & London, 1901.

——————, *Lectures on Modern Idealism* (three of the ten lectures deal with Hegel's *Phenomenology,* and one with "Hegel's Mature System"); Yale University Press, 1919; Yale paperback reprint with Foreword by John E. Smith, 1964.

Sartre, Jean-Paul, *L'Être et le Néant,* Paris, 1943. English tr. by Hazel Barnes, *Being and Nothingness,* New York, 1956. See especially Part III, Chapter I, section III: "Husserl, Hegel, Heidegger."

Schelling, Friedrich Wilhelm Joseph von, "Hegel" (pp. 126–64) in *Zur Geschichte der neueren Philosophie (aus dem handschriftlichen Nachlass,* 1827—lectures delivered in Munich), in *Sämtliche Werke, Erste Abtheilung,* X (1861).

——————, *Vorrede* in Victor Cousin, *Über französische und deutsche Philosophie. Aus dem Französischen* [tr.] *von* Dr. Hubert Beckers, *Nebst einer beurtheilenden Vorrede des Herrn Geheimenraths* von Schelling, pp. v–xxviii, especially xiii ff., Stuttgart & Tübingen, 1834. Reprinted in *Sämtliche Werke,* I, X (1861), 201–24.

——————, *Erste Vorlesung in Berlin:* 15. November 1841 (22 pp.), Stuttgart & Tübingen, 1841.

——————, *Die endlich offenbar gewordene positive Philosophie der Offenbarung oder Entstehungsgeschichte, wörtlicher Text, Beurtheilung und Berichtigung der v. Schellingischen Entdeckungen über Philosophie überhaupt, Mythologie und Offenbarung des dogmatischen Christentums im Berliner Wintercursus von 1841–42. Der allgemeinen Prüfung vorgelegt von* Dr. H. E. G. Paulus (pp. lxvi, 736), Darmstadt, 1843. (Schelling sued—for plagiarism, not for misrepresentation.)

——————, *Philosophie der Offenbarung* (posthumous authorized edition of Berlin lectures) in *Sämtliche Werke,* II, III (1858), especially pp. 86 ff. and 122.

Schilling-Wollny, Kurt, *Hegels Wissenschaft von der Wirklichkeit und ihre Quellen; I: Begriffliche Vorgeschichte der Hegelschen Methode,* München, 1929.

Schlunk, Wolfgang, *Hegels Theorie des Dramas,* dissertation, Tübingen, 1936.

Schoeps, Hans Joachim, "Die ausserchristlichen Religionen bei Hegel" in *Zeitschrift für Religions- und Geistesgeschichte,* 1955 (VII.1), pp. 1–34.

Schubarth, K. E., *Über die Unvereinbarkeit der hegelschen Staatslehre mit dem obersten Lebens- und Entwicklungsprinzip des preussischen Staates,* Breslau, 1839. See also above II.C.17.e.

Seeberger, Wilhelm, *Hegel oder die Entwicklung des Geistes zur Freiheit,* Stuttgart, 1961.

Stace, W. T., *The Philosophy of Hegel; A Systematic Exposition,* London, 1924; paperback reprint, Dover Publications, 1955.

Sterrett, J. Macbride, *Studies in Hegel's Philosophy of Religion, With a Chapter on Christian Unity in America,* New York, 1890.

Stiehler, Gottfried, *Die Dialektik in Hegels "Phänomenologie des Geistes,"* Berlin, 1964.

Stirling, James Hutchison, *The Secret of Hegel, Being the Hegelian System in Origin, Principle, Form, and Matter,* 2 vols., London, 1865; 2d rev. ed. in 1 vol., Edinburgh & New York, 1898.

Takeuchi, Yoshinori; "Hegel and Buddhism" in *Il Pensiero,* 1962 (VII.1–2), pp. 5–46.

Travis, D. C., *A Hegel Symposium,* Austin, Texas, 1962. (Contains: "A Philosopher Reconsidered" by D. C. Travis, "The Power of Negation: Hegel's Dialectic and Totalitarian Ideology" by Carl J. Friedrich, "Hegel and the Perspective of Liberalism" by Sidney Hook, "Hegel and Heine" by Helmut Motekat, "Hegel's Absolute and the Crisis of Christianity" by Gustav E. Mueller, and "Of Structure and Symbol: The Significance of Hegel's Phenomenology for Literary Criticism" by Helmut Rehder. Pp. 139.)

Trendelenburg, Adolf, *Logische Untersuchungen,* Berlin, 1840; 2d ed., 1862; 3d ed., 1870; Reprografischer Nachdruck, Hildesheim, 1964.
————, *Die logische Frage in Hegels System,* Leipzig, 1843.

Tschiževskij (Čyževśkyj), Dmitrij, *Hegel bei den Slaven,* Reichenberg, 1934; rev. ed., Bad Homburg vor der Höhe, 1961.

Wallace, William, *Prolegomena to the Study of Hegel's Philosophy and especially of his Logic,* Oxford, 1874; 2d rev. ed., 1894.

Walsh, W. H., "A Survey of Work on Hegel, 1945–1952" in *Philosophical Quarterly,* October 1953.

Index

INDEX

Arabic numerals refer to *sections,* not pages. D indicates references to Chapter VII (Documentation, arranged chronologically) and is followed by the year. An asterisk indicates a letter written by, or addressed to, the person listed. References beginning with a Roman numeral will be found in Chapter VIII which is divided into 12 sections, I.1 through IV.3.

By including first names, the Index should help to identify some persons mentioned in passing in the text.

P means Preface. Chapter IX, being very short, is not indexed; neither is the Bibliography.

Acknowledgments

For over a dozen years I have taught Hegel both in graduate seminars and to undergraduates. I want to give thanks to my graduate students for their interest and helpful discussions, above all to Professor Frithjof Bergmann who wrote his thesis on Hegel. In the spring of 1964, Ivan Soll checked my translation of the preface to the *Phenomenology* against the German original, and Richard Schacht and Charles Love compared it with Baillie's version. Much of the work on the Index was done by Michael Spence. I am grateful to Sanford G. Thatcher for his cheerful and reliable help with the proofs and other last-minute chores.

My debts to scholars are acknowledged throughout the book. But I should like to add that one of my teachers, Professor John William Miller of Williams College, who never lectured on Hegel, often remarked that Hegel's philosophy was much more open and less rigid than is usually supposed. I am most indebted to Georg Lasson, who pioneered the critical editions of Hegel's writings, to Johannes Hoffmeister, who continued this work and edited Hegel's letters—he also had my first article on Hegel translated and published in Germany—and to Rolf Flechsig, who edited the fourth volume of Hegel's correspondence after Hoffmeister's death. All Hegel scholars have reason to be grateful to Felix Meiner who, for over half a century, has published these critical editions.

For his companionship during the hours before and after midnight when much of this book was written during the summer of 1964, I thank my son, David. My debt to my wife, Hazel, is chronic by now. And thanks to Anne Freedgood and Robert Hewetson, the final stages, after the manuscript was turned over to the publisher, were free from birth pangs: one could not wish for more understanding editors.